CALIFORNIA SLAVIC STUDIES

CALIFORNIA SLAVIC STUDIES
Volume X

EDITORS

NICHOLAS V. RIASANOVSKY

GLEB STRUVE

THOMAS EEKMAN

UNIVERSITY OF CALIFORNIA PRESS
BERKELEY · LOS ANGELES · LONDON

CALIFORNIA SLAVIC STUDIES
Volume 10

UNIVERSITY OF CALIFORNIA PRESS
BERKELEY AND LOS ANGELES, CALIFORNIA

UNIVERSITY OF CALIFORNIA PRESS, LTD.
LONDON, ENGLAND

ISBN 0-520-09564-2
LIBRARY OF CONGRESS CATALOG CARD NUMBER: 61-1041
PRINTED IN THE UNITED STATES OF AMERICA

CONTENTS

EVOLUTION OF THE MEANINGS OF CHIN:
An Introduction to the Russian Institution
of Rank Ordering and Niche Assignment
from the Time of Peter the Great's Table of Ranks
to the Bolshevik Revolution

BY

HELJU AULIK BENNETT

To David P. Bennett

PETER THE GREAT promulgated a law in 1722 which is usually referred to as the Table of Ranks. Scholars have long considered it important, recognizing, for instance, that with its promulgation the status of the Russian upper classes, the structure of the Imperial bureaucracy, and even the ideas of merit and service inherited from the Muscovite past were changed.[1] Its importance, however, has been generally assessed in terms of how it helped or hindered the transplanting of western

---

I want to thank the Center for Slavic and East European Studies at the University of California, Berkeley, for giving me assistance when I began work on this article, and The Research Foundation of the State University of New York for providing me with the opportunity to finish it. I am grateful to Professor N. V. Riasanovsky for his constant encouragement, to Professor R. Zelnik for his support and detailed criticism of the paper, and to members of the Conference on Russian Officialdom (at Cornell University, Ithaca, N. Y., Spring 1975) and the History Club of Western New York (that met at SUNY in Buffalo, Fall 1974) for giving me the opportunity to present the paper in its various stages of development and for their comments and criticisms. I am particularly indebted to Professor Walter M. Pintner of Cornell University for his personal interest, encouragement, and constructive criticism and for arranging the scholarly forums that proved so helpful in testing the ideas presented here.
1. Robert E. Jones, *The Emancipation of the Russian Nobility 1762-1785* (Princeton, 1973), pp. 6-7; Paul Dukes, *Catherine the Great and the Russian Nobility: A Study Based on the Legislative Commission of 1767* (Cambridge, 1967), p. 2; N. F. Demidova, "Bjurokratizacija gosudarstvennogo apparata absoljutizma v XVII-XVIII vv," *Absoljutizm v Rossii, XVII-XVIII vv.* ed. N. M. Družinin, N. I. Pavlenko, and L. V. Čerepnin

1

influences into Russia.[2] The fundamental meaning of the Table of Ranks, as well as its consequences, can be better understood, I think, when it is viewed in the context of an evolving, complex, and peculiarly Russian institution, the *chin* system, or system of rank ordering and niche assignment. (The word *chin* will be used here to refer to this system rather than the cumbersome though more accurately rendered phrase "rank ordering and niche assignment.") That such a system existed can be seen indirectly from references in many scholarly works. Scholars with the most disparate interests—in intellectual history, state policy, military reforms, bureaucratic growth, the expansion of education—at one time or another make some mention of either *chin* rules or their consequences.[3] Its existence can also be inferred from a close reading of Russian literature. The great authors of Russia, including Pushkin, Gogol, Tolstoy, Dostoevsky, and Chekhov, often used elaborate metaphors or made allusions that were clear to Russians who were fully conversant with the etiquette, usages, and titles of the system of ranking. The language of *chin* in translation, however, often appears to foreign readers as something mysterious, something emanating from a peculiarly Russian character. If understood properly, however, the system of rank ordering that evolved in the Imperial period becomes relevant even to post-revolutionary Russia. Soviet authorities, after pointedly abolishing the *chin* system in a special decree in 1917, are in fact still using the ceremonial etiquette and even the principles of seniority and candidacy requirements for state appointments that were institutionalized in the period before 1917.[4]

(Moscow: Akademija Nauk, Institut Istorii, 1964), pp. 238, 242; Michael T. Florinsky, *Russia: A History and an Interpretation*, 2 vols. (New York, 1957-1958), 1:420-421; Nicholas V. Riasanovsky, *A History of Russia* (New York, 1963), p. 260.

2. S. M. Troickij, "Iz istorii sozdanija tabeli o rangakh," *Istorija S.S.S.R.*, 1974, no. 1, pp. 98-111. The main Russian historiography on this topic is discussed on p. 98.

3. Marc Raeff, *Origins of the Russian Intelligentsia: The Eighteenth-Century Nobility* (New York, 1966); Forrestt Miller, *Dmitri Miliutin and the Reform Era in Russia* (Nashville, 1966); Hans-Joachim Torke, "Das russische Beamtentum in der ersten Hälfte des 19. Jahrhunderts," *Forschungen zur osteuropäischen Geschichte* 13 (1967): 7-346; John A. Armstrong, *The European Administrative Elite* (Princeton, 1973), pp. 224-225, 250; Patrick Alston, *Education and the State in Tsarist Russia* (Stanford, 1969).

4. Wladislaw W. Kulski, *The Soviet Regime: Communism in Practice* (Syracuse, 1954), p. 692, makes use of photographs in analyzing power relationships in the Kremlin, thus implicitly assuming that ceremonial ranking reflects power arrangements in the U.S.S.R. Robert Conquest, *Power and Policy in the U.S.S.R.* (New York, 1967), pp. 54, 61-62, discusses the value of various types of evidence. He thinks that "formal order of appearance" and "non-alphabetical lists" can be used for analyzing personnel shifts or changes in policy, seeing in them, in fact, a greater significance than that of mere "protocol." See also Robert V. Daniels, "Participatory Bureaucracy and the Soviet Political System," in *Analysis of the U.S.S.R.'s 24th Party Congress and the 9th*

So far as I know no description or interpretation of the *chin* system as a whole exists in Russian historiography.[5] Considering its importance, reflected by the many references to it in various fields of Russian history and literature, one could easily be led to write a speculative essay on the reasons why this is so, an essay which would have to deal, no doubt, with the problems of how hypotheses brought to one's research limit one's understanding of materials and how cultural bias, present-mindedness, and so on influence historical labors. For the present, though, we need only ascribe the lack of a general description of *chin* to the cultural specificity of the institution. Such an endeavor, in which the historian would have to trace *chin's* pre-history to Kievan and Muscovite periods, clearly would be useful, I think, in explaining and interpreting certain basic problems in Russian history, such as social stratification, social mobility, westernization, modernization, and revolution. This paper, however, will be limited to analyzing the varied but fundamental meanings of *chin* as it evolved from 1722 to 1917, the Imperial period of Russian history. A particular focus of this examination will be the human problems that the institution dealt with and partially solved.

There were three specific changes in the structure of Russia's fundamental laws (changes, of course, initiated by the autocrat) that most radically affected the meaning of *chin*. These changes altered the system of social stratification upon which the meanings of *chin* depended. The first of these, as already noted, was the Table of Ranks law in 1722; the second, the Charter of Nobility in 1785; and the third, the abolition of serfdom in 1861. Each of these legislative acts will serve as a point of departure for the three major sections of this paper. The meaning of *chin* in the first period will be explored in terms of the impact of the 1722 law on the social category of nobility, since primarily it was affected. In the second period, 1785–1861, the legal categories of

---

Five-Year Plan, ed. Norton T. Dodge, Proceedings of a symposium sponsored by the Washington Chapter of The American Association for the Advancement of Slavic Studies and The Institute for Sino-Soviet Studies, George Washington University, April 30–May 1, 1971 (Mechanicsville, Maryland: Cremona Foundation), pp. 75–79; and his "Soviet Politics Since Khrushchev," in *The Soviet Union under Brezhnev and Kosygin*, ed. John W. Strong (New York, 1971). Daniels perceives that something more fundamental than simple protocol is at work in the varieties of ranking practices now used by the Soviet elite.

5. Troickij, "Iz istorii," pp. 98–111; James Hassell, "Implementation of the Russian Table of Ranks during the Eighteenth Century," *Slavic Review* 29 (June 1970): 289–290; V. A. Evreinov, *Graždanskoe činoproizvodstvo v Rossii: istoričeskij očerk* (St. Petersburg, 1887); see also "Značenie našikh graždanskikh činov v nastojaščee vremja," in E. P. Karnovič, *Očerki našikh porjadkov administrativnykh, sudebnykh, i obščestvennykh* (Petersburg, 1873), ch. 12, pp. 375–384. All the works cited above contain important information about various aspects of the development of the Table of Ranks, but do not define the institution as a whole.

the population ranked between the fully privileged nobility on the one hand, and the burdened peasantry and town populations, constituting the *raznočincy*, on the other hand, will be examined, since they were most affected by the changes resulting from the Charter of Nobility. Finally, in the third period, 1861–1917, the meanings of *chin* will be discussed in terms of the country's institutions, particularly the institution of autocracy.

I

Peter promulgated the Table of Ranks law some quarter of a century after his journeys abroad and after he had already effected important changes in methods of recruiting the army and collecting taxes, in the curriculum taught in schools, and in the organization of government institutions and social classes. (These changes were carried out for the most part during a period of intermittent wars fought against Sweden, Poland, and Turkey, the power states of the period, and against native rebels who, from time to time, challenged the authority of Peter's government.) The rules given in the *Polnoe sobranie zakonov* under a long title paraphrased as "The listing of offices, and what ranks any office is to have, and which offices are equal to which, and what grade (rank) any official is to have, and who among officials at one particular level of office list, according to seniority, is entitled to be promoted to higher offices"[6] must be considered against this background.

The Table of Ranks law had a variety of functions, arose out of multiple necessities and had important consequences. It provided for "ranking of state offices"; established guidelines for awarding "grades" to individuals who served in those offices; and spelled out the social, legal, and bureaucratic prerogatives that were to accrue to those who possessed grade.

The rank ordering of offices was established by a general chart (the *Tabel'*), a master list that brought together the hitherto separate state organs that conducted war, carried out the functions of civil service, and supported activities of the Imperial court. The chart was accordingly divided into three major sections: *voinskie*, *statskie*, and *pridvornye*, with the *voinskie* or "military" further subdivided into the four parts of infantry, guards, artillery, and navy. Each section (and each part of the military) listed "levels" or offices that were arranged to extend across

---

6. I am giving a translation of the caption to the Table of Ranks, which is based on the paragraphs appended to the law in *Polnoe sobranie zakonov Rossijskoj imperii. Sobranie pervoe 1649–1825*, 46 vols. (St. Petersburg, 1828–1830), vol. 6, law 3890 (January 24, 1722), hereafter cited as *P.S.Z.*, ser. 1.

the whole chart, thereby indicating a kind of equivalence between offices shown on the same horizontal plane. Practically speaking, the *Tabel'* did not improve the functioning of the state apparatus, nor did it accelerate the specialization of functions, a process which is usually considered a by-product of bureaucratic rearrangements or at least the motive for such reorganizations. Actually, different laws, the *štaty*, which set up or reorganized various offices like the *collegia* (the General Reglament was perhaps the most important of such laws), governed the internal relationships and subordination of offices within any one institution.[7]

What is important about the rank ordering of offices is that it brought most of the functions and activities of the state into a formal, definable, and quantifiable relationship to the Emperor, who in Russian tradition was the source of all law. Further, by assigning all state offices to a relatively limited range of fourteen levels, the Table of Ranks made easily understandable the relationship of all offices to every other office. Offices at levels 1 and 2, for instance, could clearly be seen to be better than lower-level offices; their numbers immediately indicated their proximity to the Emperor.[8] And the rank ordering provided a system of earned rewards, where appointment to each level in the ascending scale or ladder was the predictable result of duties performed in a prescribed way. This is indicated by the fact that Peter required that neophytes in state service first hold offices at lower levels.

Obviously, top-level offices could not remain vacant until officials had qualified by a process of step by step promotion. Peter in fact did not observe the stipulation that promotion to each level of office was a reward for service in a lower level; he did, however, try to salvage the orderliness of the system by allowing direct appointments to high offices in cases of necessity and then on the condition that officials so appointed remain in their offices for a specified time. He also provided for appointments to high offices of men who had served in the government before the ranking of offices established by the Table of Ranks, using their records or time spent in state service as justification.[9]

---

7. Ibid., law 3534 (February 28, 1720). The full title of the law is "General'nyj Reglament ili ustav, po kotoromu gosudarstvennyja Kollegii, takože i vse onykh prinadležaščikh k nim kanceljarii i kontor služiteli, ne tokmo vo vnešnikh i vnutrennikh učreždenijakh no i vo otpravlenii svoego čina, poddannejše postupat' imejut."

8. Ibid., law 3890; M. D. Rabinovič, "Social'noe proiskhoždenie i imuščestvennoe položenie oficerov reguljarnoj russkoj armii v konce Severnoj vojny," in *Rossija v period reform Petra I*, ed. N. I. Pavlenko, L. A. Nikiforov, and M. Ja. Volkov (Moscow, 1973), p. 137.

9. *P.S.Z.*, ser. 1, vol. 6 law 3890 (January 24, 1722), para. 14.

One aspect of the rewards accruing to the rankinj of offices was the grading of persons, or, as sometimes referred to in the Table of Ranks, *rang*, which gave social prerogatives and honor. Since in Peter's time a *rang* could be obtained in a number of ways—for instance, by birth (as was the case for princes of the blood), by time spent in office, or because of skills or actions valued by the Emperor—it did not need to correspond to the level of office one had. This can be seen from paragraphs 12 and 17 in the Table of Ranks law that made provisions for persons who had at one time or another attained high *rang* to work in offices ranked below their *rang*, though for the duration of their service in the low-level offices they were deprived of the enjoyment of the social prerogatives that went with the high *rang*.[10] Despite the fact that the grading of persons grew out of and was constantly influenced by the ranking of offices, it became almost immediately autonomous, with qualities and characteristics that can best be described when examined one by one.[11]

---

10. For consistency's sake, whenever the word *rang* is used to mean personal grade, i.e., the idea later most consistently expressed by the Russian *chin*, I shall use either the English word "grade" or the Russian word *chin*. Peter used the word *rang* in an extremely varied sense, depending on its context. *Rang* in one place clearly meant the "level" on which offices were arranged in the *Tabel'*, i.e., the horizontal tier in the chart; in another place, *rang* was used for the prerogatives or precedence an official had in public affairs; and in another, it was used as a synonym for *chin*. The word *chin* itself was also a multipurpose word and was used for "office" or "place" in a hierarchy, or for the "official" holding office, or the "grade" a person earned in office. See preamble and paragraphs 1, 2, 3, 11, 12, 13 and 14 in ibid.; Sergei G. Pushkarev, *Dictionary of Russian Historical Terms from the Eleventh Century to 1917*, ed. George Vernadsky (New Haven, 1970), p. 8.

11. Further evidence of the separateness of the two systems can be seen from the fact that information about the ranking of offices and the grading of persons is found in completely different documents. Rank of an office is often found in an *učreždenie* or *štat*, the statute or charter creating an institution, or in the *raspisanie dolžnostej* (census of offices) taken later. The grading of individuals is found in the *skazki*, *formuljarnye spiski* and other work records and private documents that were maintained by various agenciès. In the eighteenth century, copies of personnel records were assembled in the Heraldry Office of the Senate, and in the latter part of the nineteenth century, in the files of the First Section of H. M. O. Chancery. Information about promotions in grade was published in official newspapers and special documents accumulated for the purpose of providing such data. Good discussions about the location of and differences between the two types of documents can be found in G. M. Gorfejn, "Osnovnye istočniki po istorii vysšikh i central'nykh učreždenij XIX–načala XX v.," in *Nekotorye voprosy izučenija istoričeskikh dokumentov XIX–načala XX v.; Sbornik statej*, ed. I. N. Firsov (Leningrad, 1967), pp. 73-111, and, in the same volume, Z. I. Malkova and M. A. Pljukhina, "Dokumenty vysšikh i central'nykh učreždenij XIX–načala XX v.," pp. 204-229. The collection of articles, of which the two just cited are a part, was sponsored by the *Glavnoe arkhivnoe upravlenie pri sovete ministrov S.S.S.R: Central'nyj gosudarstvennyj istoričeskij arkhiv S.S.S.R.*

A rating given an office remained constant for scores of years, while the grade of an individual changed. If an office rating changed it was the result of slow social change or the creation of new offices to meet the needs of government.[12] The rating of any office, however, constituted a political act, since it affected the "established" order and traditional relationships of already ranked offices. The personal grading system changed much more rapidly, when new officials were recruited and earned their *pervyj klassnyj čin* (i.e., *chin* 14), when officials in any one office were promoted, or when officials died. When grade was considered a necessary prerequisite for officeholding, as it sometimes was, only then did the number of *chin* holders help to limit the number of competitors and hence the intensity of competition for ranked offices. The development in the *chin* system of explicit rules of correspondence between office rank and grade happened later, and the extent to which they were enforced in any one reign depended on the personalities of the Emperor and high-level officials and on the nature of the current political and social problems. A discussion of the impact of the office-ranking system and *chin* qualification requirements on politics, however, will have to be dealt with in another article. What is important for our discussion of the evolution of the *chin* system as a whole is the fact that the niche assignment system and what it meant to individuals functioned separately from the office-ranking system. In fact, *chin* can be considered to have been an attribute of a person, like an academic degree, for example, the possession of which helped to determine in important ways his social status, his legal rights, and even the rights of his spouse and children, born and unborn.

The social preferences and legal rights that eventually became dependent on possession of *chin* were spelled out in the Table of Ranks, and thus the Table of Ranks law itself constituted a kind of charter of prerogatives of *chin* possessors or graded men. It provided that men with grades, their wives and their unmarried daughters were to have "precedence rights," i.e., rights to the most deference and the best seats on all "public occasions," which included, according to the law, "gatherings

---

12. The results of a major reorganization of government can be followed in *Svod zakonov Rossijskoj Imperii, izdanija 1857 goda, tretij tom: ustavy o službe graždanskoj* (St. Petersburg, 1857), pp. 338–529, that contains "rospisanie dolžnostej graždanskoj služby po klassam ot XIV–V vključitel'no." Interesting materials relating to problems of governmental reorganization can be found on p. 77 of paragraph 363, where special provisions are made for *činovniki* who lost their places as a result of reorganization. See also *Obščee raspisanie klassnykh dolžnostej v Imperii* (St. Petersburg, 1900); Malkova and Pljukhina, "Dokumenty vysšikh," pp. 208–209.

in churches, at the mass, at court ceremonials, ambassadorial audiences, official banquets, meetings, christenings, marriages, funerals . . . and similar public gatherings."[13] Such occasions, in fact, were the times for the most part when Russians came together to celebrate bench marks of their private or official life, and according to law they were subject to regulation. Where persons were to stand and sit on such public occasions was determined by their official grades and the length of time the grades had been possessed. The kind of clothing one could wear on these occasions was also dictated by grade; i.e., those with the highest grades were entitled to wear the most resplendent and opulent clothes, such as uniforms with decorated collars, and varicolored cuffs and buttons, while those at the bottom of the grading scale had to wear clothing of drab colors with plain buttons.[14] The social visibility and hence the importance of the highest graded persons were increased by the fact that they wore imperial medals (*ordena*),[15] a kind of jewelry for men consisting of brooches, pins, chainlets, and pendants to be worn around the neck and on the breast, all enhanced by twirling sashes, ribbons, and bows.

The most important reward of *chin* was detailed in paragraph 11 of the Table of Ranks law. It stated that men who had earned *ober* officer's grade in the military service and grade 8 and above in the civil service were to be considered nobles (*dvorjane*).[16] This meant that they

---

13. *P.S.Z.*, ser. 1, vol. 6, law 3890, pars. 3, 9, 10. The law states that precedence rules need not be observed when only a few good friends got together out of good fellowship, or during general assemblies. Yet there follows a list of occasions that one would think are just such activities but that are given as occasions when observance of precedence etiquette is required. Continuous adjudication of precedence disputes continued after 1722. See *Svod zakonov I-IV*, ed. A. A. Dobrovolskij (St. Petersburg, 1913), pp. 1673-1674, which summarizes many laws that dealt with precedence disputes.

14. *P.S.Z.*, ser. 1, vol. 6, law 3890, par. 19. Catherine the Great made an attempt to contain the dress mania that broke out following the publication of the Table of Ranks; see ibid., vol. 20, law 14290 (1780). Dress codes were still officially issued in the early twentieth century. L. M. Rogovin's unofficial edition of *Ustav o službe po opredeleniju ot pravitel'stva i položenie ob osobykh preimuščestvakh graždanskoj služby v otdalennykh mestnostjakh* (St. Petersburg, 1915), pp. 364-382, contains detailed regulations for the wearing of official uniforms, dress that was different not only for each grade of officials and each agency, but for each season of the year and each occasion, whether one was on tour or traveling, etc.

15. Robert Werlich, *Orders and Decorations of All Nations, Ancient and Modern, Civil and Military*, 2nd ed. (Washington, D.C., 1974), pp. 362-376, contains pictures and short descriptions of Imperial Russian *ordena*. See also N. N. Panov, *Istoričeskij očerk rossijskikh ordenov: Sbornik osnovnykh ordenskikh statutov* (St. Petersburg, 1891), and P. F. Vinkler, "Orden," Brokgauz-Efron *Énciklopedičeskij slovar'*, 43 vols. (St. Petersburg, 1890-1907), 21: 117-121.

16. *P.S.Z.*, ser. 1, vol. 6, law 3890, pars. 11, 15.

were exempted from the labor burdens and taxes that were levied upon the lower social strata. This reward of grade also had consequences for the children. The child born after the father had attained the grade of ennoblement shared the newly attained legal status of his father, while the child born before could share the family's new legal status only if the Emperor granted him access to it in response to a petition by the father. Even so, the father could petition only on behalf of one non-noble son. The men who received grades 9 and lower in the civil service were entitled to the prerogatives of noble status, but their rights could not be passed on to their children. The category of these men was that of non-heritable nobility, a status usually translated as "personal" nobility.[17]

Peter tried to make certain property rights that Russian nobles had traditionally enjoyed, such as the prerogative to buy land and serfs, the rewards of some service and of grades earned. (He even tried to regulate the right to marry, making it contingent upon the nobleman having learned to read and write.) The right of "personal inviolability," the exemption from beating during administrative and disciplinary procedures, was now also made a reward of grade earned in the military service.[18]

A peculiarity of the grading system in Russia was that monetary rewards or salaries were only incidentally the function of grades. They were rather the function of the office one served in and therefore determined by the office's *štat*, or they were assigned by the Emperor directly to the person whom he appointed. Only in a general way were emoluments dependent on grades and the way in which they were often varied depending on the location (provincial or central) or kind of institution where the "grades" were earned.[19]

Despite the fact that payment of salaries was not rationalized by *chin*, money was an important lubricant for making the system work. For example, by disregarding rules of social precedence, by "claiming greater respect than due him by his earned grade," by demanding a more important position than he was entitled to, or by refusing to take up

---

17. Ibid., par. 15.

18. Hugh Seton-Watson, *The Russian Empire 1801-1917* (Oxford, 1967), p. 15. *P.S.Z.*, ser. 1, vol. 6, law 3760 shows just how routine were corporal punishments; it also indicates that certain kinds of exile required their own kinds of beating, for example, with *knut* or *špicruten*.

19. *P.S.Z.*, ser. 1, vol. 6, law 3876 (January 11, 1722); ibid., law 3890, pars. 3, 4; ibid., law 3876; see also *Ukazatel' alfavitnyj P.S.Z.*, ser. 1 (St. Petersburg, 1830), vol. 42, sect. 1, p. 690, where a series of laws are summarized that indicate the existence of different pay scales and even different methods of payment for various offices, grades, and locations.

his "rightful" position, an official could be fined. Even one who deferred to another of a lower grade was fined.[20] To uphold a claim to a place required evidence of possession of that right, an actual document testifying to possession of grade, a document printed on government paper given out by an official agency. The government charged a fee for certifying it and indeed had a monopoly on the production of the paper on which such documents were written. Of course, the government incurred expenses in managing this system. It hired spies to mingle in "good company" and report on the "impudent individuals and parasites" (the pejoratives can be found in the law) who did not observe *chin* rules. It also paid bounties, so to speak, to those who reported or denounced transgressors of *chin* rules, but such payments came out of the fines assessed and collected from wrongdoers. (Peter made the system of denunciation that originated in Muscovite times permanent by making it profitable.) One-third of the fine was to be given to the tattler, the other two-thirds to a hospital. A person who was fined who had a government salary had the fine deducted from his salary, while the unsalaried official who was fined had to pay a percentage of a hypothetical salary that was determined by the level of office he held when the office was compared to others of equivalent level that had salaries assigned to them.[21]

A fundamental question that must be answered is why the complex system of *chin*, with its multiple ramifications for the social, political, and cultural life of the nation, was created. Scholars who have taken note of the *chin* system, for the most part in an incidental way while dealing with other problems, have given various answers. Some of them have thought that the ranking system was created to provide rewards of social mobility to worthy non-nobles, or that as a measure against the nobility it was designed to destroy the power of the Muscovite families, or that it was devised to provide income for a state chronically short of money.[22] While these conclusions have some merit, they indicate, it seems to me, a confusion of motives with results.

20. *P.S.Z.*, ser. 1, vol. 6, law 3890, pars. 3, 4.

21. Ibid., par. 3.

22. The major standard texts cited in footnotes 2 and 19 explain not so much the motives or reasons for the establishment of the law as its consequences. Seton-Watson, *The Russian Empire*, pp. 14–15, states that the principle of obligatory service was systematized by the introduction of the Table of Ranks; Vasili Kluchevsky, *Peter the Great*, trans. L. Archibald (New York, 1961), pp. 99–200, explains that the Table of Ranks was a way to destroy the genealogical principle of promotion and claims of birth; Bernard Pares, *A History of Russia* (New York, 1926), p. 202, states ". . . in the future birth was to count for absolutely nothing; rank was to be given according to efficiency,

The *chin* system was created, I think, to solve problems that developed when Peter attempted to undertake the diversity of tasks or work done in western countries in a more "backward," institutionally less complex and less wealthy Russia. The institutions that Peter created could be considered "western" or modern from the point of view of a French or German observer of the day. From the Russian point of view the work that these institutions organized simply constituted new obligations that society had to fulfill. Peter did not simply define the tasks that Russia as a contemporary European state had to fulfill but assigned them to arbitrarily chosen social groups. Indeed, this way of getting work done in Russia was ancient, so that what Peter did in the end was merely to re-form and rearrange, but not abolish, the old system. To see how a process that appears to be "modernization" was really an ingenious modification and in fact an extension of old norms requires at least a short description of the Muscovite system of social stratification and the ways in which work was done at the time that Peter initiated his new tasks.

When Peter began to govern in his own right, Russia was already a "service state," in which the most important social groups were obligated to render labor and services (*tjaglo*) to the autocracy. The practical result of this was the construction of a system legally compartmentalizing individuals, the *soslovija* or *sostojanija* system, in which human beings were organized into groups to perform various functions. The group in which an individual happened to belong determined the kind of work, or in lieu of that, taxes or dues, that he rendered the state and defined the limits of his autonomy and choice of activities. The *soslovija* system is well known to Russian historians and has been thought of in a number of ways, as a structure, for example, like that of the German *Stände*, the French estates, or Marxist classes. In Russian legal codes, however, some categories of this system were referred to as *chiny*, whose meanings of place in a rank ordering system and grade in a personal niche assignment

---

and rank alone was to define a man's status in society," Florinsky, *Russia*, 1:420-421, thinks that the democratization introduced by the Table of Ranks was less important than the fact that official rank rather than birth gave one priority; Richard Pipes, *Karamzin's Memoir on Ancient and Modern Russia: A Translation and Analysis* (New York: Atheneum, 1966), pp. 6, 8, emphasizes the consequences of the "merging of ancient and military gentry" and their equalization; Pavel N. Miljukov, *Gosudarstvennoe khozjajstvo Rossii v pervoj četverti XVII stoletija i reforma Petra Velikogo* (St. Petersburg, 1905), Appendix IV, pp. 485, 670, 673, discusses state budgets for various years and gives information about income derived from fines and document payments. See also Jones, *Emancipation of Russian Nobility*, pp. 6-7; Dukes, *Catherine the Great*, p. 2. Most of the authors cited above also indicate an awareness of the importance of the ranking system as a means of enforcing the "service" requirement.

system we have been discussing.[23] This system of assigning persons to categories or levels by birth or tradition, or compulsorily ascribing roles to persons, was a taxation system for a backward land, one which made predictable the delivery of manpower and goods for military purposes to the autocratic state. It is not proper here to describe the long history of external and internal difficulties of the Russians that resulted in the creation of this *soslovija* or *chin* system; it is necessary only to say that in Peter's day the system of compulsory subordination of persons and groups to state service was not completed. Some groups were assigned their "roles" by birth and tradition, while other groups in society were still "free," i.e., had a degree of freedom to choose between alternative social roles or life-styles. Further, some of the groups who rendered obligatory services were not strictly confined to their roles, in that no definite method of supervision had been set up to make sure that they did not avoid their obligations. As a result, they were considered only partially bound, since their binding had not been institutionalized. If any group could be considered fully bound in Peter's day it was the

---

23. I have not been able to find anything at all in English that describes the system of social stratification, or the *soslovija*, of Russia as a whole. Good short articles about the history and development of the various major social strata can be found in Brokgauz-Efron *Énciklopedičeskij slovar'* under "Dvorjanstvo," "Meščanstvo," "Dukhovenstvo," "Kupcy," and "Služba gosudarstvennaja." A good short statement of the meaning of "role ordering" can be found in N. Lazarevskij, "Soslovija," idem, vol. 30a (St. Petersburg, 1900), pp. 911–913. N. I. Kareev, "Gosudarstvennye činy," idem, vol. 9 (St. Petersburg, 1893), pp. 401–405, gives an important clue to solving the problem of analyzing the Russians' use of *chin* by stating that in some contexts it can mean *soslovie* much in the sense of the German word *Reichsstand*, signifying *ordo* or status. Vladimir Dal'. "čin," *Tolkovyj slovar' živogo veliko-russkogo jazyka*, vol. 4 (St. Petersburg, 1909), pp. 1342–1343, defines *chin* as *stepen', zvanie, san, soslovie* and *sostojan'e*. Information about the various *soslovija* can be found in the Russian monographs: A. Romanovič-Slavatinskij, *Dvorjanstvo v Rossij s načala XVIII veka do otmeny krepostnogo prava* (Kiev, 1912); M. Jabločkov, *Istorija dvorjanskogo soslovija v Rossii* (St. Petersburg, 1876); P. G. Ryndzjunskij, *Gorodskoe graždanstvo doreformennoj Rossii* (Moscow, 1958); V. I. Semevskij, *Krest'jane v carstvovanie Imperatricy Ekateriny II*, 2 vols. (St. Petersburg, 1901). Some information about the variety of legal statuses that evolved over the centuries can be found in Jerome Blum, *Lord and Peasant in Russia from the Ninth to the Nineteenth Century* (Princeton, 1961). One meaning of *chin*, apart from the complex connotations it was to acquire during post-Petrine times and its specific meanings in the *mestničestvo* order, denoted a burdened category, work group, or level; hence it was used as a synonym for some *soslovija*. While continuing to be used in this older sense, to refer to levels in the *sostojanija* system in post-Petrine legislation, the word *chin* also acquired the meanings described above. Its variation in meaning has been extremely confusing to translators, particularly when both its earlier and later usages stand side by side. Translators sometimes tend to translate it as "rank" when it could be better rendered, given the context, by "class," etc. Examples of *chin* used as a synonym for burdened group can be found in *P.S.Z.*, ser. 1, vol. 6, law 3762 (March 15, 1721), and law 3743 (February 19, 1721). In law 3764 (March 17, 1721), it is used in the sense of "office"; in laws 3751 (March 4, 1721), and 3752 (March 1721), it is used in the sense of *soslovie*.

peasantry. It was bound to the land by the tradition of serfdom, to the authority of the lord by ownership, and to other members of the peasant community by the institution of the *mir*. The *mir* was a particularly effective institution for enforcing work because all peasants were made responsible for each peasant's conduct. When an individual or family fled the village, the group as a whole had to make up whatever loss was caused by the individual's or the family's action. The sheer volume of legal disabilities, I think, even more than his poverty, tended to keep the peasant at the lowest stratum of society, and his status, with all its restrictions, came to be the standard by which the relative binding or freedom of all other groups was judged.

Compared to the peasantry, the categories of merchants, priests, and various townsmen in the stratified social structures were more "free." The roles they were assigned—carrying out the tasks of trading, praying, informing, etc.—were not strictly hereditary, and the institutions that supervised their performance were relatively flexible and even "self-administered" (the merchants, for example, elected members of their own group to act as executors of Imperial tax laws). But though these groups were relatively free, the fact remains that their tasks were supervised, i.e., their obligations were institutionalized. If members of these groups in the middle failed to fulfill their tasks, their goods and livelihood could be forfeited. Furthermore, they could be made to bear the burdens of the peasantry, namely, recruitment into the army and payment of poll taxes. Avoiding such a possibility, of course, would be an important reason for fulfilling the work assigned at the level to which these individuals belonged, and shows, in any case, that they were bound to the service of the state.

The nobility was the least subordinated social group before Peter's day. Its service could be fulfilled seasonally, and the *pomestie* system of rewarding a noble's work for the state with land could be considered a *quid pro quo* or contractual arrangement. Moreover, what supervisory institutions there were exercised minimal control. Despite the fact that the state threatened the confiscation of land from or physical harm to the nobleman who refused to do what the state required, the pre-Petrine nobility obviously was a relatively "free" and unburdened group. But this was a condition that Peter changed radically. Having founded a permanent army and civil service, he demanded lifelong service from the nobility, a burden inevitably resisted. To make the nobility conform was a problem that he tried to solve in different ways. For example, he required that all noble offspring be registered periodically to determine their service eligibility and that they submit to inspections (*smotry*). The passport system was instituted not only to limit the movement of the lower levels of the population but of the nobility as well. Peter also confiscated the nobility's property. But, most consistently, he resorted to beating and branding to enforce the nobility's compliance.[24] These methods did not get the desired results.

The use of physical coercion not only increased the need for manpower —beatings required beaters—but also disabled the men who were to serve. The government was poor, lacking the means or wherewithal to pay its servitors, and therefore, it could be argued, had to extort service from the population. So long as its requirements of service were limited, the use of force might be justified. But when the needs and concomitant demands of the state expanded, Peter discovered that he could no longer rely upon violence to obtain servitors. To escape the paradoxical results that the large scale use of violence would have produced and yet to still "force" the nobility to serve, to make it volunteer for "hard and dangerous work"[25] for which he could not hope to pay adequately, was the problem that Peter faced. I think that he solved it by instituting the rank ordering of offices and grading of persons I have described above.

This conclusion seems valid if we notice that rewards given to individuals for service elicited a different response than threats. The *chin* system encouraged a willingness to compete and even an eagerness to earn grades. This can be explained, I think, by the Table of Ranks' way of systematizing rewards that by their nature satisfied primary human needs, both private and social, and would be given up only at great psychic cost. Actually, the Table of Ranks did not create anything inherently new, since social honor and rights of precedence had existed in Russia for centuries;[26] it merely extended the competition for that honor and those rights, which had been virtually the monopoly of the "old" families, to new men. The old families did not really lose their

---

24. Florinsky, *Russia*, 1:417–420, describes in some detail the coercive methods used against the nobility.

25. These words were used by Professor Walter M. Pintner of Cornell University, Ithaca, N.Y.

26. Kluchevsky, *Peter the Great*, p. 94. Jesse Clarkson, *A History of Russia* (New York, 1963), p. 200, states that though "service" was ostensibly made the basic principle of the new system, the "essential principle of *miestnichestvo*" was strengthened, ". . . though on a broader base." An explanation in English of the Muscovite *mestničestvo* can be found in Blum, *Lord and Peasant*, pp. 137–138. A. M. Kleimola, "Boris Godunov and the Politics of *Mestnichestvo*," *Slavonic and East European Review* 50, no. 132 (July 1975) 355–369, supplies a bibliography about *mestničestvo*; she notes that the system was relatively flexible and actually worked to safeguard "relationships" between people rather than direct "rights" to a place. I think that the principles of "ranking of offices" and "grading of persons" and the attempt, eventually, to match them—recognizing that those who have a "right" to a niche in society exercise the functions and prerogatives of that niche—clearly show a fundamental similarity between the old and new rank-ordering systems.

power, but they were required now to exert themselves in order to maintain their social advantages.[27] Since the rewards were graduated, making it easy to see what one's rights and preferences were at any step on the grading scale and what yet remained to be gained, the inclination to compete was reinforced; continued service was likely to yield improved benefits. Also, the competition for state rewards was made more attractive, I suspect even for the old families, by the fact that the rules for getting them were not based on personal whim or chance. But above all, it was, as already mentioned, the nature of the rewards that insured compliance with the system.

The rewards became "real," or existed in space and time, only when others shared them. Furthermore, social occasions became times of obligatory and elaborately choreographed *chin* displays, and since human beings get together for reasons other than just social display—to celebrate marriages, christen children, attend funerals, exchange information at bureaucratic meetings—their avoidance became nearly impossible. While one might not wish to become involved in highly regulated social situations, one could hardly avoid participating in interactions arising from the processes of living. Those who refused to play the *chin* game were almost bound to be injured since the obverse of *chin* rules was that those who did not have a right to a preferred place at the least would have to see others preferred, that those who could not claim deference were required to show it, and that ultimately those who would avoid the economic costs and reprisals that followed public resistance to *chin* rules must avoid social occasions. In sum, choosing solitude meant not only sacrificing one's own "interests" but the interests of those whose futures depended on one's success. That the system would be obeyed really derived from human psychology: most men to think well of themselves must be well thought of by others, i.e., they need social support and, consequently, will choose to live with others rather than in isolation.

What Peter the Great did to make the *chin* system work can be understood in terms of contemporary studies in psychology that recognize how essential to human beings is the attention of others or the need for "stroking" (in psychological jargon). In fact, the fundamental importance of the various forms of social interaction that yield "strokes" has only recently been admitted and investigated,[28] and has led to the development

---

27. *P.S.Z.*, ser. 1, vol. 6, law 3890 (January 1722). Paragraph 16 spells out this intention.

28. Most interesting work in "stroke economy" is being done by transactional analysts, some of whom are beginning to investigate the ways by which informal or unlegislated "stroke economies" support established hierarchies of all kinds. See Claude Steiner,

of a branch of behavioral psychology whose findings are being utilized in jails, schools, and other institutions where freedom of action is limited or where material rewards have little value. It was, I think, the exploitation of basic human needs for recognition and the use of historical precedents (such as the *mestničestvo* system) for devising ways to satisfy them that helped make the rank ordering system one of Peter's most enduring reforms. Whether he was conscious of what he was doing or not, or even intended what resulted, is a different question. Nevertheless, an institution was created whose influence was impossible for any one nobleman to escape, an institution that in the end worked independently of the will of autocrats. The fact that it assumed a character of automatism proved in some measure to be a boon to Peter; it removed the great burden of enforcement from his shoulders.[29]

There was, one can see, a certain similarity of purpose in the uses of the *mir* to enforce serfdom, the institutions of self-administration to bind the middle social levels, and the institution of rank ordering to bring the nobility under control. In the context of Russian history, the creation and subsequent development of the *chin* system can be considered a kind of logical "end" in the centuries-old evolution of the "service state," which subordinated autonomous social groups, one after another, to the will of the autocrat. But though created primarily as a substitute for the use of force against the nobility, the *chin* institution had the potential of being used to affect the behavior of other groups. In order to understand how it came to be the source of social mobility in Russia, as many western scholars think, it will be necessary to look again at the social structure as it existed in Peter's day.

When Peter began to modernize, he undertook activities that were accomplished routinely in wealthier states but had never been undertaken, at least on a large scale, in Russia. This meant new social "tasks" or burdens and a greater need for manpower. Lacking a sufficient number of nobles and skilled persons in general to perform these new tasks or functions, he turned to social categories that had in pre-Petrine days not been "ascribed" by hereditary tradition. These groups constituted, in terms of the service state model or role ascription structure, "free-floating" groups. Among these were the wanderers, vagrants, and castoffs of Peter's military campaigns; the sons of state and church servitors who had been performing the nobility's functions in

Scripts People Live: Transactional Analysis of Life Scripts (New York, 1974). pp. 131-137.

29. I owe this insight about the transfer of responsibility of enforcement from the Emperor to the peer group to David P. Bennett.

civil or military offices but without having been given documentary proof of noble status; and the Europeans brought in by Peter who chose to remain in Russia.[30] When the role ascription system was universalized, these groups became anomalous, made up of persons outside the legal rules governing the service state. In the decree of January 16, 1721 (ennobling all officers of rank 8 and above), that is, one year before the promulgation of the Table of Ranks law, Peter stated in effect that those persons who performed what amounted to the functions of the traditional nobility in the military services should be nobles.[31] One could say that the Table of Ranks law did the same thing for the non-military servitors of the state, providing a predictable and orderly method by which "non-nobles" already performing tasks that could be considered the duties of the nobility could be inscribed in that category. It should be noted, however, that the Table of Ranks law included a provision for delaying the inscription of those who were in the civil service, suggesting that Peter intended to extract more time in service from the non-ascribed subjects doing civilian work than from the non-ascribed subjects doing military work.

The practical effect of such a provision for ennoblement was that the socially unfixed or "free-floating" groups found a category in the *soslovija* system by climbing the rungs of state offices or earning grades and that in the end no group remained "outside" of the large ascription system. In addition to the traditional ways of ascription to *soslovija*, by birth, by direct Imperial action, or by census revisions, there was now added assignment to a legal category based on one's already existing mode of life. For most people, however, it was the *soslovie* into which one was born, or inherited status, that prescribed one's role. In fact, it was usually expressly forbidden to leave it at will.[32] Rarely could a nobleman become a priest, or a priest become a nobleman, or a merchant undertake a nobleman's functions. It was impossible, in particular, for

---

30. A good source in English about the various pre-Petrine social strata that Peter tried to integrate into his reformed service state is Kluchevsky, *Peter the Great*, esp. pp. 93-94. *P.S.Z.*, ser. 1, vol. 6, law 3890, par. 16, refers directly to the problems that would result if persons simply called themselves nobility.

31. Kluchevsky, *Peter the Great*, p. 100; *P.S.Z.*, ser. 1, vol. 6, law 290 (January 16, 1721); *P.S.Z.*, ser. 1, vol. 6, law 3890, pars. 11, 15.

32. *P.S.Z.*, ser. 1, vol. 22 (1739-1796), law 17212, required specific verification about a person admitted to work in the government from the lower social levels as to whether he had been granted official leave from his prior role (*zvanie*) and whether he had been released from all poll tax obligations. Given this requirement, I think sense can be made of paragraph 6 in the Table of Ranks law (see *P.S.Z.*, ser. 1, vol. 6, law 3890, par. 6) that states that no one may be given a grade (*rang*) without an exit permit (*patenta abšid*). In Basil Dmytryshyn, *Imperial Russia: A Source Book, 1700*-1917 (New

a peasant to gain a "permit" to leave his burdened estate and assume a place in the social categories through which he could earn access to noble status. In sum, only those who had been assigned to the functions of the nobility either by virtue of *soslovie* status or by direct Imperial action could undertake the work through which noble status could be earned. This statement seems paradoxical, unless we remember that it applied to the "free-floating" or pre-Petrine non-ascribed groups. The idea that the Table of Ranks law was an ascription law, i.e., one intended to fix persons in predetermined categories, is not however incompatible with the idea that it was to become a means of social mobility. The existence, however, of an ascription system that prescribed procedures for transferring from one category to another aborted the development of intermediate categories, social classes roughly similar to the middle classes of the west. All persons who undertook the activites from which middle classes could have grown were in Russia, by virtue of the Table of Ranks' ascription provisions, absorbed into the nobility.

In Peter's day, however, most of the social mobility that occurred was not the result of the Table of Ranks law. Rather, it should be labelled "sponsored" social mobility. Either the Emperor himself or a favorite of the Emperor discovered a useful or talented person in a disadvantaged social group and had him promoted to a new level. Or a low status group as a whole, for whatever reasons, could be forbidden its previous functions and then assigned new tasks, the performance of which made members of the group candidates, so to speak, for the status of nobility. Once the Table of Ranks rules were set up, however, it became an almost routine matter for "sponsors" to effect transfers between categories. (Done under the guise of correct procedure as spelled out by the new rules, these transfers contributed to dislocating the traditional *soslovija* order.)

The *chin* system, by fixing the "free-floating" groups in the ascription system as nobles and by making sponsored transfers easier, increased the number of persons who were "nobles." The *chin* laws also "equalized" the legal status of a variety of sub-categories that had comprised the upper estate in pre-Petrine times. There is no agreement yet among historians

---

York, 1967), p. 21, this has been translated as ". . . no one may be given a new rank without a release patent, unless We personally have signed that release." If one conceives of the *soslovija* order as a kind of "ranking order," it is then understandable that exit permits from their own "compartments" were required of persons from lower levels in the primary hierarchical order in order to begin competing for personal grades in a better *soslovie* level. George Vernadsky, ed., and Sergei Pushkarev, comp., *A Source Book for Russian History from Early Times to 1917*, vol. 2 (New Haven, 1972), pp 342–344, translates only a few sections of the new law and the listing of office titles by "level," and does not include this troublesome paragraph at all.

about how the social composition of the highest levels of state service was affected by these changes. High offices or high places in the rank ordering scheme seem to have remained in the main the province of the old nobility, a conclusion that is supported by detailed studies of Brenda Meehan-Waters, who investigated the Generalitet after 1730, and M. D. Rabinovich, who studied the officers' corps after 1721.[33] This makes sense when one considers that it would be the families bound by tradition to serve who would have had administrative experience and who would be accustomed to the uses of power. Even when compelled to serve, they would have most readily conformed to the demands of the highest offices.

The question arises of how much the *chin* system owed to western precedents. Some historians have thought that the Table of Ranks was modeled to some extent on the organizational charts of foreign governments, for example, of Prussia, Denmark, Sweden, or even China.[34] It cannot be denied that the titles used for classifying functions were a mixture of Latin, French, English, and German words. The important idea of "ranking and rating," of placement on a scale or assignment to a niche, each with its prescribed prerogatives, is, however, authentically Muscovite. (Some scholars, including Professor Vernadsky in *Kievan Russia*, mention the "ranking of cities" according to which the Kievan princes asserted their rights.)[35] And language explaining the procedures of ranking and grading seems to reflect Peter's personality. When one reads his communications and laws, one is impressed by the frequency of his threats, and the same menacing tone is detectable in the Table of Ranks law. If the nobility will not work, he will ennoble those who will; they will pay who will not obey the rules; they will be deprived of benefits

---

33. Brenda Meehan-Waters, "The Muscovite Noble Origins of the Russians in the Generalitet of 1730," *Cahiers du monde russe et soviètique* 12 (Janvier-Juin 1971): 28–75. Of the top 83 men in government in 1730 whose paternal records she was able to trace, Meehan-Waters discovered that 72 were descendants of men who had served in the highest positions of the Muscovite state, and that indeed 20% of the 125 men who made up the Generalitet of 1730 were descendants of the old Muscovite princely families. See also Rabinovič, "Social'noe proiskhoždenie i imuščestvennoe položenie," pp. 141–142/ (note 8, above).

34. A. Kizevetter, "Tabel' o rangakh," Brokgauz-Efron *Ènciklopedičeskij slovar'*, vol. 32 (St. Petersburg, 1901), pp. 439–441, thinks that the idea for the list of grades was given to Peter by Gottfried Leibniz, the great mathematician, and that the French, Prussian, and Swedish ranking orders influenced the formulation of the decree before the Senate began to rework and expand it. Evreinov, *Graždanskoe* pp. 26–27 (n. 5, above); Troickij, "Iz istorii," pp. 98–111 (n. 2, above). S. M. Troickij, *Russkij absoljutizm i dvorjanstvo v XVIII v: formirovanie bjurokratii* (Moscow, 1974), pp. 47–140, gives a good deal of information based on archival material about the sources used in preparing the *Tabel'*.

35. George Vernadsky, *Kievan Russia* (New Haven, 1948), p. 179.

who do not serve; and so on. The many laws that seem to show Peter's
hatred of the nobility are, I think, rather a product of style; Peter
threatened one and all alike.[36]

The fundamental impact of the *chin* system on Russia's further
development derives from the way that it extended the power of the
autocrat. While an assignment of status by niche existed in Muscovite
times, it was a niche that one had a right to, determined by service and
heredity; now the "right to place" was imprinted upon the entire
nobility by virtue of office and grade earned, i.e., one's right to a niche or
a place in the world came from the autocrat. By arrogating to the state
not only the power to rank offices and to assign any state function to a
level on a chart, but also the power to render each individual his due
by assigning him a "grade," Peter really extended the state's authority
to deal with matters of deciding claims of social usefulness and indirectly
estimating personal worth. In making use of the state's power to regulate
social distance between people, he extended the state's power regulating
human behavior, even in such matters as dress, one aspect of an area
of conduct that elsewhere was increasingly enforced by mores and rules
of etiquette and habits of politeness. (It must be noted that the state,
in claiming the right of arbitration in spheres of social propriety, inadvertently assumed responsibility for controlling social processes that
could only be very complex and contingent, a situation that in the future
would create problems by their nature impossible to deal with.)

All this was happening at a time when intellectuals in France and
England were urging their governments to policies of *laissez faire*, not
only in questions concerning the protection of hereditary status but also
in those treating economic relationships. Paradoxically, in trying to
modernize, Russia seemed to produce results that were alien to itself and
to the west. Regardless of its implications for the future, however, the
rank ordering system humanized life in Peter's Russia; the use of
physical coercion to force men to serve the state became less necessary.
For all that, however, it was a reformed Russia that was more removed
from realizing the West's ideas of freedom and equality and limited
government than backward Muscovy had been.

The behavioral restrictions and terms of competition prescribed by the
chin system, accepted for whatever reasons by the nobility, eventually
became so assimilated by it that those who behaved in consonance with
the rules did not seem to think of them as emanating from laws;

---

36. Dmytryshyn, *Imperial Russia*, pp. 15, 17, 18; Vernadsky and Pushkarev, *Source Book*, 2:125, 329; Kluchevsky, *Peter the Great*, p. 129; V. I. Lebedev, *Reformy Petra I: Sbornik dokumentov* (Moscow, 1937).

grades that determined not only official and government-related pre-rogatives but also norms of private acceptability became thought of as categories in which the world worked. As early as the eighteenth century, Russian authors began to use a vocabulary derived from the *chin* system (uniforms, grades, titles, etc.) to describe individuals and social relation-ships. Without an understanding of *chin* rules, a certain dimension of meaning in much of Russian literature remains inaccessible to a reader whose culture is untouched by such a formal and all-embracing system of ranking. A good example of a work using such language is the short story "The Nose" by Nikolay Gogol,[37] written about the middle of the nineteenth century. The hero of the story is a Collegial Assessor who arrives in St. Petersburg from the Caucasus in order to find a new post equal to his "grade." Gogol's explicit labeling of his character immediately alerts the reader familiar with *chin* lore that he is an official in the civil service who acquired his *chin* by serving in an area of the empire where promotion was easy, requiring little or no education. That he is a snob and social climber is evident from the fact that he insists on using a military title rather than the equivalent title in the civilian hierarchy; the military title gives him social precedence over those who possess the civilian title. The plot turns on the hero's nose running away and assuming the accouterments and prerogatives of an official ranked higher than it. The nose makes social and official calls in official regalia, claims service in branches of government inacces-sible to the Collegial Assessor or major (as he prefers to call himself), and snubs its owner. There are many references to the *chin* code: "place," things not "fitting ranked offices," honor to be yielded to rank, remarks that while "personal insult might be forgiven, insults to rank cannot be," etc. The story can be considered a satire on the *chin* system, and as such, one can say that Gogol's "message" is that a chunk of mindless flesh if dressed in the uniform of an official could go about without people noticing that it is not human. In more philosophical terms, the story can be seen as an imaginative speculation on the power of symbols to affect human behavior, and indeed shows that symbolizing can endow insensate things with life.

Further perspective on the evolution of the meaning of *chin* comes from the fact that while the autocracy created in the *chin* system a tool for solving an essential state problem, it also became a tool to be used by

---

37. Gleb Struve, ed., *Russian Stories: A Bantam Dual-Language Book* (New York, 1961), pp. 30–90. In this story the Russian titles are literally translated into English; for instance, *kolležskij assessor* is translated as "collegial assessor," thus maintaining the sense of peculiarity of the institutions and concepts dealt with.

various social groups for various purposes. Any interest group with access to the autocrat, or to the committees reforming *chin* rules, could make indirect use of it. By studying the changes in *chin* rules and how any change benefited one or another group, the historian can discover which social group was effectively in control of the government. From the death of Peter the Great to the granting of the Charter of Nobility (1725-1785), the predominant influence of the nobility is evident. By the end of the period the trend in Imperial legislation toward dis-nobling the gentry (as Peter had tried to do by making several of the gentry's *soslovie* rights contingent upon earning *chiny*) was stopped and reversed. The change in *chin* legislation that most strikingly reveals the influence of the nobility in government was the exclusion of lower *soslovie* persons from ranked government offices.[38] Exceptions were made, of course, for hiring non-noble persons, but the latter were not given the right to be promoted in grade. This rule effectively nullified the provision in the Table of Ranks for routinely promoting lower level, non-noble *činovniki* to the *soslovie* of nobility. One result of this limitation upon admission to the nobility was the creation of a subcategory within the *soslovija* structure, that of *kanceljarskie služiteli*.[39]

The influence of the nobility in the period can be seen not only in legislation nullifying rights earlier accumulated by non-noble categories, but also in the increase in rewards and permissible social activities that attached to *chin*. For example, as schools were created for noblemen, their children could earn grades for attending those schools. (There were instances too of pure corruption, such as the occasional enrollment of infants in government service so that by the time they began to work as

---

38. *Polnoe sobranie zakonov Rossijskoj imperii. Sobranie vtoroe 1825-1881*, 55 vols. (St. Petersburg, 1830-1884), vol. 2, law 1827 (October 14, 1827), lists those social categories that did not have a right to serve in the government. Many categories remained excluded from government service, despite the fact that Catherine II's charter to the towns had extended serving rights to new levels of the social structure. In the literature that has dealt with the subject of disparate rates of promotion for nobles and non-nobles at various times, there seems to be an assumption that promotions depended mainly upon the personality of emperors. Romanovich-Slavatinsky, *Dvorjanstvo*, pp. 227-228, thinks that Catherine's preferential treatment of the nobility was more a question of her personality than of law. Laws granting preferential promotion rights to the nobility were on the books as early as July 1762. See *P.S.Z.*, ser. 1, vol. 16, law 11,611, and *P.S.Z.*, ser. 1, vol. 17, law 12,462 (1765); these laws provided that noblemen who transferred from military to civil service were to get an automatic promotion in grade.

39. N. P. Eroškin, "Samoderžavie pervoj poloviny XIX veka i ego političeskie instituty (K voprosu o klassovoj suščnosti absoljutizma)," *Istorija S.S.S.R.*, 1975, 1 (Janvar'-Fevral'), pp. 36-59; Harold A. McFarlin, "The Extension of the Imperial Russian Civil Service to the Lowest Office Workers: The Creation of the Chancery Clerkship, 1827-1833," *Russian History*, 1, 1 (1974):1-17.

young men they had already been promoted in grade.) Legislation changing the length of time the nobility had to serve in government also indicated its influential role; by the 1740s its obligation to serve had been reduced from a lifetime to twenty-five years. Finally, the nobility's influence in government reached its culmination in 1762 when it was freed from service obligations altogether.

There is considerable historiographical controversy about whose interests were served by the "freedom" that Peter III granted to the nobility and what motives the government had in granting it.[40] A close reading of the Law or Charter of 1762[41] shows that it was a logical development in the institution of *chin*. When Peter III said "we judge it no longer necessary to compel the nobles into service as has been the practice hitherto" because "devotion and zeal for military affairs has resulted in the appearance of many experienced and brave generals; civil and political concerns have attracted intelligent people," we can see that there were enough people who served willingly for the government to be able to eschew compulsion in getting the nobility to serve. The law concluded that "zeal for public good" and "public honor," i.e., social honor and preferences of *chin*, had prompted men into service. Thus, the law really indicated the success of the *chin* system. And as if to assure its continuing success, the autocracy enumerated and further increased the "rewards" and benefits of those who served and the social disabilities of those who did not. The Law of 1762 is in fact an expansion of the application of *chin* rules and a clearer formulation of some of the ambiguous portions of the law of Table of Ranks. Even the right to leave service, granted to the nobility, was modified by *chin* rules. Those men who had earned a grade 8 could, with permission of their superiors, leave service immediately. Those who had not yet earned that grade were entitled to retire only if they had served at least twelve years. The law further provided that noblemen who retired could be readmitted to service only if there was a vacancy and could be promoted only if they had previously served three years "in grade." But subsequent promotion for them was even more qualified. They were not to be promoted over the heads of or to degrees higher than their fellows who had remained in service, i.e., they were not to be given ranks higher than those who had

---

40. Jones, *Emancipation of Russian Nobility*, p. 33, summarizes the major points of view on this question; G. V. Vernadskij, "Manifest Petra III o vol'nosti dvorjanskoj i zakonodatel'naja komissija 1754-1766 gg.," *Istoričeskoe Obozrenie* 20 (1915); Marc Raeff, "The Domestic Policies of Peter III and His Overthrow," *American Historical Review* 35, no. 5 (June 1970).

41. See Dmytryshyn, *Imperial Russia*, pp. 57-60, for excerpts of the charter in translation. The entire law is rather short as can be seen in *P.S.Z.*, ser. 1, vol. 15, law 11,444. The quotations are from Dmytryshyn.

been their equal before their retirement and who had not themselves retired. The Law of 1762, then, spelled out the seniority rules that were at least implicit in the Table of Ranks but were in any case unenforceable at the time of its promulgation. Now promotion was unmistakably contingent upon seniority in office, and the advantages that would accrue to those who remained in government were made more explicit. Peter III stated in no uncertain words that "we issue this rule in order to give preference in promotion to those now in service over those who have retired."

The provisions of the Law of 1762 altered the meaning of *chin* and, consequently, the effects of the *chin* system on the nobility. Since a nobleman was no longer punished for avoiding service, just the time he spent in service came to be considered meritorious. It was logical, then, that grades should be given for time served, and indeed, soon after 1762, an explicit promotion schedule was issued that prescribed intervals of time that had to elapse before a servitor could be considered for various promotions.[42] The amendments also made provision for accelerated promotions in cases of special distinction and special merit. Henceforth, however, the grades awarded to an individual were given more routinely, becoming in a way a "right" of the servitor, something that was his due because he had served.

When comparing the grades of the Law of 1762 to the grades in the Table of Ranks of 1722, it is apparent that they had become more valuable over time. The government increased their value by making it a matter of law that high offices would be accessible only to officials who had high degrees. Thus for the individual, a grade functioned as a license or requisite qualification that in the routine course of bureaucratic

42. Torke, "Das russische Beamtentum," pp. 53-56 (n. 3, above). Torke discusses the evolution of time requirements for promotion in some detail. See *P.S.Z.*, ser. 1, vol. 17 (1765-1766), law 12,543; the law established a lengthy time requirement for promotion of non-noble officers. See also *P.S.Z.*, ser. 1, vol. 25, law 18,894 (March 18, 1799), where the increased value of *chin* is indicated. This law provided that an official who had been subject to criminal prosecution could not lose his *chin* except with a direct confirmation by the Emperor, indicating that the possession of *chin* was as securely guaranteed as the property of the nobility after 1785. *P.S.Z.*, ser. 2, vol. 39:2, law 41,476 (November 1864), par. 945, shows that judicial reforms continued to maintain this protection. Before the time requirements for promotion became stabilized in the nineteenth century, there was considerable variation in the waiting periods of those considered for promotion. *P.S.Z.*, ser. 1, vol. 18 (1767-1769), law 12,973, required seven years "in *chin*"; *P.S.Z.*, ser. 1, vol. 23 (1789-1796), law 16,930, required eight years; *P.S.Z.*, ser. 1, vol. 23 (1789-1796), law 16,960, established different rates of promotion in the schedules of nobles and non-nobles. See also Malkova and Pljukhina, "Dokumenty vysšikh" p. 210 (n. 11, above). *Polnoe sobranie zakonov Rossijskoj imperii. Sobranie tret'e 1881-1913*, 33 vols. (St. Petersburg, 1885-1916), vol. 18, law 15,871, pars. 23-29, contains data about the promotion schedules of *činovniki* extending into the twentieth century.

affairs made him a candidate for higher office. This last change would have a profound impact on the government, its policies and personnel, but it is a topic I cannot develop here; my immediate task is to show how all these changes in the *chin* rules affected the nobility as a whole. Not only did they affect individual noblemen but the *soslovie* of nobility.

The new rules tended to divide the nobility into several "classes" with different interests. The nobility who did not aspire to service at all constituted the first "class"; the second group was made up of people who entered service on a permanent basis; and the third group comprised men who served for a time and then exercised the right to retire. The "conflict of interest" that was to develop between the last two groups is important. The nobles who accepted the reward of "freedom" that attached to the grades they had earned, i.e., those who retired, found that when they tried to reenter government service, they were routinely excluded from offices higher ranked than the offices they held at the time of their retirement. They soon discovered that only seniority qualified them for such offices, seniority earned in office.[43] Also, since higher offices were staffed primarily by men with seniority, they found that the longer they remained "in retirement," the more difficult it became for them to catch up with the men who had remained in the government. Thus, having chosen not to serve, these men were automatically handicapped for the kinds of activity that in Russia were considered the particular province of the nobility. In a real way, the men who retired became superfluous men, since nearly all the work necessary for the survival of the Russian community (its feeding, defense, administration) was done without their contributing.

Paradoxically, the wealthy and prestigious noblemen who could afford to retire were the first to suffer the experience of "alienation." If they tended to become anti-bureaucratic, however, they remained "pro-autocratic" and pro-establishmentarian. M. M. Shcherbatov, who wrote *On the Corruption of Morals in Russia* in the reign of Catherine II, N. M. Karamzin, who wrote *Memoirs of Old and New Russia* in the reign of Alexander I, and the emigré N. I. Turgenev, who wrote *Russia and the Russians* in the reign of Nicholas I, were all retired aristocrats.[44] They

---

43. Peter Dolgorukov, quoted in Richard Pipes, *Russia under the Old Regime* (New York, 1974), p. 136, states the problem of the excluded nobility most clearly.

44. Mikhail Mikhailovich Shcherbatov, *On the Corruption of Morals in Russia*, trans. and ed. A. Lentin (London, 1969), pp. 29, 30, 39, 43, 230–240; Pipes, *Karamzin's Memoir*; Nikolai Ivanovich Turgenev, *La Russie et les russes*, 2 vols. (Paris, 1847), 1:98, 2:17; Marc Raeff, "State and Nobility in the Ideology of M. M. Shcherbatov," *American Slavic and East European Review* 19, no. 4 (October 1960): 363–379, 381. Raeff states that Shcherbatov had no direct access to the councils of the Empress, which was also the situation for Karamzin, as Pipes explains.

all exhorted the autocrat to rule "without bureaucrats" and to rely rather upon the loyal nobility, protesting that it should be given access to the autocrat, that it alone should influence him, not through institutions, but through his "heart." What these men were really asking was that the autocracy rule without the institution of *chin*. (It has been usually thought that the old nobility was against the parvenus in government and wanted to restrict the government to the ancient nobility. In fact, the men in government were those who continued to serve without interruption, and some of them were of as old a lineage as those who had retired. The basis of the "outs' " hostility was that they were institutionally excluded from service because they were not qualified to hold high offices in keeping with their hereditary status since they did not have the requisite seniority or grades.)

As mentioned above, the *chin* rules also had an impact on the government. In trying to use grades as inducements to keep noblemen in service, by implicitly making office the reward of service, the government inadvertently limited its powers of appointment to those men who had chosen to remain "in service."[45] Eventually, the systematic or routine application of the exclusion provisions would determine the psychological, social, and cultural make-up of the bureaucrats. They would be those men in Russia who knew least about "life" as it was lived in the provinces of Russia or in Europe. Those who availed themselves of education or of travel rights, or left the government to manage their estates, would always be behind the men who stayed and accumulated the time in service necessary for promotion. Until the 1820s, however, the power of *chin* rules to exclude the wealthy and independent nobility from service was obviated by the existence of the court *chiny*, grades that were given not for "time" served but for any quality the emperors prized. Until 1806, all of the court *chiny* and even Imperial *ordena* (the jewelry of favor) were considered the equal of earned grades in the sense that their possessors were qualified for appointments to highly ranked offices.[46] Yet most court grades were given to those who could be seen by the autocrat, i.e., to those who had enough social importance to be admitted to court. These grades could be and indeed were used in an *ad hoc* way to qualify men

---

45. Malkova and Pljukhina, "Dokumenty vysšikh," pp. 209-211, 214-217, in describing the mass of biographical documents produced by the processes of appointments and promotions, have inadvertently shown the increasing tendency to evaluate every in-service action as something that merited consideration for promotion.

46. *P.S.Z.*, ser. 1, vol. 32 (1820-1821), law 28,517, forbade the awarding of *ordena* to *činovniki* of less than ninth grade. This indicates that all those awarded *ordena* would already be nobles. Other restrictions on awarding *ordena* and the rank-ordering of *ordena* can be found in Malkova and Pljukhina, "Dokumenty vysšikh," pp. 217-218.

for high ranked offices who did not have seniority, and obviously their existence tended to restrict the exclusion processes implicit in the routine operation of the *chin* system as a system rewarding seniority. When the power of court grades to qualify officials for appointments was limited (by a law supported by the priest's son Speransky),[47] the automatism of the *chin* system became inexorable.

The structure of rules established by Peter the Great to ensure the nobility's allegiance to the state and its cooperation in carrying out the tasks of the bureaucracy had evolved by 1785 into an institution whose routine operations tended to have the opposite effect. *Chiny* began to exclude, if not the "brightest and best," then the independent and the affluent from high office. A whole class found itself useless and there ensued that sense of malaise or "dis-ease" commented on by many writers and critics. If an institution is obsolete when it no longer serves the purposes for which it was created, then the institution of *chin* had become obsolete. It should have been abolished, but it was not. It continued to evolve, acquiring other functions and developing new meanings.

II

The second period of the evolution of *chin* began with Catherine the Great's promulgation of the Charter of Nobility in 1785.[48] As in the case of the freeing of the nobility in 1762, there is some question about Catherine's motives for granting rights to the nobility and about the interests served. Since, however, the meaning of *chiny* is dependent on *soslovie* laws, as shown above, it is necessary to concentrate on the question of how the Charter affected all the *soslovija* in Russia, even though the *gramota* addressed itself to the nobility.

Fundamentally, the Charter recognized the "honor and inviolability" of the nobility (*neprikosnovennost' ličnosti*). In effect, the nobleman could no longer be dis-nobled or demoted to another *soslovie*, nor could he be

---

47. Marc Raeff, *Michael Speransky: Statesman of Imperial Russia, 1772–1839* (The Hague, 1957), pp. 177–178; Erik Amburger, *Geschichte der Behördenorganisation Russlands von Peter dem Grossen bis 1917* (Leiden, 1966), p. 508; *P.S.Z.*, ser. 1, vol. 30, law 23,711 (August 6, 1809). Laws promulgated in the years 1806 and 1809 in fact abrogated the power of *ordena* to qualify their possessors for high offices. The provision that officials, in order to get grade 5, were first to pass educational achievement tests was abrogated. The provision that lower-level degree holders pass educational tests was reinterpreted, in practice, by allowing those who had educations to start on higher rungs than those who did not.

48. *P.S.Z.*, ser. 1, vol. 22, law 16,187, contains Catherine's Charter to the Nobility. Partial translations of the Charter can be found in Dmytryshyn, *Imperial Russia*, pp. 98–102, and in Vernadsky and Pushkarev, *Source Book*, 2:412–415. The excised portions seem to me to be particularly important for understanding the growing influence of *chiny* in Russia.

beaten (the whole *soslovie*, rather than just certain degree holders of noble status, was now exempted from corporal punishment). He could not be arbitrarily exiled or have his properties confiscated. If accused of a crime, he had a right to predictable treatment in law, a kind of due process, and he was to be tried in court by his peers. Besides these rights of personal inviolability, he gained some other personal rights, such as the right to passports (for travel both in Russia and abroad) and the right to choose his profession. The Russian nobleman also was granted some civil rights, for example, a right to private property, to own land and serfs, to sell or inherit both, and to use them to operate factories and stills (this last right, limited to be sure, infringed on the *soslovie* right of the merchant category). A new political right, after a fashion, was the right to "assemble," to form corporate bodies or associations that were empowered to deal with *soslovie* problems. In terms of the "rights of man and citizen" that the French Revolutionists were to codify less than a quarter of a century later, these new rights of the Russian nobility seem basic. According to French thought, they were due to all men since Nature and Nature's God had created men free and equal. What is particularly interesting, though, and a fact not usually noticed by western commentators on the subject, is that the Russian nobility's charter extended rights that went beyond any to be subsequently guaranteed the European. The Russian nobility was granted explicitly and clearly "a right to service" and a "right to *chin*."[49] In western terms, the Charter granted to the Russian nobility a preemptive right to a specific role, a monopoly, as it were, on the valued and honored work that was available in Russia. It is this last-mentioned right that was important in the further evolution of *chin*. As far as the nobility was concerned, the obligation to serve was finally completely abrogated; serving became instead a kind of a "reward," and the autocrat in 1785 showed special honor to the nobility by reserving to it the "right" to serve. Since the rewards for service remained grades and the social prerogatives attached to them, grades became quite naturally the preserve of the nobility, i.e., grades became the nobility's *soslovie* rights. This was a change indeed; the burdens of the nobility of 1722 had evolved by 1785 into its perquisites and privileges.

---

49. M. D'jakonov, "Dvorjanstvo," Brokgauz-Efron *Énciklopedičeskij slovar'*, vol. 10 (St. Petersburg, 1893), p. 206, summarizes most cogently the kinds of "rights" the nobility enjoyed after the Charter, among them the "freedom not to serve and the freedom to serve and to be promoted." See also Baron Sergej A. Korff, *Dvorjanstvo i ego soslovnoe upravlenie za stolet'e 1762-1855 godov* (St. Petersburg, 1906), pp. 143-144. Dukes, *Catherine the Great*, pp. 222-299, describes the integral connection between Catherine's provincial reforms and the Charter of Nobility.

Such a radical restructuring of the nobility's rights implied a fundamental change for the whole *soslovija* structure. For practical purposes, one level or category of the Russian *soslovija* was no longer subject to the laws governing the others. The nobility had no obligations, while the remaining categories were stratified, as before, according to the quantity and degree of difficulty of the obligations imposed on them, i.e., according to the extremity of their binding. The nobility also had rights while the other *soslovija* did not. In comparison to the rest of the *soslovija*, then, the nobility was doubly privileged: in its exemption from obligations and tax burdens and in its possession of rights. Its position could have meaning only in Russia, where simply having "rights" was to be privileged. In terms of Enlightenment ideas, the possession of rights was the natural condition of man, and a class was not really privileged unless it had powers beyond "rights." From this perspective, the Russian nobility was not "privileged," unless one asserts that its power over the peasantry made it so. If the Russian system of stratification had remained stable and all the "rights" granted to the nobility had remained its prerogatives alone, the changes in the following period would have been fundamentally different from what actually developed.

At the very time that the autocracy granted a Charter to the nobility, it issued what amounted to partial charters to several other *soslovija*. In the Charter of Towns (1785),[50] the autocracy gave, for example, the *kupečestvo* of the first guild and some artists and academicians some "nobles' rights" and some of the exemptions long since possessed by the nobility (such as freedom from poll taxes, billeting obligations, and personal recruitment obligations, a right of personal inviolability, and a right to private property in towns). Most importantly for our purposes, some categories were also given a "right to government service" and a "right to *chin*." In 1827, these rights were extended to the *kanceljarskie služiteli*, and their children, the officials who had been recruited from lower *soslovija* groups during the eighteenth century but were excluded from holding ranked offices and receiving personal grades in service. Several other levels of society were given rights to government service and *chin*, but they could only be received indirectly, through universities,[51] academies, and other educational institutions that were empowered to award their graduates, in addition to academic certificates,

---

50. *P.S.Z.*, ser. 1, vol. 22, law 16,187 (April 21, 1785); *Svod zakonov* (1857), vol. 13, articles 88-351 (note 12, above), describes the rights of institutions to *chin* by the rather complex method of comparing newly emergent institutions to others that had already been included in the scheme of rights and privileges.

51. Evreinov, *Graždanskoe*, pp. 48-50, lists dates when institutions were given rights to award "*chin* rights"; S. V. Roždestvenskij, *Očerki po istorii sistem narodnogo*

these *soslovie* rights of the nobility. The graduates, if they came from non-noble social strata, attained a new *soslovie* status as a by-product of having attended such schools.

The extension of "rights" to new levels of society changed the very principles by which Russian society was stratified, and hence its structure. In the years from 1785 to 1830 Russian society became more complex since some groups were stratified on the basis of obligations, others on the basis of rights (the nobility), and yet others on the basis of some exemptions as well as some rights.[52] Those who had no rights were non-privileged. Those who had rights and no obligations were considered to be "privileged," but even those who had some rights were considered to be privileged, as indeed they were under Russian conditions. The privileged and unprivileged groups generally inherited their status and transmitted it by birth to their children, but members of the partially privileged groups, those with some rights, were generally created by government policy or actions and drawn from the less privileged categories, and they had to depend on their own efforts (work in the government) to maintain for themselves the legal condition they had acquired. (By the same token, they could improve their status.) What is important in these social developments for our discussion here is that the word *chin*, through the restructuring of the *soslovija*, changed meaning. It was no longer used as a synonym for most *soslovija* categories but was applied more nearly, though not consistently, to those categories—the partially privileged groups—that had been created by the autocracy. The *raznočincy* were created when some burdened categories were given some nobles' rights, a process that continued piecemeal during the entire period from 1785 to 1861.[53] Among them, however, there were substantial differences. Some subcategories had a right to education, a right to service, and a right to *chin*, rights that when exercised had the potential

prosveščenija v Rossii v XVIII–XIX vekakh, vol. 1 (St. Petersburg, 1912), gives much information about the connections that developed between education and government service.

52. N. I. Kareev, "Gosudarstvennye činy," pp. 401–405 (n. 23, above); "Raznočincy," Brokgauz-Efron *Ènciklopedičeskij slovar'*, vol. 27 (St. Petersburg, 1899), sect. 1, pp. 179–180; N. M. Korkunov, *Russkoe gosudarstvennoe pravo*, 2 vols. (St. Petersburg, 1908–1909), 1: 288–315; G. N. Vul'fson, "Ponjatie Raznočinec v XVIII–pervoi polovine XIX veka," *Očerki istorii narodov Povolž'ja i Priural'ja* 1 (Kazan', 1967): 107–123. I am grateful to Professor W. M. Pintner for making this article available.

53. A. D. Gradovskij, *Sobranie sočinenij*, vol. 7, *Načala russkogo gosudarstvennogo prava* (St. Petersburg, 1901), pp. 200–201, states that freedom from obligations began to signify noble status, differentiating those who were "privileged" from those who were still bound. D'jakonov, "Dvorjanstvo," Brokgauz-Efron *Ènciklopedičeskij slovar'*, vol. 10 (St. Petersburg, 1893), pp. 208–209, lists the various dates when the nobility's rights were extended to other social categories.

of taking their possessors not only from their hereditarily ascribed order but also from the subcategory to which they had been elevated. These "rights" gave their possessors access to the ladder of ranked offices or prerogatives of grade that in terms of the rules of the Petrine Table of Ranks, still in force, could give them all of the nobility's rights. If persons who had the *soslovie* rights to grade, education, and service actually took advantage of them, they became a socially mobile "class" and became, in fact if not in name, an "emergent" nobility.

What this meant can be made clear by comparing the social stratification order in Russia at the beginning of the nineteenth century to the social stratification structures that had emerged in Europe by the same time. The Russian nobility's legal status (measured by the number of rights and opportunities granted it) most nearly resembled the legal status of citizenship that was adopted by nations influenced by the reforms of the French Revolution. In European terms, then, the highest level of the socially stratified Russian order could be called citizens (also "middle classes" or "bourgeoisie"). If the status of nobility was the "best" in Russia, defining the inferiority of all other categories, then the *raznočincy* were partial "citizens", with some noble rights, or citizens in the process of acquiring full citizenship rights or, we would say, earning civil rights. This definition of *raznočincy* in terms of nobility (and of nobility in terms of European citizenship) brings the real status and condition of the *raznočincy* into sharper focus than the usual definitions of them found in Russian historiography as commoners, non-nobles, middle classes, etc.[54] It is also useful because it makes it possible to continue describing the evolution of the meanings of *chin* for individuals in the proto-nobility in a more precise and understandable way.

The *raznočincy* who took advantage of the "right to *chin*" given their *soslovie* and who entered the government discovered that *chin* was used to pre-select officials for promotion in ranked offices and to reward servitors with personal and social preferences. These uses of *chin*, of course, were understood and taken advantage of by the hereditary nobility. For the socially mobile group, though, a certain number of the rewards accruing to *chin* (which to the nobility were meaningless, since it already had all the personal, civil, and political rights available in Russia) had special meaning; to them, the accumulation of *chin* meant acquiring more personal and civil rights, a way of attaining the status of full nobility. Which of the rewards implicit in *chiny* any one emergent nobleman would specifically work for, or focus on, depended on his

---

54. Christopher Becker, "*Raznochintsy*: Development of the Word and the Concept," *American Slavic and East European Review* 18, no. 1 (February 1959).

"objective" social situation (on the number of noble rights he already had) and on his "subjective" or private state of mind, a matter of goals aspired to dictated by education, experience, even friends and acquaintances. Hence, the specific or personal values that *chin* had for individuals within the group of emergent nobility varied. For instance, a proto-noble of modest goals who had only the *soslovie* right to work in government might aspire only to a ranked office that guaranteed a relatively more predictable livelihood than would be likely outside the government, given his *soslovie* status. *Chin* rewards, then, were valued by him mainly for their economic worth, as a means to sustaining life. Another proto-noble, better off economically, might try to earn "grades" for the "personal inviolability" they provided, e.g., exemption from corporal punishment (a precondition to maintaining a sound psychological life). For a more ambitious person of *raznočincy* origins, the chief aim of earning degrees in government might be to achieve equality with the "ancient nobility," to have the nobles' rights to own land and serfs, to participate in corporations of the nobility, to choose a profession (i.e., to leave service without the attendant loss of noble status), and to have the right to transmit the secure legal status to his children. These were the rights that conferred on the individual a legal personality and social standing in the community, indeed they were rights the possession of which meant to be fully "human," according to Russian intelligentsia thought. *Chiny* did not lose their importance for the *raznočinec* who became ennobled and who was ambitious. For him as a "new man" (a newly created nobleman), grades might mean a right to occupy an important government post and a right to be admitted to "court." He might aspire to earn more grades in order to qualify for powerful offices either because he wanted to do good for others or because, as a "new man" of *raznočincy* origins and a parvenu in Russian society where the codes of the hereditary nobility dominated, he wanted power and access to court as means of winning acceptance.

The different meanings of grades to individuals during 1785–1861 had important consequences in the psychology of social classes, in government policy, and indirectly in social dynamics, and these in turn produced changes in social stratification in Russia. How social psychology was affected by the changes in the *chin* system can be seen by the effect of these changes on *raznočincy* groups. When social mobility became legal, not all *raznočincy* technically entitled to improve their status were able to do so. For example, some of those who were legally permitted to go to school did not have the means to do so, or some who went to school could not finish, while still others who graduated and thus earned a "right to government service" and a "right to *chin*" could not find positions. And even among those who did find positions, some might not be noticed and promoted by their superiors. For all practical purposes, the legal right to "social mobility" was limited by "the rules of life."[55] Individuals who knew the way to legally improve their condition but were unable to take advantage of it would feel more frustrated and possibly more angry than if merely an accident of good fortune or chance made social change possible. Some, of course, succeeded, and what is discovered are the signs of discontent that we associate with losses resulting from social and geographical change, by-products of social mobility. Thus, the sense of malaise among the *raznočincy* groups can be attributed in large measure to the existence of an institution for social mobility.

Government policy was affected more indirectly by the changes in the *chin* system. Despite the difficulties inherent in any attempt to improve one's condition and despite downright discrimination, non-nobles were being ennobled. There emerged, as a result, what the older nobility labeled "proletarian nobility," a service nobility or non-landed, non-gentry nobility—in other words, a "citizen-nobility." Given the time during which the citizen-nobility was created (a period of revolutions in Europe and a time when the autocratic Russian government was still staffed by the landed nobility), the nobility who governed thought that its "estate" with its traditions and prerogatives, indeed the social order itself, was endangered by the process. The response of the government was to try to stop it by changing the regulations governing promotion in grades. According to new legislation,[56] members of the proto-nobility were required to wait longer than those who were born nobles before they were eligible for promotion to another *chin*, and they had to wait much longer before getting their first grade when working in a ranked

---

55. Two persons restricted by the "rules of life" were Vissarion Belinsky (1811–1848), who was expelled from school before graduation, and N. G. Chernyshevsky (1828–1889), who though having successfully defended his master's dissertation was not awarded the degree because of official highhandedness. See P. O. Morozov, "Belinskij, Vissarion Grigor'evič," Brokgauz-Efron *Ènciklopedičeskij slovar'*, vol. 5 (St. Petersburg, 1893), pp. 191–194; "Černyševskij, Nikolaj Gavrilovič," *Russkij biografičeskij slovar'*, 25 vols. (St. Petersburg, 1896–1918), 3: 284–293.

56. The most important restrictive legislation was enacted in the reign of Nicholas I and late in the reign of Alexander III. See Malkova and Pljukhina, "Dokumenty vysšikh," p. 212, for a chronological list of all the legislation which attempted to control the creation of hereditary nobility by raising the grade required for admission to the nobility. On pp. 206–208, legislation is cited that differentiated the promotion rights of various classes of people upon entrance into service. See also *P.S.Z.*, ser. 2, vol. 20, par. 1, pp. 450–451.

office, which the hereditary nobility usually received within a year after entering service. The degree level for admission to the *soslovie* of hereditary nobility was also raised. Later in the century, the department of government that certified admission to the nobility, the Heraldry Office, raised its fees for papers certifying attained noble status.[57]

The politics of "reaction," as these policies are usually labeled, did not stop the creation of the new hereditary nobility; they did succeed, however, in keeping those who aspired to be nobles from their goal for a longer time. The consequence was the rise of a new social category that must be considered a permanent half-nobility, a category that in Russia was hidden beneath a variety of labels—honorary hereditary citizenship, personal honorary citizenship, personal nobility, and *razno-čincy*. Aspiring nobles could enter this class with fewer degrees than required for admission to hereditary noble status. Since some members of the half-noble groups sensed that they could never earn enough degrees to achieve full nobility (the ancient nobility was staffing high offices with candidates of its own kind), the more confident and ambitious of them tried to make their way in the "free professions," such as journalism, teaching, medicine, and publishing, access to which was not limited by prescribed *soslovie* status. It was these half-noble groups that were to supply some well-known figures in Russian history, who represent a great variety of psychological types ranging from the super-conservative M. Pogodín to the radicals V. Belinsky and N. Chernyshevsky.[58] The opponents of autocracy, the revolutionary intelligentsia, have been given the most attention by intellectual and social historians, but they, I think, were the exceptions within the group. They tended to be people with experiences that led them to conclude that the *soslovija* and *chin* rules not only restricted opportunity but also destroyed life and "humanity" and therefore should be abolished. It was inevitable, I think, that after 1861 the braver and more stubborn of the revolutionary intelligentsia would find it necessary to resist the autocracy by force; if the autocracy did not exactly forbid thinking, it nevertheless made the communication of ideas concerning the "human condition," and the formation of associations dedicated to explaining it, illegal, enforcing its proscriptions with repression and persecution. In the protracted struggle with the state, many of these "outsiders" were destroyed either physically or psychically, but some survived and dedicated their lives to extirpating "the evil thing" in Russia, which came to include not only the autocracy, but the

57. Evreinov, *Graždanskoe*, p. 50; Dukes, *Catherine the Great*, p. 145.

58. Biographies of Pogodin and Shevyrev can be found in N. V. Riasanovsky, *Nicholas I and Official Nationality in Russia, 1825–1855* (Berkeley, 1959).

church, officialdom, and the liberals, in fact anyone who found life in Russia tolerable.[59]

From our vantage point, it is possible to see that during the period from 1785 to 1861 the interaction of *chin* laws with *soslovija* laws made it difficult, even impossible, for some individuals to survive as "human beings." In so far as *chin* laws increased human problems and social conflict, they were more than obsolete, they were decadent. More ominous for the state was the fact that by routinizing social mobility, *chin* began to dissolve the *soslovija* order itself by continually increasing the number of subcategories within *soslovija* and the number of men within the subcategories. The *soslovija* order, however, was still fundamental to life in Russia and had to be maintained because it made predictable the supply of goods, human beings, and administrative talent to the autocracy. As a result, it was imperative that the government do something to make the *soslovija* order work with some precision and efficiency. The existence of *chin* promotion rules in the government, however, made fundamental change difficult, even when the autocrat supported it. When the Crimean War demonstrated that the autocracy could no longer defend the country with society organized as it was, the autocracy undertook reforms, but it did not abolish the *soslovija* order; rather, it "re-formed" it in terms of *soslovija*. This meant that the *chin* system was also maintained and, consequently, evolved once more. As before, an understanding of *chiny* after 1861 requires that we analyze the changes made in the *soslovija* structure.

III

The *soslovija* order was restructured as a result of the cumulative effects of several legal enactments,[60] the most important of them abolishing serfdom, abolishing corporal punishment (for several categories of half-nobility), setting up universal military conscription, and establishing the institutions of the *zemstvo* and the judiciary. There were also some later changes made in education, in press and poll tax laws, and in regulations for founding joint-stock companies. Taken together, these reforms altered the distribution of rights, duties, and privileges of the *soslovija*.

The enactments of 1861 and 1874, the Emancipation Proclamation of February 14, 1861, and the Universal Military Statute of July 21, 1874,

---

59. See Dmytryshyn, *Imperial Russia*, p. 184 for "Belinskii's Letter to Gogol July 15, 1847," p. 241 for "The Catechism of the Revolutionary, 1868," and p. 247 for the "Demands of the Narodnaia Volia."

60. D'jakonov. "Dvorjanstvo," p. 208, (n. 53, above) lists various pieces of Great Reform legislation and discusses their impact on the *soslovija* structure.

profoundly vitiated the basic principles of the service state, namely, that groups in society were different by birth and remained so in law according to the obligations they rendered to the state. By requiring now that all men bear arms according to their ability rather than their birth, the state really equalized them before the law. If any group or *soslovie* was "merged" with the nation, it was the nobility; in principle, it was no longer "privileged" in the sense of being exempted from state burdens. The confiscation by the state of the body of the peasant (which had been a machine of labor for the landowning nobility), by making the peasant a person in law, which was literally what the Emancipation Statute of 1861 accomplished, had the effect of abolishing the nobility's economically privileged status. But the Law of 1861 also undermined the nobility's privileged status by granting many more persons some rights similar to its own rights. To the proto-nobility and the permanent half-nobility, the *raznočincy* of the pre-1861 period, the ideal estate had become less attractive; now the exemptions the nobility had exclusively enjoyed were taken away or at least shared with others.

Other enactments of the Great Reforms reduced the differences between the partially privileged groups and the groups below them. The Judiciary Reform of 1864, the Zemstvo Reform of 1864, the abolition of corporal punishment and judicial tortures in 1863, and the exemption of townsmen categories from the payment of poll taxes struck directly at the rights that had made the different levels of partial nobility preferable to the social levels below them in the *soslovija* order. By abolishing the poll taxes of the townsmen, the state extended the exemption of the *raznočincy* from state dues to categories of persons who, though not as burdened as serfs, had been at least inferior to the groups earlier liberated from poll taxes by special state action. Even the peasantry came to possess some rights that the emergent nobility had enjoyed exclusively before. And the abolition of corporal punishment (by the Law of April 17, 1863), which exempted many persons from branding, beating with rods, and general physical punishment, meant that, through state decree, the half-nobility now had to share with others what they themselves earlier had had to earn.

The acts ratifying the legality of the town *dumy* and the *zemstva* struck at other principles that made for differences between varied categories of emergent and attained nobility, such as, for instance, the principle that taxing persons and their property was to be done according to their juridical status. Both of these enactments taxed lands, i.e., property, irrespective of the juridical status of its owner. The laws instituting town *dumy* and the *zemstva* even permitted persons who had property to vote for deputies to those institutions, hence, to participate in public life. In effect, they abolished the claim of the nobility to exclusive access to "public life," which had formerly distinguished them. The founding of the institutions of courts made the protection of due process (that had been the patrimony of those born noblemen and an earned right of attained nobility) available to many individuals of lower juridical statuses.

All these changes in fact obviated the meaning and the value of *raznočincy* statuses,—partial nobility statuses—as they existed before 1863, by the relatively simple expedient of granting their rights to all *soslovija* that were not peasant. In sum, the varieties of proto-nobility were immersed in and equalized with the nation by the "elevation" of those below them to their level, while the nobility was equalized by being "demoted," i.e., by the dissolution of its exclusive rights and privileges. Since the categories we have dealt with as partial nobility of various kinds were in a sense abolished in law, *chin* as a subcategory in *soslovie* and as a valued legal device for social mobility should have disappeared from Russian public life. This would have been the case if the categories of *raznočincy* had been defined only by their condition of partial liberation from state burdens and as possessors of some noble rights. Actually, substantial differences remained after the Great Reforms to define the various old *soslovija* categories and subcategories. Since they continued to count in the dispensing of passports, admission to school, entrance to government, and even limited access to the newly created judicial, *zemstvo*, and educational professions, they continued to determine life paths. This meant that it was still important for members of categories whose opportunities were abridged (because of their *soslovie* of birth) to strive for admission to categories that had been granted greater opportunities. Since the *chin* in government had not been abolished either, government service could still serve as a ladder for social mobility. Thus, the effect of fundamental alterations in the *soslovija* structure was not to decrease but rather to increase the number of persons aspiring to improve their status,[61] particularly when police state restrictions were loosened and economic opportunity increased. What each competitor hoped for by striving for grades in government and, consequently, what value *chiny* had as rewards, depended now to a much greater degree than before on many individual factors. These can be best assessed by dealing with individuals, a process that cannot be undertaken here. What is important for us in this social development is the fact that *chin* rules as a device for social mobility increased competition for posts

---

61. *Ibid.*, p. 209, states that in Russia in 1858 there were 609,000 hereditary nobles and 276,809 personal nobles, but that by 1870 the number of hereditary nobility had declined, while the number of personal nobles had risen to 316,994, an increase in twelve years of 40,185 persons.

in the government.[62] This, combined with the continued ranking of government offices, seniority rules, and the proviso that the government only gave the *chiny* that counted in social mobility, changed the social composition of the governing elite. It is this last development in the *chin* system and its impact on government during 1861–1917 that has to be considered here.

During 1861–1917, the government not only maintained a system for ranking offices and *chiny* for grading individuals, but increasingly enforced a more rational and predictable system of rules governing the correspondence between *chin* and office. The system for classifying offices, for instance, had been modernized in the 1830s. Offices that had been added to the bureaucracy since Peter the Great's day were incorporated into the classification system, and the number of "classes" in the hierarchy of offices had been reduced to twelve (from Peter's original fourteen).[63] Some levels of work below or outside the classification system, such as the secretarial offices, were incorporated into the ranked office scheme and their officials given "grades." A grade and office correspondence law was made explicit in the latter half of Nicholas I's reign.[64] It stated that each level of office in government should be held only by persons with grades not more than two degrees lower or one degree higher than the office rank. The seniority rules for each grade were reiterated and applied with more rigor. No official with less than a grade 8 was to be promoted in *chin* more than once every three years. After earning grade 8 and until he earned grade 5, every official was to serve four years before his next promotion.[65] Theoretically, the Emperor was free to make all appointments for offices above the fifth rank, although he was at least implicitly limited to choosing officials only from among those who had the prerequisite *chiny*. Seniority rules were increasingly strengthened by a more consistent application of the rules

---

62. Armstrong, *European Administrative Elite*, p. 223, states that the Russian civil service, in contrast to the civil services of France, England, and Germany, inducted more persons at entrance level positions than could ever hold higher offices. The ratio he gives is 40 to 1.

63. McFarlin, "Extension of the Imperial Russian Service," pp. 17–18. (n. 39, above). Charts indicating the office and grade correspondence requirements can be found in *Svod zakonov* (1857), p. 332, pars. 358, 362, 556, 560 (n. 12, above).

64. Torke, "Das russische Beamtentum," pp. 80–81 (n. 3, above).

65. McFarlin, "Extension of the Imperial Russian Service," pp. 16–17, has constructed charts showing the waiting periods required for various classifications of *soslovija* before they could be promoted to the first *klassnyj čin* and the rates at which they were to be promoted thereafter. See also *Svod zakonov* (1857), p. 122, sect. 2, pars. 591–592 (n. 12, above). Similar information for a later period is in Rogovin, *Ustav o službe*, pars. 19–49 (n. 14, above).

that "outsiders," the people who did not have time in service, could be given government grades and appointments only under extraordinary circumstances, and that those with grades earned more or less as a matter of routine were to be considered qualified for any and all work in the government.

The rules of correspondence between office rank and grade established in the 1830s and 1840s, combined with the *chin* rules that worked as a device for social mobility (bringing those who wanted to earn better *soslovie* rights into the government, as explained above), operated to favor the men who had the greatest vested interest in earning grades in government. These happened to be the socially declining hereditary nobility (men who were losing land) and the partial and recently attained nobility (men who wanted secure noble rights.)[66] Under ordinary conditions, when the Emperor or members of high society did not intervene in the process of granting *chin* by "arbitrarily" promoting men in *chin*, the *chin* system worked to increase the number of grade holders—those legally qualified for appointment to office of higher levels—coming from the poor sections of society rather than from among the well-established, secure, and rich, who had less incentive to "sit out time" in government. And, of course, the time servers, viz., the poorer hereditary nobility (the attained noblemen were as yet not in positions to make decisions that would affect the government at large), had no interest in altering the social structure, which was damaging to others, or the *chin* order that had elevated them to prestigious posts in the government.[67] Whatever changes there were, were made by an energetic Emperor, or gadflies whom he listened to, and then usually only in times of emergency. Otherwise, the great inertia of the bureauracy prevailed, an inertia that

---

66. This conclusion can be reached, I think, on the basis of a detailed analysis of the work done by historians who have devoted themselves to studying the social origins of the governing elite of the late nineteenth and early twentieth centuries. See Walter M. Pintner, "The Russian Higher Civil Service on the Eve of the Emancipation," unpublished article lent by the author. P. A. Zajončkovskij, "Vysšaja bjurokratija nakanune Krymskoj vojny," *Istorija S.S.S.R.*, 1974, no. 4 (July–August), pp. 154–165, analyzes landownership of high officials on the basis of institutional affiliation. P. A. Zajončkovskij, *Rossijskoe samoderžavie v konce XIX stoletija (političeskaja reakcija 80kh–načala 90kh godov)* (Moskva, 1970), pp. 112–117, analyzes the extent of landownership among high officials in Alexander III's reign, listing officials by "grade." See also Don Karl Rowney, "Higher Civil Servants in the Russian Ministry of Internal Affairs: Some Demographic and Career Characteristics, 1905–1916," *Slavic Review* 31, no. 1 (March 1972):101–110; Erik Amburger, "Behördendienst und sozialer Aufstieg in Russland um 1900," *Jahrbücher für Geschichte Osteuropas*, n.f. 18, Heft 1 (März 1970):127–134.

67. Helju Aulik Bennett, "The *Chin* System and the *Raznochintsy* in the Government of Alexander III, 1881–1894" (Ph.D. diss., University of California, Berkeley, 1971). I argue that reaction in the government originated in the experiences of the ex-*raznočincy* as new nobility when the *soslovija* system was disintegrating.

might have prevented even the Great Reforms, save for the determination
of a few strong-minded men.

After the early period of the Great Reforms, the bureaucracy again
continued elevating the lesser or poor hereditary nobility to high offices.
Now, however, some attained noblemen (new men) were in high-level
positions, having been promoted by the Emperor in recognition of their
services on various committees that prepared the legislation of the Great
Reforms. These two groups of nobility, the poorer hereditary and the new,
had the responsibility for dealing with the social developments set into
motion by the Great Reforms. Although the autocracy had not been
altered—it was still the only institution legally empowered to initiate
changes in society—a number of old Russian noble statesmen thought
that at least its effectiveness could be improved.[68] One suggestion offered
was to institutionalize (by making it an advisory branch to the old Senate)
the information-gathering apparatus that had developed informally during the preparation and drafting of the Great Reforms, i.e., the commissions, committees, and *sovety* (councils) attached to the central
institutions and the committees of nobility at the local level.[69] But any
such innovative activity was against the interests of the new governing
elite of attained nobility and petty or declining nobility, whose preferment
in goverment depended on the routine operation of *chiny* and limiting
competition; any governmental reorganization, however minimal, would
have disturbed the existing ranking and *chin* relationships from which
they profited.

Instead of modernizing the autocracy, the government embarked on
a policy of "reaction," much of which is too well-known to repeat here
(restrictive measures in education, the *zemskie načal'niki*, press restrictions, etc.) but whose tendency in general was to reconstruct the old
soslovija structure. An even more important development during the
reactionary period, especially during the reign of Alexander III, was the
modernization of the office ranking and *chin* systems in government.[70]

---

68. Marc Raeff, ed., *Plans for Political Reform in Imperial Russia, 1730-1905*
(Englewood Cliffs, N.J., 1966). See, for instance, "Memorandum of the Secretary of State
Valuev, April 13, 1863," on pp. 120-121, and "Memorandum of Count M. T.
Loris-Melikov, January 28, 1881," on p. 132.

69. Ibid., p. 132; Gorfejn, "Osnovnye istočniki," p. 86 (n. 11, above), lists documents
helpful for investigating the advisory apparatus used unofficially by the Imperial government
when consulting with "society."

70. *P.S.Z.*, ser. 3, vols. 1-33. A useful book for surveying the development and expansion of the *chin* system after the 1860s is Rogovin, *Ustav o službe*. The growing complexity
of the *chin* system can be seen from sampling the laws in the 33 volumes of the
Polnoe sobranie zakonov, using Rogovin as a guide. In paragraph 107:5, p. 503, we find
that some state offices have been given the power to award their officials grades that are
two or three degrees higher than offices at the same level in another institution. On

Various government committees (staffed by the attained nobility and declining nobility) worked out rules for integrating institutions created by the Great Reforms (the *zemstva*, town *dumy*, reformed police, new schools, etc.) into the *chin* system. Chiefly, this was done by providing that persons who "served" in these institutions could be awarded "seniority rights" on the *chin* ladder should they transfer to government service. The newly established schools were licensed to award *chin* rights as a part of certain degrees granted to their students, who, if they sought government positions, would in turn be given certain preferences. Most military officers or rank holders in the military services (from whom many high Imperial officials in the civil service had been recruited) were disqualified from transferring to civilian offices, or at least could not transfer without great difficulty. Seniority requirements were extended to levels 5 through 3 of the ministerial offices[71] that provided the political advisory corps to the Emperor. (Improvements were also made in the salaries, pensions, and emoluments of state officials, but this need not concern us here.)

Not all of these reactionary changes endured, but some did and profoundly affected the governing personnel for the rest of the Imperial

---

p. 503 there is a law enacted in 1892 that made the awarding of *ordena*, hitherto ostensibly given for excellence, dependent on time served in government and level of office attained. For example, the Order of St. Anna of the 3rd degree could not be requested for persons without a grade 10 or for those who served in an office at level 10 or below. On p. 499 offices are given that have been exempted from *chin* and office correspondence rules, in this instance, judicial offices. Paragraph 6 on p. 461 indicates that the *zemskie načal'niki*, the "land captains" created in 1890, were exempted from having to possess the grade usually required of men serving at the level of office that their institution had been assigned. It is clear that the niche assignment system survived the revolution of 1905. On p. 523 a law of 1908 is given permitting the secretarial offices serving the State Duma to hire persons who do not have a right to the grades of ranked offices, or who have no grade at all. On p. 347 are references to *neklassnye štatnye činy*, one instance of which were those awarded to Imperial musicians giving them personal rights as if they were state civil servants but not entitling them to compete for offices in the ranked office system of the regular state service.

71. Rogovin, *Ustav o službe*, p. 152, pars. 328, 329. According to laws enacted in July 1892, August 1898, and August 1900, certain conditions had to be met before one could be recommended for grades higher than those of *statskij sovetnik*, grades that would qualify one to hold fifth-level offices. A grade 4 (*dejstvitel'nyj statskij sovetnik*) could be awarded only to persons who had had grade 5 (*statskij sovetnik*) for no less than five years and who held office at the fifth level in the hierarchy of offices. Grade 3 (*tajnyj sovetnik*) could be given to persons who had had grade 4 for no less than ten years and who held a position at no less than the fourth level of offices. Further restrictions on promotions seem to have been made by imposing time intervals before officials could make recommendations, two years for grade 4 and three years for grade 3. In any case, an official would have to have served in lower-level offices for a certain minimum period of time before promotion to the highest degree grades could be approved; for example, for *chin* 4, it was no less than twenty years. Even a recommendation for promotion for "excellence" (*otličie*) could not be entertained until a twenty-year service requirement had been satisfied.

period. First of all, extending *chin* seniority rules to public and educational institutions indirectly extended the ranking of offices, found in the government, to institutions in society. Despite the fact that the Imperial Law School and the *zemskaja uprava* (the executive committee of the *zemstvo*)—institutions included in the *chin* seniority rules—were not formally designated as levels or classes in the ranking of offices in government, individuals serving in them accrued seniority in the same way that bureaucrats in government did.[72] Rights or powers to grant *chin* preferences, however, were unevenly distributed among these institutions created after the Great Reforms. The personnel from those institutions licensed to grant preferential rights (higher *chin* rights or more seniority rights) were the individuals most likely to be appointed to higher government posts; thereafter, by the regular seniority process, they would emerge as candidates for the highest offices and become advisors to the Emperor. What is significant is that the more modern, technologically oriented institutions of industry, the railroads, law, and journalism did not get *chin* seniority rights, while the older quasi-governmental institutions of *zemstva*, town *dumy*, universities with classical curricula, etc., did. Consequently, few of the Imperial administrators of the late nineteenth and early twentieth centuries had much awareness of or experiences with the problems, economic and social, that we identify as modern. Also, by applying rules of seniority even to appointments to the highests offices, the autocrat was further limited in his choice of administrative and political talent. In effect, the *chin* rules, made more rational and explicit (i.e., an obsolete system made more efficient) and combined with an increasing commitment to the ideas of *Rechtsstaat* even among the bureaucracy, created a situation in which it was extremely difficult for the government to get even its ordinary business (of hiring, firing, and promoting officials) done. An extraordinary amount of energy and effort was required merely to keep the bureaucrats' official records straight. Further effort and imagination were required to legislate

---

72. Ibid., pp. 64–65, pars. 142–145, refers to laws abrogating *chin* requirements for technical professions. They were usually enacted after the 1860s. In paragraph 138, p. 58, Rogovin refers to laws enacted in 1905 that granted local administrative heads of the Ministry of Interior permission to hire officials without *chiny* for offices ranked up to level 6, provided that they had fulfilled certain educational requirements or had served in the *zemstva*, town *dumy*, or assemblies of nobility as elected representatives. To be appointed to offices higher than the sixth level, however, one had to satisfy stiffer educational requirements or have served a longer term in the *zemstva*, *dumy*, etc. Rogovin's *Ustav* is also a convenient source for following alterations in the grade and office ranking correspondence rules that were made in the years 1835, 1853, 1854, 1856, 1857, and 1874 (see p. 55). On p. 56, Rogovin refers to a law enacted in 1894 granting the Minister of Finance the right to hire officials without *chiny* for all offices below level 5 if they had the right education or work experience in offices of the *zemstvo*, *dumy*, etc.

exceptions to rules that plainly did not work. Important appointments had to be made "out of turn" (one of the more able and energetic of modern Russian statesmen, Count Witte, could be appointed to his office from the South Russian Railroad Administration only by having the Emperor personally grant him a series of grades).[73] Bound as it was by its own *chin* rules, then, the Russian Imperial government acted very slowly and oftentimes, in terms of its own laws, "arbitrarily" or "illegally."

In a country where the autocratic principle reigned supreme but where the autocracy could not act, a revolutionary situation was inevitably bred. Here was an institution where, as a matter of course (of organization), individuals with no interest in making any changes were placed in positions of command and, conversely, persons to whom change was essential had no way of assuming positions of power. Furthermore, even if persons willing to make change were admitted to powerful offices, a massive abolition of old laws that made necessary human activities illegal would have been required. Given these conditions, the autocracy could only maintain a policy that became increasingly "unrealistic," and in the end could only appeal to the hearts and minds of men to help solve the country's problems.

The Imperial autocracy did, however, continue to muddle through for many years. Many of the essential changes that enabled it to endure, though, took place in spite of and not under its direction. It even survived the revolutions of 1905–1906, when more significant changes were made in the laws on social stratification and even new procedures for policy making were instituted, as for example in the creation of the Duma. Even so, the *chin* system in the government remained in force. Finally, during the First World War, the autocracy fell, and shortly thereafter the *soslovija* and *chiny* were formally abolished by the Bolsheviks.[74]

---

73. S. Ju. Vitte, *Vospominanija*, vol. 1 (Moscow, 1960), pp. 208–210. Witte was a *tituljarnyj sovetnik* (i.e., had grade 9) in retirement. He was awarded the fourth grade by the Emperor himself; he was also given money from the Emperor's private purse to supplement the salary that came with his *chin*, a salary much less than what he received as an administrator of the railroad system.

74. A. Drobinskij, "Chiny," *Bol'šaja sovetskaja ènciklopedija*, ed. V. V. Kujbyšev and N. I. Bukharin, vol 61 (Moscow, 1934), pp. 611–612. A decree of November 25/12, 1917, abolished *soslovija* and *chin*. After the revolution of March 1917, civil rights were extended to all Russians and restrictive police regulations abolished; still, tax assessing continued and criminal procedures were conducted according to the old Imperial laws. In effect, *soslovija* rules continued to be enforced.

RUSSIA'S BANQUET CAMPAIGN

BY

TERENCE EMMONS

> . . . The Russian liberals, those solemn
> gentlemen, dining *ad majorem libertatis gloriam* . . .
> ROSA LUXEMBURG

IN THE EARLY stages of Russia's revolutionary crisis at the turn of this century, the urge among the country's rapidly growing minority of educated, politically conscious inhabitants to organize themselves politically was confronted by an "absence of political life";[1] that is, by a general prohibition not only on formal political parties, but on any kind of public gatherings for political purposes, and by strict control over the political content of the periodical press—measures all enforced by the autocratic state so long as it was able to do so. Under these conditions, efforts to mobilize politically significant numbers of people—a process which might be called primitive party formation in the pre-constitutional period —took a number of imaginative and original forms. The general situation was by no means peculiar to Russia (as demonstrated, for example, by the history of Japan in the first decades of the Meiji Restoration before the introduction of the 1890 constitution),[2] but the specific forms taken there are revealing about Russian political conditions and possibilities.

Considering the conditions prevailing in Russia prior to the 1905 Revolution, it is not surprising that the most radical opponents of the old

This article is part of a longer study of political mobilization in early twentiety-century Russia which is being undertaken with the support of a grant from the American Council of Learned Societies and a fellowship from the John Simon Guggenheim Memorial Foundation.

1. The phrase was used by a Moscow correspondent of *Iskra*, no. 81 (23 December 1904).

2. Nobutaka Ike, *The Beginnings of Political Democracy in Japan* (Baltimore, 1950); R. H. P. Mason, *Japan's First General Election, 1890* (Cambridge, 1969).

45

regime should have been the first to organize, clandestinely and, in the beginning, for the most part abroad. By definition, only "professional revolutionaries" could take the risk and the time required for such activities. By the time the crisis of the old regime was sufficiently advanced to propel significant numbers of "non-professionals" into political action, the revolutionary organizations were already some years in existence and relatively well established (although for the period before 1905, emphasis definitely should be on "relatively," rather than "established"). The revolutionaries had stolen a march on the reformers, and this was to have a profound impact on political developments.

Under the prohibition on political activity prior to the weakening of state authority, group discussion of political affairs did, of course, occur. For landed gentlemen there were the *zemstvo* institutions of limited local self-government and, on a few occasions, national gatherings of zemstvo leaders. For professional men there were national and local meetings of their professional societies (whose numbers proliferated around the turn of the century), as well as special problem-oriented convocations. (As is well known, the zemstvos were also outlets for the political energies of many professional people who possessed, ordinarily by dint of their landed gentry backgrounds, the property qualifications necessary for voting and standing in the zemstvo elections). Then there were the scientific-cultural associations: the Imperial Free Economic Society, the Imperial Geographic Society, the Imperial Juridical Society, etc. And there were birthdays of famous men, *Tatjanin Den'* (the anniversary of the founding of Moscow University), and other anniversaries to be celebrated. Most of these institutions, including particularly several provincial zemstvos and several professional societies, had altercations with the authorities over "abuse" of their convention rights: some meetings were closed down prematurely, elected officers were removed, and several professional groups were ordered dissolved. The frequency of such punitive measures increased markedly in 1903–04 under V. K. Pleve, whose ministry represented the regime's last attempt before the onset of the 1905 Revolution to use repression as the main method of dealing with the "social movement."[3]

As is usual in such circumstances, political activity grew bolder and more intense as authority grew weaker. The first clearly marked stage in this process opened with the appointment of Prince P. D. Svyatopolk-Mirsky to replace Pleve on 26 August 1904, more than a month after the death of his predecessor by an assassin's bomb (15 July). The arrival of what was quickly dubbed "governmental springtime" (*pravitel'stvennaja*

---

3. On these developments see, inter alia, I. P. Belokonskij, *Zemskoe dviženie* (M., 1914) and S. Galai, *The Liberation Movement in Russia, 1900-1905* (Cambridge, 1973).

vesna) was punctuated by a variety of measures intended to soothe those who were considered to be the tractable members of the political opposition: abolition of corporal punishment, amnesty of some political offenders, tax relief for the peasants. In a much-noticed speech upon taking office (16 September), Svyatopolk-Mirsky spoke of an attitude of "sincere benevolence and sincere confidence toward public (*obščestvennye*) and class (*soslovnye*) institutions and toward the population in general";[4] he then proceeded to call off Pleve's campaign against the zemstvo (by restituting elective authority to the zemstvo of Tver' province, restoring full rights to a number of prominent zemstvo activists, and several other acts), relaxed censorship, and allowed several new national newspapers to be founded.

The momentum of the political opposition was by this time such that, far from producing a moratorium on political agitation by the nonrevolutionary opposition, these actions encouraged further activity and a testing of the bounds of such activity under the new conditions. The leaders of the constitutionalist Union of Liberation (*Sojuz Osvoboždenija*), in clandestine operation since January, 1904, rejected the idea of calling a moratorium on agitation for a constitutional representative order,[5] immediately set to work on new tactics, summoned a new (second) congress of the Union for late October to endorse them, and went ahead with plans to send their delegates to a general meeting of "oppositional and revolutionary organizations" in Paris at the end of September, where they would subscribe to a united front with the revolutionary parties (minus the Social Democrats, who refused to send representatives) to "hasten the inevitable doom of absolutism" and its "replacement by a free democratic regime on the basis of universal suffrage."[6] The leadership of the zemstvo movement, in the form of the bureau of zemstvo congresses (two of whose members were also on the Council of the Union of Liberation), set about planning a new national congress scheduled for 6 November.[7]

It was far from clear to anyone at the onset of the autumnal "spring" how much open political agitation would be tolerated by the regime. Symptomatic of the state of uncertainty were the tortuous negotiations between the planners of the zemstvo congress and Mirsky over the granting of official approval for the congress, whose purpose was

---

4. Quoted in N. Smith, "The Constitutional-Democratic Movement in Russia, 1902–1906" (Ph.D. diss., University of Illinois, 1958), p. 208.

5. On the pages of P. B. Struve's émigré organ, *Osvoboždenie*, no. 57 (15/2 October 1904).

6. *Listok Osvoboždenija*, no. 17 (19 November/2 December 1904).

7. D. N. Šipov, *Vospominanija i dumy o perežitom* (M., 1918), pp. 240–258; Kn. D. I. Šakhovskoj, "Sojuz Osvoboždenija," *Zarnicy*, 1909, no. 2 (M.), pp. 130–131.

clearly the making of a political declaration (in the end, it was held as a private meeting, with the police looking the other way but editors being warned that no news stories about the congress nor any of its documents were to be allowed into print). The newspapers played cat and mouse with the censors, alluding in editorials to constitutional reform without mentioning the word.[8]

It was to be anticipated (hence Mirsky's hesitation vis-à-vis the zemstvo congress) that established institutional channels would be used under the partial relaxation to mobilize pressure on the government for political reform. But these channels were no longer wide enough nor numerous enough to contain the momentum of the movement, especially after the first definite signs that the war with Japan was going badly; pretense was soon abandoned, and public meetings organized for exclusively political purposes began to take place. At these meetings people began, at first guardedly, but very shortly in the most explicit terms, to demand political changes. This was a phemonenon without precedent in Russian history. It found its clearest expression in the so-called "banquet campaign" (*banketnaja kampanija*) during the last two months of 1904.

I

The banquet campaign was a series of public political banquets attended by persons of various professions and circumstances. Admission to the banquets was ordinarily by ticket, for which a fee of several rubles was charged to pay for the meal that was usually served, although non-paying "gate crashers" were usually on hand in some numbers. The banquets merit systematic study for the light they can shed on processes of political mobilization and the development of the revolutionary situation. The results of such a study are presented below.[9] Although the banquets can be isolated for analytical purposes, they formed an integral

---

8. The liberal editors of the lawyers' newspaper *Pravo* made bold to declare in their issue for 3 October: "We need reform, not reforms (*ne reformy, a reforma*)," and the word "reform" immediately became a euphemism for "constitution" in the legal press.

9. Despite the considerable importance generally attributed to the banquet campaign in the literature on the Revolution, it has never been studied systematically, with one partial exception—the contribution by N. Cherevanin (pseudonym of F. A. Lipkin) to the second volume of the SD–Menshevik sponsored *Social Movement in Russia at the Beginning of the Twentieth Century*: "Dviženie intelligencii," *Obščestvennoe dviženie v Rossii v načale XX-go veka. Tom II, čast' vtoraja* (St. P., 1910), pp. 146–201; discussion of the banquet campaign is on pp. 146–63. Cherevanin's work is only a "partial exception" for two reasons. 1) It does not deal with the banquet campaign as a distinct phenomenon. Cherevanin's analytical category was what he called "intelligentsia manifestations" (*intelligentskie vystuplenija*), in which he included every kind of meeting productive of political resolutions in the period November, 1904–9 January 1905 for which he could find information, with the exception of the zemstvo and town council assemblies, student gatherings, and workers' meetings. 2) His study, based on reports in several legal national

part of a broader development in which politically centered professional meetings, zemstvo and town council (*duma*) assemblies, working class convocations, student meetings, and street demonstrations were also elements. Some of these other elements of the developing revolutionary situation prior to its entering a new phase with the tragic workers' demonstration in Petersburg on 9 January 1905 will also have to be examined briefly before satisfactory conclusions can be drawn about the significance of the banquet campaign.

The legal press, the émigré press, and the police files yield information on thirty-eight banquets in twenty-six different cities.[10] (See Appendix I for data on the banquets' places and dates, and sources consulted.) All but five were held in provincial or regional capitals; a majority of these were capitals of zemstvo provinces, although eight zemstvo provinces were not represented, while all the major regions of European Russia without zemstvo institutions—the Baltic provinces, the Western provinces, the far South, and the Caucasus—were represented.

---

newspapers and in the émigré press—both highly imperfect sources due to censorship in the first case and problems of communication (as well as some deliberate selectivity) in the second—took account of no more than about half the total number of "intelligentsia manifestations" and about the same proportion of banquets in the strict sense among those known to me to have occurred in the period in question as a result of a reasonably careful reading of the newspapers together with the files of the Department of Police. The latter, in addition to fuller general coverage, provide much important information on names, numbers, and categories of banquet participants generally omitted from the newspaper accounts. Some of Cherevanin's interpretive points and conclusions will be dealt with later in the article.

10. Cherevanin uncovered in all forty-four cases, or forty-two "meetings" and two declarations by the academic councils of the Petersburg and Kiev Polytechnic Institutes. He was unaware of the existence of at least fourteen banquets. My records, using the same inclusive principle of selection as Cherevanin's, yield between eighty and eighty-five such events (the precise number depending on some rather fine distinctions concerning the character of a few events and lack of information about a few others). Reporting on the political banquets and other meetings was severely restricted in the legal press, and for all but about a week between 24 November and 2 December was limited to brief general descriptions; publishing of resolutions, particularly those with constitutionalist demands, was generally excluded except during that week. As late as its issue of 22 November, the Petersburg paper *Naša Žizn'* could refer only in the most general terms to the great Petersburg banquet of the twentieth and apologized to its readers for not being able to reprint the banquet's resolutions (no. 17, 22 November 1904, p. 3). *Russkie Vedomosti* reported on the Petersburg banquet only in its issue for 24 November (no. 327), where it described the resolutions "in a general way," but did include reference to the demand for a constituent assembly. After the twenty-fourth, there is a flood of reporting on the campaigning in various cities until 2 December. On that day, the Ministry of Internal Affairs' director of press affairs circularized the editors of periodicals with a warning against publishing "accounts, communications, or articles about any addresses, resolutions, declarations or speeches whatever concerning change of our regime that may have occured in zemstvo, town or gentry assemblies, or for that matter in meetings of scientific and other societies, or of private persons (so-called 'banquets')." Šakhovskoj, "Sojuz Osvoboždenija," pp. 141–142n.

The banquets date from 5 November 1904 (a banquet in Saratov organized to express support for the zemstvo congress due to convene the next day in Petersburg) to 8 January 1905, the eve of Bloody Sunday (also in Saratov). Only eleven of the banquets were held on the anniversary day of the 1864 judicial statutes, 20 November, although a majority of them (twenty-five) were officially called in celebration of that anniversary. Seventeen were held between 21 November and 12 December, inclusively, while only seven were held after the publication of the Ukaz of 12 December and its accompanying communiqué of the fourteenth, which threatened disciplinary action against all persons (but especially government employees) who participated in public meetings where there occurred discussions of "questions of a general political character outside their competence."[11]

The idea of undertaking a banquet campaign as a means of mobilizing public support for political reform in Russia appears to have owed less to the historical example of the French banquet campaign of 1847–48 than to direct experience with surrogates for political activity, although the phrase "banquet campaign" that was generally used in reference to the meetings probably does owe its origin to the French example.

In 1897, a group of Petersburg writers and journalists founded the "Russian Writers' Union for Mutual Aid." The most important role in this union was played by men attached to the editorial staff of *Russkoe Bogatstvo*, the "thick journal" of populist orientation. The Union's leaders had a regular practice of organizing suppers and banquets; the suppers were held on a weekly basis, the banquets on anniversaries dear to progressive intelligentsia hearts, such as the fortieth anniversary of the peasant emancipation on 19 February 1901. The Union was disbanded at the order of the minister of internal affairs Sipyagin on 12 March 1901 in the wake of the political demonstration on Kazan Square (4 March 1901), in which most of the Union's officers had participated.[12] A rump of the Union's members continued to organize informal suppers of Petersburg writers and journalists as a

---

11. *Pravitel'stvennyj Vestnik*, no. 283 (14 December 1904). Quoted in Smith, "Constitutional-Democratic Movement," pp. 273-274. The ukaz, whose several promised concessions to the opposition in the area of civil and individual liberties were, as it were, thought by the government to be sufficient to stop all further political agitation—hence the communiqué—made no promises about political representation. *Pravo*, no. 51 (1904); described in Galai, *Liberation Movement*, p. 233.

12. See Galai, *Liberation Movement*, pp. 99-101, 115. The Union had a meeting immediately after the Kazan Square episode and sent a letter of protest to the minister against the brutality exercised by the police in dispersing the demonstrators. The order to disband followed shortly, and most of the Union's leaders were exiled. A copy of the letter of protest may be found in *CGAOR*, f. 518, op. 1, no. 56, p. 20

politically inoffensive substitute for the disbanded Union. Most of the seven-man "culinary committee" that arranged these suppers were either among the founders or early joiners of the Union of Liberation. When one of its members, G. I. Schreider, went to Moscow in the autumn of 1903 to help organize the Union of Liberation branch there, he proceeded with the help of colleagues in the Union to organize similar suppers of *literati* there.[13] It is easy to see how the Union's leadership came to the idea of organizing a series of banquets all over Russia for the purpose of mobilizing support for constitutional reform.

According to the memoirs of I. V. Gessen, one of the leading figures in the Petersburg organization of the Union, the Council of the Union began to plan for a series of political banquets all over Russia as one of its first activities almost immediately after it was elected at the Union's First Congress in Petersburg at the beginning of January, 1904.[14] The plan was to use the occasion of the anniversary of the peasant emancipation (19 February) for this purpose, but when preparations were in full swing, the war with Japan broke out (27 January); public attention was diverted to the war, and it was decided to postpone the campaign to the next anniversary deemed suitable, namely the fortieth anniversary of the promulgation of the 1864 judicial statutes on 20 November 1904.[15] That this long delay was unobjectionable to the Union leadership shows that the country had not yet entered a revolutionary situation; such a schedule would have been unthinkable in 1905.

By selecting such occasions as 19 February or 20 November, the organizers hoped, first of all, to be able to receive the permission required for any such gathering from the local authorities. By late autumn, as it turned out, the political situation was such that in a number of cities permission could be gotten for less prominent occasions or, in a few

---

13. The members of the "culinary committee" were: N. F. Annensky, N. P. Asheshov, Ya. Ya. Gurevich, V. B. Carrick, A. V. Peshekhonov, M. A. Slavinsky, and G. I. Schreider. Schreider used the Moscow "technical group" of the Union, consisting of I. A. Petrovsky, A. I. Maksimov, and himself, to organize the banquets. *Poslednie Novosti* (Paris), no. 3607 (6 February 1931).

14. The first council of the Union of Liberation elected at the January, 1904 congress consisted of N. F. Annensky, V. Ya. Bogucharsky, S. N. Prokopovich, A. V. Peshekhonov, I. I. Petrunkevich, Petr D. Dolgorukov, N. N. Lvov, D. I. Shakhovskoy, N. N. Kovalevsky, and S. N. Bulgakov. *Puškinskij Dom, Otdel rukopisej*, f. 334: D. I. Šakhovskoj, no. 651. Zapisnaja tetrad' "Khronologija poslednego desjatiletija," 1901-1934, pp. 40-41, 63; T. Emmons, ed., "The Statutes of the Union of Liberation," *Russian Review* 33, no. 1 (Jan. 1974): 80-85. See also Šakhovskoj, "Sojuz Osvoboždenija," pp. 122, 136.

15. I. V. Gessen, *V dvukh vekakh: žiznennyj otčet* (vol. 22 of *Arkhiv Russkoj Revoljucii*) (Berlin, 1937), p. 176. The Union leaders anticipated a patriotic rally in response to the Japanese declaration of war and did not wish to risk failure for their campaign under those conditions.

cases, was not even solicited, the banquets being held, as the phrase went, *javočnym porjadkom*, that is, without seeking permission; but this situation was not, of course, foreseen by the planners early in the year. Secondly, they hoped that by attaching the political demands that they anticipated would be endorsed at the banquets to congratulatory messages on the occasion of the great reforms and to exhortations to return to the progressive statecraft which had produced the reforms, these demands would be looked on with relative goodwill and receptiveness, and without reprisals, in the central government. In all this, they were of course operating within the tradition of the zemstvos and gentry assemblies, which customarily used an occasion like the coronation of a new tsar or the birth of an heir to the throne to forward their petitions to "the highest instance."

In the absence of a reasonably unfettered press, a series of banquets in virtually all the important urban centers in the country appeared to be the best method for "uniting the bulk of the country's intelligentsia around the constitutionalist banner."[16] This plan was adopted as Point Two of the Council's tactical report by the Union's Congress in October 1904: "To organize on November 20, in view of the fact that the fortieth anniversary of the judicial statutes falls on that day, *banquets* through . . . members in Petersburg, Moscow, and as many other cities as possible, at which constitutionalist and democratic resolutions of a much more decisive tone than those which are to be anticipated from the congress of zemstvo and town duma men [scheduled for 6 November] are to be adopted." The plan also called for mobilizing support for constitutionalist resolutions in the forthcoming zemstvo congress and also in the zemstvo assemblies due to meet at the end of the year (for the most part in December, 1904 and January, 1905). A final point (which may or may not have been adopted by the second congress, but was being acted upon by the Union before the end of the year) called for agitation to form professional unions of lawyers, engineers, professors, writers, "and other persons of the liberal professions," and to unite them through their respective directorates with the zemstvo and duma men into a "Union of Unions" which, in its turn, was to "establish contacts with the central institutions of all the Left political parties, work out a common platform and become a sort of preparliament."[17]

---

16. Šakhovskoj, "Sojuz Osvoboždenija," pp. 141–142.

17. Belokonskij, *Zemskoe dviženie*, pp. 210–211 (note 3, above). Cf. Šakhovskoj's comments about Belokonskij's rendition of this plan—the only one known—in "Sojuz Osvoboždenija," p. 132. According to his version, the German word *Vorparlament* was used, in evident reference to the Frankfurt *Vorparlament* convened on 31 March 1848, which had organized the election to the Frankfurt National Assembly (*National-Versammlung*) by direct male suffrage. The inference, if true, gives a valuable insight into the political expectations of the Union leadership.

It was not made clear just what the content of the "constitutional and democratic resolutions" to be adopted at the banquets was to be: in the first place, it was not yet known precisely what would be demanded at the zemstvo congress; in the second, there was no official position in the Union either on the question of how the transition to the constitutional order was to be made, or on the precise character of that order. The "credo" adopted by the Union's first congress did not go beyond mentioning, under the general rubric of "the political liberation of Russia," "the broadest and, in addition, absolutely equal participation [i.e., representation] of the entire populace in state administration," and no binding program or constitutional charter was ever adopted by the Union. The immediate task of the Union was described as the "destruction of autocracy and establishment of a constitutional regime in Russia," but the question of how this was to be accomplished was left open; the perennial question of whether change was to come "from above" or "from below," that is, through the tsar's grace (or capitulation) or through revolutionary violence, was only referred to: "In determining the concrete forms in which free political institutions can be realized in Russia, we will, of course, take into consideration the historical conditions of the given time and the disposition of forces obtaining in the country at the decisive moment."[18] The options were left open.

All this reflected the diversity of views obtaining in the Union, and first of all in its leadership, on political and social issues. This was symbolized most clearly in the makeup of the Union's councils, where two groups—the at least nominally socialist (populist and marxist) professional intellectuals on the one side, and the zemstvo constitutionalist reformers on the other—were represented in near parity. All subscribed to the idea that the Union was a pre-party coalition which would break up into several parties when the conditions allowing for the free activity of political parties with concrete programs had been won. (In the end, of course, this fragmentation did take place, but it occurred before the anticipated conditions had been firmly established.)[19]

It is hard to avoid the conclusion that a sizeable proportion of the Union leadership in late 1904 shared with the revolutionary parties a commitment to the summoning of a constituent assembly on the basis of universal, direct, equal, and secret ballot (the *četyrekhvostka* or "fourtailer" of current parlance) as the preferred way of ushering in the new constitutional order. In subscribing to the declaration of common principles elaborated at the September "conference of oppositional and revolutionary parties" in Paris, the Union had only committed itself

---

18. Emmons, "Statutes," pp. 82–83.
19. See below, p. 00.

to replacing the autocracy with "a free democratic regime on the basis of universal suffrage," but in a statement accompanying the text of the conference resolutions the Union announced that it considered it "absolutely essential that the principle of universal, direct, secret and equal balloting be made the basis of political reform";[20] and Article XII of a constitutional project worked up by the Union's Petersburg and Moscow leadership before the second congress (but never officially adopted by the Union) declared: "The exclusive correct path to realization of the program outlined in the attached project we consider to be the summoning of a constituent assembly, freely elected by universal, direct, equal and secret ballot, for the elaboration and implementation of the Fundamental State Law;" and the program, prepared for the same congress by "Liberationists" in Paris, including Peter Struve, editor of *Osvoboždenie*, repeated the same proposition in the form of a demand. Although it was adopted only at the third congress (25-28 March 1905), and then not made binding on individual members, the program was described as representing "the consensus of all groups in the Union of Liberation."[21]

Nevertheless, although there was a vocal minority present supporting a formulation including the demand for the "fourtailer constituent assembly," the Moscow meeting of the zemstvo-constitutionalist group (most of whose leaders were members of the Union of Liberation), where draft resolutions for the forthcoming zemstvo congress were prepared (2-3 November 1904), endorsed only a general demand for "participation in the realization of legislative authority, in the formulation of the state budget, and in the control over the legality of the administration's activities." More detailed than the formula already elaborated by the congress' bureau, this was clearly meant to exclude the possibility of a merely consultative assembly, but it said nothing about a constituent assembly or the system of suffrage.[22] This was the resolution in fact

---

20. *Listok Osvoboždenija*, no. 17 (19 November/2 December 1904). Some years later, Milyukov referred somewhat cryptically in his memoirs to "left-wingers" of the Union in Paris who included the "fourtailer" in the statement after his departure. He had been the chief author of the resolutions of the Paris Conference, including the deliberately (for the sake of adoption by all parties) imprecise one on the future form of government and the suffrage system: "a free democratic regime based on universal suffrage." *Vospominanija*, 2 vols. (New York, 1955), 1: 244-45.

21. *Osnovnoj gosudarstvennyj zakon Rossijskoj imperii* (M. 1904). Another edition was printed in Paris by Struve in 1905. Šakhovskoj, "Sojuz Osvoboždenija," pp. 135-36, 151-56. An English translation of the program is in S. Harcave, *The Russian Revolution of 1905* (London, 1970), pp. 273-79.

22. Baron R. Ju. Budberg, "S'ezd zemskikh dejatelej 6-9 nojabrja 1904g.," *Byloe*, no. 3 (1907), pp. 72-74.

adopted by the zemstvo congress, although there too a minority at first supported the constituent assembly formulation in the resolution on political change; a minority strong enough, according to Budberg, that it looked for a time as if the congress would be deadlocked over the issue. It is significant that in both cases the more radical formulation was decisively rejected by the majority of zemstvo constitutionalists for fear of alienating D. N. Shipov and other zemstvo leaders whose idea of constitutionalism and popular representation did not at the time go much beyond the "crowning of the zemstvo edifice," that is, a consultative assembly of zemstvo (and duma) representatives.[23] The Union of Liberation tactic toward the zemstvo congress was to get it to adopt a united resolution in favor of substantive constitutional reform without structural details, i.e., without the congress assuming constituent functions for itself. As a convocation of "notables" only, it was judged to have no right to do so and could only appeal to the throne.[24] The tactic succeeded in the main.[25] Other resolutions taken at the congress called for guarantees of personal and civil rights and expressed the hope that the tsar would "summon a freely elected popular representative body" to cooperate in elaborating the constitutional reforms.

II

Clear evidence of the initiative of the Union of Liberation in organizing the banquets is available in thirteen cases, while Union initiative seems quite likely in another twenty.[26] Of these thirty-three banquets, fourteen

23. Ibid., pp. 85–86; Šipov, *Vospominanija*, p. 265 (note 7, above).

24. Cf. Smith, "Constitutional-Democratic Movement," p. 238 (note 4, above).

25. A minority of 27 voted for adopting the formulation worked out earlier by the congress' bureau, which did refer to "regular participation in legislation of popular representation through a special elected institution," while the majority of 71 voted for the version worked out by the zemstvo constitutionalists, which added the phrase "participation in the realization of legislative authority, in the formulation of the state budget, and in control over the legality of the activities of the administration." Once the majority had adopted the more clearly "constitutional" version, the congress in virtual unanimity voted in favor of endowing the legislature with budgetary authority (91–7) and controls over the administration (95–3). Šipov, *Vospominanija*, pp. 265, 269.

26. In the thirteen cases (see A below), men whom I have been able to identify as members of the Union of Liberation are reported in the sources as principal organizers of banquets. In the twenty cases (see B below), initiative from the same source seems likely because of reported important roles in the proceedings by known members of the Union, by marked similarity of arrangements, dates, program, and resolutions with the definitely Union sponsored banquets, or both.

A.	Place and date	Principal Union member(s)
	Saratov 5xi	S. A. Unkovsky
	Kiev 20xi	Prof. Wagner, V. V. Vodovozov, I. V. Luchitsky, S. A. Bulgakov

explicitly endorsed the resolutions of the November zemstvo congress.[27] Two of the fourteen endorsements added the qualification that public representation be elected by fourtail suffrage, and two others added the demand for a constituent assembly elected by fourtail suffrage.[28]

Of the remaining nineteen, four adopted resolutions close in spirit and detail to the zemstvo resolutions; that is, they called in general terms for a popularly elected assembly which would generate legislation and exercise some control over the activities of the administration, in addition to calling for guarantees of civil and individual rights, but without

Place and date	Principal Union Member(s)
Kostroma 8xii	Yu. A. Spassky
Petersburg 20xi	I. V. Gessen, N. F. Annensky
Petersburg 5xii	L. I. Lutugin
Petersburg 14xii	N. F. Annensky, A. V. Peshekhonov, M. P. Miklashevsky, V. Ya. Bogucharsky, G. I. Schreider, V. A. Myakotin
Odessa 20xi	A. S. Izgoev
Voronezh 20xi	V. I. Kolyubakin, D. A. Pereleshin
Chernigov 20xi	A. A. Svechin, L. L. Shrag
Orel 2xii	A. A. Stakhovich
Saratov 17xii	(organized by a committee of representatives of the Union, the Social Democrats, and the Socialist Revolutionaries)
Saratov 8i	(arranged by "Osvoboždency")
Moscow 5xii	(arranged in coordination with the Petersburg banquet of the same day)

B.	Place and date
Ekaterinodar 10xii	Ekaterinoslav 28xi
Kaluga 1xii	Vladimir 21xi
Nizhny Novgorod 2xii	Baku 20xi
Kharkov 5xii	Nizhny Novgorod 20xi
Rostov/Don 5xii	Tiflis 31xii
Yaroslavl 20xi	Balashov 14xii
Baku 25xi	Moscow 21xi
Libava 21xi	Moscow 14xii
Tiflis 8xii	Tambov 17xi
Smolensk 20xi	Saratov 20xi

There were at least two other banquets planned by the Union which failed in realization: one planned for 7 December in Novocherkassk by local lawyers, cancelled by the head of the local lawyers' guild; and one planned for 12 December in Kursk by a group of zemstvo constitutionalists and lawyers who were also Union members (Petr Dolgorukov, V. E. Yakushkin, A. N. von Rutsen, N. V. Shirkov, E. K. Zagorsky, Anshelson, Isakov, and Rastorguev). (It is worth noting that all these Kursk zemcy had been delegates to the November zemstvo congress, and that the group as a whole formed the nucleus of the Kadet party organization in Kursk in late 1905.)

27. Nizhny Novgorod 20xi and 2xii, Rostov/Don 5xii, Odessa 20xi (majority resolution), Vladimir 21xi, Voronezh 20xi, Baku 20xi, Orel 2xii, Tiflis 8xii, Balashov 14xii, Tambov 17xi, Saratov 17xii, Kiev 20xi, and Smolensk 20xi.

28. Smolensk 20xi and Saratov 17xii added the suffrage clause; Nizhny Novgorod 2xii and Kiev 20xi, the resolution on the fourtail constituent assembly.

explicitly endorsing the November zemstvo resolutions.[29] One other banquet adopted resolutions which were essentially of the same order, but were even less explicit about the nature of the representative body and its authority than had been the November resolutions.[30]

Six banquets in the group of thirty-three made resolutions calling for convocation of a constituent assembly (in two of these cases election to the constituent assembly by fourtail suffrage was specified).[31] The remaining eight either failed to adopt resolutions or, if they did do so, the resolutions are not reported in the sources.[32]

Of the five banquets from the total group of thirty-eight for which reasonably positive evidence for the initiative of the Union of Liberation is lacking (the possibility of such initiative is not ruled out), one passed a resolution calling for the convocation of a fourtail constituent assembly;[33] two called for a constituent assembly without reference to electoral principles;[34] one in effect endorsed the resolutions of the zemstvo congress;[35] and one passed no resolutions.[36]

In all, twenty banquets either explicitly endorsed the resolutions of the November zemstvo congress (fourteen) or produced resolutions analogous to them, particularly in regard to changes in the political system (six). Sixteen restricted themselves in resolutions essentially to that.[37] Eleven, or slightly less than a third of the known banquets called for the convocation of a constituent assembly (including the two banquets which did so in addition to endorsing the November theses); of these, six specified that election to the constituent assembly should be by fourtail suffrage.

To judge from Shakhovskoy's testimony, the leadership of the Union of Liberation found that the banquet campaign "took place with great inspiration and complete success . . . These banquets, even without the

---

29. Moscow 21xi, Saratov 20xi, Saratov 8i, Libava 21xi.

30. Moscow 5xii. The main purpose of the "Banquet of Engineers" on 5 December in Moscow was not the production of political resolutions, but organization of a Union of Engineers; the same was true of the Petersburg banquet on the same day, and of the Petersburg "doctors' banquet" on 18 December. S. D. Kirpičnikov, "L. I. Lutugin i Sojuz Sojuzov," *Byloe*, no. 6 (1925), pp. 134–46.

31. Petersburg 20xi, Kaluga 1xii, Kharkov 5xii. Petersburg 5xii, Petersburg 14xii, and Tiflis 31xii; the fourtailer was specified in the resolutions of Petersburg 14xii and Kharkov.

32. Saratov 5xi, Ekaterinodar 10xii, Yaroslavl 20xi, Chernigov 20xi, Kostroma 8xii, Moscow 14xii, Baku 25xi and Ekaterinoslav 28xi.

33. Petersburg 18xii.

34. Novozybkov 7xii and Samara 20xi.

35. Kutais 31xii.

36. Samara 1i.

37. That is, the twenty banquets minus the four which added other points.

support of the press, united the mass of the intelligentsia in the country around the constitutionalist banner."[38] As can be seen from the preceding figures, the "constitutionalism" of the banquets was expressed in a variety of ways. It was this problem of variety that Cherevanin, author of the study of the banquet campaign mentioned earlier (see footnote 9), tried to analyze. After grouping the resolutions of the "banquets" he knew of in categories approximating those presented above (and with proportional results not radically different from those above), Cherevanin came to two basic conclusions: 1) the "degree of democratism" of the intelligentsia (Cherevanin uses the term *imuščaja intelligencija*, "well-off" intelligentsia, by which he refers generally to professional people who were the "fee-paying" participants of the banquets by and large) was not very high; 2) the "democratic" orientation of what was nevertheless a sizeable minority of the banquets (which he measured by resolutions calling for the fourtailer constituent assembly, or the constituent assembly at least) was to be explained "only by the influence of the democratic mass . . . in which, along with advanced workers and professionals of the revolutionary organizations, a very prominent role was played by student youth. This democratic mass, acting under the predominant influence of the Social Democratic Party, exerted an undoubtedly enormous influence on the actions of the well-off intelligentsia."[39] Elsewhere in the Menshevik collection in which Cherevanin's work appeared, the banquet campaign was characterized as an arena of conflict between "society" and the "working masses."[40]

Cherevanin had good reason to emphasize the role of the Social Democratic Party and of student youth in the manifestation of the "democratic mass" at the banquets. The SD leadership centered around the newspaper *Iskra* in Geneva (i.e., the Mensheviks), with the advent of the "governmental springtime" and the animation of the non-revolutionary opposition in the autumn of 1904, had worked up in relation to the activity of the opposition an elaborate plan of action, whose aim was simultaneously to exploit the opposition for mobilizing elements of the working class and to push the political demands of the moderate opposition as far to the left as possible. The details of the rather tortuous scheme, designed initially for application by local party organizations to the zemstvo assemblies but easily adapted to the banquets and other public meetings once they began, were spelled out in a secret

---

38. Šakhovskoj, "Sojuz Osvoboždenija," pp. 141–42.

39. Čerevanin, "Dviženie intelligencii," pp. 155, 157 (note 9, above).

40. E. Maevskij, "Obščaja kartina dviženija," vol. 2, part 1, pp. 30–40 (note 9, above, for volume title).

"letter to party organizations" distributed in November.[41] Basically, it called for presentation of the "democratic" demands for a fourtailer constituent assembly (an SD slogan since the 1903 second party congress) to the intelligentsia banquets by SD-organized "workers' delegations"; this action was to be preceded by extensive agitation and organization among local workers by SD activists in support of these demands and their presentation at the intelligentsia meetings "in the name of the people."

This plan was implemented, in whole or in part, by a number of local committees, some of which were apparently led to these tactics by independent assessment of the local situation quite without knowledge of the *Iskra* plan.[42] They included some that were, at least nominally, Bolshevik dominated, despite Lenin's condemnation of "*Iskra's* zemstvo campaign."[43] The Socialist Revolutionary émigré organ *Revoljucjonnaja Rossija* also roundly criticized the *Iskra* plan and developed its own tactic vis-à-vis the non-revolutionary opposition (about which something will be said below), but SR organization in the provinces appears to have been so ephemeral at the time that SR involvement in the banquet campaign outside the capitals is virtually imperceptible in the sources.[44]

SD "professionals" and students generally far outnumbered *bona fide* workers in the manifestations of the "democratic mass" at the banquets.[45]

---

41. The letter is published in Lenin, *Sočinenija*, 2d ed., vol. 7, pp. 410–16. On the origins of the plan laid out in the letter, in which Pavel Axelrod played the primary role, see P. A. Garvi, *Vospominanija socialdemokrata* (N.Y., 1946), pp. 411–26, and the recent studies by S. Schwartz (*The Russian Revolution of 1905: The Workers' Movement and the Formation of Bolshevism and Menshevism* [Chicago, 1967], pp. 32–50) and A. Ascher (*Pavel Axelrod and the Development of Menshevism* [Cambridge, Mass., 1972], pp. 215–223).

42. Such, in any event, was the situation in Saratov according to an SD participant: I. L.-ij (Ivan Mikhajlovič Ljakhoveckij), "Banketnaja kampanija v Saratove (1904–1905)," *Minuvšie Gody*, 1908, no. 12 (Dec.), pp. 29–62.

43. Lenin's critique, and alternative tactic, was laid out in a pamphlet published a few weeks after the circulation of the "letter," *Zemskaja kampanija i plan "Iskry"*; cf. Schwartz, *Russian Revolution*, pp. 41–49 on the polemic. It should be noted that Lenin's position could not have been widely known among the local committees until fairly late in the development of the banquet campaign. As Schwartz points out, Lenin performed a *volte-face* in the second half of December on this tactical question, apparently because of his appreciation of the appeal of the plan to local SD organizations. In an *Iskra* article of August, 1905, Martov mentioned the SD committees of Odessa, the northern region, Nizhny Novgorod, Tver, Saratov, and Samara as examples of Bolshevik dominated SD organizations which took part in the "zemstvo campaign." ("Na očeredi," *Iskra*, no. 109 [29 August 1905]). My records on the banquet campaign confirm Martov's examples for Odessa, Nizhny Novgorod, Saratov, and Samara, at least.

44. *Revoljucionnaja Rossija*, no. 61 (15 March 1905), "Nekotorye itogi Parižskoj konferencii."

45. "In fact," Cherevanin wrote in an earlier work, "the proletariat as a broad working-class mass took no part whatsoever in the zemstvo campaign; the whole affair

The worker orators who read the SD slogans were tutored and demonstratively put forward by the SD *intelligenty*. Thus Garvi, in his reminiscences about SD activity in Kiev—one of the cities where "democratic" involvement in the banquet campaign was most extensive —recalled that the "worker" who spoke up at the meeting of the Kiev Society for the Advancement of Literacy (14 December) had been "ordered" from Petersburg along with another worker by local Menshevik activists expressly for such purposes. Both were already "party professionals."[46] The role of university and technical institute students appears to have been very important in the propaganda and organizational activities of local party organizations.[47] Cherevanin claims that the politically conscious part of Russian students was in its overwhelming majority sympathetic to the revolutionary parties.[48] The evidence of student meetings and street demonstrations in the last months of 1904 (their frequency increasing rapidly toward the end of the year) confirms this claim, with the Social Democrats much more popular than SRs, one might add. Of twelve student convocations (*skhodki, večera*) in this period, nine adopted what appears to have been SD-inspired resolutions (generally calling for the fourtail constituent assembly, amnesty to all political prisoners, and immediate end to the war), while in two of the remaining three, revolutionary speeches predominated and corresponding resolutions were forestalled only by the arrival of the police to break up the meetings.[49] The two mass street demonstrations of the capitals in the period immediately preceding Bloody Sunday—in Petersburg on

---

amounted only to the appearance at liberal banquets of social-democratic *intelligenty* and small handfuls of advanced workers." *Proletariat v revoljucii* (Moscow, 1907), p. 21. While this underplays the extent of the campaign, the evidence of the individual banquets does confirm the general proposition that workers played a relatively insignificant role.

46. Garvi, *Vospominanija*, p. 437.

47. Ibid., p. 440.

48. Čerevanin, "Dviženie intelligencii," pp. 160–61.

49. See Appendix II for the list of student meetings and sources. The nine:
   Kiev University student convocation ?xi
   Kiev convocation of Polytechnic Institute students 12xi
   Odessa student evening 23xii
   Petersburg University student convocation 1xi
   Petersburg convocation of students of Women's Medical Institute 4xi
   Petersburg University student evening 31xii
   Moscow resolution of *Bestuževki* n.d. (but during the zemstvo congress)
   Moscow University student resolution to the zemstvo congress n.d. (but during the congress)
   Moscow University student meeting 7i.

At least three of these appear to have been Bolshevik-oriented (Odessa 23xii, Petersburg 1xi, and Petersburg 31xii). It is interesting to note that a minority resolution of the latter meeting was of a mild constitutional character similar to the zemstvo resolutions—a

28 November and Moscow on 5–6 January—were both almost exclusively student affairs (although there were large crowds of bystanders in both cases), and both were dominated by slogans of the revolutionary parties (in Petersburg, the demonstration was organized by the SDs; in Moscow, the SRs apparently had considerable student support.)[50] Like the large student gathering in Nizhny Novgorod on 29 December 1904, both were dispersed, with considerable violence, by police cavalry.[51]

The question, however, remains: How numerous were cases of "democratic intervention" at the banquets, and how successful were they in pushing the gathered intelligentsia leftward in their political demands? The available evidence indicates some kind of "democratic" participation or intervention in thirteen of the thirty-eight banquets.[52] In six of these the resolutions went beyond endorsement of the zemstvo resolutions and included the demand for the constituent assembly.[53] This was half the number of banquets to demand the constituent assembly in their resolutions. In only three of the six banquets in question (Kiev 20xi, Nizhny Novgorod 20xi, and Petersburg 14xii) can a clear role in shaping the banquet resolutions be assigned to SD intelligentsia, students, or workers, and in one of the three, Petersburg 14xii, there was debate only over one element of the resolution, the wording of the suffrage clause; the issue of the constituent assembly had already been endorsed by essentially the same public at the banquets of 20 November and 5 December (all the Petersburg banquets passed resolutions calling for the fourtail constituent assembly). In Kharkov, there was one speech by a Social Democrat but no organized intervention, and the resolutions that were adopted had been prepared in their entirety beforehand by the banquet organizers. In Petersburg (18xii) at the "doctors' banquet,"

---

unique phenomenon in the student meetings. There appears to have been considerable SR influence among the Moscow students at the meeting of 7i. The remaining three:

    Nizhny Novgorod student evening 29xii

    Moscow student meeting at Petrovsko-Razumovskaya Academy 20xi

    Zhitomir charity evening for poor students of Kiev University 29xii

50. *Revoljucionnaja Rossija*, no. 56 (5 December 1904), pp. 11–12; no. 57 (25 December 1904), pp. 17–18; *Iskra*, no. 80 (15 December 1904), p. 3. See also Schwartz, *Russian Revolution*, pp. 255–256.

51. The Nizhny meeting, attended by about fifteen hundred, was held inside a large hall, into which a hundred cavalry police charged with bared sabres. Resistance was offered with sticks and chairs, but the floor caved in almost immediately, with many injuries on both sides. The crowd dispersed and only a few arrests were made.

52. Odessa 20xi, Nizhny Novgorod 20xi, Kiev 20xi, Saratov 20xi, Nizhny Novgorod 2xii, Rostov/Don 5xii, Kharkov 5xii, Ekaterinodar 11xii, Petersburg 14xii, Saratov 17xii, Petersburg 18xii, Tiflis 31xii, and Saratov 8i.

53. Kiev 20xi, Nizhny Novgorod 2xii, Kharkov 5xii, Petersburg 14xii, Petersburg 18xii, and Tiflis 31xii.

where there was a large non-medical attendance including about 100 workers and students in roughly equal proportions (as compared to 250–300 doctors), the resolutions, including one on amnesty for political and religious prisoners and one on the fourtail constituent assembly, had been prepared beforehand by the organizers. According to *Iskra*, the only issue raised, by at least two SD speakers, was whether to include a specific resolution on the right to strike. This proposition was rejected (only doctors were allowed to vote on the resolutions). In Tiflis, there was a fairly vocal Social Democratic presence, but the "democratic" resolutions adopted there had been prepared well in advance by the banquet's "bourgeois-intelligentsia" organizing committee (the characterization is that of the police report). If one looks further at the six banquets adopting resolutions on the constituent assembly which appear to have been organized by the Union of Liberation, direct influence of the "democratic mass" is evident in none, with the partial exception of the 14 December banquet in Petersburg noted above. On the same note, it is worth mentioning two cases—Odessa 20xi and Saratov 8i (two provincial cities in which SD activity was extraordinarily intense) —in which SD-sponsored resolutions were put up for vote in formal competition with the "intelligentsia" resolutions of the banquets' organizers. In both, the latter got over twice as many signatures as the former.

The case of Saratov 17xii requires special notice. A banquet was held on the date (according to the published source, the article by Ljakhoveckij [see Appendix I], the date is 14xii, but he is clearly in error about that date, as about several others) to honor the memory of the recently deceased A. N. Pypin. It was, uniquely among the banquets to my knowledge, sponsored by a committee representing the three "political parties" in town—the SDs, the SRs, and the "Osvoboždency." It was an exceptionally large affair, up to 850 attending by formal tickets and nearly 1000 in all, a crowd including *zemcy*, professional people, some liberal entrepreneurs, "*raznočincy* of the extreme parties" (Ljakhoveckij), and up to 200 workers. The terms of the resolution for presentation to the banquet were argued out in the three-party organizing committee beforehand. The bone of contention was the suffrage formula, with SDs sticking to the fourtailer, and the "Osvoboždency" insisting on reference only to "universal suffrage." Eventually the two factions compromised on the formula "universal and equal." There was no quarrel about the constituent assembly. The resolutions were adopted by the banquet and sent by telegram to the Committee of Ministers.

There was at least one other case of prior formal negotiations between the intelligentsia organizers of a banquet and the local SD organization— a possibility provided for from the SD side in the "*Iskra* letter"—that of

Odessa 20xi. They were initiated by the banquet's organizers in the hope of dissuading the SDs from disrupting the proceedings, which had occurred in a meeting of the juridical society earlier the same day when a crowd of SD students invaded the proceedings. The result of these negotiations was that the SDs were allowed to have a speaker on the agenda and to present their "democratic resolutions" to the public for a vote in competition with the organizers' resolution (in support of the zemstvo congress); the lawyers' resolution, as mentioned above, collected about 300 signatures, the SDs, 116. There is no evidence of other such arrangements. A "democratic mass" of some five thousand students and workers (according to the police report, "Jewish workingclass youth") gathered outside, shouting SD slogans. It was attacked and dispersed by cossacks and police cavalry wielding rubber clubs. Parts of the crowd regrouped in other quarters of the city over the course of the evening. According to *Iskra's* correspondent, there were fifty arrests and twenty-six wounded in the mêlée. This was, to my knowledge, the first big street demonstration of the 1905 Revolution. It was followed within a week by the street demonstrations in Petersburg, and then a week later in Moscow.

One must conclude that so far as the banquets in the strict sense are concerned, the demonstrable influence of the "democratic mass" on the "democratic orientation" among them was not great.[54] In any direct way, it may have been restricted to the resolutions of two or three banquets.[55]

---

54. It is curious that in his earlier book, *Proletariat v revoljucii*, Cherevanin had been of this opinion: "With their 'manifestations,' these handfuls of Social Democrats created a good deal of excitement and irritation in liberal circles, but they could not produce any kind of serious effect in the sense of pressure on the government or on the liberals." (p. 21)

55. In both cases, Kiev 20xi and Nizhny Novgorod 2xii, the "democratic" formula was appended to endorsements of the November zemstvo resolutions apparently as a result of Social Democratic engineered demonstrations at the banquets and expression of sympathy for their position by significant numbers of those attending. The Kiev banquet was arranged by two Union of Liberation members and delegates to the Union's October congress, where the banquet campaign tactic was adopted (Professor Wagner of the University and the political writer V. V. Vodovozov). The attendance, of three to four hundred, appears to have been nearly evenly balanced between representatives of the established intelligentsia (professors, writers, lawyers, journalists, doctors, etc.) and a youthful crowd of students, *raznočincy*, and workers. The resolution presented by Professor Wagner—an endorsement of the November resolution followed by the demand for the four-tail constituent assembly and political amnesty—was a transparent accomodation to the radical position (quite possibly by prior arrangement with the Social Democrats in order to avoid disruptions and permit the demonstration of support for the zemstvo congress, as in Odessa and Saratov). The local Union of Liberation group had intended to restrict its activities to mobilizing support for the zemstvo resolutions, but pressure to go beyond that in the direction of the "democratic" demands had been exerted in a number of confrontations with Social Democratic sympathizing students, for the most part, in the days immediately preceding the banquet. (In a meeting of the Society for Advancement of Literacy a few days earlier, there had been a noisy altercation between Vodovozov

Of much greater importance in explaining the views obtaining at the banquets was the composition of the banquets themselves. Most of the banquets that endorsed the zemstvo resolutions were held in provincial zemstvo capitals and were organized by Union members who were also zemstvo activists, often participants in the recent congress (see footnotes 26-28); of the endorsements and analogs of the zemstvo resolutions that were not of this type, most were from non-zemstvo regions where the role of lawyers in the banquets' organizations appears to have been predominant in most cases.

The banquet in Voronezh on the anniversary of the court reforms was typical of the Union-sponsored zemstvo province banquets endorsing the zemstvo resolutions: some 160 zemcy, doctors, lawyers, engineers, "third element" people, and a few merchants gathered in the "Grand Hotel," where all present signed a telegram to Svyatopolk-Mirsky expressing solidarity with the resolutions of the Petersburg zemstvo congress. This was followed by dinner and the approval of more telegrams—to Shipov and to the Moscow zemcy, to local zemstvo activists in exile—and toasts—to the memory of N. F. Bunakov, the recently deceased zemstvo activist, to all present who had been arrested in the past "for their convictions," etc. Then there were speeches by the zemcy who had just returned from the Petersburg congress, A. I. Urusul and D. A. Pereleshin (chairman and member, respectively, of the provincial zemstvo board). According to the police report, the banquet was organized by Pereleshin and Kolyubakin, former chairman of the zemstvo board. Both were prominent members of the Union of Liberation.[56]

Essentially the same scenario was repeated in Orel on 2 December. A banquet sponsored by the local bar in honor of the judicial statutes attracted the same sort of public: gentry, local bureaucrats (*činovniki*),

---

and V. M. Khizhnyakov, a prominent zemstvo liberal from Chernigov and delegate to the zemstvo congress, on the one hand, and a group of students in the hall.)

In Nizhny Novgorod some 300 lawyers, magistrates, zemstvo and duma men, professional people of various kinds, and journalists gathered to honor the court statutes on 2 December. About half those attending (151) signed a resolution addressed to the minister of justice, similarly endorsing the zemstvo resolutions, but adding the demands for the fourtail constituent assembly. The émigré press reports suggested that these added demands were made in response to a delegation of workers from Sormovo, whose representative read a political declaration which was "enthusiastically received." This delegation was presumably arranged by the local SD committee, then dominated by Bolsheviks. Cf. M. F. Vladimir-skij, *Očerki rabočego i social-demokratičeskogo dviženija v Nižnem Novgorode i Sormove* (M. 1957).

56. Kolyubakin was for a time a member of the Union's council (by cooptation); Pereleshin was a delegate to several Union congresses. Both were founders of the Kadet party organization in Voronezh at the end of 1905. The third organizer of the banquet, according to the police report, was one Koryakin.

professional people, most of the deputies to the provincial zemstvo and the town duma, journalists, and teachers. Presiding was A. A. Stakhovich, returning delegate to the zemstvo congress and prominent member of the Union of Liberation. At the end of the dinner, Stakhovich read the resolutions of the zemstvo congress and proposed a resolution adhering to them (the majority position on point ten). It was signed by 158 of the 200-odd diners (the *činovniki* present probably fearing to sign) and sent to Mirsky by wire, with a copy to the zemstvo congress bureau. Telegrams of congratulation were sent to Shipov and M. A. Stakhovich (provincial marshal of nobility).

Much the same procedure was followed in Vladimir 21xi, Nizhny Novgorod 20xi,[57] Tambov 17xi,[58] Balashov (Saratov province) 14xii, and Smolensk 20xi.[59]

In the banquets in Moscow on 21 November and Saratov on 20 November, where resolutions analogous to the zemstvo resolutions but without explicit reference to the latter were taken, the banquets were arranged by people who were not directly associated with the zemstvo campaign. In Moscow, the banquet in the Hermitage restaurant, organized by Prince S. I. Shakhovskoy, was attended by "the flower of literary and artistic Moscow." It endorsed the resolutions taken the previous day by the association of Moscow lawyers, which had called for a constitutional regime in general terms.[60] In Saratov, the local lawyers' association organized a banquet on the anniversary of the court reform. Attendance appears to have been mainly by urban professional people. The resolutions, calling for constitutional guarantees of individual and civil rights

---

57. In Nizhny Novgorod, the banquet adopted a second resolution for the minister of justice with a long list of desiderata in the area of individual and civil rights.

58. In Tambov the banquet was organized expressly to honor the delegates returning from the zemstvo congress, Kolobov and Bryukhatov, chairman and member, respectively, of the provincial zemstvo board. Both were founders, along with Yu. Novosiltsev, of the zemstvo constitutionalist group in Tambov; Bryukhatov was a member of the second council of the Union of Liberation and later a leading Tambov Kadet.

It may be noted in passing that the Tambov banquet provoked a "counter-banquet," apparently unique in the history of the banquet campaign. On 21 November (*Osvoboždenie* incorrectly dates it 11 November), the chief of police gathered together some merchants, small tradesmen, priests, and twenty-five peasants rounded up from the countryside in the local hotel for a "patriotic banquet." The peasants among them were installed in a separate room, whence they were instructed to shout "hurrah" upon command from the adjoining chamber.

59. The Smolensk resolution added the demand for election of popular representatives by fourtail suffrage, an end to the war, and amnesty for political prisoners. The cases of Kiev 20xi and Nizhny Novgorod 2xii, where the demand for the constituent assembly was added to endorsement of the zemstvo resolution, and of Saratov 17xii, have already been described (notes 55 and 57).

60. See Appendix II.

and, in a very general way, for popular representation in government, were sent to the minister of justice.

Much the same pattern prevailed among the banquets organized in the outlying areas where zemstvos did not exist: in Rostov/Don, where the banquet of 5 December was arranged by local lawyers, in Baku on 20 December and 25 November (the former was for lawyers alone; both celebrated the anniversary of the judicial reform), in Libava on 21 November (a banquet on the anniversary of the reform organized by local lawyers and members of the magistracy), in Tiflis on 8 December (also arranged by the local lawyers' association), and in Kutais on 31 December.

If we look at the nine banquets which made no endorsement of the zemstvo resolutions and called for the constituent assembly, we see that only three of them (Kaluga lxii, Kharkov 5xii, and Samara 20xi) were held in zemstvo capitals (besides Petersburg); four were Petersburg banquets; and the remaining two were held in Tiflis and in Novozybkov (Chernigov province).

The Kaluga banquet in most respects followed the pattern of the other zemstvo province banquets: it was held in honor of the judicial statutes; it was organized by a group of zemstvo constitutionalists who were probably also members of the Union of Liberation; and the attendance (of somewhat over a hundred) appears to have been the usual provincial mix of zemstvo men, local gentry, professional people, and also officers of the local garrison and some ladies (a group to which the reporting police agent affixed the term "the local intelligentsia"). Its resolutions, however, were not modeled on the zemstvo congress resolutions but the resolutions of the 20 November banquet in Petersburg (to which they were practically identical).[61] The Kharkov banquet was also typical in attendance and organization, but its resolutions, preceded by nine theses describing the current situation in the country, called for the summoning of a fourtail constituent assembly and amnesty for political offenses. According to the police report, the lawyer who presented the resolutions was an SD.[62] No details are available on the Samara banquet.

There is no need to dwell on the details of the Petersburg banquets,

---

61. The main organizers of the banquet were D. D. Goncharov and I. L. Tolstoy, and Goncharov presented the resolution. Both were zemstvo deputies, probably members of the Union of Liberation, and—along with L. N. Novosiltsev, who chaired at the banquet—founders of the Kadet party organization in Kaluga at the end of 1905.

62. The banquet was organized by the chairman of the local zemstvo board, V. G. Kolokoltsov (also a deputy to the November congress, member of the Union of Liberation, and future Kadet), another zemstvo deputy, and a lawyer (Troitsky?), who may have been the SD in question. The local party took no part in the banquet, although there was at least one speech by a Social Democrat (and one by an SR, too).

which were well reported in either the legal or émigré press. All, as mentioned above, took resolutions calling for the convocation of a constituent assembly. Of the four, two were banquets of "representatives of the intelligentsia professions" (20 November and 14 December), and two were banquets primarily for men of a single profession (the doctors' banquet 18xii) or a limited group of professions (the "engineers' banquet" 5xii). The first Petersburg banquet, the best known of all the banquets, was organized by N. F. Annensky and his "legal populist" colleagues at *Russkoe Bogatstvo*, all of whom played important roles in the Union of Liberation organization in the capital (the so-called "Big Group"). Main speakers were I. V. Gessen, V. G. Korolenko, Annensky, and V. I. Semevsky. The paper *Naša Žizn'* printed a full list of the 676 participants (apparently all present) who signed the resolutions, divided into professional categories. The largest of these were writers, lawyers, scientists, professors, and teachers (each category in excess of sixty persons). Doctors, engineers, publishers, actors, artists, and zemstvo men were represented in smaller groups.[63] The resolution, presented by the populist publicist A. V. Peshekhonov, had four points on the reorganization of "the entire state order of Russia on constitutional principles," the demand for the "summoning without delay of a constituent assembly of freely elected representatives from the entire population of the Russian state," and a demand for amnesty for political and religious offenders. The second Petersburg "banquet of the intelligentsia professions" was organized by largely the same group, with the addition of one prominent "legal marxist" writer, V. Ya. Yakovlev (Bogucharsky). This time, 780 participants registered a protest against the war and proclaimed the conviction that "the people itself is best prepared to lead the country out of its present difficulties through representatives freely elected by it on the basis of a universal, direct, secret and equal for all suffrage law." The makeup of the attendance appears to have been roughly the same as of the earliest banquet; this time, however, there was a contingent of 30–40 workers led by SDs. According to the report in *Iskra*, the resolution was devised by SD intelligentsia participants in the banquet who managed, with the help of some worker oratory, to get the support of the gathering for it over the objections of Annensky and his colleagues, who preferred their earlier version of the phrase on suffrage ("freely elected representatives of the people") to the fourtail formula.[64]

---

63. *Naša Žizn'*, no. 22 (27 November 1904). There were fifty-odd doctors, about forty engineers, and one or two dozen of the other categories.

64. The resolution in fact began "We, representatives of the intelligentsia professions and the working class . . ." Some SRs present objected to the term "working class,"

Of the two Petersburg "professional" banquets, the first was almost certainly arranged by members of the Union of Liberation pursuing both the tactic of political banquets and that calling for the organization of professional political unions (the main purpose of the banquet was discussion of organization of a nationwide union of engineers and technologists and a banquet for the same purpose was held simultaneously in Moscow).[65] Most of the 485 persons signing the resolutions were engineers, although there were at least 26 non-engineer teachers from technical schools attending. *Osvoboždenie's* correspondent also remarked the presence of 15 generals, many owners of industrial enterprises, and directors of some of the biggest factories in Russia. At the "doctors' banquet," as mentioned earlier, there were in attendance 250–300 medical doctors and about 100 students and workers.

The Tiflis banquet was arranged by a group of lawyers and deputies of the city duma. The organization committee apparently borrowed from earlier banquets in Russia in preparing the speeches and resolutions for the banquet. The attending crowd was described in the police report as "bourgeois-liberal intelligentsia." Attendance was by invitation (issued by the committee), but some SDs, SRs, and a few workers got in without invitations. During supper the floor was yielded to any speaker, including representatives of the revolutionary parties. According to *Iskra*, some invited guests were offended by the behavior of the SDs, but the majority was interested in what they had to say and impressed by their solidarity and the skill of their orators.

The small "political banquet" in Novozybkov was attended, according to the police report, by third element employees, professional people, and "local Jews." In attendance were the old *Narodovolec* writer-ethnographer Bogoraz-Tan (later one of the founders of the Popular Socialist party) and five lawyers who had been participating in the Gomel trial (S. A. Kalmanovich, M. L. Mandelstam, N. D. Sokolov, M. I. Ganfman, and Krasilschikov). According to *Iskra*, this banquet addressed a statement to the Chernigov provincial assembly, then about to convene, exhorting it to demand a constituent assembly; according to the police report, the resolution called for "participation in legislative work by representatives of the zemstvo."

It appears that in those provinces where the most active role in

---

preferring "the people" (*narod*) or "the working masses" (*trudjaščiesja massy*), but the SD sponsored workers insisted and the phrase remained.

65. The organizing bureau, consisting of a group of Petersburg engineers, included L. I. Lutugin, member of the Petersburg Union of Liberation leadership and, for a time, of the Union's council, and later a founder of the Union of Unions and of the Popular Socialist party.

political affairs (including the organization of the banquets) was played by zemstvo men (and this seems to have been the case in most of the zemstvo provinces where banquets were held, with the special exceptions of Petersburg and Moscow), the zemstvo institutions were still considered the main arena of political activity and protest in the country. Accordingly, the tactic of supporting the zemstvo congress was generally accepted by the banquet participants, who were by no means predominantly zemstvo men (although that contingent appears to have been quite large at most of the zemstvo province banquets); professional men as a rule and even the representatives of the "lower intelligentsia" in attendance (zemstvo and city government employees, salaried railway personnel, etc.) in these areas generally supported this tactic. Whether the specific tactic of support for the zemstvo resolutions would have been widely followed had those resolutions been significantly different—say, considerably more modest and vague about the desiderata of political change— is a moot question. In view of the strong constitutionalist convictions of most of the zemcy organizers of the banquets[66] and the presumption of an even less compromising stand on such issues on the part of the urban intelligentsia participants, it seems likely that the tactic would have been different. But the chances are that the banquets in these areas would have, in one way or another, linked their political demands to the zemstvo. *Par contre*, in the metropolises, in non-zemstvo provinces, and in a few zemstvo provinces where banquets appear to have been the affairs almost exclusively of the non-zemstvo intelligentsia, this linkage was usually absent.

A brief survey of the numerous meetings of learned, cultural, and professional societies during the period November, 1904–9 January 1905, will help to clarify the interrelationships between the zemstvos, professional groups and political strategies in the political movement of late 1904.

III

Of forty-two "political" meetings of such organizations for which I have records (see Appendix II), thirty-two produced formal resolutions.[67]

---

66. This may be assumed from their membership in organizations like the Union of Liberation and the group of zemstvo constitutionalists, and in many cases by their future involvement in the Kadet party.

67. These included meetings of:
    5 juridical societies
    15 professional societies, including:
        9 lawyers' organizations
        2 doctors' organizations

(Of the other ten, all but three failed to adopt resolutions only because the meetings were prematurely ended by disruptions caused either by intervention of "the democratic mass" or by the police, or both.)[68] Of these thirty-two resolutions

A. 5 called for convocation of a constituent assembly by fourtail suffrage

B. 8 endorsed the zemstvo congress resolutions (with two adding a clause on fourtail suffrage as the basis of the electoral system)

C. 19 were similar to the zemstvo resolutions or were even less specific __about matters of political change

    32 total

If we look at the large majority of such gatherings that produced resolutions of a moderate and general constitutionalist character (groups B and C), we find relatively few clear outright endorsements of the zemstvo resolutions (possibly as few as four; another four are unclear from the sources but appear to have been explicit endorsements).[69] These were all, apparently, the affairs of the liberal professions, with no participation by the "lower intelligentsia."[70] Most of the remaining meetings of professional organizations (professors, lawyers, and doctors) and of voluntary educational and health organizations produced resolutions roughly

---

  3 engineers' and technologists' organizations
  1 teachers' organization
12 voluntary organizations for aid to health, education, etc.
  1 agricultural society
  2 academic councils
  7 others, including:
    2 public meetings in Baku and Maykop, respectively
    1 artists' supper in Petersburg
    1 meeting of political exiles in Arkhangelsk
    2 New Year's parties
    1 society for aid to salaried employees of private enterprises

68. The meeting of the Kharkov Juridical Society, 6xi; Odessa Society for Preservation of Public Health 18xi; Odessa Juridical Society 20xi; Samara "Family Pedagogical Circle" 19xi; Permanent Commission on Technical Education of the Moscow Section of the Russian Technical Society 29xii; Kiev Society for Literacy 14xii; Saratov Parents' Circle of the Section on Children's Hygiene of the Saratov Pharmaceutical Society 15xi.

69. Congress of Science Teachers in Kiev 29xii; an artists' supper in Petersburg (fifteen signatures) 30xii; a meeting of "persons of the Free Professions on the anniversary of the court reforms" in Baku 22xi; and one New Year's party (ca. sixty-nine signatures) in Piatigorsk 31xii. It is not entirely clear whether the lawyers' meeting in Petersburg 21xi, Kutais (n.d. but ca. 23xi), and Rostov/Don 24 or 25xi, and the meeting of the Kharkov Juridical Society made explicit endorsement of the zemstvo resolutions or passed resolutions quite similar to them.

70. With the partial exception of the Teachers' congress. It appears to have been attended primarily by gymnasium and technical institute professors.

analogous to those of the zemstvo congress. Thus the meetings of barristers (*prisjažnye poverennye*) of the Moscow Judicial District on 20 November adopted a protocol with a list of twelve resolutions on constitutional reform, including demands for changes in state structure that would guarantee civil and individual liberties through a system of representative government. It also called for an immediate end to administrative abuses and use of extraordinary legislation and voted that the minutes and protocols of the meeting be sent to the ministers of justice and interior. Similar resolutions were taken by the Petersburg lawyers' association the next day, and telegrams of solidarity with the lawyers of the capitals were sent by their colleagues in Rostov/Don and Kutais.

The academic council of St. Petersburg Polytechnic Institute, in an extraordinary session devoted to the crisis created at the institute by a confrontation between students and police, declared that

> for Russian institutions of higher learning it is a matter of urgent and unavoidable necessity that there be a genuine establishment of the rule of law which would guarantee security of the individual and home for every citizen, freedom of speech and convocation, and equality of all regardless of class, nationality, confession or other differences. The necessary condition and exclusive guarantee of such a rule of law is the broad participation of freely elected popular representatives in legislative work and control over the actions of the administration.

A quite similar declaration was adopted by about two hundred and fifty members of the Petersburg Pedagogical Society.

Five meetings in this category added specification of fourtail suffrage as the basis for popular representation:

Kostroma Agricultural Society 3xii

Vologda Enlightenment Society 26xi

Voronezh meeting of the Fifth Russian Congress of the Society for the Protection of Public Health 2xii

Yaroslavl Society for Aid to Education 1xii

Address to the minister of interior signed by sixty-two residents of Maykop 12xii

Other meetings producing constitutional demands essentially like those of the zemstvo congress were: the Kharkov Juridical Society 18xii, the Academic Council of Kiev Polytechnic Institute (n.d.), the Saratov Technological Society 6xi, the Directorate of the Society of Russian Doctors 29xi, the association of Vologda lawyers, and the Kostroma Pushkin Society.

A few meetings, such as the 6 December meeting of the Nizhny Novgorod Society for Aid to Salaried Employees of Private Enterprises, made reference to the system of desired representation in very general terms only ("active participation of public representatives in legislation and administration"). A declaration of similar vagueness was adopted by a meeting of Smolensk medical doctors.

At least two societies made resolutions calling for introduction of individual and civil liberties in some detail, but without specific demands concerning public representation (the meeting of the Society for the Advancement of Primary Education of Nizhny Novgorod 27xi, and the Kursk meeting of the Society for Aid to Education 8xi).

Of the five formal endorsements of the radical formula calling for the constituent assembly, one was made by a meeting of a voluntary organization, the Kharkov Public Library Association 11xii; one by the congress of the Russian branch of the International Union of Criminal Lawyers in Kiev 4i; two by meetings of assistant barristers (*pomoščniki prisjažnykh poverennykh*) in Moscow 20xi and 4xi, respectively; and one by a group of political exiles in Arkhangelsk on 7 November. In the Kharkov meeting, the resolution calling for "summoning of an assembly of popular representatives elected by means of direct, secret and equal [sic] vote for elaboration of the fundamental statute of the Russian State" was adopted by a vote of 135; a minority resolution endorsing the zemstvo congress resolutions was proferred by Professor Gredeskul. It got 43 votes.[71]

At the congress of criminal lawyers, a number of resolutions were taken, including one (presented by I. A. Kistyakovsky) with political demands calling for democratic reforms to be elaborated by "representatives of the people, freely elected on the basis of universal, direct, equal and secret vote." This resolution was adopted by a vote of 77–37, after some pleading by the same Professor Gredeskul and others to tone it down. As they had feared, the governor closed the congress after this resolution was adopted.

---

71. It may be noted that this meeting was held behind closed doors by order of the governor in order to avert disturbances such as had occurred at the 6 November meeting of the Juridical Society. There Gredeskul, as chairman, had proposed sending a telegram to Svyatopolk-Mirsky, congratulating him for his intention to "trust the genius of the Russian people." This proposal was shouted down in the hall containing 600–700 people (1000 according to *Iskra*), of whom 200–300 appear to have been SD-led students and workers. Gredeskul shut the meeting down after an SD orator got up to propose a resolution calling for the constituent assembly. The SDs tried then to turn the gathering into a public meeting, but were unable to regain order; the SD-led crowd went into the streets shouting radical slogans, and had largely dispersed when the cossacks arrived. The Kharkov banquet of 5 December, from which students were systematically excluded and which was thus a purely "intelligentsia" gathering, adopted the radical formula in its resolution.

The Moscow district organization of assistant barristers, in contrast to the district organization of barristers, appears to have been predominantly sympathetic to the revolutionary parties throughout. In their meeting of 4 November they put 105 signatures (unanimous) to a declaration to the forthcoming zemstvo congress urging its support for convocation of a constituent assembly. Its meeting of 20 November endorsed the constitutionalist resolution passed the same day by the lawyers' association but added the demand for the constituent assembly to it (168 signatures).

The apparently unique Arkhangelsk meeting of some sixty exiles on 7 November also prepared a resolution intended for the zemstvo congress, declaring that the congress was not armed with a popular mandate for working out the new fundamental laws and that its task ought to be restricted to demanding the convocation of a fourtail constituent assembly from the tsar.

The evidence of the meetings of the professional and voluntary organizations shows quite clearly that the moderate constitutionalist position adopted by the zemstvo congress and supported by a large majority of the banquets in zemstvo provinces reflected views that were not confined to zemstvo circles alone.

What we see in the constitutionalist opposition movement in late 1904 is a fairly broad grouping of men around a vision of the future that might be described in the following way. Constitutional reforms would be granted from above under pressure from the educated elements of society, without revolutionary violence. These would guarantee basic civil and individual liberties and would bring into the exercise of political power men like themselves as public representatives. The guarantee of the latter proposition they may have seen either in established patterns of deference, a system of indirect elections (most likely involving the existing representative institutions), a literacy test for the franchise and the same for holding public office (the latter possibly with an education requirement as well), or some combination of these. The view is relatively free of "populist" mythology: there is no belief that the people, the *narod*, is wise or that it must rise up before the new order can be installed.

It is probable that many who saw the immediate political future in these terms had a longer-range vision of development toward mass democracy. Their avoidance of the slogan of fourtail suffrage in the banquets and professional meetings they dominated was less a judgment about the intrinsic merits of that system than it was an act of political strategy; the general terms of that strategy, designed to provoke reform from above without resort to revolutionary violence, dictated avoidance of demands so radical as to be certain of rejection by the regime. If they applied this rule of thumb to the fourtailer slogan, the same rule applied in spades to the slogan of the constituent assembly: that demand was quite unacceptable to the government and adherence to it by the opposition could only lead to revolutionary confrontation. Moreover, a constituent assembly elected by universal direct suffrage, however it might come to be convened, involved (to use a phrase often employed in zemstvo constitutionalist circles in those years) too great a "leap into the unknown" to have any appeal to the moderate reformist mentality.

Alongside this outlook there is a coalescence of views of a more democratic orientation—more democratic in the sense that it is attached to a vision of an immediate transition to popular democracy and appears to be grounded in a belief in the political wisdom and "creativity" of the masses. It does not fear revolutionary confrontation. Accordingly, the demands for universal suffrage and a constituent assembly are acceptable to it; it has no fear of the ideologies of the revolutionary parties—its own program is surely "revolutionary" in the context of the times—and tends to be sympathetic toward their activists. It is not, however, wedded (as the "revolutionary" ideologies are) to the idea that the old order can be brought down and the new ushered in only by the revolutionary struggle of the popular masses.

There are, of course, intermediate positions between these two primary groupings of political attitudes among the intelligentsia constituencies of the banquets. Thus those resolutions that added the fourtail suffrage formulation to endorsement of the zemstvo resolutions reflected, it seems, an intermediate position on the scale of attitudes in which a strong commitment to political democracy is tempered by apprehension about such radical departures as a constituent assembly and, conversely, by faith in the existing processes and institutions of the constitutionalist movement to bring about the desired reforms. The two major orientations —which for purposes of convenience may be called the "liberal" and the "democratic" respectively—appear to account, however, for the large majority of the campaign's participants.

The analysis of the political movement of late 1904 presented on the preceding pages has, I hope, at least sufficed to demonstrate that the prevalence of the liberal or democratic orientation at one or another gathering cannot be explained for the most part by the degree of pressure exerted there by the revolutionary parties (Cherevanin's "democratic mass"); and this conclusion leads necessarily to the problem of the sociology of the banquets and other political meetings of late 1904.

It would distort the complexity of relations between political attitudes and what Karl Mannheim called "social location" to associate either the liberal or the democratic outlooks with specific categories within the banquet constituencies in a rigid, mechanical way. Neither social origin, occupation, nor age are sure guides. Among the democrats it would be easy to find many examples of men of gentry origin, zemstvo men, lawyers and practitioners of other liberal professions, and men who were no longer young. Simple correlations based on the banquet resolutions are also ruled out by the fact that the resolutions were always in some sense the product of tactical compromise, the common denominator acceptable to the large majority attending a given banquet; multiple resolutions would have defeated the purpose of the undertaking.

Nevertheless, the evidence shows that banquets and other political meetings dominated by zemstvo men and men in the more prestigious and remunerative modern professions—law, the academic professions, and medicine—adhered, for the most part, to the liberal position; while the democratic orientation is to be found most frequently in the populous banquets of major cities and in meetings of practitioners of less prestigious, lower-paying, often technical professions, or those traditionally associated with democratic attitudes (such as journalism and zemstvo employment).[72] But there were obviously other factors than status and profession involved in the differing degrees of radicalism observable at the banquets and meetings of late 1904.[73] I have already mentioned the influence in the zemstvo provinces of political traditions associated with the zemstvo institutions. By the same token, the more radical orientation of most of the banquets in the two capitals and in a few other large and relatively "modern" cities such as Kiev and Odessa must be attributed in significant measure to the more intense political culture of those cities, to the higher degree of political mobilization prevailing in them, to the fact that the tensions leading up to the revolutionary situation of 1905 were building up earlier there than elsewhere. The general, more or less constant leftward drift of political attitudes in Russia that was characteristic of the period November, 1904–October,

72. The political physiognomy of the medical profession was complex, as a comparison of the resolutions of the Petersburg "doctors" banquet and the Smolensk medical meeting suggest.

73. As a point of speculation, in view of the apprentice-like character of some of these professions (such as that of assistant barrister) and the rapid proliferation at the turn of the century of others due to the expansion of zemstvo services from the early 1890s and the country's rapid industrial development beginning about the same time, it seems reasonable to associate the banquet attendance from these constituencies with relative youthfulness as well.

In 1903, Peshekhonov characterized the liberals and the revolutionaries as two generations —the "fathers" and the "sons", respectively—of the intelligentsia, rather than as

1905 was always most advanced in the big cities. It is probably fair to say that the level of mobilized political discontent prevailing among educated and professional people in the large cities by late 1904 was reached by their provincial counterparts, in most cases, only toward the middle of 1905.

Taking the constitutionalist campaign of late 1904 as a whole, the more moderate liberal tone clearly prevailed. The disposition of the participating intelligentsia public at large at that time appears to have been rather more moderate, less "risk oriented," than that of the Union of Liberation, not to mention the revolutionary parties. No doubt this disposition betrayed a lack of political realism: it is easy with hindsight to see the futility of anticipating that the regime would surrender any of its authority in response to mere resolutions. Yet many of the people who entertained such hopes in late 1904 became involved in succeeding months in efforts to mobilize more serious forces in the political struggle with the autocracy, and in doing so they courted a revolutionary confrontation. At the same time, the basic dichotomy between "liberals" and "democrats" in the political movement outside the revolutionary parties remained in evidence throughout, as can be seen in the history of the union movement in 1905 and in the processes of political party formation before and after October, 1905.

IV

It is instructive to consider briefly in conclusion the response to this development by several interested parties.

Both the Socialist Revolutionaries and the Social Democratic Mensheviks were at this time committed to a united front or at least the

---

representatives of different social classes, and he accordingly concluded that "the Russian revolutionaries and the Russian liberals are moving in essentially the same direction; they only stop at different points" (and therefore there was no reason why they could not cooperate) (*Revoljucionnaja Rossija*, no. 32 [15 September 1903]). Considering what is known of the average age of members of the revolutionary parties in this period (late teens to mid-twenties), the political attitudes of students, and their social background, there appears to be a good deal of truth in this characterization. One is inclined to associate the more radical, but "non-revolutionary," intelligentsia with the intermediate age group between "fathers" and "sons" (bearing in mind of course that, biologically, age differences are spread along a continuum, rather than being divided into "generations"), but the evidence is so limited as to rule out anything beyond speculation.

For the figures on the growth of the professions see V. R. Lejkina-Svirskaja, *Intelligencija v Rossii vo vtoroj polovine XIX veka* (M., 1971), ch. 2; and L. K. Erman, *Intelligencija v pervoj russkoj revoljucii* (M., 1966), ch. 1. On the ages of revolutionaries, see D. Lane, *The Roots of Russian Communism; a Social and Historical Study of Russian Social-Democracy 1898-1907* (Assen, 1969); M. Perrie, "The Social Composition and Structure of the Socialist-Revolutionary Party before 1917," *Soviet Studies* 24, no. 2 (October 1972): 223-250.

avoidance of disruptive conflict with the non-socialist constitutionalist opposition.

If one looks through the pages of their émigré organs *Revoljucion- naja Rossija* and *Iskra* in the autumn and winter of 1904-1905, one finds remarkable similarity in the assessments of the political scene. In the diversity of elements participating in the current constitutionalist movement, both saw two basic groups: the "zemstvo" or "agrarian" liberals, and "non-socialist" (for the SRs) or "bourgeois" (for the SDs) democracy. It was the entrance of large numbers of men from the ranks of "democracy" (its own ranks swelling as a result of capitalist development) that had made the constitutionalist movement into a significant phenom- enon in Russian life; and this growing involvement of "democracy" in the constitutionalist movement in recent years was the product, in part, of the contacts established with the veterans of the constitutionalist move- ment in the zemstvo and cultural institutions, into which representatives of both groups had been increasingly drawn ever since the "cult of small deeds" had taken root during the reaction of the 1880s.[74]

Both the SRs and the SD Mensheviks were apprehensive that the zemstvo liberals might dominate the movement and, having done so, compromise with the autocracy or otherwise stop short of destruction of autocracy. The danger, at the outset of the banquet campaign period (it will be remembered that the zemstvo congress and zemstvo institu- tions were still the center of political attention in the country), was perceived as very real: the zemcy had experience and the prestige of the zemstvo institutions behind them, and the zemstvos still appeared to many democrats as (in Potresov's phrase) "the Archimedes fulcrum by which democratic agitation could move the monolith of autocracy." Moreover, the movement was made up of diverse elements, of which no others were so well organized as they.

At the same time, both parties at the outset of the "governmental springtime" saw considerable perspectives of support in this recently mobilized element. Bourgeois democracy, it was observed by the *Iskra* publicist, is part of bourgeois society, but not a part which has a direct role in the exploitation of labor. It is consequently disposed to economic reformism and political democracy; it does not feel an "organic antago- nism between itself and the popular masses"; it is attached by tradition to "the cult of the people" and has no fear of revolutionary ideologies. (The SRs had no need to split hairs in this fashion, since they did not consider "democracy" to be a part of the bourgeois class, but rather a

---

74. On the "cult of small deeds" cf. A. A. Kizevetter, *Na rubeže dvukh stoletij* (*Vospominanija, 1881-1914*) (Prague, 1929), pp. 167-71.

basically anti-bourgeois element of the intelligentsia—a distinct social formation.)[75] It can therefore be brought to support the revolutionary party, without being assimilated by it. The task of the revolutionary party (as Potresov wrote for *Iskra*) was to split the "opposition conglomerate" and draw the democratic elements in it into the party's sphere of influence. This would mean that

> All groups, organizations, and even unformed trends in which there is even a grain of democratism are pulled toward rapprochement with [Social Democracy] in the name of the current task . . . It means that under the hegemony of the strongest and only consistent democratic organization [i.e., the SDs], popular Russia mobilizes against anti-popular Russia, even though wearing the uniform of constitutionalism. It would mean . . . splitting the opposition conglomerate; a splitting of it, so to speak, along the lines of democratism, and, in accordance with this division, a new combination of social forces.[76]

The dividing line in question (following the resolution Potresov had himself introduced at the second party congress) was acceptance or rejection of the slogan of the fourtail constituent assembly. Although the "hegemony" for social democracy to which Potresov referred applied only to the struggle against the autocracy and, in keeping with the general Menshevik position, not to the political order which was expected to emerge from that struggle (the "bourgeois revolution"), there was ambivalence, not to say outright contradiction, in a tactic that in effect called simultaneously for cooperation with the "bourgeois opposition" and for splitting it up. In this regard, the contemporary tactic of the Bolsheviks was more consistent: Lenin and his faction also called for splitting up the "opposition conglomerate" in order to draw "bourgeois democracy" into a union with the proletariat and peasantry for the revolutionary struggle (indeed, they made much more of this tactic in the course of 1905 than did the Mensheviks), but, except for a brief moment following the October Manifesto, they consistently rejected any possibility of cooperation with the liberal movement and had no intention of relinquishing "hegemony."[77]

---

75. "Demokraty na rasput'i," *Iskra*, no. 77 (5 November 1904); Starover [A. N. Potresov], "Naši zaključenija. I. O liberalizme i gegemonii," *Iskra*, no. 78 (20 November 1904); "Socialisty-revoljucionery i nesocialističeskaja demokratija," *Revoljucionnaja Rossija*, no. 56 (5 December 1904); "Nekotorye itogi Parižskoj konferencii," *Revoljucionnaja Rossija*, no. 61 (15 March 1905).

76. Starover, "Naši zaključenija."

77. L. Martov, *Istorija rossijskoj Social-Demokratii*. Izdanie tret'e (P.-M., 1923), pp. 81–157, *passim*; L. K. Erman, "Bor'ba Bol'ševikov za demokratičeskuju intelligenciju v 1905 godu," *Voprosy Istorii*, 1955, no. 2, pp. 17–31.

While the particular idea of hegemony by the revolutionary party was the special property of the Social Democrats, the SR publicists outlined the same task of differentiating the liberal-democratic opposition as a means of forwarding the revolution and avoiding compromise with the autocracy. In short, the ranks of bourgeois democracy had to be competed for by the revolutionary parties.

If it was clear to the SR and SD theorists at the outset of the banquet period that the constitutionalist movement had reached a point of organization and activation where it could no longer simply be assumed that it would serve their ends, by the end of the year a tone of real disquiet had crept into the discussion of the movement. In late December *Iskra* printed a Moscow correspondent's warning that, while the opposition was showing a dangerous tendency to compromise with the "non-democrats"—either in the hope of carrying the movement as a whole or by the inertia of their habit of relying on "influential elements." This had been demonstrated by the large number of signatures supporting the resolutions of the zemstvo congress. Moreover, "a significant portion of the democrats, if not the majority, are trying to demonstrate the 'eternal character' of this union of diverse elements and are finding fertile soil for such propaganda in contemporary political conditions." There was talk of "pure liberalism" and "pure supraclass liberalism."[78]

If the optimism of the SR and SD publicists became clouded with apprehension by developments in the opposition movement, Struve, with the encouragement of a correspondent writing in *Osvoboždenie*, was moved by these same developments to resume his call (which he had first made as early as February 1903) for the formation of a liberal-democratic party of the intelligentsia. Already by the end of October, Struve was writing that it was "necessary to take advantage of this in all respects extraordinarily propitious moment to gather energetically minds around a broad democratic program and, in the heightened social temperature, to forge a strong organization." Struve's strategy was quite clear: by adopting a "broad democratic program" (in which the main platform would be "universal and equal suffrage" as the basis for all elections), the "liberal-democratic party" would be able to count on the allegiance of the bulk of the intelligentsia and could mount a national movement, even enlisting the popular masses, for a *peaceful* transition to the new order. He anticipated, moreover, turning the tables on the revolutionary parties in the competition for the support of "democracy": after the winning of basic political liberties (by early 1905 he was arguing that this could be begun right away even before the

78. "Iz Moskvy nam pišut," *Iskra*, no. 81 (23 December 1904).

destruction of autocracy), the working class movement, led by the Social
Democratic Party, could be gradually turned over to the workers themselves (he foresaw it becoming a "trade unionist" organization on the
German model) and the intelligentsia who currently constituted the main
population of that party would move, he implied, to their natural
home: the liberal-democratic party.[79]

In the long run Struve was to be disappointed in his anticipation that
the intelligentsia at large could be united in a single liberal-democratic
party, but the revolutionary publicists, as future developments were also
to show, had good reason to be apprehensive about the political inclina-
tions of "democracy." In fact, they tended to underestimate the possibility of a strong formation immediately to their right because of the
inadequacy of the categories of social class analysis with which they
approached the contemporary political scene.[80] This is particularly true
of the *Iskra* publicists. To be sure, they recognized that through interaction in the zemstvos and cultural institutions and through the continual
entry of sons of landed gentry into the bourgeois professions, the boundaries between "gentry liberalism" and "bourgeois democracy" had
become blurred, but in their view the basic duality of the constitutionalist
movement, grounded in social differences, persisted.[81]

---

79. "Organizacija i platforma demokratičeskoj partii," *Osvoboždenie*, no. 58 (27/14
October 1904); "K očerednym voprosam," ibid; "Komitet ministrov i komitet reform,"
ibid., no. 63 (20/7 January 1905); "Nasuščnaja zadača vremeni," ibid., no. 63 (20/7
January 1905).

In giving "universal and equal suffrage" the central place in his program, Struve
could not have been unaware that recognition of that principle had been established by the
second SD congress as the fundamental prerequisite for the party's cooperation with
"liberal democracy." (Martov, *Istorija*, p. 72.)

80. It is symptomatic of the situation that *Revoljucionnaja Rossija* apparently saw no
danger of the Union of Liberation growing into a party organization, despite the clear
import of Struve's writing in *Osvoboždenie*. (That journal was not, to be sure, the official
organ of the Union, but it certainly reflected views that were current there.)

81. Cf. *Iskra*, no. 78 (20 November 1904), and *Revoljucionnaja Rossija*, no. 56
(5 December 1904). *Iskra* quoted a recent speech of the gentry liberal N. N. Lvov. Lvov
had argued that as a result of the practice of equal distribution of inheritances, the
sons of gentry landowners were having to seek livings in the liberal professions: "Becoming
doctors, lawyers and teachers, the young generation of gentry is going over to the ranks of
the *raznočinnaja intelligencija* and is absorbing its democratic frame of mind. At the same
time, it is building a bridge between the landlord class (*zemlevladenie*) and the bourgeoisie,
is forging a single entity out of historically separated social groups and is transforming
narrow zemstvo liberalism into the broad social stream of the democratic movement." The
Iskra commentator agreed that "the left wing" of zemstvo liberalism had been brought into
close contact with democratic elements of Russian society and had been given new strength
by this, but warned that the tactics of the zemstvo liberals were futile and that democracy
must "throw off the political hegemony [of the liberals]" and join with social democracy.
"As long as bourgeois democracy follows the zemstvo flag at the heels of moderate

This was a highly simplified view of the complex formation on which the opposition movement was drawing. It was one thing for the revolutionaries to predict that a large part of the landed gentry currently sympathetic to the opposition would abandon it as soon as their social status and property appeared to be seriously threatened[82]—in this they were soon proven quite correct. But they underestimated the degree to which "gentry" Russia and "bourgeois" Russia were intertwined in a society where there were vast differences within the nobility in economic and occupational status; where the census of 1897 showed that the vast majority of all living persons with higher education were still technically of noble origin; where the sons of "nobility and *činovniki*" still constituted an absolute majority of the student bodies of the major universities; and where a "bourgeoisie" in the Western sense existed only in embryo.[83] And therefore they underestimated the potentialities for a political party that would encompass significant numbers of men of diverse backgrounds whose most significant shared attribute was a higher education.[84]

In terms of political mobilization, the immediate fruits borne by the banquets and meetings of late 1904 were the "political professional" unions (that is, organizations formed along professional lines for the pursuit of political goals). The first of these unions—the Doctors' Union, the Academic Union (the "Professors' Union"), and the Engineers' Union—were in fact organized at the banquets and professional meetings of late 1904. Their example was followed in a rapid proliferation of unions in the winter and spring of 1905 and by the formation in May, at the initiative of the Engineers' Union, of the "Union of Unions." Consisting at first of thirteen member unions, the Union of Unions may have had a combined constituency of more than a hundred thousand persons by October, 1905; its leadership and several of its constituent unions, most particularly the Union of Railway Employees and Workers,

---

liberalism it will always be open to the danger of falling under a cross-fire and suffering complete defeat." *Iskra*, no. 77 (5 November 1904).

82. *Iskra*, no. 77 (5 Novembr 1904).

83. Cf. Lejkina-Svirskaja and Erman, note 73 above.

84. Gregory Freeze has made an intelligent critique along these lines of conventional wisdom in Western scholarship on the character of the liberation movement ("A National Liberation Movement and the Shift in Russian Liberalism 1901-1903," *Slavic Review* 28, no. [March 1969]: 81-91.) He may be wrong, however, in attributing the source of the conventional view primarily to the writings of V. A. Maklakov. The writings of the Mensheviks (the *Iskra*-ites of 1904) in the volumes of *Obščestvennoe dviženie* which appeared just before the first world war seem to have been at least as influential as Maklakov's. Indeed, one wonders if they might not have had an influence on Maklakov himself, who elaborated his views long after the revolution.

played crucial roles in the organization of the country's first general strike, which resulted in the tsar's Manifesto of 17 October promising substantive constitutional reforms.[85]

The chief beneficiary of the potentialities for a political party encompassing significant numbers of educated men was, of course, the Constitutional Democratic (Kadet) party. Having met in constituent congress only in the midst of the October general strike, the Kadets, working quasi-legally in the conditions created by the October Manifesto, built provincial party organizations in nearly all the provinces, hundreds of local party groups, and had a registered membership of about a hundred thousand by early 1906.[86] This was an organization comparable in size and rate of growth to that of the revolutionary parties in the same period; but whereas the latter drew primarily on a reservoir of student and working class youth, the Kadets drew primarily on the intelligentsia of the capitals and provincial towns of Russia.[87] In a sense, the architects of the Kadet party, who for the most part possessed the moderate constitutionalist attitudes described earlier, had won the battle for the allegiance of the "democratic intelligentsia" which had begun in the banquet campaign when they emerged as the most powerful party in the first national legislature convened in April, 1906.[88] They were, of course,

---

85. See Kirpičnikov, "L. I. Lutugin i Sojuz Sojuzov" (note 30, above), for the constituent unions and the estimate of total membership. A recent and balanced discussion of the role of the Railway Union in the general strike is W. Sablinsky, "The All-Russian Railroad Union and the Beginning of the General Strike in October, 1905", in A. and J. Rabinowitch and L. Kristof, eds., *Revolution and Politics in Russia: Essays in Memory of B. I. Nicolaevsky* (Bloomington–London, 1972), pp. 113–133. An authoritative history of the Union of Unions and of the professional union movement in general remains to be written.

86. *Alfavitnyj spisok adresov mestnykh grupp Konstitucionno-Demokratičeskoy partii (partii Narodnoj Svobody)* (St. P., 1906); *CGAOR*, f. 523, ed. khr. 27 (*Alfavitnyj spisok adresov mestnykh grupp partii Narodnoj Svobody*). The estimates of aggregate party membership are discussed by J. E. Zimmerman, "Between Revolution and Reaction: The Russian Constitutional Democratic Party: October, 1905 to June, 1907" (Ph.D. diss., Columbia University, 1967).

87. See note 73 above in regard to data on the social composition of the SD and SR parties. No formal studies of the social composition of the Kadet party in this formative period exist. Evidence to support the general proposition stated here is to be found in the archives of the Kadet party secretariat, *CGAOR*, f. 523, op. 1, which circularized local party groups with a questionnaire on the composition of membership, among other things, in the spring of 1906 (see ed. khr. 33a for a copy of the circular).

88. According to questionnaires filled out by deputies in May, 1906, there were 153 Kadets in the Duma, or 37.4% of the deputies. (The theoretical size of the Duma was 524 deputies, but only 499 had appeared from the various extremities of the Empire by July, when the Duma was prorogued.) The political complexion of the remainder of the deputies was highly variegated. See S. M. Sidel'nikov, *Obrazovanie i dejatel'nost' pervoi gosudarstvennoj dumy* (M., 1962), ch. vi.

aided enormously in that struggle by the dismal failure of the revolutionary parties' tactic of "definitive confrontation" with the autocracy in November-December, 1905, and then by the revolutionaries' equally ill-considered boycott of the first national elections.

Events soon demonstrated, however, that allegiance to the Kadet party among the "democratic intelligentsia," while remaining in the long run significant, was neither universal nor constant. Participation by the revolutionary parties in the second Duma election (February, 1907) drew off considerable support in the urban (non-working class) curia, which the Kadets had swept in the first elections; and in the atmosphere of widespread disenchantment with the Duma experiment that set in after the Stolypin coup d'état of 3 June 1907, the national network of Kadet organizations shrank to a mere vestige of what it had been in the heady spring of 1906.[89]

ABBREVIATIONS USED IN APPENDICES I AND II

ARCHIVAL SOURCES

CGAOR—*Central'nyj gosudarstvennyj arkhiv Oktjabr'skoj Revoljucii i socialističeskogo stroitel'stva*, Moscow. Unless otherwise indicated, all references are to *fond* 102, *Department policii, edinica khranenija* 1250, 1904g. Roman numerals identify the volume number in the archival unit; arabic numerals the page number.

NEWSPAPERS (ALL NEWSPAPER ENTRIES ARE IDENTIFIED BY CONSECUTIVE ISSUE NUMBER AND, WHERE NECESSARY, YEAR)

Emigré newspapers

I —*Iskra*. Central organ of the Russian Social Democratic Labor Party. Geneva.

O —*Osvoboždenie*. Edited by Peter Struve. Paris.

LO —*Listok Osvoboždenija*. Irregular addendum to *Osvoboždenie*.

RR —*Revoljucionnaja Rossija*. Central organ of the Socialist Revolutionary Party. Geneva.

V —*Vpered*. SD organ edited by Lenin. Geneva.

---

89. On the later history of the party, see Zimmerman, "Between Revolution and Reaction;" the contributions by Zimmerman and W. Rosenberg to C. Timberlake, ed., *Essays on Russian Liberalism* (Columbia, Missouri, 1972); and W. Rosenberg, *Liberals in the Russian Revolution: The Constitutional Democratic Party, 1917-1921* (Princeton, 1974).

Legal newspapers
ND   —*Naši Dni.* Petersburg.
NZ   —*Naša Žizn'.* Petersburg.
P   —*Pravo.* Petersburg.
RV   —*Russkie Vedomosti.* Moscow.
SO   —*Syn Otečestva.* Petersburg.

APPENDIX I

POLITICAL BANQUETS, NOVEMBER, 1904–JANUARY, 1905

Locations by city in alphabetical order, with dates and source references.

1. Baku 20xi. *CGAOR* I:188
2. Baku 25xi. *O* 63
3. Balashov (Saratov Province) 14xii. *ND* 5
4. Chernigov 20xi. *CGAOR* I:126-7
5. Ekaterinodar 11xii. *CGAOR* II:78-80; *I* 82; *ND* 11
6. Ekaterinoslav 28xi. *CGAOR* I:164; *I* 80
7. Yaroslavl 20xi. *NZ* 23
8. Kaluga 1xii. *CGAOR* f. 102, opis' 5, ed. khr. 2425, ch. 37, 1905g., 11-13; *O* 63; *NZ* 32
9. Kharkov 5xii. *CGAOR* I:147, II:45-58; *I* 81, 82; *NZ* 36
10. Kiev 20xi. *CGAOR* I:49-50, 128-30; *V* 1; *NZ* 20
11. Kostroma 8xii. *CGAOR* I:194
12. Kutais 31xii. *I* 87
13. Libava 21xi. *CGAOR* II:293
14. Moscow 21xi. *CGAOR* I:98; *I* 81; *NZ* 21, 29
15. Moscow 5xii. *CGAOR* I:189
16. Moscow 14xii. *CGAOR* II:37-8
17. Nizhny Novgorod 20xi. *CGAOR* I:99; *NZ* 20
18. Nizhny Novgorod 2xii. *O* 63
19. Novozybkov (Chernigov Province) 7xii. *CGAOR* III:21-3; *I* 79, 80, 83, 84
20. Odessa 20xi. *CGAOR* I:33, 38, 177-181; *I* 79, 80; *V* 2; *O* 62; *RR* 57; *NZ* 22
21. Orel 2xii. *CGAOR* I:204-6; *NZ* 29
22. Rostov/Don 5xii. *CGAOR* I:223-4, 233-4, II:114; *I* 80, 81; *O* 63; *V*3; *NZ* 36
23. St. Petersburg 20xi. *CGAOR* I:69-71; *I* 79; *NZ* 17, 22; *LO* 19
24. St. Petersburg 5 xii. *CGAOR* I:269; *I* 82; *O* 62
25. St. Petersburg 14xii. *CGAOR* I:264-7, II:155; *I* 82, 83; *O* 63; *V* 1
26. St. Petersburg 18xii. *CGAOR* I:275-7, II:155-6, 159-60; *O* 63; *I* 83; *V* 1
27. Samara 20xi. *SO* 13
28. Samara 1i. *CGAOR* III:58-59
29. Saratov 5xi. *V* 2; *NZ* 5; *I* 80; L-ij [I. M. Ljakhoveckij], "Banketnaja kampanija v Saratove (1904-1905)," *Minuvšie Gody*, 1908, no. 12 (Dec.), pp. 29-62

30. Saratov 20xi. *CGAOR* I:89–95; *I* 80; *V* 2; *NZ* 22; Ljakhoveckij
31. Saratov 17xii. *CGAOR* I:281–85; *ND* 11; Ljakhoveckij
32. Saratov 8i. *CGAOR* III:50–53; Ljakhoveckij
33. Smolensk 20xi. *CGAOR* I:77–8; *NZ* 21
34. Tiflis 8xii. *CGAOR* I:196
35. Tiflis 31xii. *CGAOR* III:109–112; *I* 86
36. Tambov 17xi. *O* 62; *NZ* 18
37. Vladimir 21xi. *CGAOR* I:79–80; *NZ* 21
38. Voronezh 20xi. *CGAOR* I:42–44; *NZ* 19

APPENDIX II

OTHER POLITICAL CONVOCATIONS,
NOVEMBER, 1904–JANUARY 9, 1905

A. Meetings of cultural, professional, and learned societies and charitable organizations. Location by city in alphabetical order, with dates, name of organization, and source references. Unless otherwise indicated, references are to meetings of local branches of the Imperial Societies.

1. Arkhangelsk 7xi. Meeting of political exiles. *I* 79
2. Baku 22xi. Public meeting in honor of court reforms. *CGAOR* I:188
3. Bogorodsk (Moscow Province) n.d. Imperial Technological Society. *O* 63
4. Yaroslavl 1xii. Society for Aid to Education. *CGAOR* I:54–57
5. Kharkov 6xi. Imperial Juridical Society. *CGAOR* I:20–23; *I* 78, 79
6. Kharkov 11xii. Library Society. *CGAOR* II:44; *I* 82
7. Kharkov 18xii. Imperial Juridical Society. *ND* 11
8. Kiev 20xi. Lawyers' supper. *RV* 329
9. Kiev 14xii. Society for Advancement of Literacy. *I* 82
10. Kiev 29xii. Congress of Teachers of Natural Science. *CGAOR* II:181–82; *NZ* 60
11. Kiev 4i. Congress of Russian Group of International Union of Criminal Lawyers. *P* 5 (1905)
12. Kiev n.d. Council of Professors of Polytechnic Institute. *I* 80
13. Kostroma 3xii. Imperial Agricultural Society. *O* 63
14. Kostroma [n.d.] xii. Pushkin Society for Aid to Public Education. *V* 3
15. Kursk 8xi. Society for Aid to Public Education. *NZ* 8
16. Kursk 20xi. Imperial Juridical Society. *CGAOR* I:41
17. Kursk 21xi. Imperial Juridical Society. *CGAOR* I:41
18. Kutais n.d. (but ca. 20xi). Lawyers' meeting. *ND* 1 (1905)
19. Maykop 12xii. Public meeting. *CGAOR* II:144–45
20. Moscow 4xi. Meeting of assistant barristers. *I* 78; *LO* 18; *RR* 56
21. Moscow 20xi. Meeting of assistant barristers. *CGAOR* I:235–46; *NZ* 19
22. Moscow 20xi. Meeting of barristers. *CGAOR* I:98, 235–46; *NZ* 19
23. Moscow 29xi. Directorate of Society of Russian Doctors. *O* 63

Terence Emmons

24. Moscow 29xii. Standing Committee on Technical Education of Technological Society. *CGAOR* II:167–70; *I* 84
25. Nizhny Novgorod 27xi. Society for Dissemination of Primary Education. *CGAOR* I:225–6; *V* 1
26. Nizhny Novgorod 6xii. Society for Aid to Salaried Employees of Private Enterprises. *CGAOR* II:81–2
27. Novorossiysk 31xii. New Years Party. *CGAOR* III:6–7
28. Odessa 18xi. Society for Protection of Public Health. *CGAOR* I:177–181; *I* 79; *V* 2
29. Odessa 20xi. Juridical Society. *I* 79; *V* 2
30. Pyatigorsk 31xii. New Years party. *CGAOR* II:161, 166
31. Rostov/Don 24-25xi. Lawyers' meeting. *RV* 333
32. St. Petersburg 21xi. Lawyers' meeting. *SO* 5
33. St. Petersburg 28xi. Pedagogical Society. *O* 62
34. St. Petersburg 30xi–2xii. Academic Council of Polytechnic Institute. *O* 62
35. St. Petersburg 30xii. Artists' supper. *NZ* 58
36. Samara 19xi. Family Pedagogical Circle. *CGAOR* I:84; *I* 83
37. Saratov 6xi. Technological Society. *NZ* 7
38. Saratov 15xi. Parents' circle of *fel'dšer* school. *I* 80
39. Smolensk 5i. Society of Medical Doctors. *I* 83, 86
40. Vologda 16xi. Lawyers' meeting. *CGAOR* I:240
41. Vologda 26xi. Educational-aid society.*CGAOR* I:154–57; *NZ* 23
42. Voronezh 2xii. Society for Protection of Public Health. *CGAOR* II:84

B.   Student meetings
1. Kiev 12xi. *Skhodka* of Polytechnic Institute students. *I*79
2. Kiev [n.d.]xi. *Skhodka* of university students. *I* 79
3. Moscow 6–9xi. Resolution of Bestuzhevki. *I* 78
4. Moscow 6–9xi. Resolution of university students. *I* 78
5. Moscow 20xi. Meeting of students of Petrovsko-Razumovskaia Academy. *I* 79
6. Moscow 7i. University student evening. *RR* 56, 57
7. Nizhny Novgorod 29xii. Student evening. *NZ* 56
8. Odessa 23xii. Student evening. *V* 3
9. Petersburg lxi. *Skhodka* of university students. *O* 60
10. Petersburg 4xi. *Skhodka* of students of Women's Medical Institute. *I* 78
11. Petersburg 31xii. University student evening. *CGAOR* III:1–2
12. Zhitomir 29xii. Charity evening for poor students of Kiev University. *CGAOR* II:176–79

A RUSSIAN IMPRESSIONIST:
Leonid Osipovich Pasternak, 1862-1945

BY

GUY DE MALLAC

LEONID OSIPOVICH PASTERNAK[1] was born in Odessa on 4 April (22 March, O.S.) 1862. In his memoirs he vividly recalls the sights, smells, and sounds of what he calls "our legendary courtyard." His father rented out that courtyard to peasants spending the night in town. To the yard was attached an eight-room inn whose lodgers were small gentry and aging former serfs. Teeming with all manner of people, carts, and animals, this court-yard appeared awesome and even terrifying to the young, impressionable Pasternak. Here he found remnants of Old Russia—topknotted peasants, petty landowners, and rural merchants. He writes: "All this courtyard, with its carts and wagons, with its horses and oxen, with its Ukrainian ox-cart drivers, coachmen, and Tatars, in no little way contributed to the enrichment of my artistic fantasy and the development of my observation."[2]

Artistic ability appeared early. When the boy was only seven, an old house porter—to whom he later referred as "my first Lorenzo Medici"—had already commissioned him to draw pictures of borzois hunting rabbits. This patron valued the boy's work enough to decorate the walls of his hut

---

1. The noun *pasternak* means "parsnip" in Russian, Polish, and Ukrainian. According to a family tradition, the Odessa Pasternaks are descended from a Sephardic family that settled in Russia in the eighteenth century, rather than from Ashkenazy Jews of central or eastern Europe, which is the background of most Jewish families in Odessa. Leonid Pasternak tells us in his memoirs that the family counts among its ancestors Don Isaac ben-Iuda Abravanel (also: Abrabanel, Abarbanella, 1437-1508), a theologian and exegete sufficiently favored by Alphonse V of Portugal to be made Minister of State to Ferdinand and Isabel. (He later became Minister in the employ of the Republic of Venice.) See L. O. Pasternak, "Vier Fragmente aus meiner Selbstbiographie," in Max Osborn, *Leonid Pasternak* (Warsaw: Stybel, 1932), p. 44. Pasternak claims to have seen the family's genealogical tree.

2. "Iz zapisok Leonida Pasternaka," *Novyj Žurnal* 69 (Sept. 1962): 143. (This first installment of Pasternak's memoirs will be cited hereafter as "Iz zapisok L. P.," I.)

with his pictures. Pasternak, later recalling the incident, expressed surprise that as a boy of six or seven he was capable of fulfilling his customer's
orders to the latter's full satisfaction, receiving for each hunt five copecks
(which he spent immediately on sweets for himself and his sister Asya).[3] In
a general way, the vivid, swarming Italianate harbor town of Odessa had
a decisive impact on the budding artist's sensibility.

Before he entered the gymnasium, the adolescent had talked his mother
into letting him take "lessons" from various artistically inclined boarders,
paying for the lessons with her meager savings. Out of this poor, simple
family of nine, unfamiliar with art, both Leonid Osipovich and his older
brother David (who was to die after graduation from the gymnasium)
showed artistic ability. In his memoirs Leonid Osipovich observes, "It
is incomprehensible that there could have been two sons blessed with
artistic talent in a family as simple, poor, and unfamiliar with art as were
my parents." He goes on to say that his father's remarkable gift for
humorous imitation on the one hand, and his mother's immense love for
nature, flowers, and colorfulness (*vsë koloristiČeskoe*) on the other, somehow acquainted him, respectively, with the elements of *form* and *color*,
essential to the graphic arts. Yet, to pursue his vocation Leonid had to
wage a long and unrelenting struggle against the prejudices typical of the
extremely modest, unsophisticated, and unenlightened milieu to which his
parents belonged. To them "daubing" (*"maljuvan'e"!*) held out no significant guarantees for the future. To the best of their knowledge (as Pasternak points out in his memoirs), painting (*malevan'e*) was the occupation of
house-painters—workmen who were seen going around stained and soiled.
For the child they loved they had other ambitions (that he become a
professional—"a doctor or a lawyer"). As a result, even his usually
tender mother occasionally took extreme, cruel measures—such as burn-
ing his drawings in the stove, in order to nip the problem in the bud.[4]

At the age of thirteen he completed a self-portrait which revealed a
considerable degree of talent. In his last year at the gymnasium and then
as a young student Leonid Osipovich contributed to such humoristic
journals as *Osa* (The Wasp), *Majak* (The Lighthouse), and *PČëlka* (The
Little Bee). In *PČëlka* (which appeared in Odessa) Pasternak published
various caricatures and satirical compositions as well as depictions of
Odessa types, and characteristic street and harbor scenes. One of his types
was a harbor tramp (*bosjak*) who, as he found out later, did not escape
Gorky's attention.[5] During that period he also attended courses at what he

3. L. O. Pasternak, *Zapisi raznykh let* (Moscow: Sovetskij khudožnik, 1975), p. 13.

4. "Iz zapisok L. P.," I, pp. 147-49.

5. "Iz zapisok Leonida Pasternaka," *Novyj Žurnal* 77 (Sept. 1964): 201-02. (This second
installment of Pasternak's memoirs will be cited hereafter as "Iz zapisok L. P.," II.)

terms the "half-Italian" Odessa School of Drawing—he tells us that the techniques favored by that institution (where Vrubel also studied) were heavily slanted toward the Italian tradition.[6]

Although they appreciated his talents, Pasternak's parents preferred him to choose a more stable profession, so after finishing his courses at the classical gymnasium in 1881, he moved to Moscow to study medicine. Later, when one semester of dissecting unnerved the sensitive artist, he switched to law, simultaneously taking private lessons from the renowned academician Evgraf Sorokin. He remarks later in his memoirs that he benefited greatly as an artist from the study of anatomy which he pursued at the faculty of medicine.[7]

In 1882 Pasternak applied for admission to the Moscow School of Painting, Sculpture, and Architecture.[8] There was only one opening, however, and the competition was between the unknown young artist and Countess Tatyana Lvovna Tolstoy. Failing in his bid for entrance, Pasternak returned a few years later to teach classes there, one of which was attended by the Countess herself. Later, when the Tolstoys and the Pasternaks became good friends, they could look back on this incident and laugh. After his unsuccessful application, the undaunted Pasternak continued obtaining private tuition from Sorokin while continuing his study of law.

In 1883 Leonid Osipovich changed over to the University of Odessa. In October he left for the Royal Academy of Art in Munich (at which the classes in draftsmanship were considered to be among the best in Europe), where he studied painting with enthusiasm but at the cost of many personal privations.[9] (Over the next few years numerous Russian artists—including

---

6. See "Iz zapisok L. P.," II, p. 192. "Lively draftsmanship and a very immediate perception of color" were acknowledged characteristics of the alumni of the Odessa School. N. M. Moleva and È. M. Beljutin, *Russkaja khudožestvennaja škola vtoroj poloviny XIX-načala XX veka* (Moscow: Iskusstvo, 1967), p. 165. (This work will hereafter be cited as Moleva and Beljutin.)

7. "Iz zapisok L. P.," II, p. 209.

8. The Moscow School of Painting, Sculpture, and Architecture (Moskovskoe Učilišče Živopisi, Vajanija i Zodčestva) was affiliated with the Academy of Arts in St. Petersburg. It will hereafter be referred to as the (Moscow) School of Painting. The School played an outstanding and progressive role in the history of Russian art. Its forerunner was a life class organized in 1832 by several lovers of painting. Later it was reorganized into an art class, attached to the Moscow Art Society. In 1843, it became a school of sculpture as well as of painting; in 1865, courses in architecture were added to the curriculum. During the latter half of the nineteenth century, the Moscow School of Painting was a center for the development of realism in art. Cf. Ja. D. Minčenkov, *Vospominanija o peredvižnikakh* (Leningrad: Khudožnik RSFSR, 1963), p. 326.

9. Thus, Pasternak recounts in his memoirs that, in view of the inadequate funds he had at his disposal (savings he had set aside from his fees for doing illustrations for magazines in Odessa), he often could not afford even the most modest meal, and went round the Munich galleries on an empty stomach. L. Pasternak, *Zapisi raznykh let*, pp. 26–27.

Jawlenski, Grabar, Dobuzhinsky, Shcherbatov, Kandinsky, David and
Vladimir Burlyuk, Verevkina, Bekhteev, Kogan—were to follow in Pasternak's footsteps and go on an artistic pilgrimage to Munich.) At the competitive entrance examination Pasternak ranked first in his class. There,
while working under Ludwig Herterich,[10] he decided once and for all
to devote himself exclusively to painting. Upon his return to Russia after
a two-year stay in Germany, he performed a year's military service in
Odessa, and graduated in law at the University there (1885). In 1887 he
went to Moscow where within a few years he was to assume a prominent
place in artistic circles because of the popularity of his sketches.

All Moscow was stirring with talk about this young artist's work,
especially his widely-exhibited sketches and portraits. P. M. Tretyakov,[11]
having learned of Pasternak's work, bought a few of his more dramatic
drawings. When, in 1889 (while staying in a small furnished room on
Lubyansky Passage), Pasternak finished his first major canvas, *Vesti s
rodiny* (News from Home),[12] Tretyakov bought it straight from the easel
for 2,000 gold rubles, before its appearance at the exhibition of the
Peredvizhniki (Itinerants). The exacting jury of the Peredvizhniki had
accepted it by an overwhelmingly strong vote.[13] *Vesti s rodiny* was the first
major life-size genre painting in Russia—up to then genre paintings (i.e.,
paintings on themes other than historical subjects) were done on a scale
smaller than life. Pasternak, who began as a genre painter working mostly

10. The Munich Academy was the stronghold of the so-called Diez school of painting.
Pasternak studied most closely under Ludwig Herterich, but also with A. von Liezen-Mayer
and L. Löfftz. Rejecting the historical-didactic approach that at that time prevailed in
most schools of painting in Europe, Herterich encouraged the painting of sensuous,
bright, color-oriented canvases in which very strict attention was also paid to composition.

11. Pavel Mikhaylovich Tretyakov (1832–98), major patron of Russian art and founder of
the gallery which now bears his name, was actively interested in the periodical Peredvizhniki
exhibits and sought out worthwhile achievements of the best contemporary talent.

12. The painting *Vesti s rodiny* is also referred to in certain sources (such as Polenov's
letters) as *Pis'mo s rodiny* (Letter from Home). In view of the universal acclaim which
this picture has since received, it is curious to note that at the time some of Pasternak's
colleagues, such as Repin and Polenov, had reservations about it, wishing the artist had
polished up his draftsmanship even more. This is pointed out in letters of Polenov to
his sister: "Pasternak risunok počti ne ispravil i ot ètogo očen' terjaet . . . Pasternakom on
[i.e. Repin] nedovolen za risunok." (V. D. Polenov, letter of 20 February 1889 to N. V.
Polenova, in V. D. Polenov, *Pis'ma, dnevniki, vospominanija*, 2d ed. [Moscow: Iskusstvo,
1950], pp. 249–50). "Pro Pasternaka Repin skazal, čto èto plokhaja vešč', čto tol'ko
èkspressii nedurny." (V. D. Polenov, letter of 21 February 1889 to N. V. Polenova, in
Polenov, *Pis'ma, dnevniki, vospominanija*, p. 251).

13. *Vesti s rodiny* received fourteen votes out of a possible sixteen. It is interesting
to note that during these same deliberations, the jury gave three pictures of Levitan only
nine, thirteen, and ten votes, respectively. (Another picture by Levitan, *Maj*, was turned
down.) Polenov, letter of 19 February 1889 to his sister, and appendix to that letter, in
Polenov, *Pis'ma, dnevniki, vospominanija*, pp. 249, 485.

in charcoal to make pictures such as his *Jewish Musicians*, started using more watercolors, pastels, and oils, and was soon to become, along with Serov, perhaps the most prominent portraitist in Moscow.[14]

Around this time, a fateful event occurred in Pasternak's artistic life. The first All-Russian Conference of Artists, created by the Moscow Society of Art Lovers (of which Pasternak was a member), took on a broad program for the designing and executing of stage sets and costumes for musical/theatrical performances. Although Pasternak knew artists with experience in this area and had even attended a meeting of the Society where this problem was discussed, he himself had never attempted anything of this sort. It was decided, however, that Pasternak should design and paint the stage set for the opera *Raphael* by Arensky. He accepted but only with misgivings. The set, despite the author's inexperience, turned out successfully. Leonid Osipovich himself was surprised by the effect he had produced: "So much air! How everything shines, illuminated by the sun!"[15] He insists that his association with this group and his subsequent commission influenced the decision of the Council of Instructors of the School of Painting, Sculpture, and Architecture to accept him in 1894 into the Faculty of the School as an instructor in figure painting.[16]

Shortly before this, in 1889 in Odessa, Leonid Osipovich was asked unexpectedly to be art editor of the Moscow-based *Artist* (The Artist), a journal that Balmont, in a conversation with Pasternak, referred to as ". . . for us, the precursor of [Diaghilev's] *Mir Iskusstva* (The World of Art)."[17] While he was editor Pasternak did the illustrations for a one-act study by Chekhov, entitled "Kalkhas" and appearing in *The Artist*. Evidently he did not read the script carefully enough to notice that one of the characters he drew was described as having a beard, but when Chekhov saw the illustration, he liked it so much that he changed the description of the character to fit the drawing.

During a previous stay in Odessa (in 1885), Leonid Osipovich had met Rosalia Isidorovna Kaufmann,[18] a concert pianist who was teaching there in the Conservatory of Music. After his initial success in Moscow reassured

---

14. Cf. Academician Igor' Grabar', "Pamjati Leonida Pasternaka," *Sovetskoe Iskusstvo*, no. 28 (13 July 1945), p. 4.

15. "Iz zapisok L. P.," I, p. 152.

16. Pasternak was to teach the figure class at the School from 1894 to 1897, and from 1897 until the Revolution was, with A. E. Arkhipov, one of the leaders of the life class. See Moleva and Beljutin, pp. 243–44, 252.

17. "Iz zapisok L. P.," I, p. 156.

18. She is variously referred to in different early documents as Rozalija or Roza Kaufmann, or Rosa Koffmann or Koffman.

him about his own professional future, he married the brilliant young pianist on 14 February 1889. A native of Odessa, Rosa Kaufmann had given her first public recital in 1875, at the age of eight, and had then studied under the Odessa pianist and composer Ignatz Tedesco. In 1880, at thirteen, she gave the first of her numerous concert tours in southern Russia, and was met everywhere by enthusiastic audiences, particularly in Kiev. In 1881 she met the famous composer Anton Rubinstein, who from then on gave her considerable encouragement and professional support. In 1883 Rosa Kaufmann gave about twenty highly successful concerts in most large cities of Russia and Poland. Starting in 1883 she studied for several years in Vienna under the famous pianist Theodor Leschetizky,[19] who also counted Paderewski among his pupils. After her return to Odessa Rosa Isidorovna was, in 1888, appointed instructor of the most advanced piano classes in the Conservatory. Her marriage to Leonid Osipovich meant a radical change in professional orientation: gradually, and with a few brief resumptions of her activity as a concert pianist, she gave up her brilliant career in favor of total devotion to family life[20] and to her husband's own professional development. She took upon herself a great number of tasks, from entertaining the numerous models who sat for him to planning and organizing exhibitions of his works. To these combined ends she continued applying all her energies and affection, in spite of failing health (in 1911 she had her first heart attack, soon taking a rather successful cure in Germany, followed by another cure there in 1921).[21] In the 1890s and 1900s, however, musical evenings frequently took place at the Pasternaks, occasionally attended by the Tolstoys, at which Rosa Isidorovna often performed, while other musicians as well participated or attended, such as Mogilevsky, Grzhimali, Skriabin, and Brandukov.[22]

---

19. Or, according to the original Polish spelling of his name, Teodor Leszetycki (1839–1915).

20. The Pasternaks had four children: Boris (1890–1960), poet and novelist, won the Nobel prize for literature in 1958; Alexander (b. 1893) became a noted architect; Dr. Josephine Pasternak (b. 1900) pursued philosophical studies; Dr. Lydia Pasternak-Slater (b. 1902) specialized in biochemistry. Both the artist's daughters wrote and published poetry.

21. For more details on Rosa Pasternak, see Serge Levitsky, "Rose Koffman-Pasternak: la mère du poète," *Etudes Slaves et Est-Européenes* 8 (1963): 73–80.

22. Josephine Pasternak says of her mother's playing: "Like the rest of us, like the audiences in her younger days, he [Leonid] became overwhelmed by the manifestation of life's drama, of its irreconcilable duality of pain and joy, as one experienced an almost mystical identity of life and music when mother played." Josephine Pasternak also recalls that in the thirties, after a particularly stirring private performance on the piano by his wife, Leonid said in a voice of pure admiration: "I now realize I ought to have married you. It was my fault. You have sacrificed your genius to me and the family. Of us two you are the greater artist." J. Pasternak, "Last Years," in the catalogue *Leonid Pasternak 1862–1945* (London: Oxford University Press, March–May 1969).

After their marriage in 1889, the young couple settled down in Moscow at their first permanent residence, Dom Lyžina (Lyzhin's House), a red brick building on Oruzheynaya (Armory) Street. The Pasternaks were to live in this house until 1894 when they moved to Myasnitskaya Street. Once settled in Moscow, Leonid Osipovich continued his career as an artist, making his way as an illustrator for various periodicals (including *Svet i Teni* [Light and Shadows]), retaining his editorship of *The Artist*, and founding his own school of drawing. Still, the period after the move to Moscow was one of financial stress for the family of the struggling young artist (awareness of these difficult times is reflected in the original lullaby that the nurse of the Pasternak children used to sing to Boris, according to Leonid Osipovich's memoirs).[23] Nonetheless, in 1889 Pasternak took a trip to Paris where he saw numerous examples of French Impressionism in the original.

Upon returning to Moscow, Leonid Osipovich frequented his former teacher Vasily Polenov,[24] a member of the Peredvizhniki and an established professor at the Moscow School of Painting, Sculpture, and Architecture. Polenov would prove to be a true friend and an important artistic influence. Indeed, friends such as Polenov would prove invaluable to Pasternak's career: Polenov himself helped publicize Pasternak's newly founded school, and Repin, a most distinguished painter, even sent pupils to Pasternak. In the artistic world, Leonid Osipovich's other friends were Levitan, Korovin, Serov, and N. N. Gué.[25]

More and more challenging commissions came. Thus in 1890 the Kushnerev publishing house decided to bring out the first illustrated edition of Lermontov's works on the occasion of the fiftieth anniversary of the poet's death, and asked Pasternak to be its chief art editor; in that capacity he invited a *pléiade* of Russian artists to contribute, including V. and A. Vasnetsov, K. Korovin, Polenov, Repin, and Serov, but also such a controversial figure (for a "respectable" publishing house of the 1890s) as Vrubel. Vrubel's illustrations for that edition (1891) were revolutionary for the time, and exerted considerable influence on the new generation of Russian artists. Pasternak points out in his

---

23. "Sleep, my child; when you grow older, your papa won't have to paint any more, but will have hired hands (*spodručnykh*) instead." L. Pasternak, "Vier Fragmente," p. 58 (note 1, above). For the Russian version, cf. "Mastityj L. Pasternak," *Rubež* [Kharbin], no. 28 (1 June 1933).

24. In the 1880s Pasternak had attended as a student the private drawing and watercolor sessions held at Polenov's. Cf. E. V. Sakharova, *Vasilij Dmitrievič Polenov. Elena Dmitrievna Polenova. Khronika sem'i khudožnikov* (Moscow: Iskusstvo, 1964), pp. 5, 25.

25. Nikolaj Nikolaevič Ge (1831–1894), the distinguished elder Itinerant. His name is often transliterated as Gué or Gay.

memoirs that the leading artists of the day viewed this edition as a
competitive event, and vied with each other in making a significant
contribution to it.[26]

In the autumn of 1892, Pasternak was invited with the more famous
Repin, Vereshchagin, and Kivshenko to illustrate a deluxe edition of
War and Peace, which appeared in installments in the journal *Sever*
(The North). Countess Tatyana Tolstoy reported to have said about
Pasternak's illustrations: "We have never had anything like that!" Com-
menting on this remark, Leonid Osipovich wrote in his autobiography:
"I was then perhaps the first Russian painter to consider the illustrating
of books earnestly as an independent form of creative work, sufficient
unto itself."[27]

It wasn't until the following year, however, that Pasternak was to be
introduced to the man with whom he was to stay on friendly terms
for the next seventeen years. At the annual Peredvizhniki exhibition
in the spring of 1893 (where his picture *Debjutantka* enjoyed great
success), a senior "Itinerant" introduced Leonid Osipovich to Tolstoy,
a regular visitor of Peredvizhniki exhibitions and a secret admirer of
Pasternak's works. Pasternak called on Tolstoy at his residence on
Khamovniki Street in Moscow to submit for Tolstoy's comments his
illustrations of *War and Peace*, and he and his wife became frequent
visitors of the Tolstoys both in Moscow and at Yasnaya Polyana.[28]

In 1894 the Pasternak family moved into lodgings at the School of
Painting, Sculpture, and Architecture, after Pasternak was offered a
professorship at this school, which under the leadership of Prince A. E.
Lvov became one of the most progressive art schools in Europe.[29]
In his reminiscences, the artist relates the circumstances of this offer:

26. "Èto lermontovskoe izdanie s illjustracijami počti vsekh našikh togdašnikh russkikh
khudožnikov bylo svoego roda smotrom i sostjazaniem." "Iz zapisok L. P.," II,
pp. 190–91, 193 (note 5, above). Cf. also I. S. Zil'berštejn and V. A. Samkov, eds.,
Valentin Serov v vospominanijakh, dnevnikakh i perepiske sovremennikov, 2 vols. (Leningrad: Khudožnik RSFSR, 1971), 1: 701, 709.

27. L. Pasternak, "Vier Fragmente," p. 78.

28. For the details of Pasternak's contacts with Tolstoy, see his text "My Meetings with
Tolstoy," *The Russian Review* 19 (April 1960): 122–31. A somewhat different version of
this is to be found in his "Vier Fragmente," pp. 58–94.

29. In the early 1890s, Prince Lvov submitted the curriculum of the School to a
thorough overhaul. One of his innovations consisted in inviting the famous historian
V. O. Klyuchevsky to give lectures on Russian history. The prestigious scholar liked the
public there very much. Pasternak, who as a young law student had already attended
Klyuchevsky's lectures, was delighted to have a chance to encounter him as a colleague and
have long conversations with him. His oil painting of the scholar (the only extant
portrait of Klyuchevsky, it seems) and the eloquent vignette of him he gives in his
memoirs are complementary—and very forceful—depictions of Klyuchevsky. Cf. "Iz zapisok
L. P.," II, pp. 209–14.

I thanked Prince Lvov for his kind offer, which I was delighted to accept. At the time, however, I pointed out that I doubted the realization of this proposal, as it still had to be formally confirmed by the trustee of the school, the Grand Duke Serge Alexandrovich, and I feared that my being of Jewish origin would stand in the way of the latter's approval. I added that although I had been brought up in a Jewish family—admittedly religious but free from adherence to ritual—whose members, including myself, felt completely assimilated to our Russian surroundings, and although I believed in God but did not in practice belong to any religious denomination, I would never consider baptism as a means of facilitating my progress in life or raising my social status. The very humane and tolerant Prince Lvov understood me very well, and promised to inform Serge Alexandrovich of my standpoint. Contrary to my expectations, the Grand Duke sanctioned my appointment, a thing unusual in those days, when civil servants had to belong to the Russian Orthodox Church, or at least to profess another Christian creed.[30]

Thus was the Pasternak family established in a position from which it could develop contacts within the highest artistic and social spheres in Moscow.

When Pasternak's appointment was approved by the Grand Duke in 1894, the family moved into the quarters of the School of Painting at 21 Myasnitskaya Street. (The street was renamed after Kirov in 1934.) Boris Pasternak remembered of the new lodgings that "the main building, which was old and beautiful, was remarkable in many ways."[31] It was, like others on the street, originally built in the eighteenth century for a noble family, but by the second half of the nineteenth century the neighborhood had become the heart of the business district.[32] The Pasternaks were to reside at No. 21 Myasnitskaya Street without interruption until 1911, when they moved to new lodgings provided by the School of

---

30. Quoted in Lydia Pasternak-Slater, "Letter to the Editor," *The New York Times Book Review*, 29 October 1961, p. 50.

31. Boris Pasternak, *I Remember: Sketch for an Autobiography*, trans. David Magarshack (New York: Meridian, 1960), p. 21.

32. Myasnitskaya Street had become one of the main thoroughfares leading from the center of town to the three main railroad stations. Wealthy merchants and industrialists had replaced aristocratic families as the owners of the buildings, and their shops and offices, which lined the street, had turned it into the business street of Moscow. As early as 1890, it had been lit with electricity, but was still paved the old-fashioned way, with cobblestones, until the 1900s. Like the street, the house at no. 21 went through considerable alteration after its construction by Bazhenov in the eighteenth century. In the middle of the nineteenth century, it was transformed into the Moscow School of Painting, Sculpture, and Architecture. Boris Pasternak describes the further transformations which the building underwent in the late 1890s:

Painting: 14 Volkhonka Street, Apartment 9. Pasternak was to remain active on the staff of the School for over a quarter of a century.[33]

During the first few years of their residence at Myasnitskaya Street, Pasternak began to attend evening parties given by artistically inclined members of the Russian aristocracy:

> If there was even the smallest chance to sketch from real life, as at Korovin's, Polenov's, and especially at Prince Golitsyn's, I was always there participating most ardently. I can say the same about Serov. . . . Almost all the best artists frequented such parties. . . . I remember [I was painting] one of the most attractive women of that aristocratic circle . . . Princess Yusupov, Countess Sumarokov-Elston. Standing behind me for a long while, the General [-Governor of Moscow, Grand Duke Serge Alexandrovich] . . . [was] comparing my sketch with our sitter. . . . At the next periodical exhibit of the Moscow Society of Art Lovers . . . [he then] bought this sketched portrait of Princess Yusupov.[34]

Apart from exhibiting with the Peredvizhniki (which he was to do during the whole of the period 1888-1901),[35] Pasternak was active in other circles. In the 1890s he co-founded with Polenov the Moscow Group of the 36 Artists (*Tridcat' šest' khudoznikov*), which, like the better-known and better-publicized *Mir iskusstva* that was to come into being shortly afterwards, was created in reaction against the rigid and stifling policies of the Itinerants.[36] Pasternak was also a member of the *Mir iskusstva* (World of Art) society, which came into being in 1900 in St. Petersburg (comprising the artists who had exhibited in the *Mir iskusstva* exhibitions to date).[37] In 1903 the *36 khudožnikov* and

---

"The fever of the nineties had an effect on the School of Painting, too. The government grants were not sufficient for its maintenance. Businessmen were therefore entrusted with the raising of additional funds to cover its budget. It was decided to build on the land belonging to the school large apartment houses for letting to private persons, and to erect in the middle of the property, on the site of the former garden, glass exhibition galleries, also for letting." B. Pasternak, *I Remember*, p. 32.

33. In 1918 the School was renamed *Vysšie khudožestvenno-tekhničeskie masterskie* (Advanced Art Studios)—also known as *Vkhutemas* (the acronym), and Pasternak continued on its staff until 1921.

34. "Iz zapisok L. P.," I, pp. 157–59 (note 2, above).

35. Moleva and Beljutin, p. 365 (note 6, above).

36. Unlike *Mir iskusstva*, which concerned itself with theater, ballet, and literature, as well as painting, the *"36"* were concerned solely with painting and the freedom of artistic expression. Until 1903 *Mir iskusstva* and the *"36"* at times engaged in open rivalry. Cf. I. È. Grabar'; V. N. Lazarev; A. A. Sidorov; and O. A. Švidovskij; eds., *Istorija russkogo iskusstva*, vol. 10, pt. 2 (Moscow: Nauka, 1968), pp. 28–31.

37. The periodical *Mir Iskusstva*, founded by Dyagilev and Benois, was published from 1898 until 1904. The *Mir iskusstva* society was founded on 24 February 1900, and counted

certain members of the now defunct *Mir iskusstva* banded together to form the *Sojuz russkikh khudožnikov* (Union of Russian Painters); this union required compromise between the two groups, but solidarity was seen as a necessity in the face of the ever-popular—and unyielding— Itinerants. Pasternak was a member of this new group, which was to last until 1923.[38] With its program centering upon "nature and life," the new society heralded a departure from stereotyped historical themes and a return to reality in its concreteness and soon became the focal point in the development of modern art in Russia.

Apart from these annual exhibitions, Pasternak showed his work on various occasions such as the exhibition Blanc et Noir, the Munich International Exhibition, and various shows in Berlin, Vienna, London, and elsewhere. His famous painting *Studenty pered èkzamenom* (Students Before the Final Examination) (1895) was awarded a gold medal at the Munich Exhibition, and at the Paris World Exhibition in 1900 it was purchased by the French Government for the Musée du Luxembourg.[39]

It is interesting to compare this canvas both with *News from Home* (1889) and another group composition by Pasternak, *Soviet Moskovskogo Učilišča Živopisi* (Council of Instructors of the Moscow School of Painting—sometimes referred to in English as *Moscow Artists*—1902), in which we see Arkhipov, S. Ivanov, K. Korovin, Serov, Kasatkin, A. Vasnetsov, and the artist himself in session in the Russian Museum. These three significant canvases, done within a thirteen-year period, exhibit certain common traits. In these pictures, which all portray indoor scenes, the artist is interested in meticulous draftsmanship, composition, and psychological portraiture, rather than in depicting bright and sensuous sunlight effects in typically Impressionist fashion. We have here a subdued, restrained use of Impressionistic techniques; not Renoir or Monet, but Degas.

A bright era in Leonid Osipovich's career began when Tolstoy requested the artist to illustrate his new novel, *Resurrection*. During these years, Pasternak frequently visited the Tolstoys; before and during work

---

among its members Bakst, Benois, Vasnetsov, Lanceray, Levitan, Malyavin, Nesterov, Somov, Serov, Vrubel', Golovin, Korovin, Mamontov, P. Trubetskoy, Baksheev, Pasternak, Roerich. For the minutes of the organizational meeting of the society, see the "Khudožestvennaja khronika" section of *Rossija*, no. 321 (17 March 1900).

38. The *Sojuz russkikh khudožnikov* was also joined by some Itinerants who had left that society. The greater part of *Sojuz* members upheld the principles of realism in their art, while others exhibited impressionistic and at times modernistic tendencies. In 1910 the former adherents of *Mir iskusstva*, led by A. N. Benois, left the *Sojuz*. Minčenkov, *Vospominanija o peredvižnikakh*, p. 327 (note 8, above).

39. Since then it has been hanging in the Musée du Luxembourg in Paris.

on *Resurrection*, he sketched many convincing, informal drawings of Tolstoy, his family, and life around the estate. In his autobiography, Pasternak tells us that on a dark October day in 1898, Tolstoy's daughter Tatyana came to inform the painter that her father wanted him to illustrate a novella he was writing. He promptly took the night train to Yasnaya Polyana where he spent a few days with Tolstoy going over the text and planning his task.[40] The text of that novella grew and grew, finally to become *Resurrection*. In *Sketch for an Autobiography* Boris Pasternak vividly describes his father's work:

> Tolstoy held back the proofs, constantly revising them. The danger a-
> rose that the illustration made for the original text would not agree with
> Tolstoy's subsequent changes. But Father made his drawings from the
> same source used by Tolstoy for his observations: the courtroom, the
> transit prison, the country, the railway. This supply of living detail
> and realistic understanding common to both saved Father from any
> danger of digression. Joiner's glue boiled on the stove. The illustra-
> tions were hurriedly wiped off, dried with fixative, glued onto card-
> board, rolled up and tied. The finished illustration was then sealed with
> wax and sent off.[41]

Pasternak had to work intensively to meet the deadlines, since the Petersburg publisher A. F. Marks (who published the magazine *Niva*, in which the novel was being serialized during all of 1899) put great pressure on both artist and writer.[42] At Yasnaya Polyana, the artist read the text of the novel during the day, discussed the illustrations with Tolstoy in the evening, and worked on the drawings themselves at night. In six weeks he finished thirty-three illustrations (black water-colors), and when the assignment was over he fell ill from exhaustion.

Tolstoy assigned grades for each illustration like a schoolteacher; Pasternak would often score an "A plus" (*pjat' s pljusom*). Once, when he had done an exceptionally remarkable illustration for a chapter which Tolstoy had in the meantime decided to discard, Tolstoy was so enthusiastic about the illustration that he re-introduced material into the text in order to retain the illustration.[43] The illustrations and the text

40. L. Pasternak, "Vier Fragmente," pp. 86-90 (note 1, above). Cf. also his text, "My Meetings with Tolstoy" (note 28, above).

41. B. Pasternak, *I Remember*, pp. 27-8 (published translation revised by me). The illustrations referred to here might well be the photographic reproductions of the originals. The originals went to *Niva*, the photographic reproductions to the foreign publishers.

42. Tolstoy himself was in a hurry to publish *Resurrection*, for the proceeds were to be devoted to helping the Dukhobors emigrate to Canada.

43. German Svet, "U L. O. Pasternaka. K otkrytiju ego vystavki v Berline" [an interview with Pasternak], *Segodnja* [Riga], no. 286 (18 December 1927).

were sent to the publisher while copies were mailed to Paris, London, and New York, where the novel was appearing simultaneously. Pasternak's illustrations for *Resurrection* had a larger circulation than any other pre-revolutionary Russian graphics: while it also appeared in book form, the novel was serialized in the magazine *Niva*, which had a circulation of 200,000—the largest of all Russian periodicals at the time.[44]

It has been said that these illustrations by Pasternak constituted "a very serious, realistic, and intensely psychological narrative."[45] Since then, no other Russian artist has attempted illustrations of *Ressurection* —which is testimony enough to the unique excellence of Pasternak's achievement in capturing both the psychological truth of the characters, and the details of Russian *byt* (costumes and uniforms, courtroom and prison scenes, town and country backdrop, lower- and upper-class background). Such close attention to the characteristics of everyday life and reality was a central tenet of the Itinerants' esthetic—here we have proof of Pasternak's debt to that school which dominated Russian art in the last quarter of the 19th century. The originals of these illustrations, with Tolstoy's grades, are in the Tolstoy Museum in Moscow.

Shortly after work on *Resurrection*, Pasternak painted his famous pastel *L. N. Tolstoj v sem'e* (Family Portrait of the Tolstoys—1902-03), in which the strongest impression is made by the figure of Tolstoy himself, sitting on a chair with his left hand resting on the back of a neighboring chair. This expressive profile is one of the most exquisite, perceptive portraits of Tolstoy extant. In the opinion of the former curator of the Tolstoy Museum (and one-time secretary of Tolstoy) V. F. Bulgakov, Pasternak's portraits of Tolstoy (in oil, tempera, and pencil) are more successful than those of all other artists—not excluding Repin—in capturing the old writer's likeness, insofar as they faithfully render the sharpness of outline, and the angular and emaciated aspect of the novelist, without being guilty of a defect of Repin's portraiture (which, Bulgakov says, exaggerates the "corporealness" [*telesnost'*] of Tolstoy in depicting too powerful a chest and shoulders).[46]

44. A. A. Sidorov, *Russkaja grafika načala XX veka. Očerki istorii i teorii* (Moscow: Iskusstvo, 1969), p. 50.

45. Sidorov, *Russkaja grafika*, p. 59. For additional comments and information on these illustrations, see p. 50. It should be noted that in addition to the black and white illustrations for the novel (which have since become famous), Pasternak did a series of *color* illustrations for the same text, which were discovered in the artist's studio by the curator of the Tolstoy Museum, V. F. Bulgakov, and acquired for the Museum. In the opinion of Bulgakov this series is esthetically less convincing than the black and white illustrations. Val. Bulgakov, "L. O. Pasternak," *Iskusstvo*, no. 7 (1961), p. 66.

46. Bulgakov, "L. O. Pasternak," p. 67. A number of Pasternak's drawings of Tolstoy were printed in the periodical *Mir Iskusstva*, no. 8 (1902).

After *Family Portrait of the Tolstoys*, Pasternak did (also in Yasnaya Polyana) a watercolor *Tolstoy Reading*, which is significant in that it represents a departure from the more sedate form of Imprssionism practiced so far by the artist, in favor of a bolder manner, with a considerably lesser degree of obvious concern for draftsmanship, and marked by coarser brushstrokes and more sensuous use of color. Sedate masses of green and dark green are enlivened by the glaring yellow mass of the lampshade and the lamp's reflection, and smaller red and ochre patches. Both as an essay in psychological portrayal and technically, as a study in contrast of color masses, this picture is an outstanding achievement of Impressionist technique. Evidencing bravura (though of a kind different from that achieved by Serov in his *Portrait of Countess Orlov*), this picture of Tolstoy is perhaps Pasternak's most memorable portrait.

In 1900 Pasternak traveled to Paris where his illustrations for *Resurrection* were shown in the Russian Pavilion of the Paris World Exhibition, earning him a Silver Medal. Four years later, Leonid Osipovich for the first time journeyed through Italy, visiting Venice, Verona, Florence, and finally Rome. In the latter city he was overjoyed to meet Rainer Maria Rilke, with whom he had developed friendly relations when the poet visited Russia.[47] A short while later, in 1905, Pasternak received important recognition—he was elected a member of the Petersburg Academy of Arts.

In the wake of the 1905 Revolution, Pasternak was liberal enough to sign, together with another 112 artists, a *Rezoljucija khudožnikov* (Resolution of the Artists), which was issued in May 1905, calling for the immediate reform of the government, within the context of "full freedom of conscience, word, and the press, freedom of assembly and meetings, and personal immunity."[48] He and Serov often contributed to political and satirical journals. Towards the end of 1905, Pasternak often saw Gorky, who invited him to the editorial offices of *Bič* (The Whip), *Župel* (The Bugbear), and other such journals.[49]

The School of Painting proved to be one of the principal hotbeds of

---

47. The degree of friendship and warmth between the two artists is convincingly conveyed in Pasternak's memoirs, "Iz zapisok L. P.," II, pp. 203–07; see also 'Vier Fragmente," pp. 94–106. For some additional background, cf. André von Gronicka, "Rilke and the Pasternaks: A Biographical Note," *The Germanic Review* 27 (Dec. 1952): 260–71, and Christopher J. Barnes, "Boris Pasternak and Rainer Maria Rilke: Some Missing Links," *Forum for Modern Language Studies* (St. Andrews) 8, no. 1 (Jan. 1972): 61–78.

48. "Rezoljucija Khudožnikov," *Pravo*, no. 18 (8 May 1905), cols. 1510–11. Quoted in Minčenkov, *Vospominanija o peredvižnikakh*, p. 330.

49. B. Pasternak, *I Remember*, p. 48.

revolutionary agitation, to the same extent as the University and the Technical College (*Tekhnologičeskoe učilišče*). That in February, 1905 studies at the School were suspended "until further notice" (presumably on the orders of the Curator of the School) in no way affected the constant stream of political gatherings and meetings which continued in full swing—without the Council of Instructors in any way speaking out against this.[50]

However, the October events were to bring more turmoil to the School. Things got out of hand when students took up arms and joined the demonstrators, actively seeking weapons and endeavoring to enlist the support of their professors. At that point the administration of the School requested help from the city authorities, which sent troops.[51] In the midst of the ensuing panic, Pasternak remained staunch and was of great support to the Director of the School.[52] We have a description of these events from a uniquely well qualified witness, Boris Pasternak:

> In response to the student demonstration following the manifesto of the 17th of October [1905], the rabble from Okhotny Ryad, the game market of Moscow, got out of hand, and began to smash up the higher educational institutions, the University and the Technological College. The School of Painting was also in danger of being attacked. On the instructions of the Principal of the School, heaps of cobblestones were piled up on the landings of the main staircase and hoses were screwed into the fire-cocks to repel any attack by the looters.
>
> Demonstrators turned in to the school from the processions in the neighboring streets, held meetings in the Assembly Hall, took possession of rooms, went out on the balcony, and made speeches to those who stayed in the streets below. The students of the school formed militant organizations, and a fighting detachment made up of them kept watch over the building at night.
>
> Among my father's papers are some sketches he made at the time: a woman agitator, who was making a speech on the balcony, is being shot at by dragoons who swooped down on the crowd. She is wounded, but she goes on with her speech, catching hold of a column to prevent herself from falling.[53]

The Pasternaks' daughter Lydia had fallen seriously ill, and when the veritable siege to which the School had been subjected was over, the

---

50. Moleva and Beljutin, p. 281 (note 6, above).

51. Ibid.

52. Princess Vera A. Lvov [Lwoff], daughter of Prince A. E. Lvov, Director of the School of Painting. "Vospominanija", personal recollections communicated to the author in May, 1963.

53. B. Pasternak, *I Remember*, p. 47.

family left for a sojourn of about a year (late 1905–early 1907) abroad, staying mainly in Berlin. There, Pasternak met Gorky,[54] as well as the German painters Max Liebermann and Lovis Corinth.

In 1907, after teaching for fourteen years at the Petersburg Academy of Arts, Repin resigned his post at that institution. Shortly thereafter, a search for his successor was initiated. Students at the School of Painting selected four candidates, including Serov and Pasternak. Serov was first offered Repin's professorship, and declined. At that point, in a letter addressed to a colleague at the Petersburg Academy, Pasternak withdrew his candidacy, invoking the following argument: "as a Jew, I would in any case not be selected by the Academy";[55] he then goes on to list other reasons: "(1) Why should I leave our School of Painting which I love with all my heart, and to which I have given my best strength; [very modestly he goes on to say:] (2) I don't feel worthy to replace someone of the magnitude of Repin; (3) To go to the Academy with its present atmosphere—many thanks!"[56]

That same year, Pasternak and his wife started on a journey that took them, through Holland and Belgium, on their first visit to England. There, at the invitation of a Mr. Vincent, who had seen reproductions of his work in the English art magazine *The Studio*, Pasternak spent a few days painting a portrait of his host's daughter. This stay in London afforded him the opportunity to inspect the originals of the great eighteenth-century English portraitists, whose work he had until then seen only in reproductions. Perhaps more interesting for the artist, however, was the chance to examine first-hand the art of Turner, whom in his reminiscences he singles out as the ancestor of the French Impressionists. The Pasternaks were then invited by Vincent's brother and sister to visit them at their country home in Esher, Surrey. After a tour of the estate's remarkable picture gallery, their host, Edgar Vincent, tried to persuade Pasternak to settle in London, assuring him of a successful career in England. Pasternak, however, once again would not leave Moscow and the School of Painting he so loved.[57]

---

54. Pasternak met Gorky both in Berlin and in the suburban sanatorium-pension in Zehlendorf where the writer was residing. Pasternak made an etching of Gorky (in connection with which Andreeva told Pasternak: "You haven't understood him. He is Gothic.") Cf. B. Pasternak, *I Remember*, p. 55.

55. "Menja Akademija vse-taki ne vybrala by kak evreja." Pasternak, letter to S. P. Kračkovskij, Vaksel' Archive No. 3269, Department of Manuscripts, Saltykov-Ščedrin State Public Library; quoted by Moleva and Beljutin, p. 365. However, things might have turned out differently; Pasternak himself had been surprised thirteen years earlier when the curator of the Moscow School of Painting had approved his appointment.

56. Moleva and Beljutin, p. 365.

57. Vincent's prediction of a successful career in England might well have been fulfilled. In 1914, Vincent was made Baron d'Abernon of Esher, and in 1920 was appointed the

Shortly after the death of his fellow artist and friend Serov (1911), Pasternak again went abroad, in 1912, this time because of the poor health of his wife (Rosa had just had her first heart attack). The Pasternaks stayed at Bad Kissingen, of which the painter gave a witty description.[58] Horribly bored by the stilted, sterile life of the conventional spa visitors, Leonid Osipovich fled to Kassel to seek artistic stimulation in that city's first-rate museum. There paintings by Rembrandt (in particular *The Blessing of Jacob*) were an important aesthetic experience for him.[59] During the summer Leonid Pasternak also visited the university town of Marburg where his son Boris was studying philosophy under the famous Hermann Cohen, of whom the artist drew a notable sketch. The Pasternaks then paid a visit to Italy (Leonid Osipovich's second journey to that country) where they stayed near Pisa.

In 1914, for a charity collection in Moscow in aid of the war victims, Pasternak drew a poster of a wounded soldier, which became immensely popular—it was reproduced in various forms, and millions of copies were sold. The artist believed he was the first in Russia to produce such a poster by the method of auto-lithography (whereby the artist himself makes an auto-lithography, i.e., draws on the lithographic stone). The poster turned out to be spectacularly popular.[60] The Tsar

first ambassador to the new German republic. Later, in England, his trusteeship at both the National and Tate galleries gave him an influential position in the arts. Undoubtedly, Lord d'Abernon would have been a useful sponsor for Pasternak. For more details concerning the contacts with the Vincent family, see David Buckman, *Leonid Pasternak: A Russian Impressionist* (London: Maltzahn Gallery Ltd., 1974), pp. 55-60.

58. Pasternak wrote: "[Among European resorts] Kissingen is one of the most fashionable and most frequently visited. And visited particularly by Jews. They come from everywhere, from every corner of the world and they are of the most varied types: from Hasidic, Polish, Galician Jews to those who have acquired an exterior European varnish—the representatives of the stock exchange and financial aristocracy. All types are represented, from those in traditional, long-flapped frock-coats, with long sidelocks, to dandies; from old women in black- and red-haired wigs to fashionably attired ladies. Who is not acquainted with those peculiar, unattractive, and flashy types of self-satisfied, *nouveau riche* ladies—the *parvenu* types, to be found everywhere promenading, near the spring founts, in the Kursaal, ostentatiously flashing in front of each other their arsenals of diamonds and valuable sets of jewelry?" L. Pasternak, *Rembrandt i evrejstvo v ego tvorčestve. S 30 snimkami s proizvedenij Rembrandta* (Berlin: S. D. Saltzmann, 1923), pp. 14-16.

59. This experience prompted him to elaborate his views in the volume he wrote on Rembrandt within the next few years. See further in the text.

60. L. Pasternak, *Zapisi raznykh let*, p. 84 (note 3, above). He goes on to tell us (p. 84): "I was amazed by its success and popularity, when my poster was stuck all over Moscow on the day of the collection. Crowds gathered in front of it and would not move. Village women cried . . . Famous artists were in charge of the collection. They sold picture postcards of my poster, too, hundreds of thousands of copies . . . The material success of this venture, both in Moscow and in other Russian cities, also exceeded the expectations of the organizers of this charitable collection. From Petersburg, the State Duma President Rodzyanko asked me to let him have about a hundred thousand copies for

104 Guy de Mallac

criticized it on the grounds that it aroused pity rather than admiration for bravery, and four years later the same poster was used as anti-war propaganda by the Soviet Government. One of Pasternak's most successful psychological studies dates from this period—a portrait of Lenin addressing the Praesidium of the Seventh Congress of the Soviets, which captures the leader's vitality and aggressive intelligence. This dramatic drawing forcefully conveys the polemic personality of the subject.[61]

Pasternak's concern for esthetic appreciation and the various dimensions of the art of painting took many forms. Thus in 1918-20 he wrote a short volume, the Russian edition of which was to come out a few years later in Berlin under the title *Rembrandt i evrejstvo v ego tvorčestve* (Rembrandt and the Jewish ethos in his work).[62] He composed this essay in Russian with the intention of having it translated into Hebrew (in which language it was also published). The writer's aim in presenting this study of Rembrandt was, according to the introduction, to carry out "the first endeavor to be made" to acquaint "the Jewish masses" with the plastic arts—an area which, the author points out, "is entirely unknown to . . . [them] up to now." Thus, the fact that the Pasternaks counted among the most sophisticated and privileged[63] of Jewish families in the Empire does not mean that Leonid Osipovich lost awareness of his Jewish identity. His earnest devotion to the missionary tasks he outlines (the esthetic education of the "Jewish

---

his collection of donations . . ." The English art magazine *The Studio* reproduced the poster (Feb. 1915, p. 63).

61. Of this drawing Frederick Laws remarked that it "suggests daemonic force but has the immediacy of a note made by a cartoonist of genius covering a political conference." Laws, "Paintings, Drawings and Watercolours of Pasternak," *The Manchester Guardian*, 10 October 1958.

Pasternak's depiction of Lenin has consistently been received favorably by the Soviet press—cf., for example, the following statements: "Dukhovnaja sila voždja rasširila gorizont talantlivogo živopisca, zakhvatila ego voobraženie v te dni. . . . Naprjažennaja živaja mysl' osveščaet kharakternoe lico Vladimira Il'iča s udivitel'no točno skhvačennym vyraženiem volevoj sosredotočennosti i glubokogo intellekta." S. Burdjanskij, "Dorogie čerty," *Izvestija*, 6 November 1965 (Moscow evening issue), p. 3.

62. See note 58 above.

63. The Pasternak family personally did not suffer much as a result of the poor treatment and lack of consideration which was the lot of many Jews in Old Russia; such prejudice was not exercised against a family whose head had gained access to a high position. Nonetheless, it is worth noting that in *Doctor Zhivago* Boris Pasternak had Yury Zhivago exclaim at the time of World War I: "Under enemy [i.e., German] rule they [the Jews] enjoy equal rights, and we [in Russia] do nothing but persecute them." (Boris Pasternak, *Doctor Zhivago*, trans. Max Hayward and Manya Harari [New York: Pantheon, 1958], p. 119). For a general discussion of the condition of Jews in Russia, see Jacob Frumkin, G. Aronson and A. Goldenweiser, eds., *Russian Jewry 1860-1917*, trans. Mirra Ginsburg (New York: T. Yoseloff, 1966). (The book contains a brief section devoted to L. Pasternak [pp. 326-27] in the chapter "The Russian Jew in Art" by Rachel Wischnitzer).

masses") is but one instance of the recrudesence in the 1910s of his serious interest in Judaic life and values, after a few decades during which his awareness of such values had been dormant and his main concern had been assimilation into the mainstream of Russian life.[64]

Why choose Rembrandt as subject matter for this task of popularization or semi-popularization? Pasternak claims that: "In truth, in the long succession of ages and up to the present, neither in Jewry itself nor among the people who have been singing the praise of Jewry, has there been an artist more 'Jewish' than the great Rembrandt."

He further adds that, were it not for the circumstances of Rembrandt's non-Jewish ethnic background, "there would be everything in him for him to be considered a [Jewish] national artist." Of all the great painters, "no one came so close to the spirit of the Bible as Michelangelo and, especially, Rembrandt."[65] How is it possible, the author asks, that Rembrandt, a non-Jew and always a strict, earnest, and practicing Calvinist, was capable of recapturing the heart of Jewish psychology, the essence of Jewry, its very "taste" as it were (in Yiddish: *dem tam*)?[66] Pasternak gives several converging explanations: Rembrandt's decision to elect as his residence a house in the very center of Amsterdam's *"Judenviertel,"* his close friendship with the learned Rabbi Menasse ben-Israel and the famous physician Ephraim Bonus, the warm and friendly feelings held towards his neighbors in an exotic district that appealed to him as an artist and as a man, and finally the tragic overtones of his personal life, which gave him the deepest understanding of the long-suffering Jewish people.[67] One of the author's most worthwhile contributions is his detailed and convincing interpretation of some of Rembrandt's paintings (in particular *Jacob's Blessing, David and Saul,* and *The Prodigal Sons*), showing how they reflect the artist's profound

---

64. On the one hand, it might well be exaggerated to speak of Pasternak's Zionist sympathies, as I have done in the past (Guy de Mallac, "Pasternak and Religion," *The Russian Review* 32, no. 4 [Oct. 1973]: 366). On the other hand, it has been claimed with some justification that around 1918–20 (i.e., during the writing of *Rembrandt i evrejstvo*), as a result of the impact of the war and the revolution, Pasternak was drawing much closer to Jewish society and culture, from which he had kept at a distance for several decades, and that he paid frequent visits to the Jewish writer David Frishmon and other Jewish personalities. (M. Z. Ben-Ishaj, "With the Pasternaks in Moscow," *Ha-doar* [New York], 12 December 1958). Pasternak was in contact in Moscow with the Marburg philosopher Hermann Cohen, who undertook lectures in the Russian capital in 1913 in support of the cause of Judaic culture (and whose extensive writings on Judaism have been analyzed in Jehuda Melber's 503-page volume, *Hermann Cohen's Philosophy of Judaism* [New York: Jonathan David, 1968]). For further discussion of the relationship of the Pasternak family to Judaism, see my article "Pasternak and Religion."

65. L. Pasternak, *Rembrandt i evrejstvo,* pp. 11–12, 30, 79.

66. Ibid., p. 46.

67. Ibid., pp. 46–57, 63, 77–9.

understanding of the Jewish ethos and psychology. Like all of Pasternak's writings, the book on Rembrandt is highly readable and characterized by an extremely concrete, pictorial, and lively style.

The year 1921 marks the end of the Pasternaks' thirty-two-year stay in Moscow and the artist's long professorship at the School of Painting. On account of Rosa Isidorovna's deteriorating heart condition, they and their daughters moved to Berlin. There was another obvious motivation for the family's trip: although practically no direct information is available on the subject, one can reasonably assume that during the period 1918–1921 Pasternak's position at the School of Painting, restructured as the Vkhutemas, could only have been uncomfortable, in an atmosphere pervaded by the revolutionary aesthetics of Malevich, Tatlin, Pevsner, and Kandinsky, which he thoroughly disliked. In the art world, this was a time of great turmoil, during which even Chagall was ousted by Malevich from the Vitebsk Art School on the grounds that his work was old-fashioned and irrelevant. There is no reason to believe that, politically speaking, Pasternak was in disagreement with the Soviet regime; while his contributing to satirical journals in 1905 in no way meant he was a radical, his eagerness to portray Lenin and subsequent good relations with the Soviets bespeak his sympathy toward the new government.

Relocated in Berlin, Pasternak began to become as famous to German art lovers as he was in his own country and held many exhibitions not only in Germany but in other countries as well. Because of the prolonged treatment necessitated by Rosa Isidorovna's illness, the Pasternaks stayed in Berlin longer than intended. It then turned out that this prolonged stay in such an enlightened and sophisticated capital as Berlin became extremely significant for Pasternak's career. However, he nonetheless always considered Soviet Russia as his true home, retaining his Soviet citizenship, and maintaining a friendly relationship with Soviet embassies and officials throughout his life. In 1927, for example, Lunacharsky, the head of Narkompros (the Soviet Commissariat for Education), took the time, during a visit in Berlin, to preview his one-man exhibit at the Galerie Hartberg before the official opening a few days later. Nevertheless, recognition of Pasternak's achievement has been hampered because Soviet critics have long felt uneasy about commenting on the work of this "émigré." Only in 1975 did the Moscow publishing house Sovetsky Khudozhnik bring out his collected writings *Zapisi raznykh let.*

In 1924 Leonid Osipovich visited Palestine and Egypt as a participant in an art expedition organized by the publisher Aleksandr Kogan, the editor of the Berlin-based Russian journal *Žar-Ptica* (Firebird). That visit lasted a little over a month. Pasternak's daughter Lydia remembers the striking impression the country made on her father: "He . . . fell in love with the magnificence of the country, raved about the sun-drenched colors of the landscape, the street scenes, the Biblical picturesque types of Hebrew and Arab alike, brought back with him a large series of wonderful sketches, portraits and landscapes . . ."[68] He also brought back remembrances of his new friendship with Viscount Samuel, whose portrait he painted while in Jerusalem.

After his trip, there followed many exhibits; among the largest was one held at the Galerie Hartberg in Berlin in March–April, 1927, consisting of about sixty pastels, drawings, and watercolors. Conspicuous among Pasternak's paintings was a portrait of his friend (and erstwhile fellow-student in Munich), the German painter Lovis Corinth, which the well-known art critic Fritz Stahl rated among the most brilliant achievements of portrait painting that he had ever encountered.[69] Because of the warmth and incisiveness with which it depicted the ecstatic concentration of the German artist, that watercolor of modest proportions stood out from other works (which included portraits of the Zionist Naum Sokolov and the German theologian Adolf von Harnack, as well as certain somewhat less successful oil paintings done in Munich). Another important one-man exhibition took place in the Galerie Hartberg, commemorating the painter's seventieth birthday in 1932, and was accompanied by the publication of a monograph on Pasternak in German, with reproductions of his works, excerpts from his memoirs, and an introductory text by Max Osborn.[70] This monograph is also remarkable for the technical and artistic excellence of the reproductions —Pasternak drew some of the originals on the lithographic stone, and had the overall responsibility for the graphics.

The Pasternaks stayed in Berlin until 1938. At that time, they were profoundly disturbed by an act of the Nazi government—the impounding at the printer's and then the destroying of all copies of a monograph devoted to Pasternak (and containing illustrations by him and photographic reproductions of his works).[71] As a result of this incident, and because of their growing distaste for the generally darkening climate of Nazism, Leonid Osipovich and his wife planned to return to Moscow. Before their actual return home, the family decided, upon the doctor's advice, to pay a visit to England (where their daughters lived)

68. Lydia Pasternak-Slater, "Letter to the Editor" (note 30, above).

69. Fritz Stahl, "Ausstellungen," *Berliner Tageblatt*, 21 December 1927.

70. Osborn, *Leonid Pasternak* (note 1, above). The essay by Osborn at the beginning of this volume contains much interesting background information.

71. Bulgakov, "L. O. Pasternak," p. 67 (note 45, above).

so that they should have a chance to recover (Rosa Isidorovna's health was not improving, and her husband had suffered from an angina pectoris). There, on 23 August 1939, Rosa Pasternak died suddenly. A week later, World War II started, and Pasternak, with his two daughters and their families, moved to Oxford. Pasternak only slowly found consolation in his work and owing to the war, old age, and his poor health, led a very retiring life. Apart from his work (*The Oxford Mail* of 25 March 1942 reported that he was painting an historical representation of Bach),[72] he spent his leisure time with his children and grandchildren, and in visits to the Ashmolean. Pressed by his daughters, he also wrote a series of reminiscences. During his last years, Pasternak was often in a pensive mood. Paucity of news from his sons and relations in Russia disturbed him profoundly. A born pacifist and friend of Tolstoy, he suffered from the news of atrocities committed in the war. He still expressed the desire to go back to the Soviet Union and to spend the last years of his life active as an art professor there.[73] Still painting until the very end, when an unfinished portrait of Lenin was on his easel, he died in Oxford on 31 May 1945.

Leonid Pasternak's development as an artist took a unique path. Influenced by the French Impressionists and the German "Secessionists,"[74] he early developed an exceptionally subtle sense of texture, and an ability to record transient effects of light and movement, retaining a firmness and vitality of color. Such characteristics, typical of icon painting, reveal his awareness of Russian tradition. Using the palette typical of Russian iconography, with its oriental dusty blues and darkish reds, he developed into one of the most representative of Russian artists. Sir Maurice Bowra suggested that Pasternak's artistic goal was: ". . . to bring more light and color into painting, and to get away from the sombre tones and the glutinous quality of the preceding generation. The firm, unshakable foundation of Pasternak's art was his drawing. He himself was convinced that without this nothing could be

---

72. During the war years Pasternak did complete paintings on themes borrowed from the history of music, such as *Bach and Frederick the Great* and *Mendelssohn Conducting Handel's "Messiah"*. He also completed other paintings, including *Tolstoy at his Writing Desk*, *Scenes from Soviet Life*, and *Pushkin and his Nurse*.

73. L. Pasternak, *Zapisi raznykh let*, pp. 95–96, 104 (note 3, above).

74. Some Munich painters (under the leadership of Franz von Stuck [Franz Stuck] and others) severed themselves from their older colleagues in 1892, and were the first group to adopt the name "Sezession"—setting an example for similar movements, e.g., for the Berlin impressionists (including Max Liebermann, Walter Leistikow, Arnold Böcklin, Lovis Corinth), who, also in 1892, left the *Verein Berliner Künstler* (first calling themselves the "Eleven," then adopting the name of "Sezession").

really right, and he concentrated on it from his student days."[75] Even when he focused on movement and nuances of color in the background, he was always aware of the underlying structure. An extraordinary draftsman himself, whose artistic credo was bound up with his faith in the continuity of art, he believed that draftsmanship (*risunok*) was the cornerstone of all art (not just the graphic arts, but also painting and architecture) and in this connection referred to statements by Michelangelo, Ingres, and Delacroix. The supreme mastery of Rembrandt's drawings and sketches served him as an ideal and inspiration. He insisted that draftsmanship constituted the rudiments of artistic literacy.[76] If his first sketch did not catch the essential character of his subject, he felt he had failed and must start again. His extraordinary talent as draftsman hinged upon the way in which he was obviously fascinated by the linear patterns afforded by subjects in a number of familiar, domestic poses (sitting, reading, sewing, stitching, leaning over a table to write or to drink).

Pasternak introduced significant innovations on the Russian artistic scene as he resolutely broke with the subject-dominated, historical approach of the Itinerants. He greatly admired Renoir, Manet, and Degas—from whose technique he drew inspiration. Among his countrymen he most respected A. Ivanov, Polenov, Serov, Vrubel, Levitan, and Repin. He greatly contributed to the renaissance of Russian art at the turn of the century through his pioneering efforts in the graphic arts of engraving, lithography, etching, and illustrating (highlights of these efforts being his work as chief art editor of the illustrated edition of Lermontov's works of 1891, and his illustrations for Tolstoy's *Resurrection).*[77] Under his influence, these pursuits, which Pasternak regarded as an independent aspect of the fine arts, began a revival in the early nineties in Moscow, where they were sadly neglected at the time. In addition to his epoch-making illustrations of Tolstoy's *Resurrection,*[78] Pasternak attracted the attention of connoisseurs by an altogether different kind of achievement, typical of which were the illustrations for Lermontov's *Maskarad* that he did for the Lermontov jubilee edition of 1891.[79] This contourless, contrastless type of line drawing consists not of

75. C. M. Bowra, "Leonid Pasternak," in the catalogue *Memorial Exhibition of Paintings and Drawings by Leonid Pasternak* (Oxford: Ashmolean Museum, April 1958).

76. L. Pasternak, *Zapisi raznykh let*, pp. 225-26.

77. See nn. 26, 44, 45 above.

78. See text, pp. 12-13.

79. Cf. above, n. 76.

"lines" properly speaking but of extremely tenuous strokes and of combinations of hachure-thin strokes. One critic pointed out that such contrastless and contourless art comes close to defeating the definition of modern graphics as practiced by Beardsley and Somov, and stressed the merits of this original "impressionistic" and "tonal" variant. A. A. Sidorov went on to indicate that during the pre-revolutionary period Pasternak became perhaps the most typical representative of tonal and chiaroscuro graphics among Muscovite artists.[80] Furthermore, it should be mentioned that Pasternak deserves the credit for enriching the curriculum of the School of Painting with graphics and engraving. There he helped establish a special graphics department for the students, and tried (unsuccessfully) to create a workshop where tempera, fresco, and pigment research could be conducted.[81]

As an artist who experimented in remarkable ways with modes of conveying masses of light and air, he did not adapt to specifically post-Impressionistic techniques, and his method remained pre-cubist, and also predominantly pre-expressionist (with the reservation that his much bolder use of colors in his oil paintings of the 1920s possibly shows the influence of contemporary trends in German painting). One sees in this respect a difference between his work and that (more complex) of his friend Lovis Corinth—much of whose *oeuvre* is clearly impressionistic, while some of his later achievements, characterized by extremely vivid, vibrant, and vigorous coloristic effects, definitely approached the style of expressionism.[82] Pasternak was definitely opposed to non-figurative art in its various forms, and often condemned it.[83] The epoch-making manifesto of expressionism and "absolute painting" promulgated in 1912 by Pasternak's fellow countryman and contemporary Vasily Kandinsky (1866–1940), *Concerning the Spiritual in Art*, was never acknowledged by the impressionist artist. While admiring in Picasso an

---

80. Sidorov, *Russkaja grafika*, p. 105.

81. His achievement in this area is acknowledged by Moleva and Beljutin: "Imeja v vidu bolee širokoe khudožestvennoe razvitie učaščikhsja, Pasternak, po suščestvu, vpervye v praktike Moskovskogo Učilišča vvodit novye vidy iskusstva: stankovuju i illjustrativnuju grafiku, gravjuru." Moleva and Beljutin, p. 256 (note 6, above).

82. On the one hand, Corinth's portraiture is recognized as belonging among the best achievements of German impressionism, and Corinth, in his capacity as president of the impressionist Berlin Sezession, most virulently fought the expressionists on the Berlin art scene. On the other hand, it has been pointed out that in his last portraits, religious paintings, and well-known Walchensee paintings, he does approach the style of expressionism. See Peter Selz, *German Expressionist Painting* (Berkeley, Los Angeles, London: University of California Press, 1957), pp. 34–5.

83. Pasternak "scorned his fellow Russian, Kandinsky" ("Boris Pasternak's Father," *Time*, 24 August 1962, p. 48). Regarding Pasternak's negative feelings toward non-figurative art, see also Grabar', "Pamjati Leonida Pasternaka" (note 14, above).

accomplished draftsman, Pasternak never recognized the rest of his achievement. The tensions that occasionally developed between such professors of the School of Painting as Serov and Pasternak, on the one hand, and certain students on the other, do indicate that a "conflict of generations" existed there, as a result of the divergence of esthetic conceptions.[84] (Such generational esthetic conflicts should not be confused with the politically motivated confrontations that occurred between students and the *administration* of the School—with professors such as Serov, Pasternak, and Korovin sometimes caught in the middle.)[85]

The emergence of esthetic divergences between professors and students is certainly not surprising if one remembers that among these students were such iconoclasts as Vladimir Mayakovsky, M. F. Larionov,[86] and I. I. Mashkov.[87] In spite of such divergences, Pasternak should be given

---

84. A former student of the School, M. F. Shemyakin (see n. 91), indicated that there were occasionally discipline problems at the School—e.g., disrespect, or inadequate respect, toward Serov, and sallies of such students as L. A. Sulerzhitsky (1872-1916, a future producer at the MKHAT) against certain instructors—and mentioned the general fermentation of new ideas during the 1890s and 1900s, a period fertile in new developments and upheavals ("sumburnoe vremja") at the School. Shemyakin, "Vospominanija," in Zil'berštejn and Samkov, *Valentin Serov*, vol. 2, p. 231 (note 26, above).

85. A notable instance of such confrontations was the incident which occurred at the School in 1910 and was reported in the press, e.g. in *Russkie Vedomosti*, at the time. (This incident is referred to here and there, though no source contains a full account.) K. A. Korovin (Pasternak's colleague at the School) was ill and had asked Pasternak to replace him, but when the latter showed up at Korovin's portrait studio, a group of students walked out on him (or, according to other accounts, refused him access to the studio). Pasternak felt deeply offended by this and wanted to resign. The veteran Serov (who had resigned a short time before from the staff of the School to protest the administration's unfair and politically motivated attitude toward one of his students) wrote a strong letter to the students of the portrait studio, criticizing their behavior and protesting the offense to Pasternak. It is clear that the students' action was in no way directed against either Pasternak or Korovin, but rather against the administration. In the end, Pasternak did not resign, and disciplinary measures were taken against the students involved. Cf. V. A. Serov, *Perepiska. 1884-1911* (Moscow: Iskusstvo, 1937), pp. 380-81; Moleva and Beljutin, p. 366; Zil'berštejn and Samkov, *Valentin Serov*, vol. 1, p. 375.

86. Mikhail Fedorovich Larionov (1881-1964) was little appreciated by most instructors at the School, where he was one of the most unruly students and from which he was dismissed (1910). He soon began organizing exhibitions (e.g., the Symbolist "Blue Rose" exhibition of 1907; the "Golden Fleece" exhibitions of 1908 and 1909). Larionov became famous as the initiator of a new concept in painting, *lučizm* (Rayonnism), based on the perception of rays emanating from the object. In 1915 he left Russia, to which he never returned.

87. Ilya Ivanovich Mashkov (1881-1944) soon departed very sharply from the principles of his teachers such as Pasternak and Korovin. He experimented with such techniques as black contour lines, sharp contours, primitive color schemes, hyperbole, geometricization, and exaggerated naiveté inspired by the *lubok* (naive popular print). Some of his work reveals an interesting convergence between the *lubok* and cubism. Mashkov was a member of the *Bubnovyj valet* (Jack of Diamonds), a formalistic group hostile to realism (active 1910-26). Later he departed from his earlier experimentation to fit into the context of Soviet painting.

the credit for training a considerable number of notable artists, who benefited from his solid pedagogy while attending his drawing classes and receiving training and encouragement from him in the area of graphics. Among his students the following diverse figures should be mentioned: Mashkov, K. F. Yuon,[88] K. S. Petrov-Vodkin,[89] A. M. Gerasimov,[90] M. F. Shemyakin,[91] D. D. Burlyuk.[92] Still another of his pupils, Prince S. A. Shcherbatov, was to give a highly positive appraisal of Pasternak, representing him as the most competent, professional, conscientious, and helpful of teachers—in an eloquent testimony that very few professors would elicit.[93] Others have similarly lavished praise on him for both acquainting his classes with the latest developments in Russian and Western European art, and for paying very special attention to the

---

88. Konstantin Fedorovich Yuon (1875-1958) studied under Pasternak and Serov at the School of Painting. He soon was to become—along with his former teachers—a member of the *Sojuz russkikh khudožnikov*. Yuon excelled in the depiction of peculiarities of Russian landscapes: nature as well as architectural landscapes, Muscovite and provincial (including the Monastery of St. Sergius in Zagorsk, Novgorod, Pskov, Rostov the Great). Together with the architectural monuments, his pictures usually portrayed the picturesqueness of religious festivals and traditional Russian *byt*. In addition to using oil, watercolor, and tempera, he did notable work in graphics (specifically, his series of line drawings *Sotvorenie mira*). Yuon was the author of numerous theoretical and critical works on art.

89. One of the most original of Russian artists, Kuzma Sergeevich Petrov-Vodkin (1878-1939), went against the Impressionists' conception of color, volume, and space. In his work new, formal viewpoints influence relationships between color, shape, volume, space, and surface, while his manner is characterized by philosophical depth, even an intellectualization of the subject, which remains compatible with an emotional dimension. Staying in Russia after the advent of the Soviet regime, he eventually had to conform to the tenets of socialist realism.

90. Aleksandr Mikhaylovich Gerasimov (1881-1963) studied at the Moscow School from 1903 to 1915 and later was to become one of the most successful exponents of socialist realistic art during the Stalinist period. "Heavy," "pompous," and "monumental" are epithets most often used by discriminating critics to qualify the manner of this four-time winner of the Stalin Prize.

91. Mikhail Fedorovich Shemyakin (1875-1944) studied at the School of Painting during the period 1895-99, then again from 1902 to 1905 (in Serov's studio). Later he became a professor at the Moscow Art Institute. He was to write of Pasternak: "Isključitel'no obrazovannyj i kul'turnyj čelovek i khudožnik, on vnosil v metod princip khorošej zapadnoj školy." M. F. Šemjakin, "Vospominanija," Vaksel' Archive No. 3269, Department of Manuscripts, Saltykov-Ščedrin State Public Library. Quoted in Moleva and Beljutin, p. 256.

92. David Davidovich Burlyuk (1882-1967) studied painting in Kazan and Odessa before studying at the Moscow School. He was active both as a poet and a painter, and was "the man without whom there probably would have been no Russian futurism" (V. Markov). In 1911 Burlyuk became associated with Mayakovsky, whome he attracted into the Futurist movement.

93. In his memoirs, Prince Sergey Aleksandrovich Shcherbatov (died 1962) tells us that after paying his due to Moscow mundanities, he "finally met a serious teacher, Leonid Osipovich Pasternak"—whose student he became, attending his private classes for many years. He goes on to describe Pasternak and his pedagogy as follows:

student's individual development as a creative artist (neither of which was being practiced by the typical art instructor at the Moscow School).[94]

Pasternak began by painting Russian scenes, but widened his scope as he traveled abroad. He was noted for the wide range of his subject matter (portraits, still life, interior, genre, landscape, illustrations, etc.) and for his versatility of expression. Apart from the traditional media,[95] he worked in a new technique of his own invention (a combination of tempera and pastel), which enabled him to achieve a subtlety of expression unobtainable otherwise. To the intrinsic value of Pasternak's portraits is added their documentary importance: noted and distinguished men of arts and letters, science, and politics were among his sitters.[96] Such prominent figures as Lenin, Chaliapin, the statesman V. A. Maklakov, the learned Chief Rabbi of Moscow Jacob Mase, the poet Sh. An-ski (author of *The Dybbuk*), Tchaikovsky, Prince Kropotkin, Gorky, Rainer Maria Rilke, the writer Remizov, the famous English *homme de théâtre* Edward Gordon Craig, Rachmaninoff, Tolstoy, Solovyev, and the Belgian symbolist poet Verhaeren sat for him in Moscow. After he was relocated in Berlin, his impressive list of sitters expanded to include Albert Einstein, Chancellor Gustav Stresemann,

---

"Evrej, s licom Khrista s kartiny Munkačio, on prepodaval v Škole Živopisi i Vajanija, no narjadu s ètim vel častnye klassy na otdel'noj kvartire s naturščikami (tol'ko dlja golovy), kotorye ja poseščal dva raza v nedelju. Na dom on zadaval kompozicii 'na temu' i tolkovo razbiral ikh. On prinosil v klass reprodukcii khorošikh kartin, pojasnjal ikh kačestva, govoril ob iskusstve i khudožnikakh s učenikami, slovom, v nem ne bylo toj zatkhlosti, kotoraja, v silu nekoego moskovskogo provincializma, tak suživala gorizont mnogikh khudožnikov i prepodavatelej. Pasternak imel vozmožnost' putešestvovat' po Evrope, znal muzei. A skol' nemnogie iz russkikh khudožnikov mogli sebe dostavit' ètu 'roskoš' ', javljajuščujusja neobkhodimost'ju?" Kn. Sergej Ščerbatov, *Khudožnik v ušedšej Rossii* (New York: Chekhov Publishing House, 1955), p. 30.

Later, Pasternak was to have a decisive influence on Shcherbatov, encouraging him to study in Munich rather than in Paris. (Ščerbatov, p. 72).

94. "V svoem prepodavanii èti khudožniki [i.e., Pasternak, Serov and Korovin] stremilis' sočetat' zaveršenie akademičeskogo kursa obučenija s èlementami tvorčeskoj podgotovki učenika, i ego znakomstvom s poslednimi dostiženijami russkogo i zapadno-evropejskogo iskusstva. Vse èto dolžno byt' napravleno na poiski molodym khudožnikom svoego individual'nogo tvorčeskogo puti i metoda. Osobaja rol' zdes' prinadležala Pasternaku." Moleva and Beljutin, p. 256.

95. Pasternak used oil, watercolor, line and wash, pastel, chalk, charcoal, bodycolor, pencil, red pencil, sanguine, sepia, etching, line drawing, and lithography.

96. Pasternak also did portraits of several people who did not formally sit for him as models. Thus the remarkably learned librarian of the Rumyantsev Museum, N. F. Fedorov (1828–1903), an extremely modest and self-effacing man, had always declined to sit for any photographer or painter, but in the course of his visits to the Rumyantsev Library, Pasternak surreptitiously made sketches that enabled him to portray the thinker in an interesting and well-known group portrait that depicts him in the company of his friends Vladimir Solovyev and Leo Tolstoy.

the Moscow philosophers Lev Shestov and Mikhail Gershenzon, the painters Max Liebermann and Lovis Corinth, the Jewish poets Chaim Nachman Bialik and Saul Chernichovsky, and the dramatist Gerhart Hauptmann. Sir Maurice Bowra sees in all of Pasternak's portraits the same unerring sense of personality, the gift for presenting a man not through his superficial traits but through his inner character.[97] Pasternak was able to do this because he was passionately interested in human beings and had a most unusual gift for understanding human nature. He was uniquely perceptive in his depiction of children and youngsters—this appeared clearly to Serov when he remarked that Pasternak had become a master in the art of capturing children;[98] coming from the creator of *The Girl with Peaches*, that remark was no small compliment.

He brought to his paintings an unfailing sense of rhythm, a vibrating, animated quality, technical skill, and an overwhelming sense of integrity and purpose. His several portraits of Tolstoy are prime examples of his many-sided talent. One, suffused with warm yellow light, shows Tolstoy at ease with his family; another, a rough, brooding, and weathered profile against a gray background, suggests King Lear. Years later, Boris Pasternak wrote to his father: "I think that your best subjects were Tolstoy and [the artist's daughter] Josephine. How you drew them! Your drawings of Josephine were such that she grew up according to them, followed them in her life, developed through them more than through anything else."[99] Pasternak was thus equally felicitous in depicting youth and the old father figure.

In his tiny pastel landscapes, we meet a gentler, more lyrical Pasternak than is evident in the often somber strength of the drawings. His *Seascape at Haifa* is permeated with a languid beauty and simple, delicate color harmonies; *Landscape with Grey Sky* is another such economical statement. His striking Palestine landscapes have tender tones and occasional dusty-violet hues. His watercolor *Moscow in Winter* also stands out as an example of consummate achievement in the balancing of delicate tones. While his bold, at times florid use of watercolor reveals a sensuous joy in color, the arrangement of interrelated, yet clashing masses in some of his pastels creates an intensely dramatic atmosphere. By and large, one can say that his watercolors and pastels yield

97. Bowra, "Leonid Pasternak" (note 75, above).

98. Serov observed to Pasternak: "Vy ovladeli det'mi." Cited in: Iv. Lazarevskij, "L. O. Pasternak," *Novyj Žurnal dlja Vsekh* 9 (1909): 82.

99. Boris Pasternak, letter of 1934 to his father, quoted by Lydia Pasternak-Slater, "Introduction to Boris Pasternak," in Boris Pasternak, *Fifty Poems* (London: Allen & Unwin, 1963), p. 16.

stronger evidence of his originality. However, in his oil paintings too he can achieve excellence: some of his still-lifes reveal an exuberant, yet sensitive colorist, unafraid of bright colors, but not dominated by them. In his oils, not the same fluency is achieved as in other media, yet a few notable works (for example, a study of his daughters) have some distant, pleasing reminders of some of Gauguin's canvases. The technique of his painting *Late Summer* definitely has something of Van Gogh about it. Aside from his work in pastel and oil, Pasternak's sketches done in red pencil, chalk, and charcoal stand out conspicuously as his most abundant and successful achievement. The life that is expressed in the color of his oil paintings is conveyed through the lines of his sketches in charcoal or pencil—here movement may originate with a chair or table, continue into a figure, and eventually reach the background. In a striking parallel with Boris Pasternak's critical aesthetic formulation stressing how he strove "to seize this whirling world as it was rushing headlong, and reproduce it,"[100] Leonid Osipovich's whole endeavor was to sketch nature *in movement*, and in his uniquely talented way of accomplishing this through his mastery of the graphic media rests the originality of his achievement.[101]

The qualification of Pasternak as a "Russian Impressionist" may appear paradoxical—primarily because of the paradox inherent in the very concept of "Russian Impressionism." To start with, Impressionism came late to Russia: only since the turn of the century were French Impressionist paintings introduced to Russia—by Sergey Shchukin who started purchasing them in 1897, and by *The World of Art* which started exhibiting them in 1899,[102] while it was not until the major "Golden Fleece" exhibition of 1908 (i.e., twenty-two years after the eighth and last exhibition of the French Impressionists in Paris) that a considerable number of Impressionist paintings were shown.[103] Although individual Russian painters such as Serov, Pasternak, and Korovin had become acquainted with French Impressionism during their stays in France before 1900, Impressionist techniques were essayed by Pasternak with the above-mentioned qualifications, by Korovin more timidly in the 1880s and quite frankly in the 1900s, by Golovin essentially in the

---

100. For a discussion of this statement, see Guy de Mallac, "Pasternak's Critical-Esthetic Views," *Russian Literature Triquarterly* 6 (Spring 1973): 515 ff.

101. In Pasternak's formulation, the ideal is to "na letu skhvatyvat' naturu." L. Pasternak, *Zapisi raznykh let*, p. 80 (note 3, above).

102. Aleksandr Benua, *Vozniknovenie "Mira iskusstva"* (Leningrad, 1928), quoted in Camilla Gray, *The Great Experiment: Russian Art 1863-1922* (New York: Harry N. Abrams, 1962), p. 38. See also Gray, p. 45.

103. Gray, *Great Experiment*, p. 70.

sphere of theatrical design, by Serov only to a limited extent in certain portraits. "Impressionist" was a term used very loosely in Russia—e.g., to describe Malevich's early works[104] or Larionov's work in the period 1902-1906.[105] Only in a derivative sense was there such a phenomenon as "Russian Impressionism." Thus, Pasternak's belief in draftsmanship as the cornerstone of all art is the very opposite of Monet's or Pissarro's position—and the main thrust of French Impressionism does go against the tradition inherited from Ingres, whom Pasternak so much admired. It is not surprising that among contemporary French artists Pasternak admired most Manet and Degas, the least "Impressionist" of the Impressionists.

It is very difficult to claim that there existed in Russian painting a specifically Impressionist transitional period between the heyday of the Peredvizhniki and the success of Modernism: very soon after the Itinerants went out of fashion as a result of the growing success of *Mir iskusstva*, various groups or movements started coalescing and within a matter of years occupied the forefront of the artistic scene: *Mir iskusstva* (1898), Primitivism (1909), Rayonnism or *lučizm* (1913), Suprematism (1913-1915). Significantly, the 1900s was the decade during which the majority of Russian artists and art lovers simultaneously discovered the French Impressionists of the 1870s-1880s *and* the Post-Impressionists (Bonnard, Vuillard, Matisse, Derain, Cézanne, Van Gogh, Gauguin, Picasso).

No more than such other "Russian Impressionists" as Levitan, Korovin, or Serov did Pasternak have any direct impact on the Russian modernists who proclaimed their discoveries in the 1900s and the 1910s. Like these artists of his generation, however, he fulfilled an essential function—representing the transitional link between Itinerants and Modernists, and (clearly so in his case), in the demanding role of art professor, providing rigorous training for two generations of artists. Even though we feel today that, outside the realm of illustration and graphics, Pasternak's *oeuvre* was by and large less innovative than that of such students of his as Yuon, Mashkov, Petrov-Vodkin, and especially Larionov, his achievement remains original and highly significant.

APPENDIX I: LOCATION OF
LEONID PASTERNAK'S WORK

Much of Leonid Pasternak's work has remained in his native Russia. There hangs the bulk of his work—in the Tretyakov Gallery, the Tolstoy and Gorky

104. Ibid., p. 128.
105. Ibid., p. 92.

Museums, the Historical Museum (the Kremlin collection), the Skriabin Museum, the Teatralnyj Muzej and the Lenin State Library in Moscow, the State Russian Museum and Tolstoy collections in Leningrad, and in about forty other galleries, such as those in Smolensk and Odessa. Some of his paintings are also in private collections in the Soviet Union. In the West his work can be found in the Musée du Luxembourg and Musée national d'art moderne in Paris, the Berlin Kupferstichkabinett, the Pinakothek (Munich), the Schiller Museum (Marbach), the Ashmolean in Oxford, the British Museum, the Tate Gallery, the Victoria and Albert Museum, the City Art Galleries of Bristol, Birmingham, and Southampton, at Harvard University, the University of Jerusalem, and in many museums around the world, including those in America, Asia, and Australia. A considerable number of his paintings and sketches are in private collections in Western Europe, particularly those of his daughters, Dr. Josephine Pasternak and Dr. Lydia Pasternak-Slater of Oxford. At the same time certain of his works have been displaced, damaged, or lost over the past forty years.

Among the most significant showings in recent years were the exhibits of 1958 at the Ashmolean, of 1962 in Bristol and at the Herbert Art Gallery and Museum (Coventry), at the Munich Stadtgallerie im Lenbachhaus that same year, of 1969 at the Oxford University Press, Ely House, London, of 1973 in Moscow (an exhibition of work owned by private collectors), and of 1974 at the Maltzahn Gallery in London.

Work on a *catalogue raisonné* of Pasternak's paintings and drawings is in progress in England.

APPENDIX II: BIBLIOGRAPHY

Barnes, Christopher J. "Boris Pasternak and Rainer Maria Rilke: Some Missing Links." *Forum for Modern Language Studies* (St. Andrews) 8, no. 1 (Jan. 1972): 61–78.

Ben-Ishaj, M. Z. "With the Pasternaks in Moscow." *Ha-doar* [New York], 12 December 1958.

Benois, Alexandre [Benua]. *Memoirs.* Translated by Moura Budberg. London: Chatto and Windus, 1960.

"Boris Pasternak's Father." *Time*, 24 August 1962, p. 48.

Bowra, C. M. "Leonid Pasternak." *Memorial of Paintings and Drawings by Leonid Pasternak.* Oxford: Ashmolean Museum, April 1958. (Foreword to exhibition catalogue of Pasternak's works.)

Buckman, David. *Leonid Pasternak: A Russian Impressionist.* London: Maltzahn Gallery Ltd., 1974 (Published by the Maltzahn Gallery in connection with the exhibition of Pasternak's works organized in 1974 by the Gallery. Contains 20 reproductions of works by Pasternak.)

Bulgakov, Valentin. "L. O. Pasternak." *Iskusstvo* 7 (July 1961): 65–7.

Burdjanskij, S. "Dorogie čerty." *Izvestija.* 6 November 1965 (Moscow evening issue), p. 3.

―――. "Novaja vstreča s Il'ičem." *Nedelja*, 28 November–4 December 1965, p. 2.

Čertkov, Leonid. *Rilke in Russland auf Grund neuer Materialien.* Österreichische Akademie der Wissenschaften. Philosophisch-historische Klasse. Sitzungsberichte, No. 301. Band 2. Abhandlung. Veröffentlichungen der Kommission fur Literaturwissenschaft, Nr. 2. Vienna: Österreichische Akademie der Wissenschaften, 1975.

———— and Konstantin Azadovskij. "Russkie vstreči Ril'ke." In R. M. Ril'ke, *Vorpsvede—Ogjust Rodèn—Pis'ma—Stikhi,* pp. 357-385. Moscow: Iskusstvo, 1971.

Dobužinskij, Mstislav. "Iz vospominanij." *Novyj Žurnal* 52 (March 1958): 109-39.

Èttinger, P. "The Drawings of L. Pasternak." *The Studio* 37, no. 158 (15 May 1906): 306-13.

Frumkin, Jacob; Aronson, G.; and Goldenweiser, A.; eds. *Russian Jewry 1860-1917.* Translated by Mirra Ginsburg. New York: T. Yoseloff, 1966.

Grabar', I. È. "Pamjati Leonida Pasternaka." *Sovetskoe Iskusstvo,* 13 July 1945, p. 4.

Grabar', I. È.; V. N. Lazarev; A. A. Sidorov; and O. A. Švidovskij; eds. *Istorija russkogo iskusstva.* Vol. 10, pts. 1 & 2. Moscow: Nauka, 1968-1969.

————. *Valentin Aleksandrovič Serov. Žizn' i tvorčestvo 1865-1911.* Moscow: Iskusstvo, 1965.

Gray, Camilla. *The Great Experiment: Russian Art, 1863-1922.* New York: Abrams, 1962.

Gronicka, André von. "Rilke and the Pasternaks: A Biographical Note." *The Germanic Review* 27 (Dec. 1952): 260-71.

Herrmann, Luke. "Portraits by a Pasternak." *The Sunday Telegraph,* 8 April 1962.

Klimov, E. "Arkhipov, Bakšeev, Pasternak. K 100-letiju so dnja ikh roždenija." *Novoe Russkoe Slovo,* 23 December 1962, pp. 6-7.

Laws, Frederick. "Paintings, Drawings and Watercolours of Pasternak." *The Manchester Guardian,* 10 October 1958.

Lazarevskij, Iv. "L. O. Pasternak." *Novyj Žurnal dlja Vsekh* 9 (1909): 82.

Levitsky, Serge. "Rose Koffman-Pasternak: la mère du poète." *Etudes Slaves et Est-Européennes* 8 (1963): 73-80.

L'vov [Lwoff], Princess Vera A. (daughter of Prince A. E. L'vov). "Vospominanija (UNPUBLISHED)." Personal recollections communicated to the author in May, 1963.

Mallac, Guy de. *Boris Pasternak.* Paris: Editions Universitaires, 1963.

————. "Pasternak and Religion." *The Russian Review* 32, no. 4 (Oct. 1973): 360-75.

————. "Pasternak's Critical-Esthetic Views." *Russian Literature Triquarterly* 6 (Spring 1973): 503-32.

Markov, Vladimir. *Russian Futurism: A History.* Berkeley and Los Angeles: University of California Press, 1968.

"Mastityj L. Pasternak." *Rubež* [Kharbin]. no. 28 (1 June 1933).

Mayer, Anton. [Report on Leonid Pasternak's exhibition at the Hartberg Gallery, Berlin.] *8-Uhr-Abendblatt,* 17 December 1927.

Meissner, Carl. "Leonid Pasternak." *Westermanns Monatshefte*, November 1932, pp. 213-20.

Melber, Jehuda. *Hermann Cohen's Philosophy of Judaism*. New York: Jonathan David, 1968.

Minčenkov, Ja. D. *Vospominanija o peredvižnikakh*. Leningrad: Khudožnik RSFSR, 1963.

Moleva, N. M. and È. M. Beljutin. *Russkaja khudožestvennaja škola vtoroj poloviny XIX-načala XX veka*. Moscow: Iskusstvo, 1967.

Mullaly, Terence. "Pasternak the Elder." *The Daily Telegraph*, 24 May 1959.

Osborn, Max. "Leonid Pasternak." *Vossische Zeitung*, 29 May 1932.

————. *Leonid Pasternak*. Warsaw: Stybel, 1932.

————. "L. O. Pasternak." *Žar-Ptica* [Berlin] 13 (1925).

————. [Report on Leonid Pasternak's exhibition at the Hartberg Gallery, Berlin]. *Vossische Zeitung*, 24 December 1927.

The Oxford Mail, 25 March 1942.

Pasternak, A. "Leto 1903 goda." *Novyj Mir* 1 (Jan. 1972): 203-11.

Pasternak, Boris. *Doctor Zhivago*. Translated by Max Hayward and Manya Harari. New York: Pantheon, 1958.

————. *An Essay in Autobiography*. Translated by Manya Harari. London: Collins and Harvill Press, 1959.

————. *Fifty Poems*. Translated by Lydia Pasternak-Slater [Lydia Leonidovna Pasternak]. London: Allen & Unwin, 1963. (With an introduction by Lydia Pasternak-Slater.)

————. *I Remember: Sketch for an Autobiography*. Translated by David Magarshack. New York: Meridian, 1960.

————. *Safe Conduct: An Early Autobiography, and Other Works*. Translated by Alec Brown. Five lyric poems, translated by Lydia Pasternak-Slater [Lydia Leonidovna Pasternak]. London: Elek Books, 1959.

Pasternak, Josephine [Leonidovna]. "Last Years." *Leonid Pasternak 1862-1945*. London: Oxford University Press, March-May 1969. (Foreword to an exhibition catalogue of Pasternak's works.)

Pasternak, L. O. "Iz zapisok Leonida Pasternaka." *Novyj Žurnal* 69 (Sept. 1962): 138-60; 77 (Sept. 1964): 190-214.

————. "My Meetings with Tolstoy." *The Russian Review* 19 (April 1960): 122-31. [Extract from the unpublished memoirs of Leonid Pasternak, translated by Lydia Pasternak-Slater and Josephine Pasternak.]

————. "O Serove." In *Valentin Serov v vospominanijakh, dnevnikakh i perepiske sovremennikov*, edited by I. S. Zil'berštejn and V. A. Samkov, 2 vols. Leningrad: Khudožnik RSFSR, 1971.

————. "Pis'ma k R. I. Sementkovskomu." *Russkaja Literatura* 3 (March 1975): 186-191.

————. "Pis'mo v redakciju." *Lebed'* 7 (1909): 41-2.

————. *Rembrandt i evrejstvo v ego tvorčestve. S 30 snimkami s proizvedenij Rembrandta*. Berlin: S. D. Saltzmann, 1923.

————. "Vier Fragmente aus meiner Selbstbiographie." In *Leonid Pasternak*, by Max Osborn. Warsaw: Stybel, 1932.

_____. *Zapisi raznykh let.* Moscow: Sovetskij khudožnik, 1975.

Pasternak-Slater, Lydia [Lydia Leonidovna Pasternak]. "Letter to the Editor." *The New York Times Book Review,* 29 October 1961, p. 50.

Rilke, Rainer Maria. "Pis'ma v Rossiju" [edited by Konstantin Azadovskij]. *Voprosy Literatury* 9 (Sept. 1975): 219-242.

Russell, John. "Pasternak." *The Studio* 161 (March 1961): 98-101.

Sakharova, E. V. *Vasilij Dmitrievič Polenov. Elena Dmitrievna Polenova. Khronika sem'i khudožnikov.* Moscow: Iskusstvo, 1964.

_____. *Vasilij Dmitrievič Polenov. Pis'ma, dnevniki, vospominanija.* Edited by A. Leonov. 2d ed. Moscow: Iskusstvo, 1950.

Ščerbatov, Sergej, knjaz'. *Khudožnik v ušedšej Rossii.* New York: Chekhov Publishing House, 1955.

Šebuev, N. "Vystavki." *Russkoe Slovo,* no. 357 (28 December 1902).

Selz, Peter. *German Expressionist Painting.* Berkeley: University of California Press, 1957.

Šemjakin, M. F. "Vospominanija." Vaksel' Archive No. 3269, Department of Manuscripts, Saltykov-Ščedrin State Public Library. Quoted by N. M. Moleva and È. M. Beljutin, *Russkaja khudožestvennaja škola vtoroj poloviny XIX-načala XX veka.* Moscow: Iskusstvo, 1967.

Serov, V. A. *Perepiska. 1884-1911.* Moscow: Iskusstvo, 1937.

_____. *Vospominanija.* Moscow, Leningrad: Iskusstvo, 1947.

Sidorov, A. A. *Russkaja grafika načala XX veka. Očerki istorii i teorii.* Moscow: Iskusstvo, 1969.

Stahl, Fritz, "Ausstellungen." *Berliner Tageblatt,* 21 December 1927.

Svet, German. "U L. O. Pasternaka. K otkrytiju ego vystavki v Berline." *Segodnja* [Riga], no. 286 (18 December 1927). (An interview with Pasternak.)

Svet, Geršon. "Leonid Pasternak. K stoletiju so dnja roždenija." *Novoe Russkoe Slovo,* 3 April 1962, p. 3.

Tarasov, N. "L. O. Pasternak." *Niva,* no. 48 (1917).

Tatarinov, V. "L. O. Pasternak." *Rul',* 30 December 1927.

Webb, Kaye. "Tolstoy's Artist in Oxford." *Lilliput,* January 1944, pp. 63-6.

Zil'berštejn, I. S. and V. A. Samkov, eds. *Valentin Serov v vospominanijakh, dnevnikakh i perepiske sovremennikov.* 2 vols. Leningrad: Khudožnik RSFSR, 1971.

COUNTERPOINT OF THE SNAPPING STRING:
Chekhov's *The Cherry Orchard*

BY

JEAN-PIERRE BARRICELLI

To THE AUTHOR of *The Cherry Orchard*, to be a member of the human race meant to be a confused victim of oppositions or paradoxes, of counterpoints. For this reason, paradox is inherent in Chekhov's concept of dramaturgy, and something provoking bewilderment does not necessarily constitute an extraneous element in a play. A case in point is the unexpected and vaguely disconcerting sound of a snapping string that is heard in the distance and from the sky twice in *The Cherry Orchard*, once toward the end of Act II, and again at the conclusion of the fourth and final act. Critical bewilderment before the sound has persisted since the first rehearsals in Moscow, attended by the author during December and January of 1903–1904.[1] To our way of thinking, the two soundings, contrapuntally placed, are central to the play: to its structure and symbolism and therefore to its innermost meaning. More than a psychological device for the audience, the double sounding is a substantive and structural device embedded deep in its heart, though all too often it has not been considered in this light. J. L. Styan declares correctly that "To interpret that sound is to interpret the play,"[2] although his interpretation follows that of many others who simply relate the sound to the passing of time, to the demise of the old social order and the ushering in of a new one. H. Pitcher contends that by it Chekhov did not intend "one specific meaning,"[3] and F. Fergusson hears it as a "sharp, almost warning signal,"[4] but nothing more. And C. B. Timmer,

---

1. See Ronald Hingley, *Chekhov: A Biographical and Critical Study* (New York: Barnes and Noble, 1966), p. 230.

2. J. L. Styan, *Chekhov in Performance* (Cambridge: Cambridge University Press, 1971), p. 337.

3. Harvey Pitcher, *The Chekhov Play* (London: Chatto and Windus, 1973), p. 182.

4. Francis Fergusson, "The *Cherry Orchard*: A Theater-Poem of the Suffering of Change," in *Chekhov: A Collection of Critical Essays*, ed. R. L. Jackson (New Jersey: Prentice Hall, 1967), p. 154.

in an otherwise enlightening article on Chekhov's use of the bizarre, the grotesque, and the absurd—that is, in an article which, by drawing careful distinctions among these aspects of his art, would seem, therefore, to lend itself somewhere to a consideration of the weird, bizarre, and potentially absurd sound—makes no mention of it.[5]

As might be expected, Soviet criticism, which eschews the exploration of metaphysical or symbolical forms that are not directly related to "social realism" and that may in fact controvert its goals, engages in no discussion of the meaning of the snapping string. Vsevolod Meyerkhold once came close when in criticizing Stanislavsky's interpretation he sought the key to the play in its acoustics and inner rhythm (comparing it to a symphony of Tchaikovsky!), and concluded that the producer "must first of all understand it with his hearing."[6] Clearly for Chekhov words are not the best vehicle to express thoughts and feelings. But more recently, Georgy Berdnikov, who speaks of "devices" as coordinated with the characters, of "pauses" as revealing their inner substance, and of "sounds" as adding to the lyrical idea of the play, is silent on how this special sound may reveal the inner substance of *The Cherry Orchard.*[7] Aleksandr Revyakin merely calls our attention to how the generally sad mood "finds correspondence in the words of Lopakhin, in the melancholy song of Epikhodov, and is diffused in the sounds of a breaking string," though a few pages later he returns to the sound, suggesting that it has "an especially large, realistico-symbolic meaning"—but only, again, because it "announces a coming catastrophe."[8] Again, no attempt is made to come to grips with the actual sound of the snapping string, which, in this non-formalistic body of criticism, is totally ignored. Abram Derman, whose chapters on "The Structural Elements in Chekhov's Poetics" or

---

5. Charles B. Timmer, "The Bizarre Element in Čechov's Art," in *Anton Čechov: Some Essays*, ed. T. Eekman (Leiden: E. J. Brill, 1960), pp. 277–292.

6. Quoted from Nils Åke Nilsson, "Intonation and Rhythm in Čechov's Plays," in *Anton Čechov: Some Essays*, ed. Eekman, p. 180. The quotation in turn is to be found in S. D. Balukhatyj & N. V. Petrov, *Dramaturgija Čekhova* (Kharkov, 1935), p. 120. Meyerkhold, of course, predates Soviet criticism. Except for *The Cherry Orchard* itself, for which I have used the translation of Avrahm Yarmolinsky in *The Portable Chekhov* (New York: The Viking Press, 1968), all translations, unless otherwise noted, are by me. For the original text of the play, I have consulted the following edition: *Višnevyj sad: komedija v četyrekh dejstvijakh* (Vstup. stat'ja V. V. Ermilova, Moskva: Gos. Izd-vo Detskoj Lit-ry, 1963).

7. Gerogij P. Berdnikov, *Čekhov dramaturg* (Leningrad and Moscow: Gosudarstvennoe Izdatel'stvo "Iskusstvo," 1957), p. 200. The author is silent about the string in his other book, *A. P. Čekhov* in the series *Russkie dramaturgi* (Moscow and Leningrad, 1950), too.

8. Aleksandr I. Revjakin, *"Višnevyj sad" A. P. Čekhova* (Moscow: Učebno-Pedagogičeskoe Izdatel'stvo, 1960), pp. 177 and 182, respectively.

"The Poetry of Chekhov's Creativeness" would otherwise be likely places for such a discussion, overlooks it,[9] as do Korney Chukovsky and Vladimir Ermilov.[10] One of the most striking omissions occurs in Sergey Balukhaty's study of Chekhov as a dramatist, where a whole chapter is devoted to *The Cherry Orchard* with no mention of the sound despite an important comparison between Act II and Act IV.[11] And we are not farther advanced in our inquiry by consulting the works of Aleksandr Roskin or Vasily Golubkov.[12]

Maurice Valency, in his fine study of Chekhov's plays, despite its revealing title (*The Breaking String*) as well as its concluding chapter called "The Sound of the Breaking String," accepts the sound metaphorically, but does not explore its more intimate meanings, either contextually or intextually. While he recognizes that "*The Cherry Orchard* centers upon the sound of the breaking string," he prefers to leave it shrouded in mystery: "The sound of the breaking string remains mysterious, but it has finality. The symbol is broad; it would be folly to try to assign to it a more precise meaning than the author chose to give it. But its quality is unequivocal. Whatever of sadness remains unexpressed in *The Cherry Orchard*, this sound expresses."[13] And later, following up the observation that the sound is heard when the young people, Varya, Anya, and Trofimov find the aging Gaev's lyrical tribute to Nature unbearable and force him to silence, Valency explains the metaphor in terms of a generation gap: "The golden string that connected man with his father on earth and his father in heaven, the age-old bond that tied the present to the past, was not to be broken lightly. When at last it snapped, the result . . . was both world-shaking and soul-shaking."[14] We agree with Pitcher that the interpretation is forced.[15] In any event, no further sense is made of the mysterious occurrence.

To be sure, the sound bespeaks a mood (and as such should not be

9. Abram Derman, *O masterstve Čekhova* (Moscow: Sovetskij Pisatel', 1959).

10. Kornej I. Čukovskij, *O Čekhove* (Moscow: Izdatel'stvo "Khudožestvennaja Literatura," 1967), and Vladimir Ermilov, *A. P. Čechov* (Moscow: Sovetskij Pisatel', 1954).

11. Sergej Balukhatyj, *Čekhov dramaturg* (Leningrad: Gosudarstvennoe Izdatel'stvo "Khudožestvennaja Literatura," 1936), pp. 243–244.

12. Aleksandr I. Roskin, *A. P. Čekhov: Stat'i i očerki* (Moscow: 1959), and Vasilij V. Golubkov, *Masterstvo A. P. Čekhova* (Moscow: 1958).

13. Maurice Valency, *The Breaking String* (New York: Oxford University Press, 1966), pp. 284 and 287.

14. Ibid., pp. 289–290.

15. Pitcher, *The Chekhov Play*, p. 182 (note 3, above).

explained with specifics), what Mirsky would call one of Chekhov's
"purely atmospheric creations."[16] For, as the critic remarks, in Chekhov,
where no one person seems to listen to his neighbor, there is not
straight line but a series of moods. It was reported by Stanislavsky that
during the December rehearsals, one of the actors casually made an
imitative sound with his lips of the kind the author had described,
and Chekhov turned to him exclaiming: "That's just what we want!"[17]
Yet, because of its highly unusual quality—even for Chekhov—Styan
believes that he took "an extraordinary risk" in introducing it in Act II,[18]
and Mirsky goes even further: ". . . in his search for suggestive poetry
he sometimes overstepped the limits of good taste— . . . for instance,
the bursting of a string in *The Cherry Orchard* . . ."[19]

The implication here is that, while Chekhov's world is filled with
noises, they are not necessarily strange noises, and that in *The Cherry
Orchard* he planned something much out of the ordinary. The apocalyptic
sound, as Mirsky describes it, is not typical of Chekhov. It is different
from the guitar string which snaps in a dark room in the story
The Dream Fiancée (1903). It is even different from the *"Takh! t! t! t!"*
that reverberates across the steppes' thin air in *Happiness* (1887): it may
be equally mysterious and receive a similar explanation ("It must have
been a bucket falling in a mine shaft," says Pantelei, unperturbed, just
as in *The Cherry Orchard* Lopakhin attempts to identify the sound the
same way), but it is nowhere near as "apocalyptic," and furthermore
it only sounds once. The episode recalls the passage in *A Rolling
Stone*, of the same year, where the hero falls to the bottom of a mine
when the chain holding his bucket snaps.[20] Hence Hingley's comment
about the extraordinary sound which baffles stage directors: "One
remarkable sound effect has caused some embarrassment to producers,
and illustrates the production of *nastroenie* on a more surrealist level . . .
The play does not make it entirely clear how this noise is supposed to
have originated, but Chekhov certainly regarded it as important in
evoking the right sort of mood in his audience."[21]

16. D. S. Mirsky, *A History of Russian Literature*. ed. F. J. Whitfield, (New York:
Random House, 1926), p. 381.

17. Quoted from Revjakin, *"Višnevyj sad"*, p. 177.

18. Styan, *Chekhov in Performance*, p. 287 (note 2, above).

19. Mirsky, *Russian Literature*, pp. 381–382.

20. From David Magarshack we learn that Chekhov had heard the sound as a child, in a
little hamlet in the Donets Basin, where he used to spend the summer: "It was there
that he first heard the mysterious sound, which seemed to be coming from the sky, but
which was caused by the fall of a bucket in some distant coal mine" (*Chekhov the
Dramatist* [New York: Hill and Wang, 1960], p. 286).

21. Hingley, *Chekhov*, pp. 238–239 (note 1, above). We might mention, too, the

If the enigmatic sound stands out, however, it does so because it does more than provoke the "right sort of mood." Chekhov was too precise and self-conscious an artist to allow a gratuitous or solely mood-setting, isolated incident to enter his work. As we know, he insisted that all specifics in his plays be executed down to the last particular, but, by the same token, not over-executed.[22] The Chekhovian pattern of understatement obtained even in expressing the significant detail. He used all sound effects in his stage directions with great subtlety, and did not fill his plays with mysterious happenings which require a spectator to turn detective. There are no "secret connotations which must be pieced together like a jigsaw puzzle."[23] The sound in *The Cherry Orchard* cannot be said even to fit the musical dimensions of the play; it may be "a musical sound in its way, but contrasting so strangely with the thoroughly familiar sounds of Epikhodov's guitar"[24] or the Jewish orchestra that it commands direct attention. The simple fact that Trofimov and Gaev *hear* it suggests that the incident is woven firmly into the fabric of the play. That Chekhov wanted his characters to take note of the sound is best suggested by his change of setting from a river to a chapel, as if to allow the greater quiet to bring out better the distant vibrations: "In the second act I have substituted the river with an old chapel and a well. It is quieter so."[25] Furthermore, Chekhov's direction or description concerning the sound is expressed verbatim both times it is heard—as sure an indication of the importance he placed on it as we might wish to have. So if *ultimately* it is a mere sound effect, *intimately* it has much to say.

The most important thing it has to say, regardless of Chekhov's own paradoxical assertions about his plays being comedies and not tragedies (another counterpoint!), is that the play is not an "undramatic drama" (as Mirsky likes to call Chekhov's dramas) but indeed a tragic drama. It

reference to the sound by Siegfried Melchinger (*Anton Chekhov*, in the series *World Dramatists* [New York: Ungar, 1972]): "its eeriness startles people, who then make it into a mystery. Therefore, Chekhov utilized, for his own ends, the possibility that such a sound can exist and have this effect" (p. 147)—an opinion he repeats later (p. 154). But the idea here, as worded, is not entirely clear.

22. In fact, Stanislavsky often eagerly overdid such sound effects (out of place bird calls, croaking frogs, chirping crickets, etc.), much to Chekhov's annoyance.

23. Nilsson, "Intonation and Rhythm," p. 179 (note 6, above).

24. Fergusson, "The *Cherry Orchard*" (note 4, above).

25. Letter to Vladimir Nemirovich-Danchenko, August 22, 1903, in Anton Chekhov, *The Cherry Orchard*, trans. T. Guthrie and L. Kipnis (Minneapolis: The University of Minnesota Press, 1965), p. 121. Cf. also *The Cherry Orchard* in *The Oxford Chekhov*, vol. 3, trans. and ed. R. Hingley (London: Oxford University Press, 1971), p. 319. Valency states: "Chekhov's world, in general, is quiet, so quiet that when a string breaks in the sky, we hear it" (*Breaking String*, p. 301).

is not a cheerful message the story conveys; yet, strange as it may sound, an optimistic interpretation is not uncommon. For there are those like Ermilov who in good Soviet fashion see the play's ending as bright, as introducing a new, powerful, and decisive force in society, the Russian working class, and who accordingly entitles his chapter on *The Cherry Orchard*: "Welcome, New Life." To put an end to the past: this is the emotional significance of the play. "Laughter, gay and unrestrained, penetrates every situation in the play . . . Karl Marx expressed a profound thought when he called laughter a way of 'bidding farewell' to the old, exhausted forms of life."[26] Similarly, outside the Soviet periphery, Sophie Lafitte, while recognizing that the basic theme of Chekhov is the "constant affirmation of inner solitude," insists that at the end of *The Cherry Orchard* (and *Uncle Vanya!*) there "bursts the hope of a better future, of happiness which is not only possible, but certain, though still far off."[27] Pitcher, more cautiously and neutrally, sees no *real* pessimistic or tragic implications.[28]

We believe the opposite, however, and concur with Aimée Alexandre: "*The Cherry Orchard* is the drama of death, the disappearance of a past with all that it contained that was good and bad, with all the nostalgia it will create, with all the sadness over the passage of time."[29] The important concept is the "drama of death," and the snapping string is the surrealistic symbol relating to it, reminiscent of the final snipping of the thread by Atropos. It provides a mood not just of "wonder" but of "regret," stressing nostalgically "time past and time passing"[30] rather than "bidding farewell" to them with "bursts of hope" for time future. Let us not forget, among other indications, that at the end Mme. Ranevskaya and Gaev—not villains in any way—sob in each other's arms, according to the stage directions, "in despair" (*v otčajanii*) that the family is dispersed, and that the final posture and situation of good Firs *does* remind us of death. It should not be surprising that, running down the aisle during a rehearsal, Chekhov had insisted that the sound be made "more painful" or dolorous (*žalobnee*).[31] Therefore, many critics and directors have indeed associated the sound with death, generally relating it, like Styan and Valency, to the death of values and way of life of the

26. Ermilov, *A. P. Čechov*, pp. 391, 393, and 395 (note 10, above).

27. Sophie Lafitte, *Tchékhov* (Paris: Hachette, 1971), p. 268.

28. Pitcher, *The Chekhov Play*, p. 201 (note 3, above).

29. Aimée Alexandre, *A la recherche de Tchékhov* (Paris: Editions Buchet / Chastel, 1971), p. 257.

30. Styan, *Chekhov in Performance*, pp. 287 and 288.

31. In Revjakin, *"Višnevyj sad"*, p. 177 (note 8, above). He also wanted the sound to be "more melancholy and soft" (*grustnee i mjagče*). Revyakin's source is Stanislavsky.

older Russian society of the Ranevskayas and Gaevs, symbolized by the cherry orchard—nostalgically "a sort of requiem for the 'unhappy and disjointed' lives of [Chekhov's] characters."[32] But in doing so, they have indicated at best only *what* the sound seems to signify, and if its meaning is tragic, we must still be able to say *how* it got to have this meaning, and *how* it reveals it structurally within the play. Given the dissension over the optimism or pessimism of the message, we should look for clues to validate the latter interpretation *inside* the play, for the former interpretation is little more than a superimposition.

To begin with, and with no intention of detracting from its arcane quality, the background of the snapping string must be sought in folklore. The sound establishes the folklore element inside the play. This possibility is hinted when Mme. Ranevskaya refers to the sound as "ill-omened" (ominous or foreboding: *nesčastnyj*). Perhaps this is what led a German critic to claim that it is used "as a symbol for the end of the aristocracy's splendor, as a ghostly omen"[33] (*Menetekel*). There can be no question that Chekhov used the motif in its most widespread folklore application concerning unhappiness associated with the end of life. Its homeopathic aspects appear all over Western and Central Europe, Western Slavic countries included. Though one cannot yet locate immediate evidence of the motif's presence in Russia itself, folklorists find it legitimate (and logical) to suppose its existence in Russian folklore because it is well known, for example, in Slovak folklore which in turn shows frequent links with Russian popular traditions. And Chekhov, being well acquainted with Eastern Slavic folk traditions, was undoubtedly familiar with this motif.

In folklore, a player may leave his instrument behind as a "life token," an extension of himself, and if during his absence a string breaks, this is considered an evil portent. The chord that snaps involves the idea of a separable soul.[34] One may come upon several such examples of a breaking string: "If a string of an instrument breaks for no special reason, then there will soon be a wedding, or, according to a more widespread superstition, one must expect a death."[35] With reference to

---

32. Magarshack, *Chekhov the Dramatist*, p. 286.

33. Wolf Düwel, *Anton Tschechow* (Halle [Sale]: Veb Verlag Sprache und Literatur, 1961), p. 172.

34. Cf. Johannes Bolte, ed., *Zeitschrift des Vereins für Volkskunde* 20 (1910): &, note 9: Motiv E761.5.2: Life token: zither string breaks. Secondary reference in Bächtold-Stäubli below. I am grateful to Dr. Andrew Cincura for his counsel in the area of folklore.

35. Hanns Bächtold-Stäubli, ed., *Handwörterbuch des deutschen Aberglaubens*, vol. 7 (Berlin und Leipzig: W. de Gruyter & Co., 1935-36), pp. 889-890 (see *Saite*). The wedding

The Cherry Orchard, it is clearly the more common belief, the *Todesfall*, that draws our attention. A typical illustration of the "snapping-chord-of-death" motif is the story of the Swiss fiddler:

> A fiddler living in the wilds of Elvig used to visit his loved one, who used his fiddle, twice a week in the Balmen Lötschenpass. She always knew exactly at what time he would walk into her house. Suddenly a chord of another violin snapped. "Oh Lord," cried she, "now something unfortunate has happened to my beloved," and correctly, at that exact moment he had been struck dead.[36]

Again, there is the story from Syra of Strong Hans, who could not be made to do anything except play the zither, and who sallied forth one day to fight the ogre (who had ravished the king's daughter), telling his mother: "If you see that the strings of my zither are broken, then come and seek me [for I shall be dead]."[37] Folk tales such as these form the tradition underlying the question of how the breaking string got to mean what it means in Chekhov's play.[38]

How this sound reveals its meaning structurally in the play is a

---

omen is further explained elsewhere: "When during an orgy a chord on the instrumentalist's fiddle snaps, then there are either married couples on the dance floor or a dancing pair will soon become engaged" (Bächtold-Stäubli quotes Evald Tang Kristensen, *Gamle folks fortaellinger om det jyske almveliv* [Fortfatterens forlag, Århus, 1900], p. 889). While the *Todesfall* omen has greater relevance for our purposes, it may still be marginally interesting to note that there are dancing couples in the ballroom in *The Cherry Orchard*, and that several of them perhaps will be getting engaged (dancing the *Grand Rond* when Act III opens are Pishchik and Charlotta, Trofimov and Mme. Ranevskaya, Anya and the Post Office Clerk, Varya and the Stationmaster, Dunyasha and others). No snapping string is heard at this point, of course; however, it has just been heard (near the close of Act II).

36. Cf. Fr. X. Pritz, *Überbleibsel aus dem hohen Altertum* (Linz: 1854), p. 86. Also *Sagan und Märchen aus dem Obersallis*, vol. 2 (Basel: Verlag der Schweiz. Gesellschaft für Volkskunde, 1913), p. 176, note 63. Secondary references in Bächtold-Stäubli above.

37. Pritz, *Überbleibsel.* Cf. also Johann Georg von Hahn, *Griechische und albanesische Märchen*, vol. 2 (München und Berlin: G. Müller, 1918), p. 18, note 64; also Bolte, *Zeitschrift des Vereins für Volkskunde* 20 (1910): 70, note 9. According to Bächtold-Stäubli, von Hahn's motif is similar to the one given by Edwin S. Hartland, *The Legend of Perseus*, vol. 2 (London: D. Nutt, 1895), p. 11.

38. We might note here that translators (into English) have needlessly complicated the issue by attempting to identify the instrument. Lyricized by the creative imagination, the raucous, metallic bucket's clang of childhood recollection became the vibrating, melancholy tone of a breaking chord on a string instrument—*any* string instrument, since the word is *struna*. But we may find the translation commonly pointing to a harp (because the sound comes from the sky?), or to a violin (because Chekhov's father, an excellent musician, played the violin? or because the Jewish band that performs in Mme. Ranevskaya's home is dominated by violins?). Magarshack (*Chekhov the Dramatist*, p. 286) suggests a balalaika (because this instrument is most readily associated with Russia? or because one of the variants of the stage directions in Act II reads: "Someone is heard walking quietly along the road and quietly playing a balalaika"?—cf. *The Oxford*

question which leads us to the heart of Chekhov's art in *The Cherry Orchard*, the art of counterpoint. Its ingredients combine in a pattern of oppositions, establishing architectural and conceptual relationships, expressively balanced, while retaining a clear individuality of their own at all times. Fundamental are the images of the owl and heron, not only because they appear in the very center of the play (end of Act II) and just before the first instance of the snapping string, but also because of their symbolic significance juxtaposing life and death, the drama's main counterpoint. Furthermore, a number of ancillary contrapuntal motifs come forth in the same scene. Epikhodov has just crossed the stage, playing his guitar:

> GAEV: Ladies and gentlemen, the sun has set.
>
> TROFIMOV: Yes.
>
> GAEV: *in a low voice, declaiming as it were*: Oh, Nature, wondrous Nature, you shine with eternal radiance, beautiful and indifferent! You, whom we call our mother, unite within yourself life and death! You animate and destroy!
>
> VARYA: *pleadingly*: Uncle dear!
>
> TROFIMOV: You'd better bank the yellow ball in the side pocket.
>
> GAEV: I'm silent, I'm silent . . .
>
> *All sit plunged in thought. Stillness reigns. Only* FIR's *muttering is audible. Suddenly a distant sound is heard, coming from the sky as it were, the sound of a snapping string, mournfully dying away.*
>
> MME. RANEVSKAYA: What was that?
>
> LOPAKHIN: I don't know. Somewhere far away, in the pits, a bucket's broken loose; but somewhere very far away.
>
> GAEV: Or it might be some sort of bird, perhaps a heron.
>
> TROFIMOV: Or an owl . . .
>
> MME. RANEVSKAYA, *shudders*: It's weird, somehow.
>
> *Pause*
>
> FIRS: Before the calamity the same thing happened—the owl screeched, and the samovar hummed all the time.
>
> GAEV: Before what calamity?
>
> FIRS: Before the Freedom. *Pause*
>
> MME. RANEVSKAYA: Come, my dear friends, let's be going. It's getting dark . . .

Chekhov, p. 324 [note 25, above]). One translator is even tempted to remove the string and leave just the instrument: "A distant sound that seems to come out of the sky, like a breaking harp (-string) slowly and sadly dying away . . ." (*Six Plays of Chekhov*, trans. Robert W. Corrigan [New York: Holt, Rinehart and Winston, 1962], p. 340). Nor have the guitar, the mandolin, and the zither been forgotten as possibilities.

Then the poor stranger appears, in a shabby white cap, begs thirty kopecks, and Mme. Ranevskaya, who has no silver in her purse, gives him a gold piece (to Varya's annoyed astonishment).

The break in silence, like the quiet tranquility of the old world that comes to an end, is anticipated by Gaev's words concerning the animating and destructive manner of Nature, and what he exclaims literally about life and death is balanced and restated symbolically after the break in silence by the heron and the owl—the former alluded to by Gaev himself, who dreams of his tranquil, older world continuing, and the latter by the representative of the younger generation, Trofimov, who wants its demise (and who strangely, and ironically, it might appear, seems to hoot at the very end of the play, over Anya's happy calls, while the older people leave and the orchard starts falling: "Aoooo" [*Ay!*]). In folk literature, the hooting of an owl represents a bad omen, while hearing the heron's cry represents a good one. In the Egyptian systems of hieroglyphs, the owl symbolizes "death, night, cold and passivity" and also pertains to the realm of the dead sun (a sun that has set),[39] and not surprisingly Virgil speaks of the owl's mournful strain when Dido longs for death.[40] Similarly, among the Egyptians, the heron (together with the stork and ibis) symbolized morning and the generation of life,[41] and Homer has Athene send a heron to Odysseus and Diomedes as they set out on a perilous mission, in order to insure their success.[42]

Old Firs had heard an owl years before, while the graciously living society kept minding its cup of tea, after which the bad portent became reality: the emancipation of the serfs in 1861, serfs who became the Lopakhins of the next generation, the one that buys and axes the orchards.[43]

---

39. J. E. Cirlot, *A Dictionary of Symbols* (New York: Philosophical Library, 1962), pp. 235–236. Note how many references there are in the play to the sun which has set, or, conversely, to the moon which is rising.

40. *Aeneid* 4. 462–463:
> and on the roofs in doleful song the solitary owl oft complained and spun out his long notes in mournful strain.

41. Cirlot, *Dictionary of Symbols*, p. 141.

42. *Iliad* 10. 274–277:
> and on the right along the path they followed Pallas Athene sent down a heron to them; their eyes could not behold it through the dark of night, but they could hear it crying. And Odysseus harkened at the bird-sign, and he prayed to Athene.

43. In this connection, the episode of the stranger suggests a counterpoint with the unwritten portion of the play following the curtain fall. The stranger who asks for help and is given a gold piece parallels the strangers (the new society) who "ask" for the cherry orchard and are "given" it. As if enacting Lopakhin's blunt, speculative words in Act I: "You must tear down the old buildings . . . , cut down the old cherry orchard . . . [so as to let in the strangers who will pay] ten rubles per acre a year," the strangers will come after the second snapping of the string to deal a death blow to the previous style of life.

Once the heron-owl pattern is set, the rest of the counterpoint falls into place, and we come to realize that hearing the sound of the snapping string twice underscores the structure.[44] An expressive series of sometimes obvious but more often subtle oppositions between death and life forces makes up this dialectic, as it were, which creates a tension throughout the play, and how the tension is resolved—the chord snaps—can only invite a pessimistic interpretation. But this becomes clear only at the end, because before that the dialectic operates ambiguously on an optical and phonic as well as on an actional and perceptional level.

On the optical level, we note that, as the tombstones of Act II counterpoise the chapel, so do the telephone poles the cherry orchard. The industrial and the natural, the city and the meadow, the skeletal and the rounded, termination and hope, face each other in precarious balance.[45] In addition, the death instruments, the gun Charlotta carries and the revolver Epikhodov reveals, act to counterpoise the musical instruments as well the expressed desires for continued life or the rays of hope emanating from the many telegrams, torn up or not, Mme. Ranevskaya receives every day from that "savage" who needs her and whom she loves in Paris. Epikhodov's query, "Should I live or should I shoot myself . . .?" creates more tensions than the words by themselves seem to betray, as does his ominous remark, "Now I know what to do with my revolver," followed by his reassured walking off playing his guitar. In effect, his query does not differ from his double-edged, symbolic observations at the beginning of the play that while "there's a frost this morning—ten degrees below— . . . yet the cherries are all in bloom" (and at the end: "It's devilishly cold here . . . yet it's still and sunny as though it were summer"), or from Mme. Ranevskaya's romantic attempt to poison herself in Paris coupled ambivalently with her sudden magnetic attraction for life in Russia. Even the stage directions, as N. Å. Nilsson points out, are composed of "wholly opposing parts" ("cheerfully through tears" [*radostno skvoz' slezy*], as an example; the non sequiturs too [Varya's and Anya's in Act I] amount to "oppositions").[46] Almost everything we see, from tombstones to guitars, exists in dialectical relationship with other objects. And observations and events follow the same pattern.

---

44. Styan suggests that at the end of Act II Chekhov is "familiarizing us with the sound . . . , so that [at the very end] it will not then disrupt the experience of the whole by its strangeness, but tie this movement with that" (*Chekhov in Performance*, p. 287).

45. Somehow the pattern of sunrise and sunset (moonrise) throughout the play fits the optical scheme, if only because, in the dialogue and stage directions together, there are at least eight literal references to such astronomical movements, not to speak of those used figuratively.

46. "Intonation and Rhythm," p. 172 (note 6, above).

The optical level of interpretation is intensified by Chekhov's insistence on the use of the color white. White pervades the play, not merely as a refraction of the heron, but as a veritable tonality struck about a dozen and a half times during the drama: one of Mme. Ranevskaya's two rooms is white, Firs wears a white waistcoat and puts on white gloves, Charlotta appears in a tightly laced white dress, Mme. Ranevskaya imagines her mother "all in white" in the orchard, and even Pishchik discovers white clay on his land. Furthermore, the orchard, as Gaev describes it, "is all white," and Mme. Ranevskaya laughs with joy at its being "all, all white!" while she visualizes her mother in it in the form of "a little white tree, leaning over." Then she underscores: "What an amazing orchard! White masses of blossom . . ." Chekhov's intent is clear from his correspondence: in his mind, even Lopakhin has a white waistcoat,[47] and "in Act One cherry trees can be seen in bloom through the windows, the whole orchard is a mass of whites. And ladies in white dresses." Hardly any other color is mentioned in the play.[48]

Inside and outside of Western folk tradition, white has symbolized the positive and timeless. It is considered purified yellow; it is the hope of life. By the same token, yellow is considered impure white, or life in a state of decay, or, at least, of imperfection. One is reminded of Balzac's character Poiret, in *Old Goriot*, whose white ivory cane handle has turned yellow with age and use, or of the aged countess' yellow gown in Pushkin's *The Queen of Spades*. The figurative meaning of yellow as a color given in Ozhegov's dictionary[49] includes the notions of conciliation, reform, and betrayal of the interests of the working class (used contemptuously). One should not overlook, then, Gaev's many, albeit eccentric, references to the

47. Letter to V. I. Nemirovich-Danchenko, November 2, 1903, in *The Oxford Chekhov*, p. 328.

48. Letter to K. S. Stanislavsky, February 5, 1903, in ibid., p. 318. See also the Guthrie and Kipnis edition of *The Cherry Orchard*, p. 118 (note 25, above). Pitcher calls this "a Turgenevan atmosphere of white dresses" (*The Chekhov Play*, p. 161) (note 3, above). Chekhov's insistence on white stands out dramatically by comparison with the infrequency of other colors mentioned in the play. None is a "life" color. Varya is dressed in black, a figure in the ballroom wears a grey top hat, Mme. Ranevskaya's other room is violet (a tone of mourning and death, thus counterbalancing her other room, which is white), and the sky is a cold clear blue—enough to set the white cherry blossoms into pronounced relief. None of these opposing colors acquires the ubiquitous personality that white acquires throughout the work. White is a precious color: like the life of the older generation, it is so easily soiled (like the blossoms, which will so easily fall with the "frost"). It does not fit the laborer, and if the tramplike stranger wears a white cap, it is perforce "shabby," just as, conversely, Dunyasha's hands are "white, as white as a lady's."

49. S. I. Ožegov, *Slovar' russkogo jazyka*, izd. 7-e stereotipnoe (Moscow: Sov. Enciklop., 1968).

"yellow ball"[50] bank shot in the side pocket,[51] for through his very eccentricity Gaev tacitly suggests that he realizes, at least subconsciously, what is happening to Russia. Despite his white waistcoat, suggesting the higher class status he has now attained, Lopakhin still wears "yellow shoes,"[52] almost as if to sugest his peasant stock. Thus the mood of counterpoising oppositions is enforced, shaping the play with tensions as it develops, and guiding it to its final expression of the snapping string.

Actional and perceptional levels of interpretation corroborate the optical. In a spatial context, the counterpoint between Mme. Ranevskaya's kissing her "darling bookcase" or Gaev's tearful and impassioned encomium to it on the one hand, and the epidemic of knocking over furniture accidentally or breaking belongings on the other, is quite obvious.[53] Lack of control over the physical world symptomizes the collapse of the spiritual. The spatial context is corroborated in turn by the temporal: in Act I, Mme. Ranevskaya says of Varya what she will also say of Lopakhin, that she is "the same as ever," which at different times is what Yasha says of Gaev and Varya of her mother, like a variation of Lopakhin's phrase to Gaev: "You're as splendid as ever." The phrases "You haven't changed a bit" and "just the same as ever" take on the qualities of a leit-motif by the end of the first act. They imply a desire to hang on to the status quo, to have it continue as splendidly as before, to prolong the "whiteness." But as the play wears on and, let us say, the heron turns owl, we hear the opposite theme sounded, that of change: "How you've aged," exclaims Mme. Ranevskaya to Firs, the way Varya laments to Petya: "How old you look!" Together, the

---

50. Ironically, the yellow ball becomes white the last time he aims his imaginary shot. Is it not so that if the white ball is pocketed the game is over?

51. For this reason, the Oxford edition, which translates the billiard game's "yellow" references by "red," in accordance with how the sport is played "in English-speaking countries" (*The Oxford Chekhov*, p. 335), is in error.

52. Letter to V. I. Nemirovich-Danchenko, November 2, 1903, in ibid., p. 328. Need one also recall that a yellow house (*želtyj dom*) means a madhouse, or that prostitutes in Russia used to carry yellow cards, or that the color is associated with oppressiveness (cf. the yellow parlor in Mme. Bovary's home in Tostes, or the yellow hotel room Svidrigaylov rents before his suicide)?

53. As examples of the loss of control over the physical world, we might single out the following: in Act I, a bouquet, a chair, and a saucer fall, and Gaev gets something in his eye; in Act II, Dunyasha develops a headache, Mme. Ranevskaya fumbles in her bag, and gold pieces scatter from a dropped purse; in Act III, a billiard cue is broken, Pishchik thinks he has lost his money from his pocket, Lopakhin is hit accidentally on the head, later he trips, a telegram falls, and Trofimov falls down the stairs; and in Act IV, Trofimov loses his rubbers, a hat box is crushed, Varya cannot find something in her luggage, and a thermometer is broken. Each can say, with Epikhodov, "A misfortune befalls me every day."

spatial and the temporal dimensions produce a counterpoint of their own: that of the wishful, dreamy, and passive world of the *status quo* which Mme. Ranevskaya, Gaev, Firs, and Dunyasha live in, epitomized by the latter's remark: "I am daydreaming,"; and that of the realistic, pragmatic, and materialistic world of change which Anya and Trofimov look to, or the mercantile logic of Lopakhin prepares. Says Lopakhin: "I'm always handling money . . . Sometimes I lie awake at night, I think . . ."

The most encompassing counterpoint, of course, operates on the phonic level, and it climaxes with the sound of the snapping string. The meaning of *The Cherry Orchard* is rooted in a kind of recondite music, or un-music, contrasting intensely with the clumsiness of the characters or their inability to harmonize (*neskladnyj*), and is expressed on the surface in many ways—the distant sound of a shepherd's piping and the allusion to bells in Act I, the guitar (confused with a mandolin) and the band (four violins, a double bass, and a flute) in Acts II and III, the waltz and the frequent mention of the musicians in Act III, and Yasha's and Charlotta's humming in Act IV. In point of fact, however, all this music leads to naught; it represents little more than an attempt by the characters to impose happiness artificially—again, to retain the "whiteness." It echoes in an empty shell of vapid desire. The pessimism could not ring more poignantly. For in *The Cherry Orchard* the music, like the whiteness, ultimately becomes an illusion, a pathological form of wishful thinking. These two would-be positive forces resemble the orchard itself—an illusion of a past life that the protagonists perceive more easily than the audience, which sees more poplars and telephone poles through the set windows than anything else. Symbolically, the sprightly sound of a band's music yields to the dull, unmusical clicking of billiard balls—all of which lends significance to the double innuendo that people are like the balls on a billiard table, knocked about in a series of banked shots before being pocketed away, and that they are made to act like melancholy puppets on a string, dancing ritually as if in a state of benumbed dream, not knowing the reason for what they do. This is the forlorn state of those who can say soulfully with Pishchik: "Everything in this world comes to an end."

Out of a simple pair of bird images, then, Chekhov cross-weaves a network of motifs which culminates in the final counterpoint: the sounds of the snapping string and of the felling ax. That both are related intrinsically, and gloomily, is certain from Chekhov's description of them: both ring identically: mournfully and sadly (*grustno, pečal'nyj*). The first instance of the snapping string in the middle of the performance is not accompanied by the thuds of axes against trees, for at this point, like the characters, we do not know whether it is a heron or an owl that we have heard. In the reverberation there is hope rather than finality: at least there is questioning. Life and death hang in the balance, so the counterpoint may continue: the cherry orchard may still not be sold to strangers and leveled for commercial purposes. But the first sounding leads to the second, as if answering the question with death. "A feeling of emptiness" takes over, and in the shell of the house the tunes have vanished, leaving nothing but the faint echoes of humming voices. Since the string's sound and the ax's thud become synonymous (as if the ax had struck the string and broken it), it becomes painfully clear that a breaking string is after all a broken string. Here it does sound with finality, and here the counterpoint ends. This is not a case of "emotional distancing," as has been claimed.[54] *The Cherry Orchard* is written in an emotional key, deeper or more overt, perhaps, than we are used to in Chekhov, and the emotional experience finds its objective correlative in sounds. And the experience is far from optimistic: that the white illusion of life is finally crushed by the axed trees, just as the musical illusion of happiness is finally destroyed, as in the ending of folk tales, by the snapped string—all this bespeaks a pessimistic message, a "drama of death." The ending is tragic:

> FIRS: . . . Life has gone by as if I had never lived. *Lies down.* I'll lie down a while . . . There's no strength left in you, old fellow; nothing is left, nothing. Ah, you addlehead! *Lies motionless. A distant sound is heard coming from the sky as it were, the sound of a snapping string mournfully dying away. All is still again, and nothing is heard but the strokes of the ax against a tree far away in the orchard.*

In every other full-length play, Chekhov made a pistol shot dominate the climax. He was well aware that *The Cherry Orchard* represented a departure from this practice: ". . . there's something new about it . . . there's not a single pistol shot in the whole play."[55] But the snapping string is a pistol shot of a different order of magnitude: rather than limit itself immediately and primarily to the physical world, it reverberates throughout the world of the spirit, regardless of whether mortals can make sense out of it. It has contrapuntal associations which the other Chekhov "sounds" do not have, and because of its distant origin in folklore, uniting the light and dark of creation, one could say, its vibrations can be overpowering. Perhaps Chekhov was aware of this potentially deafening resonance when he tried to tone down the enthusiasm for sound effects of his directors, who were trying hard to make

---

54. See Pitcher, *The Chekhov Play*, p. 209.
55. Letter to O. L. Knipper, September 25, 1903, in *The Oxford Chekhov*, p. 320.

acoustic sense out of the enigmatic sound. Chekhov naturally spoke in terms of a simple sound effect, which, after all, is all the snapping string is when it comes to producing the play: "Tell Nemirovich that the sound in Acts Two and Four of *The Cherry Orchard* must be shorter, a lot shorter, and must be felt as coming from a great distance. What a lot of fuss about nothing—not being able to cope with a trifle like this, a mere noise, although it's so clearly described in the play."[56] For us, however, this trifle, or mere noise, well illustrates what Thomas Mann said of Chekhov: that he was one of those major writers who could embrace the fullness of life in a simple incident.

---

56. Letter to O. L. Knipper, March 18, 1904, in ibid., p. 330.

METAPOETICS AND STRUCTURE IN
BOLESŁAW LEŚMIAN'S RUSSIAN POETRY

BY

ROCHELLE STONE

Alles Poetische muss märchenhaft sein
NOVALIS
Muza—skazok žilica
A. BELYJ

ALTHOUGH LIMITED in number, Leśmian's Russian poems occupy a prominent place in his predominantly Polish creative work. His Russian works are represented by three extant cycles of poetry [*Pesni Vasilisy Premudroj*, written in 1905 and published in *Zolotoe Runo* (No. 11-12, 1906); *Lunnoe pokhmel'e*, published in *Vesy* (No. 10, 1907); *Volny živye*, published in *Pereval* (No. 11, 1907)] and the lost drama *Vasilij Buslaev* (written in 1907).[1] Dating from 1905-1906, the Russian poetry presents a curious phenomenon because it contains, especially in the cycle *Pesni Vasilisy Premudroj* ("Songs of Vasilisa the All-Wise"), a direct expression of all the ideological elements of Leśmian's mature poetry, at a time when, in his Polish poetry, they were still in their formative stages. The best example is the cycle *Oddaleńcy* ("The Distant Ones"), written the same year, in which he tries to reach the 'beyond,' the realm of metaphysics, by means propagated in Nietzsche's *Thus Spake Zarathustra*. Leśmian's refutation of these Nietzschean concepts in the closing poems of *Oddaleńcy* shows that his creed was still in the process of development, a process which can be seen in its mature phase in the Russian cycle.

---

1. A. Juniewicz, "Nowe rosyjskie wiersze i listy Leśmiana," *Przegląd Humanistyczny*, no. 1 (1964), pp. 147-148. In a letter to Bryusov, written in August, 1907, Leśmian mentions the drama, hoping to have it published and staged with the help of the Russian poet. For future discussion see R. Stone, *Bolesław Leśmian: the Poet and His Poetry* (Los Angeles and Berkeley: University of California Press, 1976), ch. 4.

137

Nowhere, not even in Leśmian's mature Polish poetry contained primarily in the volumes *Łąka* ("The Meadow") (1920) and *Napój cienisty* ("Shadowy Potion") (1936), are his views on poetic creation stated as succinctly as in the cycle *Pesni Vasilisy Premudroj*. In a sense this cycle can be considered a poetic commentary to Leśmian's entire work. It may be compared to *Szkice Literackie* ("Literary Sketches"), written mainly between 1909 and 1915, and with "A Treatise on Poetry," written in 1937. Together they form the only cohesive Symbolist program of any consequence in Polish literature. This unique position of Leśmian's Russian works strengthens my belief, and the beliefs of others,[2] that eventual access to archives in Russia might bear out the testimony of Leśmian's friends that the poet wrote an additional volume of Russian verse.[3] He may one day be acknowledged as a truly bilingual poet.[4]

How do we explain the maturity of his poetic creed, especially in the first Russian cycle of poems, at this early stage of his career? Was it cautiousness because he was writing in a foreign language, or was it because it was easier for Leśmian to crystalize his ideas in Russian? Russian was not only the language in which he received his entire education, but also the language of the poets dearest to him: Pushkin, and especially Tyutchev and Fet. He was interested in Russian thought, literary criticism, and above all, by his own admission, in the *skazki* and *byliny* of Russian folklore.[5] He dreamt of creating the Polish equivalent of a *bylina*, of writing a fairy tale "Žar-ptica". Deeply immersed in the works of Afanasyev, *Narodnye russkie skazki* and *Poètičeskie vozzrenija drevnikh slavjan na prirodu*, and in the Russian folk epic, he even considered the *bylina* as a possible source of Stefan Żeromski's *Powieść o Udałym Wałgierzu*.[6] Such titles as *Pesni Vasilisy Premudroj* and *Vasilij Buslaev* point clearly to Russian folklore as their

---

2. Cf. S. Pollak, *Srebrny wiek i później* (Warszawa; "Czytelnik," 1971), p. 253. Cf. also D. Čiževskij, "Bolesław Leśmian als russischer Dichter," *Zeitschrift für slavische Philologie* [Heidelberg] 23, Heft 2 (1955):262. The latter believes that a search in anthologies from Leśmian's time will lead to the discovery of more Russian poetry written by him.

3. A. Stern, "Powroty Bolesława Leśmiana," in *Wspomnienia o Bolesławie Leśmianie*, ed. Z. Jastrzębski (Lublin: Wydawnictwo Lubelskie, 1966), p. 344. Stern bases his belief on a letter received from the poet's friend S. Zieliński.

4. See R. Stone, "Bolesław Leśmian: The Theoretician and Bilingual Poet" (Ph.D. diss., University of California, Los Angeles, 1971).

5. E. Boyé, "Dialogi akademickie. W niepojętej zielonosci," in B. Lešmian, *Szkice Literackie* (Warszawa: P.I.W., 1959), p. 499 (henceforth referred to as SL). This article, titled "W niepojętej zielonosci," based on an interview with Leśmian, appeared in *Pion*, no. 23 (1934).

6. B. Leśmian, *Utwory rozproszone, Listy*, ed. J. Trznadel (Warszawa: P.I.W., 1962) (henceforth referred to as *UR*). See letter no. 1, Paris, 1906, p. 303.

source. Leśmian's relationship to Russian folklore merits some discussion of the literary-historical context from which Leśmian emerged as a poet. A contextual analysis will explain why Leśmian used folklore as a vehicle of poetic and ideological expression, while a textual analysis will show in what ways he benefited from it.[7]

For Symbolism, as a literary trend opposed to rationalism, folklore was a manifestation of primordial culture, still uncontaminated by urban civilization, a creative realm unfettered by the rational, a realm where the supernatural coexisted with the real. As such, folklore was, especially for the Symbolists of the second generation, not merely a source of fantastic, musically incantational motifs, but of cultural and literary ideas. Owing to their illogical, magical elements and regional motifs, folklore genres, especially fairy tales, appear in different variations, lending themselves to different interpretations, and are therefore "highly informative."[8] Thus their illusive quality suited Symbolist aesthetics. As an art which was originally transmitted and preserved orally, folklore was a medium which enabled people to share the mystery and the joy of creative art collectively, thereby strengthening communal bonds.[9] In its relationship to folklore, Symbolism continued the Romantic tradition in which *mythopoeia* was one of the most pertinent attributes. The idea that speech, music, and poetry were co-original and analogous as expressions of intuition and spirit had, in fact, become the basis for the linguistic speculations of the German Romantics.[10]

---

7. Cf. Ju. M. Lotman, *Analiz poètičeskogo teksta* (Leningrad: "Prosveščenie," 1972), pp. 216–217. Such an analytical approach has been favored by this Russian scholar, whose works made me aware of many correlations between his ideas and those of the Polish poet expressed in his *Szkice Literackie* and in the cycle *Pesni Vasilisy Premudroj*. Some of these correlations will be referred to later.

8. Ibid., p. 220. The author ascribes this high degree of information to the unpredictable elements in poetic texts, "Každyj element v posledovatel'noj stročke, sostavljajuščej tekst, ne do konca predskazyvaet posledujuščij." Cf. also V. Ja. Propp, *Morphology of the Tale*, 2d rev. ed., ed. L. A. Wagner (Austin and London: University of Texas Press, 1968), pp. 12–13, discussing the many variations of motifs in the Russian fairy tale and their "very capricious life on the lips of mankind."

9. Cf. Vyacheslav Ivanov's ideas on "sobornost' " in his: "Poèt i čern' " in *Po zvëzdam, Stat'i i aforizmy* (St. Petersburg: Izd. "Ory," 1909). Ivanov believed that "the Symbolist poet perceives atavistically, by reverting to the forgotten property (heritage— *dostojanie*) of the people's soul, and by his unconscious immersion in the elements of folklore" (p. 40). He believed that "the 'keys to mystery' entrusted to the artist are the keys to the forbidden secrets of the peoples soul" (p. 42). Therefore, he believed that the interaction of the artist with the masses is vital to creative art. Only communal art can bring universal harmony (p. 37).

10. Their ideas evolved from Giambattista Vico's *Scienza Nuova* (1725). See *The New Science*, tr. T. G. Bergin and M. A. Fish (New York: Ithaca Press, 1948), pp.

Similar linguistic speculations were continued by the Russian scholars
Aleksandr Potebnya (1835-1891), the literary historian Aleksandr Ves-
elovsky (1838-1906), and the philosopher-psychologist Ivan Chelpanov
(1862-1936), who traced the poetic word to the myth-making stage,
considering poetry to be "protonatural," primordial language governed
by intuition.[11] Their works influenced especially the second generation
Symbolists—Bely, Ivanov, and Blok—as did the last phase of German
Romanticism as a whole.

As I have illustrated elsewhere, Leśmian fits closely into this particular
Russian literary context.[12] Like the younger Russian Symbolists and the
French poet-theoretician Tancrède DeVisan (whose work was reviewed
in 1904 in *Vesy*, No. 10, by Vyacheslav Ivanov), Leśmian did not
consider Symbolism a literary school, but a lyrical attitude encompassing
all levels of contemporary thought: the scientific, the philosophical,
the religious, and the artistic.[13] At the same time he felt Symbolism to
be deeply rooted in the past. In an interview he stated: "I was fascinated
by Symbolism that was none other than Romanticism, which was in turn
none other than Greek tragedy in many cases. One of the Russian
authors in turn [Vyach, Ivanov, in "Dve stikhii v sovremennom simvo-
lizme"] says that each century draws upon its own cosmos which after

63-68. Vico equates the imaginative and instinctual activities of primitive man with man's
earliest poetic expressions, which contain the seeds of all later arts, sciences, and social
institutions. These views were expanded by Herder, Schlegel, Schelling, Novalis, et al.,
and developed into a Romantic theory, explained succinctly by M. H. Abrams, *The Mirror
and the Lamp* (New York and London: Oxford University Press, 1953), pp. 80-83,
passim. Cf. also J. G. Herder, "Abhandlung über den Ursprung der Sprache (1770),'
Sämtliche Werke (Tübingen: J. Cotta, 1805-1820).

11. In *O nekotorykh simvolakh v slavjanskoj poèzii* (Khar'kov: 1860), A. Potebnja
deals with symbols in Slavic folk poetry, while *Iz lekcij po teorii slovesnosti* (Khar'kov:
1894) contains a chapter on myth. In A. Veselovskij, *Istoričeskaja poètika* (1899), intr.
V. Žirmunskij (Leningrad: "Khudožestvennaja Literatura," 1940), p. 47, the author speaks
about the relationship of mythology to the word. According to him, "the creation of
symbols unites knowledge, cognition and incantation in one word. . . . The incantation
creates images, the word creates flesh." I. Čelpanov, the author of *Mozg i duša* (1900),
deals with the issue of causality as a stifling factor in the creative process and argues
the importance of creative, artistic intuition.

12. R. Stone, "Leśmian i drugie pokolenie symbolistów rosyjskich," *Pamiętnik Literacki*
[Warszawa] 62, z. 2 (1972): 19-50.

13. These views closely correspond to ideas expressed by Ju. M. Lotman, *Struktura
khudožestvennogo teksta*, intr. T. G. Winner (reprint ed., Providence: Brown University
Press, 1971), pp. 5-7, passim. The author points out the advantages and the added
dimension gained by studying a literary text in a specific historical and cultural
context with which it shares an extratextual, cultural code. We find also valuable
remarks on this subject in H. Markiewicz, "Literatura w świetle semiotyki (Na marginesie
prac J. Lotmana)," *Konteksty nauki o literaturze, Z Dziejów Form Artystycznych w
Literaturze Polskiej* (Wrocław, Warszawa, Kraków: Ossolineum, P.A.N. 1973), pp. 91-106.

a while, to following generations, apears to be a fantastic reverie, as the Greek cosmos . . . is for us. . . . Today's cosmos demands a different reality"[14] According to Leśmian and the Russians, Symbolism was to bring about a new and different reality, using art to improve the present and the future of mankind. For the Symbolists who were attempting to reveal the ideas inherent in various forms, ancient myth was synonymous with truth.

A highly metaphysical poet, concerned with the intuitive element in man's existence, Leśmian, as mentioned above, attempted at first to transcend the existing reality by following the path of Nietzsche's *Thus Spake Zarathustra* (see the poem "Metafizyka" in his Polish cycle *Oddaleńcy*). However, this anti-democratic "ascent" to the "beyond" as a superman did not lead him to truth, but made truth rather "distant." Instead, he decided to "descend" to Schelling's "Urgrund," to return to primordiality, to fuse his soul with nature. He wanted his creations to be like those of primitive man, whose poetic word *incarnated the idea*, and whom he considered a natural poet. [15]

In his *Szkice Literackie* ("Literary Sketches"), he evolved a comprehensive "mythology" of his own which combined folk elements, the idealistic philosophy of Schlegel, Schelling, the pantheism of Spinoza, the Indian Upanishads, and Bergsonian creative evolution with his own myths of regression to primordiality. [16] His is a mythology which has continual myth-creation as its basis. Myth as the authentic expression of the creative act is born of intuition; it captures the elusive and is, therefore, forever created anew. For Leśmian, as for Vico, myth (as the basic concept of poetic cognition) enables the poet to establish a "dialogue" with nature and with those realms of reality which in modern times are obscured by the power of rationality. Furthermore, according to Leśmian, the act of myth-creation is unpredictable, and therefore

---

14. Boyé, "Dialogi akademickie," pp. 497–498.

15. Similar theories on the genesis of poetic language can be found in works of C. Lévi-Strauss, *La Pensée sauvage* (Paris: Plon, 1962). E. Cassirer also takes important notice of this in *Language and Myth* (New York: Harper & Bros., 1946), pp. 59–62, and offers a searching analysis. Cf. also M. Eliade, chapter on "Le Mythe du Bon Sauvage," *Mythes, rêves et mystères* (Paris: Payot, 1940), p. 48, in which the author sees in regress to primordiality the restoration of the original wholeness of man within himself and with his environment. M. Głowiński, "Leśmian, czyli poeta jako człowiek pierwotny," *Pamiętnik Literacki* [Warszawa] 55, z. 2, pp. 385–417, presents us with an excellent study on Leśmian's ideas of regression to primordiality as applied in his poetry, which aims at approximating the creative act of the "natural poet."

16. F. Schlegel, *Gespräch über die Poesie*, vol. 2, ed. H. Ediner (Stuttgart: I. B. Metzler, 1968), 358–363. Here the author speaks of the need for such a "mythology" as the central unifying element for modern poetry.

approximates life. In his view only creative life is comprehensible to man,[17] so that myth (poetry) helps to understand the true essence of life. Thus, Leśmian the Symbolist believed that the myth-creating word is a true symbol, capable of expressing changing, obsolescent reality and of creating a mythogenic poetry which would raise the cultural and ethical standard of man.

Convinced that in our present reality folklore approximates myths created by primitive man, Leśmian turns toward it as a means to achieve this goal. In his view, ". . . the kinship with the folkloric world and its world of the beyond . . . will revitalize language. [Language] as the eternal disseminator of primordial impressions and immortal sights and non-sights (*widów i niewidów*) conceals within itself immeasurable . . . creative wealth. Besides, the people's ritualistically-inspired view of art will force the [present] lack of perception [in man] toward flights over the gray 'commonplaces' and will at the same time oblige [man] to fruitful encounters."[18] Here folklore, as the communal art, represents for Leśmian a superstructure on *mythopoeia*, a "derivative designate" (for term see fn. 19), and still closer to myths than is natural language.

In addition, Leśmian creates a poetic structure (or model) analogous to folklore dealing with his own convictions, and therefore representing the incarnation of his poetic creed. This type of text lends itself to a variety of interpretations. To Leśmian, the fact that it is based on folklore, which is understood by the people, gives the model a greater veracity.[19] He attributes to folklore an epistemological function, because it perpetuates the closeness of poetry with music, as in primitive languages, by means of which primitive man got to know the world surrounding him.

Leśmian's relationship to folklore is twofold. On the primary level, following the tradition of great Russian writers beginning with Pushkin,

---

17. Leśmian, "Z rozmyślań o Bergsonie," *SL*, p. 37 (note 5, above), where the poet declares: "Eternal creativity and the unpredictable are a feature of life. There is no Absolute" (p. 32). Here Leśmian states that even exact science is rooted in myth and, therefore, born of intuition. This concept of Leśmian corresponds to ideas expressed by Ju. M. Lotman in "Voprosy teorii iskusstva," *Lekcii po struktural'noj poètike* (reprint ed., Providence: Brown University Press, 1968), p.35.

18. Leśmian, *UR*, p. 346 (note 6, above). The text is taken from a letter written to the editor of the periodical "Ponowa." Cf. also the words "widów—niewidów" as an obvious example of Russian influence on his neologisms; cf. "vid."

19. Here, by using folklore, Leśmian anticipates ideas expressed by Lotman in "Slovesnyj izobrazitel'nyj znak (obraz)," *Strukture*, pp. 72-73. "Iz materiala estestvennogo jazyka-sistemy znakov, uslovnykh, no ponjatnykh vsemu kollektivu . . . , voznikaet vtoričnyj znak izobrazitel'nogo tipa."

Leśmian turns to folklore as the source of truest artistic value. In it he sees "the demystification of his [the poet's] own existence by transferring it into the mythical, fairy tale realm, a realm inaccessible to human eyes which allows the poet to reach . . . the fullest freedom of creation."[20] The motifs and devices of *skazki* appear throughout his poetry. Yet he avoids stylization à la early Bal'mont. For him folk stylization is not a means of creating a specific literary style. In general he takes liberties in his stylization, utilizing folkloric elements as a point of departure toward his own specific creed. However, on a secondary level Leśmian's poetic practices appear to be almost "identical with the creative methods of folklore—more precisely—with its primitive fantasy."[21] Like folklore, which is based on a specific culture and on common recognition, Leśmian's poetry is calculated to fulfill the anticipation of the receiver.

The fairy tale "skazka-skladka," defined by Afanasyev as a collective creation, fulfills the role of a social utopia and is, according to many East European folklorists including Boris Sokolov, "a type of dream compensation,"[22] a world where in the end good prevails over evil. Leśmian too creates a poetic utopia by means of "a language which, approximating the primitive, imposes upon [the poet] its remote 'dream world' ('śni mi się')."[23] He creates another realm governed by the anthropomorphism of the remote past, by a "metaphysics" of primitive man whose vision was unlimited because it knew no division between dream and reality, man and nature. In this realm there were no boundaries between existence and nonexistence, and the creativeness of man made him an extension of God.[24]

---

20. Leśmian, "Pieśni ludowe," *SL*, p. 390.

21. A. Sandauer, "Poezja twórczych potęg natury," *Studia o Leśmianie*, ed. M. Głowiński and J. Sławiński (Warszawa: P.I.W., 1971), p. 13.

22. R. Jakobson, "On Russian Fairy Tales," *Selected Writings*, Slavic Epic Studies, vol. 4 (The Hague: Mouton & Co., 1966), p. 99. Here the author gives B. Sokolov's definition of fairy tale, and points out that "it is not by chance that in our epoch, when borders between utopia and reality are being effaced . . . the ideology of the folk tale begins to come sharply into focus." Cf. also E. Trubeckoj, "Inoe carstvo i ego iskateli v russkoj narodnoj skazke," *Russkaja Mysl'* [Prague], 1923, who in this study tries to explain man's longing for utopia.

23. Leśmian, *UR*, p. 346.

24. Leśmian, "Znaczenie pośrednictwa w metafizyce życia zbiorowego," *SL*, p. 47-48. This is how the poet explains the relationship of primitive man, as well as his own, to God: "The anthropomorphic outlook on life is the most primitive one. God, emanating from such an outlook, is an expansion into infinity of the human being who gets to know the universe *rapaciously*, enforcing upon it his own laws and finding in it the image and likeness of himself . . . One ought not differentiate between man and god, between the creative idea and the work which bore it . . . Primitive man is a mixture of heaven and earth, an antediluvian dragon, whose torso, half human and still half divine, allows him to dwell simultaneously in two worlds."

In Leśmian's aesthetics, form is an expression of poetic creed (cf. "pesnja"—song). Just as the correspondence between word and action decides man's values, so the correspondence between content and form decides the total expression of ideas in works of art. A textual analysis of the cycle *Pesni Vasilisy Premudroj* will demonstrate how Leśmian utilized folklore in his own work.

I

Я - солнечная быль, я - мудрая царевна,

Любимица небес и леса и ручья, -

Я - голос бытия таинственно запевный, -

Всем обрученная и все же я - ничья!

Я знаю мысль цветов и думу лунных блестков,

И песню дряхлую, что мохом поросла,

И трепеты ночей, и тайны перекрестков,

И водометный сон упругого весла!

В моем коралловом, подводном захолустье

Есть жизнь бессмертная и радостная грусть.

Я много помню дней и знаю наизусть я

Все то, чего нельзя запомнить наизусть!...

Меня исполнил Бог душою благовонной,

Душою - розою и телом - жемчугом, -

Вдоль да по матушке - лазури небосклонной

Плывет моя ладья, окованная сном!

Она плывет-поет по ветру-урагану

О том, кто был в нее так сказочно влюблен!...

Поклон ему в былом - царевичу Ивану -

За тридевять земель - мой царственный поклон!

II

С улыбкой ясною твержу я неустанно

Мою пословицу: где сказка - там и Бог!

И удивляю мир тревожный и туманный

Разоблачением невиданных дорог!

Плескаясь на слепо в жемчужной суматохе

Невольно-пенных волн, заплетенных в венец,

В начале расскажу и ужасы, и вздохи,

Чтоб неожиданней был радостный конец.

И, веря, что игра - заботы мудренее,

Я всеми чарами за правду постою!

И мне легко найти забаву и затею,

И я горжуся тем, что слез не признаю!

Для сказок - нет могил! Единая могила -

Лишь эта знойная, заоблачная твердь!

Ту жизнь, что мне дана, я долго золотила, -

И смерть мне нипочем! Я видывала смерть!

III

Когда в безбрежности луна воздушно блещет,

И золотится сном догадливая бровь, -

Неслышным пламенем в груди моей трепещет,

Обильно-сладкая, святая нелюбовь!...

Я чувствую ее к минуте пробужденья

От сна заморского и полного чудес,

Хотя и страшно мне в ночном самозабвенье,

Мечтать о небесах и не узреть небес!...

Но я молюсь тогда молитвою греховной -

Да не коснется день моих недвижных плеч!

И слышен ангелам мой трепет нелюбовный

И нелюбовная, причудливая речь!

Но утро красное, что в солнце ночевало,

Ласкает грудь мою и теплится в крови, -

Я знаю: сон исчез! Я знаю: солнце встало!

И замираю вся от нежной нелюбви!...

IV

Пылают облака узорчато-цветные,

Струится в воздухе благоуханный гром!...

Поспели уж к весне кораллы наливные,

Люблю их пожинать невидимым серпом!

Уж тени мнимые в глазах от света бродят,

Стоит - не движется полуденный пожар,

И волны замерли и золотом исходят,

Как будто солнечный постигнул их удар!

Я знаю сказ весны! Я помню, как намедни

Взывал гуслярный звон у красных у ворот, -

Пора задуматься над сказкою последней,

Над той, которая придет, но не пройдет!

Пора от старого, забытого обрыва

В условленную даль уплыть мне по волне!

Чу!... лебедь сказочный встревожил гладь залива...

Чу!... время движется!... Нет времени во мне!

V

Я та, которой нет - но есть мои мечтанья,

И слышен шопот мой повсюду - на цветах,

Не чужд и мне живой огонь существованья,

И Богу я могу присниться в небесах!

Я знаю суетность разгаданных заклятий

И дивно не хочу быть видимей Любви,

И, как она, живу - вне жизни, вне объятий!

Я - только сон во сне! Я - бред в твоей крови!

Но мною бредит лес, и ветер за горами,

И вековечный дуб, склонившийся к пруду, -

И светится мой взор, моими колдовствами

Перезолоченный в полночную звезду!

И дружбою своей до гроба и загробной

Дарят меня давно богатыри всех стран!

Люби меня за то, что я жизнеподобна, -

За то, что нет меня, царевич мой Иван![25]

The external form of the cycle is quite simple. It consists of five songs, each of which is composed of four quatrains, except for the first song which has five stanzas. It is written in iambic hexameter with alternating twelve- and thirteen-syllable lines. This meter, with a fixed caesura after the sixth syllable, has been used not only in such formal genres as epic and drama but also in Polish folk songs. The rhyme pattern is traditional: a b a b. We find a number of rich rhymes: "ruč'ja:: nič'ja," "Porosla:: vesla," "vljublën::poklon," "venec::konec." There is only one compound rhyme: "zakholust'e::naizust' ja," plus a few assonances: "neustanno:: tumannyj," "zagrobnoj:: žiznepodobna." Whereas in the clausula Leśmian adheres to traditional rhymes, within the verse he uses stylized folkloric inner rhymes, such as "Plyvët— poët," "Dušoju—rozoju i telom—žemčugom." The external phonetic parallelisms of the rhyme and the highly varied inner rhymes (derived from patterns used in *byliny*) lend the verses great melodiousness. In fact, the musicality of the rhyme carries its own cognitive function in Leśmian's aesthetics. As with the primitive man the musicality is inseparable from the word and therein lies its magic quality. We find occasional enjambements in the cycle (Song I, stanza 3, lines 1-2; stanza 4, lines 3-4; etc.) which, along with the unstressed caesura, are used to express the flux of the creative process. Vasilisa's declarations represent a total correspondence between the phrase and its musical pattern. Her songs, like incantations, appeal to the mnemonic faculties,

---

25. Leśmian, *UR*, pp. 74-78.

so as to dwell easily in man's memory. Thanks to rhythm, the "Duch wichrowy" (*élan vital*) or propelling force in Leśmian's poetics, we find certain sound parallelisms in the cycle, which according to Zhirmunsky can be considered rhymes or rhymoids.[26]

The six-foot iambic verse with its fixed caesura allows for the use of inner autonomous rhythmical units which add dynamism and prevent greater monotony. Use of the fixed caesura is apparent whenever Vasilisa speaks of herself as "byl' " (song), using apostrophes, maxims, and stylized proverbs. (See for apostrophes: Song I, stanza 5, lines 3–4; Song V, stanza 4, lines 3–4; for maxims: Song II, stanza 4, line 1; Song V, stanza 2, line 4; for proverbs: Song II, stanza 3, line 1; *et al.*) The mellifluousness of the cycle is enhanced by the consonantal instrumentation with

---

26. V. M. Žirmunskij, *Rifma, eë istorija i teorija* (Peterburg: Akademia, 1923). For this discussion of "embryonic rhymes" see p. 20, for "rhymoids" see p. 14. Initially, the term "zvukovoj povtor" ("sound repetition") is limited primarily to canonical rhymes as the organizing factor in poetry. See p. 9: "Dolžno otnesti k ponjatiju rifmy vsjakij zvukovoj povtor, nesuščij organizujuščuju funkciju v metričeskoj kompozicii stikhotvorenija." However, this function is also extended by Zhirmunsky to "embryonic rhymes," which can occur in the initial, middle, and final position of the verse (p. 293). The same is true for "rhymoids." Enriching and organizing sound-orchestration (so vital to Leśmian's poetics), these "rhymoids" appear in the *Pesni Vasilisy Premudroj* in every possible pattern. The compilation which we supply below is organized according to Zhirmunsky's categories.

I. Here we have rhymoids, i.e., the phonological correspondence of stressed (italicized below) and unstressed vowels in the line with the ictus of the clausula:
   a) Cf. Song I, st. 1, ln. 1: j*a* - a - ja . . . // ja - a - ja - *a*
      Song I, st. 4, ln. 1: (-a) - *o* - *o* // *o* - *o* - *o* - o
      Song I, st. 5, ln. 2: o - *o* - o . . . - ë // (a) - o - ë
   b) Correspondence of the vowel of the ictus in the initial position and in the clausula:
      Song I, st. 5, ln. 2: *o*. . . . // . . . . ë
      Song II, st. 1, ln. 3: j*a* . . . // . . . . *a*
      Song V, st. 1, ln. 1: *a*. . . . // . . . . *a* (passim)
   c) In the a) initially stressed vowels or b) in the final position of the hemistich:
      a) Song III, st. 1, ln. 1: *a*. . . . // *a*
      b) Song III, st. 1, ln. 2: . . . . *o* // . . . . o
   d) Correspondence of the stressed caesura vowel (popular with the Symbolists; cf. Bal'mont) with the ictus of the clausula:
      Song I, st. 5, ln. 2: . . . neë // . . . -ën
      Song III, st. 1, ln. 2: . . . -om // . . . -ov'
      Song IV, st. 3, ln. 2: . . . -on // . . . -ot
      Song V, st. 3, ln. 2: *u*b // -d*u*
II. a) Correspondence based on heteroaccentual, "embryonic" inner rhyme of morphological nature:
      Song I, st. 2, ln. 1: cvet-ov:: blestk-ov
   b) Correspondence of morphemes in stressed and unstressed position:
      Song I, st. 3, ln. 1: -ëm, om, -om
      Song I, st. 3, ln. 2: -naja, -naja
      Song II, st. 4, ln. 2: -oju, -oju // -om, -om
      Song III, st. 1, ln. 1: -aja, *a*ja
      Song III, st. 2, ln. 3: -ogo, -ogo
      Song III, st. 2, ln. 4: nebes-, nebes (cf. also Song IV, Song V)

sonorants predominating. (In Song I, where the overall number of consonants equals 328, we have 51 *n*, 28 *m*, 31 *l*, and 21 *r*, = 41%.)

The title of the cycle indicates that we are about to hear songs. However, a closer examination of this title reveals a deeper meaning. In Leśmian's works the words "song" and "singing" are always associated with poetic creation. Thus in his aesthetics, song is synonymous with *true* poetry. In this he follows Vico's belief in the primordial man as a natural poet, whose "primordial, emotional language must have been at the same time poetry and song."[27] Leśmian also adheres to the Romantic tradition in general, much of which was absorbed by Symbolist aesthetics. Just as Herder called poetry "the music of the

---

c) Anaphoric "rhymoids":
    Song I, st. 1, ln. 1, 3: Ja. . . .
                  Ja . . .
    Song I, st. 2, ln. 1, 2, 3: I. . . .
                  I. . . .
                  I . . .
    Song V, st. 5, ln. 1–4: Ja . . .
                  I . . .
                  I . . .
                  Ja . . .

III. Tautological rhyme considered as "smyslovaja rifma" ("connotational rhyme") (p. 300) in a) horizontal, b) vertical, c) horizontal and vertical correspondence (cf. p. 56):
  a)   Song II, st. 4, ln. 1: . . . mogil! // . . . mogil(a)
        Song V, st. 2, ln. 3: živu (vne) žizni
        Song V, st. 2, ln. 4: . . . son (vo) sne //
        Song V, st. 3, ln. 3: . . . moj // moimi
        Song V, st. 4, ln. 1: . . . groba zagrobnoj
  b)   Song III, st. 3, ln. 3, 4: . . . . // . . . neljubovnyj
                       I neljubovnaja // . . . (epanalepsis)
  c)   Song II, st. 4, ln. 4: smert' . . . // . . . smert' (horizontal)
        Song I, st. 3, ln. 3, 4: poklon . . . // (vertical)
                . . . . // . . . . . poklon

IV. The vertical inner rhyme:
    Song V, st. 4, ln. 3, 4: . . . . davno //
               . . . . za to //
    Song I, st. 1, ln. 1, 3: byl'*ja*
               byti*ja*

V. Morphological, syntactical parallelisms (p. 58):
    Song I, st. 1, ln. 2: i lesa i ruč'ja
    Song II, st. 3, ln. 3: zabavu i zateju
    Song IV, st. 3, ln. 2: u krasnykh u vorot

It is obvious from these fugue-like sound-orchestrations that the notion of "zvukovoj povtor" of any kind, as an organizing function in modern versification, is already dominant in Leśmian, just as it is in other Symbolists.

27. Vico, *New Science*, p. 68 (note 10, above). The first to stress the synonymity of primitive poetry and song, the Italian philosopher considred it of necessity "densely figurative" (see pp. 134–139). Vico's ideas were followed by Jean-Jacques Rousseau in his "Essai sur l'origine des langues," *Oeuvres complétes*, vol. 11 (Paris: A. Sautelet, 1826),

soul," and Novalis considered "music and poetry as synonymous,"[28] so did the Russian Romantics from Zhukovsky on follow the same line of thought. It was continued by Tyutchev, who also understood the magical thought of the soul as songs, as true poetry; by Fet, who said: "Ne znaju sam čto budu pet'"; and finally by the Symbolists, who looked upon all the great Russian writers of the nineteenth century as poets, "musicians of words," and therefore singers.[29] "Song" is definitely tied with melic folk poetry, particularly in Leśmian's case.

Leśmian, an acknowledged connoisseur of folklore, must have been well acquainted with the Russian proverb "skazka—skladka, pesnja—byl' " ("The tale is an invention, the song, a truth").[30] For his title he chose, not by accident, "songs" = "byl' " (truth = myth), that is, poetry *par excellence*. Nor is the choice of the singer's name accidental. The idea that the wisdom of the people inspired myth and was contained in myth was shared by Leśmian.[31] Therefore, Vasilisa Premudraja (Vasilisa the All-wise), a positive heroine of the *volšebnaja skazka*, as the incarnation of wisdom and of truth, symbolizes myth-creating, or poetry. *Pesni Vasilisy Premudroj* can be interepreted as poems about poetry, and therefore the title bears a decidedly metapoetic connotation.[32] If the *skazka* applies to Leśmian's mode of poetic creation, as that of poetry serving as a metaphysical utopia, then *pesnja = byl'* is his primary means of expressing metapoetic views. We shall see through textual analysis that his statement "I started in song that which I shall develop in that very song"[33] is in fact indicated in the first stanza of Song I (emphasis mine):

---

pp. 221-224. He states that "the first languages were song-like . . . figurative and, therefore, the language of poets." Similar views we find are also expressed by Hegel, et al.

28. See J. G. Herder, "Kritische Wälder," *Sämtliche Werke*, vol. 4 (Leipzig: Quelle & Meyer, 1925), p. 166. See also Friedrich von Hardenberg [Novalis], *Romantische Welt: Die Fragmente*, ed. Otto Mann (Leipzig: Dieterich, 1939), p. 313.

29. Cf. B. Bugaev [A. Belyj], "Nastojaščee i buduščee russkoj literatury," *Lug zelenyj: Kniga statej* (Moskva: "Al'ciona," 1910), p. 64.

30. P. G. Bogatyrev, *Russkoe narodnoe poètičeskoe tvorčestvo* (Moskva: Gosučpedizd., 1956), p. 295. Translation is by Jakobson, "On Russian Fairy Tales," p. 98.

31. Vico, *New Science*, p. 104, states that in the primitive states "myth-poetry expressed the wisdom of the people. . . . Wisdom was myth created elementally, in the process of man's perceiving the world surrounding him, and, therefore, he considers myth as the only truth."

32 The period of Young Poland abounds in metapoetic works, because of the writers' preoccupation with poetic form and their belief in "art for art's sake." The period of Symbolism may well be viewed as a source of the present-day upsurge of metaliterary works and studies.

33. Leśmian, "Św. Franciszek z Asyżu," *SL*, p. 425. Cf. also similar ideas expressed in "U źródeł rytmu," ibid., pp. 71-74.

Я - солнечная быль, я - мудрая царевна,

Любимица небес и леса и ручья, -

Я - <u>голос</u> <u>бытия</u> <u>таинственно</u> <u>запевный</u>, -

Всем обрученная и все же я - ничья!

The "zapevnyj," i.e., the mellifluousness, is emphasized by an effective sound-orchestration based on internal rhymes of "-ja" (supported by the repetitions of "-a") within stanza 1 (italicized vowels are stressed):

The horzontal anaphorical rhymoid (*ja*) of the first line is echoed in the second line in the final rhyme, and taken up in the third line as an internal rhyme within the first hemistich, to be again resumed in the unstressed caesura of the fourth line, and finally used in an internal rhyme of the second hemistich. The vowel "ja" appears in virtually every possible euphonic combination. The vertical scheme consists of a) an anaphorical parallelism—cf. lines 1 and 3; b) an epanalepsis—cf. lines 2 and 3; c) an internal heteroaccentual rhyme—cf. the first hemistichs of lines 3 and 4. The vertical pattern is enhanced by a "rhymoid" of a ring pattern, i.e., *-ja* appears in the initial and final stressed position of the entire stanza— cf. lines 1 and 4. Since the vowel "ja" means "I", its repetition emphasizes the *Ich-Lyrik* aspect of this poem. Furthermore, this elaborate pattern of rhymoids and external and internal rhymes serves euphonic, graphic, and ideological purposes. It is an apotheosis of the lyrical "I".

The genre of the cycle can be classified as a stylization of a "contaminated" (i.e., mixed genre) lyric folk song. It is analogous with the nature of the prototype, which like the *skazka* draws upon other folk genres. We find in this lyric song stylized proverbs, incantations, riddles, and elements of tales and epics (*byliny*). As indicated, the heroine is taken from the *volšebnaja skazka* which, in terms of genre, is considered closest to prehistorical folklore in drawing upon the active, elemental magic forces of an autonomous nature.

Few but important motifs of the fairy tale appear in this cycle. We have some allusions to the origin and the habitat of the wondrous heroine, the daughter of the *Car'* of the sea, usually referred to in *skazki* as the "golden stream."[34] They appear in Song I, stanzas 1, 3, 4: "Ljubimica . . . ruč'ja./ . . . . / V moem korallovom zakholust'e / . . . . / Menja ispolnil Bog . . . telom—žemčugom;" or in Song II, stanza 2: "Pleskajas' na slepo v žemčužnoj sumatokhe / Nevol'no-pennykh voln, . . ." All the elements referring to the heroine are part of the underwater realm. In the *skazka*, Vasilisa is always victorious because of her wisdom and truthfulness. The heroine's beloved is Ivan Carevič, who is a type of a *bogatyr'* since in the end he emerges as a positive hero, a brave and noble fighter for righteousness, always ready for sacrifice.[35] In this cycle he symbolizes the poet. Both heroes represent optimism, and prophecy the victory of poetic truth. This corresponds to their folklore characterization as the "nositeli vysokoj morali, vploščenie narodnykh idealov, [kotorye] pobeždajut tëmnye sily i dobivajutsja pravdy."[36] Vasilisa plays a dual role. She is the heroine of the cycle, the inspiration of myth-creation (as Bely would say: "Muza—skazok žilica"),[37] and the very product of that inspiration—a *byl'*-myth which represents true reality and, as a word-symbol, she is for Leśmian the Symbolist *the hero* of poetic creation.

The metapoetic title might lead us to anticipate programmatic statements frequent in Symbolist works. However, what we are presented with is hardly an obvious, programmatic poetry, in the manner of Verlaine's "Art poétique." Leśmian was against programs and definitions, which he considered the product of logic and therefore not of the creative realm.[38] In his poetry mere mention of the creative act

---

34. Y. M. Sokolov, "Folk Tales," Russian Folklore, tr. C. R. Smith (New York: The Macmillan Co., 1950), p. 423. Cf. also Propp, *Morphology*, p. 116 (note 8 above).

35. Cf. E. M. Meletinskij, *Geroj volšebnoj skazki*, ed. V. M. Žirmunskij (Moskva: Izd. vost. lit., 1958), p. 177 for characteristics of Vasilisa and p. 143 for characteristics of Ivan Carevič.

36. See È. V. Pomeranceva and S. I. Minc, eds., *Russkoe narodnoe poètičeskoe tvorčestvo: Khrestomatija*, 2d ed. (Moskva: Gosučpedizd., 1963), p. 178. The main source of Russian folk tales remains still A. N. Afanas'ev's *Narodnye russkie skazki* (Moskva: 1855–1860), an edition which, according to relatives and friends, Leśmian owned and used. He agrees with Afanas'ev's views on the magic tale as a means of utopia for the downtrodden, which has been promultaged by Veselovskij in *Istoričeskaja poètika*, p. 587 (note 11, above).

37. A. Belyj, *Poèzija slova* (Peterburg: Èpokha, 1922), p. 25.

38. Leśmian, "Przemiany rzeczywistości," *UR*, p. 184. This is how the poet expressed his viewpoint: "A definition is a transparent glass coffin in which the sacred body anointed with oil is put to rest." To Leśmian definitions were a part of "secondary reality,"

alludes to metapoetic intent. The text presents a lyrical heroine—
creation personified—whose monologue, an *Ich-Lyrik*, is addressed to
the second person, the "you"—Ivan Carevič. Vasilisa speaks of herself as
"sunny" myth, a utopian creation, and as the favorite of all natural and
supernatural elements. Unlike the traditional, confessional first person
lyric, it is interspersed with elements of folklore and of descriptive
narration, the latter being Leśmian's most characteristic means of mature poetic expression. See Song III, stanza 1; Song IV, stanza 1;
especially Song IV, stanza 2:

> Уж тени мнимые в глазах от света бродят,
>
> Стоит - не движется полуденный пожар,
>
> И волны замерли и золотом исходят,
>
> Как будто солнечный постигнул их удар!

This aggregate of devices widens the scope of intepretations, and engages
the reader's participation in decoding the heroine's thoughts, which are
presented in the process of development.

The "song" represents an important compositional and ideological
element in this cycle. In Leśmian's aesthetics, "song" as one of the key
symbols is an integral part of man's cognitive process, due to its specific
relationship to the word, "which [because of it] is first of all . . . a tool
of perceiving the world, a tool which defines this process and its result
as well"[39] As in the primordial past the word-symbol, combining music
and word into an indivisible whole, became the means of a "dialogue"
with nature, but also a means of distinguishing man from nature.
Similarly, the "song" captures the elusive magic, defined by Leśmian as
an "extralingual current"[40] which the "natural" word does not possess.
Hence, Vasilisa boasts (see Song I, stanza 1): "Ja *golos* bytija *tainstvenno
zapevnyj*" (italics mine). It is this magic capacity which allows the
heroine to inspire all, perceive the thoughts of autonomous natural

---

i.e., of "natura naturata," following the tenets of Erigena and Spinoza, to whom he
refers in some of his essays contained in his *Szkice Literackie*.

39. Ibid., p. 183.

40. The poet explains his idea about this specific "song" as a tone defying logic
and grammatical rules. The "extralingual current" contained in "song" (poetry) represents
to Leśmian this unique tone, which man has to emit in order to translate his being
into an interhuman, poetic language.

phenomena (e.g., Song I, stanza 2: "Ja znaju *mysl'* cvetov i *dumu* lunnykh blestkov"), the sorcery of the dream world as well as the forgotten myth of the primitive past (cf. same stanza: "*pesnju drjakhluju, čto mokhom porosla*") (italics mine). As the "song" is the subject and the object of the lyrical monologue, we may assume that Vasilisa is not only a heroine of a dual role, but the *porte-parole* of the poet as well. Since the behavior of the heroine is determined by the tradition of folklore, the author's point of view is expressed by a folkloric phraseology. Employing a structure based on "nonconcurrence of the phraseological and ideological planes,"[41] where folkloric stylization employed by a primitive narrator becomes the means of philosophical expression, Leśmian achieves various effects: the poet's spokesman Vasilisa, given a language suitable for her, is more convincing. At the same time this phraseological plane allows for a certain authorial distance, and therefore, for authorial objectivity.

The contrast of these two planes, usual for *skaz*, proves to be a useful device for Leśmian.[42] It allows the heroine to introduce herself and lets the reader witness her speaking inner thoughts aloud. In a sense the heroine herself represents a spatial antithesis: her declarations represent the external world, her meditations the internal one. Since Vasilisa symbolizes poetry as myth-creating, her thought process corresponds to the process of poetic creation itself.

As the first two quoted verses of Song I indicate, Vasilisa has a specific way of "materializing" poetic art. A primitive heroine, she expresses herself in "concrete" images drawn from a world familiar to her: the autonomous nature of which she is a part (see the first two verses cited below). In a world governed by anthropomorphism in which limits between man and nature are erased, Vasilisa combines the secrets of nature known to her with human creative magic: cf. Song I, stanza 2, lines 1 and 2; stanza 3, lines 3 and 4 (italics mine): "ja znaju mysl'

---

41. B. Uspensky, *A Poetics of Composition: The Structure of the Artistic Text and the Typology of a Compositional Form*, trans. V. Zavarin and S. Wittig (Berkeley, Los Angeles, London: University of California Press, 1973), p. 102. "The nonconcurrence of points of view on the phraseological and ideological levels takes place when the narration in a work is conducted from the phraseological point of view of a particular character, while the compositional aim of this work is to evaluate this character from some other point of view. Thus, on the level of phraseology a particular character [here Vasilisa] emerges as the vehicle of the authorial point of view while on the level of ideology she serves as its object."

42. Ibid. Uspensky finds this device characteristic of *skaz* narration, and an effective means of creating irony. However, the irony he has in mind follows the Greek etymology of the word *eironeia*, meaning "dissimulation." Here it would apply to Leśmian's disguise under Vasilisa's appearance.

cvetov i dumu lunnykh blestkov,/ . . . ./ I trepety nočej, i *tajny* perekrest-
kov,/ I *vodometnyj son* uprugogo vesla! / . . . ./ Ja mnogo pomnju
dnej i znaju naizust' ja/ Vsë to, čego nel'zja zapomnit' naizust'! . . ."
Thus poetry is presented as the result of a fusion of two realms. The contrast does not confine itself to these realms only.

The cycle *Pesni Vasilisy Premudroj*, as is characteristic of Leśmian's
poetics, is built on antithesis of various levels, starting with semantic
nonconcurrences, i.e., oxymora: "radostnaja grust' " and catachreses:
"dogadlivaja brov'," "vodometnyj son," etc., which Ju. Lotman also
refers to as "smyslovye nesootvetstvija."[43] The text—basically folkloric
in origin and intent (as exemplified by the title)—is also philosophical,
Symbolist in origin and intent. Ideological Symbolist categories, such as
the concept of myth and its origin and the process of the creative act as
a *creatio ex nihilo*, have been projected onto a stylized folkloric background, composed of elements of various folk genres, yielding thereby
greater semantic flexibility and variety. Finally, the text is also based on
the structural contrast between the fabular aspect (which represents
certain more personal episodes imparted by the heroine; cf. Song II,
stanzas 2 and 3; Song IV, stanza 2) and the generalizing, mythological,
i.e., universal aspect (cf. Song II, stanzas 1 and 4; also Song V).[44] These
various levels become the main ideological vehicle of the cycle.

As we can judge even by the first stanza of the cycle, the phraseological
level which we would expect to be essentially homogeneous in a folkloric
text is in effect often heterogeneous, i.e., of mixed stylistic levels. We
can detect two main patterns.

I. Vasilisa a) when describing herself (i.e., poetry) as an accom-
            plished fact, or
       b) when speaking about the general characteristics of
            poetry, or
       c) when alluding to the relationship of poetry and the poet,
uses a more concrete, yet densely ornamental and ceremonious language,
usually found in the *skazka*.[45] We find in pattern I examples of:

---

43. Lotman, *Struktura*, p. 337 (note 13, above). Even in this early stage, Leśmian's
poetics seem to fit remarkably close to most of the ideas expressed by the Russian
philologist, about sixty years later.

44. Cf. ibid., p. 258. Lotman calls the fabular aspect that which represents an
episode of reality, while the mythological one is a model of the universe as a whole.

45. Jakobson, "On Russian Fairy Tales," p. 96 (note 22, above). This is how the author
describes the style of a Russian folk tale. Vasilisa's language corresponds to that of the
primitive man who, according to Leśmian, was expressing himself and "thinking in
images." Cf. his "Znaczenie pośrednictwa . . .," *SL*, p. 47.

symbols (S), fixed epithets (E), topoi (T), and internal parallelism (P), which are characteristic of the traditional homogeneous phraseology of folklore. However, as pointed out earlier, Leśmian takes liberties with the stylization of folkloric tropes, preserving them only partially.[46]

Here are some examples for categories specified under I in which the retained part of the original trope is italicized:

a) *"Solnečnaja* byl' " (E), *"mudraja carevna"* (E), "s *ulybkoj jasnoju*" (E), *"vekovečnyj* dub" (E), "lebed' *skazočnyj"* (E), *"golos zapevnyj"* (E), *"byl'* " (S), *"lebed'* " (S).

Let us examine what these images mean. Poetry (*byl'*) is an optimistic utopian song; it is the road to wisdom and serenity. The legendary swan is here also a symbol of the maiden, and it may represent, in the poetic context, the immortality of the poetry as well (cf. Derzhavin's poem "Lebed' "). In addition, for the Symbolists of the second generation, the maiden is the Eternally Feminine Wisdom—"Sophia"—and the Soul of the Earth (i.e., "das ewig Weibliche" and the "Erdgeist"); while for Leśmian the maiden represents the Wisdom of the people. The pattern dealing with the attributes and the existence of poetry is described in Song I, stanza 4; stanza 5, line 1:

b) "Menja ispolnil Bog dušoju *blagovonnoj* (E),/ Dušoju - *rozoju* (S) i telom - *žemčugom* (S), -/ *Vdol' da po matuške* . . . (T) / . . . / Plyvët moja *lad'ja* (S), / . . . ./ Ona plyvët - poёt po *vetru-uraganu* (P)" (italics mine).

The first two lines deal with anthropomorphism and reification. God has filled Vasilisa with a sacred, love-filled soul.[47] He has given her the precious body of a pearl. Precious metals, stones and gems of the underwater kingdom have been an ancient source of fairy tales and poetry. Here the pearl symbolizes ultimate truth (*byl'*), i.e., perfect poetry resulting from the synthesis of the sacred and creative spirit and the word become flesh. The pearl stands also for the concreteness, stability, and *eternal value* of poetry-myth in contrast to the changes and

---

46. It should be pointed out that the validity of the "fixed epithets" has been questioned by scholars, among them Zhirmunsky, because the epithets were interchangable already in the texts of the seventeenth century *byliny*, thus their "postojanstvo" ("stability") is relative. Cf. A. P. Evgen'eva, *Očerk po jazyku russkoj ustnoj poèzii v zapisjakh XVII-XX vv.* (Moskva and Leningrad: Izd. Akad. Nauk SSSR, 1963), pp. 328, 330. In view of this fact, Leśmian's play with stylized epithets may be built upon solid precedents.

47. The epithet "blagovonnyj" may be a stylization alluding to the Church Slavic attribute "blagoukhannyj". Cf. "blagoukhanie" used in such genres as the *Žitie*. Fragrance emanating from the body attested to the sainthood of the protagonist. According to Leśmian, the soul and body represent the fusion of the immortal, creative element of poetry with its earthly, material manifestations. See "Pieśni ludowe," *SL*, pp. 390–391.

transitoriness of nature.[48] (Cf. Song I, stanza 3, lines 1 and 2: "V moëm *korallovom* podvodnom zakholust'e/ Est' *žizn' bessmertnaja* . . . ." [italics mine].)

The semantic tautology of the juxtaposed images is reinforced by the epanalepsis (or repetition) "dušoju" in the second and third hemistich (cf. "dušoju *blagovonnoj/* Dušoju-rozoju"), and by the parallelisms in the second line (heteroaccentual internal rhyme used in the manner of *byliny*, typical of Leśmian's "embryonic rhymes").[49] All these devices emphasize the concreteness and unity of the two components in this static image, which is transformed in the subsequent three lines into a kinetic image both by means of the Romantic motif of a wandering heroine-poetry and by the frequently used motif of water-mirror reflection expressing the duality of dream and reality,[50] adapted by Symbolists, juxtaposed here with a folk topos and changed to suit Leśmian's need.

The *locus communis* "vdol' da po matuške Volge" is altered and the topos image inverted. The boat (i.e., its water reflection: "vdol' . . . lazuri nebosklonnoj") is flowing down the heavens. For Leśmian the boat signifies creative poetic life, as attested by his statement: "In *a song—a boatman* flows through the sea."[51] The dreamlike life of *true* poetry moves on "singing" despite the storms described emphatically by a semantic tautology of the synonymical pair: "vetru-uraganu"[52] while the internal rhyme: "plyvët—poët" indicates the equation of living-singing with the act of poetic creation.

The last two lines of Song I exemplify pattern

c) *Poklon* emu (T) v bylom—*careviču Ivanu* (S)—

   Za tridevjat' zemel' (T)—moj *carstvennyj* poklon (E): (italics mine).

They are directed to the prince in love with Vasilisa the poet, about

---

48. Cf. J.-P. Bayard, *Le monde souterrain* (Paris: Flammarion, 1961), where great attention is given to the subject of the origin and symbolism of precious metals and stones in tales and poetry. Cf. also M. Podraza-Kwiatkowska, "Symbolika kreacji artystycznej," *Młodopolskie harmonie i dysonanse* (Warszawa; P.I.W., 1969), dealing with the same subject.

49. Cf. Žirmunskij, *Rifma* (note 26, above), where we have examples of internal rhymes found in *byliny* in which the lack of phonetic correspondence of stress ("raznoudarnye rifmy") is compensated for by morphological correspondence of the endings (p. 273: "po carju-gradu po Kievu"). The author defines them as "embryonic" rhymes. Cf. fn. 26.

50. Cf. O. Maslenikov, "Russian Symbolists: The Mirror Theme and Allied Motifs," *The Russian Review* 16 (January 1957):42–52. Cf. Leśmian, "U źródeł rytmu," *SL*, p. 71. For similar ideas see also "Z rozmyślań o Bergsonie," *SL*, p. 41.

51. Leśmian, "Z rozmyślań o Bergsonie," *SL*, p. 41.

52. The "synonymical pairs" are often used as an intensifying device in folklore. Cf. Evgen'eva, *Očerk po jazyku russkoj ustnoj poèzii*, pp. 260–267.

whom she sings and to whom she sends regards to the land "way beyond thrice nine lands".

Both verses abound in authentic and stylized topoi and folkloric devices, representing a "homogeneous" phraseology. We may conclude that Leśmian considers the imagery of folklore a suitable metapoetic vehicle, especially when poetry is regarded as a concrete entity—as an accomplished fact—a precious gem ("žemčug").

II. However, while evoking the process of poetic creation through her feelings and thoughts, Vasilisa uses a language of mixed levels. It is a highly poetic language containing, in addition to folk stylization (F), a juxtaposition of archaisms (A), high poetic words (HP), colloquialisms (C), and images based on tautology (TT) and on catachreses and oxymora, some of which may be referred to as "synaesthetic epithets" (SE) or "antithetical epithets" (AE).[53] The (SE) and (AE) represent in themselves semantic neologisms (SN), since they resemanticize the natural language.[54]

Let us look at some examples:

F) "utro krasnoje," "u krasnykh u vorot"

A) "tverd'," "lad'ja"

HP) "blagoukhannyj," "gusljarnyj"

C) "namedni," "mudrenee," "nipočem," "zolotom iskhodit"

N) Here the neologisms, except for the (SE) and (SN), are not extraordinary; they are mostly

1) compound adjectives: "tainstvenno-zapevnyj," "nevol'no-pennye," "obil'no-sladkaja," "uzorčato-cvetnye"

2) adjectives: "nebosklonnaja," "perezoločennyj," "žiznepodobnyj"

3) nouns built on antinomies: "neljubov'," "bezbrežnost' " (also used by Russian Symbolists)

4) singularia tantum used in the plural: "koldovstva"

5) adverbs whose morphological structure could be an assimilation of the Polish comparative or of a rarely used poetic Russian form: "vidimej," "neožidannej"

SE) "blagoukhannyj grom"

---

53. The first category (i.e., SE) was defined by Čiževskij, "Bolesław Leśmian," p. 264 (note 2, above). The second (i.e., AE) is discussed by B. Tomaševskij, *Teorija literatury, poètika* (Moskva: Gosizd., 1928), p. 36.

54. Cf. Lotman, *Struktura*, p. 116. The author refers to this type of neologism as "snjatie zapretov," the result of destruction of the "zveno sintagmatiki," which may even occur "within one semantic unit—a word, or within phraseological combinations, to which the great majority of lexical neologisms belong." This type of neologism applies to Leśmian's poetic idiom.

AE) "radostnaja grust'," "molitvoju grekhovnoj," "svjataja neljubov'," "nežnoj neljubvi"

SN) "dogadlivaja brov'," "poludennyj požar," "vodometnyj son,"
"korally nalivnye," "nevidimyj serp," "(lad'ja) okovannaja
snom," "nebosklonnaja lazur'," "žemčužnaja-sumatokha"

TT) "moljus' molitvoju."

Such tautologized expressions are frequently used as a means of intensifying emotion and thought in folklore, particularly in lyrical songs. In
general, Leśmian has a tendency to create autonomous, derivative words
of identical roots in the manner of Russian folklore, which R. Jakobson
treats as "etymological figures."[55] They represent to the poet an identification of a thing with itself.

As we survey these examples, we realize that not only are they the
elements of a diversified phraseology, but are also, in themselves, images
based on semantic contrast. This is evident even in nouns of the type
"neljubov'."[56] Defying the word associations of natural language, most
of the (SN) examples bear the seed of antithesis, which, as we shall
see, is the basis of Leśmian's aesthetics and of his style, especially
when he speaks of the creative process.

Leśmian as the proponent of a creative evolution freely resorts to
antithesis in his idiom for the purpose of dramatization and hence
dynamization of various forms of poetic expression, such as descriptive
narrative. The neologisms with a negative prefix can be considered
the smallest unit of dramatization. Tautology provides Leśmian with the

---

55. R. Jakobson, "The Kernel of Comparative Slavic Literature," *Harvard Slavic
Studies* I (Cambridge: Harvard University Press, 1953): 9. The term "etymological
figures" was attributed by the author to words based on tautology. Cf. also his study,
"Poetyka w świetie językoznawstwa," *Pamiętnik Literacki*, Warszawa, 2(1960):431–473, in
which he points out that due to tautology, Leśmian's words attain an intensification of
semantics and even an autonomous lexical existence. Cf. also A. Sandauer, "Filozofia
Leśmiana," *Poeci trzech pokoleń* (Warszawa: "Czytelnik," 1962), p. 22, who demonstrates
that the strong tendency toward tautological images in Leśmian's poetic idiom serves
several functions. Repetition makes the image stand out, become more concrete. Leśmian
seems to be attracted to objects rather than to their attributes. He believes the object to
be more durable in the evolutionary process of existence. Therefore, in order to fortify the
noun, he creates tautological verbs. As Sandauer points out, "this tendency has its
counterpart in phenomenology, which attempts to define the objects in themselves,
their 'proper *what*'—as Husserl, the father of that school, would say."

56. Nouns and verbs of contrasting prefixes prevail especially in Leśmian's mature Polish
poetry, creating the effect of a paradox. They often represent a syntactical shortcut:
e.g., the verb "*za-nie*-istnieć," where a whole sentence dealing with the process of beginning,
continuity, and ceasing to exist has been replaced by the verb-neologism. This method
seems to point to folklore, more specifically to the riddle, as its source. See Stone,
Bolesław Leśmian: The Poet and His Poetry (note 1, above). Cf. also the valuable
study by J. Sławiński, "Semantyka poetycka Leśmiana," *Studia o Leśmiane*, ed. M.
Głowiński and J. Sławiński (Warszawa: P.I.W., 1971), pp. 103–117.

means of dynamization of an image or of a state: "moljus' molitvoju," which is, however, limited to a dynamization of a vicious circle. However, in order to depict the flux of the creative process and the fusion of various realms, he resorts to the dynamization of tropes, by juxtaposing various levels of expression (as illustrated by the [SN] above). This process causes one image to flow into another, resulting often in a semantic shift, especially apparent in the following image (cf. Song I, stanza 2): "vodometnyj son uprugogo vesla," where the attribute of the oar has been shifted to the *dream*, alluding to its fecundity, to its creative powers. Here, as elsewhere in Leśmian,[57] the "dream-land" seems to be ideal for abolishing all barriers between various realms of existence.

The first stanza of Song II, as a prelude to the creative process, reveals especially clearly the role of the fairy tale element which serves Leśmian as "a rainbow bridge uniting us with the illogical realm of existence, with the . . . precipice of mystery,"[58] that is, with poetic creation. Only in this realm could existence and nonexistence, reality and dream, the cognizable and the unknown, merge. By contrasting phraseology in the two distichs Leśmian is able to declare directly through Vasilisa his understanding of myth (emphasis mine):

С улыбкой ясною твержу я неустанно

Мою пословицу: где сказка - там и Бог!

И удивляю мир тревожный и туманный

Разоблачением невиданных дорог!

In Leśmian's aesthetics the wisdom of the world lies exclusively in myth creation which, according to him, is *true* divinity, God, and a constant process of discovering new existences.[59] While the idea in the first distich is stated in folkloric language, the second distich describes

---

57. There is hardly a single poem of Leśmian in which "dream" or synonyms for "dream" do not occur. To take just a few examples from the poem "Beglyj son" in his Russian cycle *Lunnoe pokhmel'e*: "Ja - tvoj blednyj *son*, neponjatnyj *son*/ . . . ./ *Son* prisnilsja ej, *son* po nej bežit!/ . . . . / Ja svobodnyj *son* . . . ," etc.

58. Leśmian, "Z rozmyślań . . . ," *SL*, p. 31, passim.

59. Ibid., pp. 42–43.

the potentialities of poetry in a highly poetic language. Here the image is based on some semantic equivalence (cf. *tuman* with *oblako*), where the "beclouded" world ("tumannyj mir") is "declouded" ("razoblače-niem"). Thus we have an example of resemanticization, since Leśmian has returned to "razoblačenie" some of its original etymological meaning.

With the charming naîveté of a simple narrator (or *bakhar'*), Vasilisa leads into the mystery of the creative process in Song II, stanza 2 (emphasis mine):

Плескаясь на слепо в жемчужной суматохе

Невольно-пенных волн, заплетенных в венец,

В начале расскажу и ужасы, и вздохи,

Чтоб неожиданней был радостный конец.

The creative process, represented by thoughts on the inner reality of the poet, conveyed through Vasilisa, takes place in her natural habitat. Owing to the concreteness of the imagery (see the first distich), we can see and hear the bustle of various elements in the water. The "strange" sound of the synaesthetic image "žemčužnoj sumatokhe" is juxtaposed with images presenting motion, precipitateness, accidental action (cf. "voln," "na slepo," "zapletennykh," "nevol'no"), reflecting the unpredictability of the creative process, and demonstrating a tendency to attach attributes or actions of one phenomenon to the other. Here the attribute "žemčužnoj" is selected as an analogy to the word symbolizing poetry. "The creative process approximates the first language, a collection of first elements of poetry, an imitation of resounding, active, evermoving nature . . . animated by interjection of human feeling."[60]

An example of shifting meaning in this stanza is the word "pleskat'-sja," usually associated with waves and the sea but here connected with Vasilisa, who blindly and precipitately splashes amidst the pearly bustle of the involuntarily foaming waves, intertwined into a wreath. The last image may insinuate the "crowning" of the poetic process, if we follow the Russian proverb: "konec delu venec" ("all is well that ends

---

60. Abrams, *The Mirror and the Lamp*, p. 82 (note 10, above).

well"). This could be a likely interpretation, judging by the rhyme "radostnyj konec." In Leśmian's and the Symbolists' aesthetics, myth, defying causality, is an unexpected, joyous expression of truth.

Equal in importance to the stylistic patterns are the sound patterns, to which folklore also ascribes semantic significance. In this case, the lexical imagery is supported, correspondingly, in the first two lines by euphonic patterns which help to realize the idea. Here we encounter inversion within syllables as an effective onomatopoeic device: "ples—slep" recreates the splashing and hissing, and moreover the ebb and the flow of the waves,[61] as does the following pattern: "vol'n—pen—, voln—plet—." The orchestration of alternating continuant and plosive consonants *v*, *p*, recreates the foaming sounds of the waves, while the sound metaphor "nevol'no-pennykh voln" strengthens the idea of the involuntariness of the creative process.

The prattling of the last two lines of Song II, stanza 2, emphasized by the partial inversion "S(k)ažu-užas," alternates with self-assured declaration (emphasis mine):

И, веря, что игра - заботы мудренее,

Я всеми чарами за правду постою!

И мне легко найти забаву и затею,

И я горжуся тем, что слез не признаю!

Для сказок нет могил! Единая могила -

Лишь эта знойная, заоблачная твердь!

In the initial lines the manner of folk narration consists of juxtaposing syntactical variants. A stylized proverb is followed by a maxim and two declarations. The last distich represents aphorisms on a higher poetic level. In addition this collage-like stylistic structure is a retardation device. It interrupts the narrative flow describing the creative process. The use of asyndeton (lines 1, 5-6, above), typical of stylized proverb

---

61. Tomaševskij, *Teorija literatury*, pp. 60-68, esp. p. 63, where this type of inversion is referred to as "obratnyj khiatičeskij povtor." Cf. also S. Pirkova-Jakobson in her "Introduction to the First Edition" in Propp, *Morphology*, p. XX (note 8, above), particularly her emphasis on the significance of sound patterns.

structure, is also an effective retardation device because of the repetitive quality in which the sequence of time corresponds to a sequence of action and of thought. In this stylization of the Russian proverb "utro večera mudrenee," the word "igra" alludes to the Symbolist concept of creation as an "umnoe vesel'e."[62] In the following maxim the word "silami" is replaced by the word "čarami," with which it can be considered almost synonymous in this fairy tale context.

The somewhat static quality of the first two declaration lines and their thought pattern is supported by the following two polysyndetic lines of reassurance. The anaphoric parallelism "I mne," "I ja," emphasizes this declaration structurally. Myth-creating, regarded as fun and play, stands for optimism and for truth. As such, it is immortal, as Vasilisa concludes in her final direct statement. The only grave for myth is earthly reality. Here we have a metaphor "zaoblačnaja tverd' " (which for Romantic poetry signifies the heavenly realm) depicting the two contrasting realms: the crusty, beclouded earth and the heavenly realm of fairy tale. In this stanza the poet has again utilized a stylized folkloric phraseology to allow poetry to express, through Vasilisa, his ideas on poetry.

Song III uses a simultaneously spatial, lexical, and syntactical change to describe the creative process. The sunny, optimistic atmosphere of the realm of poetic achievement gives way to the magic of moonlit infinity, under the spell of which the myth-creating begins (italics mine): "Kogda v bezbrežnosti luna vozdušno bleščet,/ I *zolotitsja snom dogadlivaja brov',-*/ . . . v grudi trepeščet/ Obil'no-sladkaja, *svjataja neljubov'! . . ./ . . . ./*" Cf. stanza 2: "Ja čuvstvuju eë k minute probužden'ja/ Ot *sna zamorskogo* i polnogo čudes,/ . . . ." Cf. stanza 3: "No ja moljus' togda *molitvoju grekhovnoj-*/ Da ne kosnetsja den' moikh nedvižnykh pleč!" Vasilisa's anticipation of fruitful creativity is expressed by means of a synecdoche: "dogadlivaja brov'," as the "gilded" dream-like trance envelopes her. In Leśmian's poetics the verb "zolotit'sja" is equivalent to "singing," both of which are synonymous with poetic creation (cf. fn. 48). Since dream represents poetry, according to Vasilisa's subsequent statement, the synaesthetic image "zolotitsja snom" tells of myth-creating in progress. The ripening of poetry is, according to Leśmian, a sweet and divine, but "iconoclastic" process. His poetry represents theodicy. The (AE) juxtaposition in the ninth line emphasizes this creative divine iconoclasm. It should be stated that in the cycle (see Song V, stanza 4) Leśmian refers to God as a

---

62. Leśmian, "U źródeł rytmu," *SL*, pp. 71, 73. "*With a song to work* man builds his boat [life]." "The joy of song comes through creation." Cf. also Vjač. Ivanov, "O vesëlom remesle i umnon veselii," in *Po zvëzdam. Stat'i i aforizmy* (St. Petersburg: Izd. "Ory," 1909), pp. 196–197.

finality—a "staryj obryv"—an "Abgrund."[63] In contrast to Him, poetry —as an incarnation of divinity—is timeless, boundless, created "ot sna zamorskogo i polnogo čudes," and represents another, wondrous realm— a third existence.

In Song III, stanza 4, poetry—ripened after the dream of the night—is heralded by the fixed epithet "utro krasnoe" in line 1: "No utro krasnoe, čto v solnce nočevalo." Here again poetry, the result of the creative act, is seen in the concrete image of the sun, a natural phenomenon, whose fixed epithet "krasnoe solnyško" is shifted to "utro." In the songs the moon, the sun, the dream, and shadow are among the main motifs derived from folklore. Once again Vasilisa uses folkloric phrasing in the third line: "Ja znaju: son isčez! Ja znaju: solnce vstalo!" Its syntactical, rhythmical, and internal rhyme parallelisms emphasize the elation, making it sound like a *song* of joy. Still more ingenious is the euphonic parallelism: "Ja znaju: son . . . ! Ja znaju: solnce . . . !" Utilizing the phonetic equivalent of *son* and *so(l)n-ce*, the poet emphasizes the idea that the dream has given rise to a dream, i.e., to poetry (cf. "solnečnaja byl' "). This singing phrase announces the climax expressed in Song IV, stanza 1, line 2 (emphasis mine):

Пылают облака узорчато-цветные,

Струится в воздухе <u>благоуханный гром</u>!₀..

Поспели уж к весне <u>кораллы наливные</u>,

Люблю их пожинать невидимым серпом!

All the unintelligible, natural sounds of the creative stages are merged into a "fragrant thunder" (into a "sacred" one; see fn. 47), into *true* poetry, expressed by a synaesthetic metaphor (cf. line 2). The songs have ripened like "juicy corals" ready to be harvested. This image contains a shift of meaning in the verb. The line could be considered as a semantic tautology, since "spelyj" means "ripe". Therefore the phrase could be read as: "pospeli . . . korally spelye." The metaphor presents

---

63. The theme of night as a conducive atmosphere for creativeness is inherited from Romanticism. Here we have also some echoes of Tyutchev's idea about the cosmic chaos, as well as the *Leitmotif* of the Schellingean "Abgrund." Cf. F. Schelling, *Schriften zur Identitätsphilosophie*, vol. 3 (reprint ed., Müchen: Beck, 1958–59). However, Leśmian deviates in the understanding of the "abyss" from the German philosopher, who sees in the chaos of man's psyche a microcosm of the dissonance reigning in the cosmos. For the Polish poet, "abyss" is always connected with the image of God.

poetry again as a concrete image of something precious, of a gem. It also has a spatial function reminding us that the act of poetic materialization has taken place in Vasilisa's underwater realm. In the fourth line the word "serp" has a dual connotation: as the sickle and "the moon" under whose spell the harvest takes place.

The motifs of shadow, dream, and reverie, often associated with the continuing, flowing creative process, are now replaced by the image of poetry as a golden liquid, immobilized by a sunstroke. Cf. Song IV, stanza 2:

Уж тени мнимые в глазах от света бродят,

Стоит — не движется полуденный пожар,

И волны замерли и золотом исходят,

Как будто солнечный постигнул их удар!

Here again the image is underlined by euphonic patterns emphasizing the change from a kinetic image into a static one. In the image "teni mnimye brodjat" the syllabic twins (term coined by V. Markov), which usually occur in the initial or final position of words, transgress here the word boundaries of the subject and attribute; cf. "ni-mnim" recreating the flow of the moving shadows. Yet, in line 2, the syllabic twins "po-po" ("poludennyj požar"), appearing in their usual position, serve an opposite function by stressing the, shall we say, static quality of the image, which in addition is hyperbolized (cf. "žara" substituted by "požar"). The static quality is furthered in lines 3 and 4 by "rhymoids" built on the principle of sound parallelism, consisting of syllables with corresponding stressed vowels. The sounds are associated with tangible matter: "I volny . . . zolotom iskhodjat,/ Kak budto solnečnyj. . . ."

Confident of her myth-creating and regenerating powers, Vasilisa longs to create a last immortal fairy tale, "kotoraja pridët, no ne projdët!" (see Song IV, stanza 3, lines 3 and 4). The epanaleptic, embryonic rhyme of the second hemistich in line 3, with the initial clause of line 4, and the internal ring-rhyme in the second hemistich of the line seem to emphasize this idea acoustically with the ending "-ët" resembling an echo. The creative process starts again; cf. stanza 4, lines 3 and 4: "ču . . . *lebed'* skazočnyj vstrevožil glad' zaliva . . ./ Ču! . . .vremja dvižetsja! . . . net vremeni vo mne!" The interjection "ču" bids us be silent and listen. Indeed, the "legendary maiden" (myth) has stirred the waters. The anaphora stresses the resumed flow of creative process, and the "zvukovye povtory," considered as rhymoids: "*vrem*-ja," "*vrem*-eni," emphasize its timelessness.

Vasilisa now creates her fifth and last song which, as we shall see, is immortal, i.e., it knows no time. In this last song the heroine embodies Leśmian's ideas on poetic creation: "These songs arise as an unconscious blind and magical feeling, created within itself and by itself . . . The goal is sweet and nameless, but in her loving madness and delirium there is as much knowledge as lack of knowledge . . . as much joy as there is suffering . . . She knows and does not know her lover. . . . She knows and does not know where she is running to. . . ."[64] Indeed these words could be considered as a blueprint for the cycle and especially for the last song, were they not written five years later. Throughout the cycle, except for the first and last songs, in which the poetry is presented in a finished form, we are a witness to Vasilisa's process of thinking about the poetic creative act. We discover its realization in successive creative stages.

A textual analysis of Song V will demonstrate in what way it corresponds to Leśmian's ideas quoted above:

Я та, которой нет - но есть мои мечтанья,

И слышен шопот мой повсюду - на цветах,

Не чужд и мне живой огонь существованья,

И Богу я могу присниться в небесах!

Я знаю суетность разгаданных заклятий

И дивно не хочу быть видимей Любви,

И, как она, живу - вне жизни, вне объятий!

Я - только сон во сне! Я - бред в твоей крови!

---

64. Leśmian, "Pieśni ludowe," *SL*, p. 391.

Но мною бредит лес, и ветер за горами,

И вековечный дуб, склонившийся к пруду, -

И светится мой взор, моими колдовствами

Перезолоченный в полночную звезду!

И дружбою своей до гроба и загробной

Дарят меня давно богатыри всех стран!

Люби меня за то, что я жизнеподобна, -

За то, что нет меня, царевич мой Иван!

This last poem is the most unpredictable and enigmatic of the cycle, and forms a fitting climax. It starts out with Vasilisa's direct statement, an aphorism of what poetry really is and is not. Poetry is an idea derived from the creative thought process (see the second hemistich in the opening line). Therefore, as a poem dealing with the essence of poetry, the song is *metapoetic*. The heroine, Leśmian's spokesman, expresses the poet's concept of poetry emanating from his belief in the *poetic word*, which begets poetry of its own. This is the most *programmatic* song of the cycle *Pesni Vasilisy Premudroj*, although an absence of dogma and of causal logic makes it differ from a real program.

The song is built on the negation and antithesis of a riddle, one of the oldest folkloric genres. Hence the contrast, encountered previously on various levels of poetic expression, has now emerged as the very incarnation of Leśmian's poetry. Let us examine its correlation to the riddle. It has been said that the riddle reflects the people's perception of the world: "It retained its primordial mythological character."[65] More than in other folkloric genres, the goal of the riddle is to develop in man a poetic view of reality. Therefore, it has an element of intellectual play. Customarily in fairy tales, it is the wise maiden who poses the riddle, the essence of which is a description of a phenomenon which is not named directly. Therefore, the language and the ideas of most riddles are enigmatic, as they have been since primitive times. The play of varied ideas is achieved by means of contrasting and often contradictory word associations (such as oxymora and catachreses, which

---

65. F. Buslaev, *Istoričeskie očerki*, vol. 1 (St. Petersburg, 1861), p. 33.

in this study were labeled [SN]), by strange imagery and daring metaphors.

All the statements on the riddle so far correspond to the cycle *Pesni Vasilisy Premudroj*, and apply especially to the last song. It corresponds in form to an extended riddle in which there are no obvious questions and answers given. (Like many creators of literary riddles, Leśmian develops the contradictory at the expense of the descriptive.) It also represents the object (poetry) speaking in the first person. Here the negation is inherent in the very subject: *contradictio in subiecto.* We find in almost all the stanzas of Song V an affirmation followed by negation. Especially in the first stanza the poetic idiom, partly based on stylized folkloric phraseology, is direct and transparent, almost devoid of metaphors, and yet it is highly abstract in meaning. The riddle structure is apparent in the syntax of the first line of the song, as Vasilisa declares that poetry does not exist as a reflection of mundane reality, yet it does exist after all, as a result of the inspirational powers of reverie and intuition. As such it can dwell in both realms: the real and the beyond, and can even influence the dreams of God. The element of reality in these dreams is made tangible by the association with the lyrical "I," the personification of myth. It is Leśmian's belief that these antinomies confirm "the constant and necessary contact of our logical thinking with the other, the illogical one, without which the first cannot exist, if it wants to create and investigate."[66] Therefore, myth contains an element of reality, as expressed in the third line by the metaphor "živoj ogon' suščestvovan'ja." We have a juxtaposition of nonexistence and existence which, as is the case in a riddle, is constantly questioned. A use of the hyperbole "povsjudu" in the second line gives the idea of the omnipresence of poetry, although in the following clause it is limited to flowers. We detect an element of antithesis in the "Ja ta . . . - no . . . ," of the first line, while the assertion of Vasilisa's inherent powers is expressed by the aphorism in the last line: "I Bogu ja mogu . . ." and emphasized by its heteroaccentual internal rhyme.

The second stanza expresses the poet's creed. Vasilisa admits her awareness of the futility of "secondary truths" using a highly poetic metaphor: "suetnost' razgadannykh zakljatij," which refers to the futility of art that has lost its magic, an apt representation of Leśmian's philosophy on creation.[67] In contrast, the lyrical heroine (and through

---

66. Leśmian, "Z rozmyślań . . . ," *SL*, pp. 37–38. This corresponds to Lotman's idea that we achieve full comprehension through the combination of intuition and logic (Lotman, *Struktura*, p. 36).

67. The futility of "razgadannye zakljatija" represents phenomena which are removed, for the purpose of inquiry, from the creative realm, i.e., "true reality"—*natura naturans,*

her the poet) wants her song to be as *true* and invisible as *Love,* since poetry, an intuitive creation, dwells mostly outside the realm of material life and ripens on its own. (This idea was expressed much later in Leśmian's Polish metapoetic poem "Zamyślenie" ["Meditation"].) Here the poet, using the Calderonian idea "La vida es sueño," lets Vasilisa speak of dream-myth as a dream within the dream of life, and as the irrational element born of the delirium in the poet's blood.[68]

The last two lines of the second stanza of Song V, dealing with the existence and nonexistence of poetry-myth, are appropriately of a riddle-like structure.[69] The syntactical parallelisms based on tautology and on repetitive negations (frequent also in Russian folksongs and epics): "živu—vne žizni, vne ob"jatij!" lead to the climactic revelation of the last line, in which the tautological image "son vo sne" is the key symbol to Leśmian's poetics. Its content indicates the elusiveness, the "momentary mythology"[70] of poetry, while as a formal tautological device it builds upon dynamization of the vicious circle; cf. "moljus' molitvoju." The circularity here is appropriate for ascribing to Vasilisa philosophical thoughts on her existence which imply the poet's viewpoint on poetry and life.

Despite the elusiveness of myth, its oscillation between existence and nonexistence, its eternal quality, symbolized by "vekovečnyj dub," is acknowledged by nature. The sorcery of myth is sufficient to change it into a "regilded midnight star." (Cf. line 4: "perezoločennyj v polnočnuju zvezdu.") In this stanza the repetition of personal and possessive pronouns referring to the lyrical "I" ("No mnoju, moj, moimi") is a tautological device of a myth asserting its existence as if preparing for the declaration of the last stanza. The repetitive device of assertion of the lyrical "I" is characteristic for Leśmian's mature poetry (cf. his

---

into the realm of "secondary reality"—*natura naturata,* where they become statistical entities enriching the museums of civilized man. Like A. Blok, Leśmian saw an antithesis between culture and civilization, the latter feeding on creations of culture, which is organized not by man but by the "spirit of music," that is by the primordial, creative spirit. For a discussion of the above, see V. Ivanov et al., "Tezisy k semiotičeskomu izučeniju kul'tur," *Semiotyka i struktura tekstu,* ed. M. R. Mayenowa (Wrocław, Warszawa, Kraków: Wydawnictwo P.A.N., 1973), p. 10.

68. We find an elaboration of these ideas in the *Szkice Literackie* ("Literary Sketches"), and echoes of them in his most enigmatic, metapoetic work "Słowa do pieśni bez słów" (Words to a Song Without Words"), from the third volume of his Polish poetry, *Napój cienisty* ("Shadowy Potion").

69. See Sokolov, *Russian Folklore,* pp. 282–289 (note 34, above), for a formal and ideological discussion of the genesis of the riddle. Cf. also V. P. Anikin, *Russkie narodnye poslovicy, pogovorki, zagadki i detskij fol'klor* (Moskva: Gosučpedizd., Min. RSFSR, 1957), pp. 54–86.

70. Sandauer, "Filozofia Leśmiana," p. 19 (note 55, above).

third volume *Napój cienisty*), where it expresses his desperate attempt at clinging to earthly existence. Here the repetition "do groba i zagrobnoj" serves further to concretize the forever self-renewed existence of poetry-myth which is admired by the *bogatyri*—poets of all times.

The last two lines in stanza 4 represent a final antithesis, an apostrophe to the hero Ivan Carevič—the poet. Her imploring for his love is expressed formally by various repetitions: 1) pronominal paradigmatic ones: "menja, ja, menja, moj"; 2) an internal rhyme and a syntactical phrase parallelism using an epiphora: "Ljubi menja *za to*, čto *ja*. . . ./ *Za to*, čto net me*nja*, ..."; 3) the internal rhyme of the initial phrases of lines 1 and 2: "Darjat menja davn*o* . . . ./ Ljubi menja za t*o*. . . ." Vasilisa wants to be loved for the antithesis inherent in her, for her lifelike qualities, and for her nonexistence. The neologism "žiznepodobna" has a profound meaning, contrary to Čiževskij's view.[71] In fact it is the basis of Leśmian's aesthetics. Poetry is a microcosm of life. The poem-"song" is saturated with 1) rhythm, 2) sounds, 3) colors, 4) smells of a mythic, yet palatable world, exemplified by 1) "po vetru—uraganu," "nevol'no—pennykh voln"; 2) "struitsja . . . grom!"; 3) "pylajut oblaka uzorčato—cvetnye"; 4) "blagoukhannyj grom." As a "momentary myth" it captures the phenomena of life in flux, and therefore it is also *lifelike*. In addition, as Vasilisa declares above, poetry is a riddle, a dream within the riddle of the dream of life.[72]

The cycle *Pesni Vasilisy Premudroj* follows, in a sense, a ring structure. The first and the last stanzas represent poetry as an established fact. Here Vasilisa is credible, using a language of her own—concrete, lapidary and dynamic in style—suggesting her strong convictions. In other stanzas dealing with the creative process we have a strange, "haphazard" word juxtaposition, typical of Leśmian's poetic idiom in general, which Vasilisa calls "pričudlivaja reč' " (see Song III, stanza 3) because it has not crystalized into "song." Hence, the language she uses is not yet her own. Only after having attained true poetry culminating in a "fragrant thunder" (see fn. 47) does she return to her own phraseology. Both the first and the last song end with Vasilisa as myth addressing her lover Ivan Carevič—the poet.

---

71. Čiževskij, "Bolesław Leśmian," p. 263 (note 2, above).

72. Cf. the Greek riddle in K. Ohlert, *Rätsel und Rätselspiele der alten Griechen* (Berlin: Mayer und Müller, 1912), p. 137, which parallels Song V: "The one who sees is watchful, this one does not see me; I am seen only by the one who does not see, and the one who does not speak, this one speaks, and the one that does not run, this one runs; I am a deceitful phantom, but I speak the truth." It should be pointed out that there is a similar riddle form in the Hindu epic *Rigveda*, echoes of which we find in Leśmian's later poetry, which abounds in enigmatic, mysterious, riddle-like elements. They form the core of Leśmian's poetry.

It would appear that Leśmian uses the stylized folkloric phraseology primarily for those metapoetic purposes where poetry can be expressed in concrete terms. The use of different levels of language during the creative process may be interpreted as an authorial intrusion, investing Vasilisa with an idiom characteristic of Leśmian's mature poetry. This is reasonable, as the subject is poetic creation and the cycle represents the very process, a stage of creating a poetic idiom and a poetic creed of its own. Leśmian describes the process of attaining a true "song"-poem as: "The impetus of a song, listening and looking ahead toward the final stanza, the joy of words aptly chosen and appearing on time, the sweetness of insinuations, sudden pauses, the necessity of naive expressions, of *seemingly haphazard* rhymes. In short, the whole range of often elusive pleasures known to the poet when he *sings*, and when the *songs* are successful." (italics mine)[73] This explains the naîveté of the lyrical "I" of Vasilisa's measured, dense, laconic idiom, contrasting with antithetical juxtapositions such as "obil'no-sladkaja, svjataja neljubov' " and "nežnoj neljubvi," as Vasilisa—the myth—looks ahead to the final stanza, her immortal song. What Vasilisa, the *porte-parole* of the poet, started in song, she finishes in song.

In the cycle *Pesni Vasilisy Premudroj*, Leśmian has created a near-perfect example of a literary model which, based on intuitive cognition, recreates the original folkloric realm. Vasilisa's last song is indeed a song which "ne projdët," which will be immortal. The song is a riddle, rooted in life and reverie, which will be forever interpreted anew and, therefore, will always be alive. In terms of metapoetics, the song reminds us that the process of creation is more important than its result.

---

73. Leśmian, "Pieśni ludowe," *SL*, p. 390.

THE FIRST CIRCLE
OF ALEKSANDR SOLZHENITSYN:
Symbolic Visions

BY

NINA LARIONOFF

AN ANALYSIS of the stylistic devices used by Solzhenitsyn in *The First Circle* shows that, in the compact precise style of this novel, the choice of every trivial detail, every character-type, event, and situation has been dictated by its inherent symbolic possibilities: only those details have been chosen which assist the author in his exposure of the Soviet system and in the presentation of his moral-philosophical ideas.

All the more conspicuous are the few instances in which the author appears to be indulging himself in long, seemingly superfluous descriptions of ordinary scenes and objects, such as the whole chapter devoted to Yakonov's memories of his visit to a small church, some twenty-two years before; or the meticulous descriptions of the paintings of the imprisoned artist Kondrashov-Ivanov. However, the strangely tense, visionary atmosphere of these passages, and particularly the thematic content of these seemingly arbitrary retardations of the narrative, point to a startling truth: namely, that far from being irrelevant and expendable, these passages are really complex symbolic structures, utilizing the full arsenal of Solzhenitsyn's literary devices and expressing the most significant ideas of the novel. In fact, these passages represent independent and self-contained complexes of ideas, something akin to prophetic visions and revelations. It is through these passages that Solzhenitsyn projects his interpretation of Russia's historical destiny and of the effect of the Revolution on the old cultural traditions, his organic theory of history, and his conception of the national character of modern Russia, as well as his prophetic vision of Russia's immediate future. For the lack of a more precise term these passages will be referred to in the following pages as "visions."

Six such symbolic visions can be singled out in *The First Circle*.[1]

---

1. It is possible that some additional symbolic visions are contained in one of the nine chapters not included in the published (New York: Harper & Row, 1968; Frankfurt/Main:

174 *Nina Larionoff*

Four of these are presented through the paintings of Kondrashov-Ivanov: "The Maimed Oak," "Moscow, 1941," "Autumnal Stream," and "The Castle of the Holy Grail"; the remaining two visions are incorporated into the direct authorial narrative and occupy two whole chapters, entitled respectively "The Church of St. John the Baptist" (chapter 23) and "The Ark" (chapter 48).[2] The symbolic messages contained in each of these visions are so complex and so vital to the central idea of *The First Circle* that they must be discussed individually. With the exception of "The Maimed Oak," which has been placed first because of the all-embracing nature of its symbol, these visions are discussed in the order of their appearance in the novel.

NATIONAL DESTINY: "THE MAIMED OAK"

The latent symbolism of Kondrashov-Ivanov's painting "The Maimed Oak" has been noted by several reviewers of *The First Circle*. Their interpretations range from the casual remark by Abraham Rothberg that " 'The Maimed Oak' is typical of Russia,"[3] through the somewhat broader approach of John B. Dunlop, who sees in it "a depiction of the tenacity of the human spirit which refuses to capitulate despite unrelenting and perpetual attack,"[4] to, finally, Rosette C. Lamont's extensive analysis of this symbol, in which she comes to the conclusion that the "The Maimed Oak," besides being a symbol of Russia, is also a symbol of frustrated and maimed but indestructible creative genius—like Solzhenitsyn himself.[5] Strangely enough, Georges Nivat,

Possev-Verlag, 1969; Paris: YMCA-Press, 1969) editions of *The First Circle*. Their forthcoming publication will provide an answer on that point. So far, three of these chapters have been published in the various 1974 issues of the *Vestnik R.S.Kh.D.*: chapter 44, "Na prostore" (vol. 111, pp. 70–89); chapter 61, "Tverskoj djadjuška" (vol. 112–113, pp. 160–173); and chapter 90, "Slovo razrušit beton" (vol. 114, pp. 193–203).

One more chapter (88, "Dialektičeskij materialism—peredovoe mirovozzrenie") has been published in *Kontinent* 1 (1974): 125–142. None of these chapters contains anything resembling symbolic visions.

2. Solzhenitsyn mentions also a fifth painting, with the intriguing title "Utro neobyknovennogo dnja," but, in a striking departure from his usual exhaustive symbolic exploitation of every detail, neither mentions it elsewhere in the novel nor gives a description of its contents. If it is used in one of the remaining unpublished chapters, it is probably with reference to chapter 85, "Utro streleckoj kazni."

3. Abraham Rothberg, *Aleksandr Solzhenitsyn: The Major Novels* (Ithaca: Cornell University Press, 1971), p. 123.

4. John B. Dunlop, "The Odyssey of a Skeptic: Gleb Nerzhin," in *Aleksandr Solzhenitsyn: Critical Essays and Documentary Materials*, ed. John B. Dunlop, Richard Haugh, and Alexis Klimoff (Nordland Publishing Co., 1973), p. 254.

5. Rosette C. Lamont, "Solzhenitsyn's 'Maimed Oak'," *Review of National Literatures* 3, no. 1 (Spring 1972): 153–182.

in his highly perceptive study of Solzhenitsyn's symbolism,[6] passes over in silence the symbolic implications of this painting and of this image.

All of the above interpretations of "The Maimed Oak" are valid, of course; the nature of this symbol is such that it comprises a variety of meanings. However, its very universality seems to suggest that with this image Solzhenitsyn wanted to present something just as big and indestructible as this old tree—the entire Russian nation.

This is how Solzhenitsyn describes the painting as seen through the eyes of his literary alter ego, Gleb Nerzhin:[7]

> It showed a solitary oak which grew by some mysterious force at the summit of a barren cliff, to which a perilous path wound upward along the precipice and to which the onlooker seemed elevated. What hurricanes had not blown here! How had they twisted that oak! And the skies over the tree and all around were stormy now as ever.
> The skies had probably never known the sun. This stubborn, sharp-clawed tree, with its twisted, broken branches, maimed by the ceaseless struggle with the eternally blowing winds trying to tear it from the cliff, refused to give up its battle and continued to cling to its God-forsaken place over the abyss. [222-223]

What a superb visual symbol of Russia and of its historical destiny and how convincingly it expresses Solzhenitsyn's awed recognition of tremendous physical and spiritual forces slumbering under his country's unprepossessing, enigmatic countenance. Translated into words, it could read something like this:

Russia . . . A remote, barren country, placed by its destiny onto the vast plains between East and West, never included in the family of European or Asian nations, it has been lonely, indeed.

Born in the darkness of the Middle Ages and burdened with the heritage of Byzantine mysticism, it has never felt the warming sun of the Renaissance or the liberating storms of the Reformation. Only devastating foreign invasions and bloody internecine wars swept over the country in never ceasing onslaughts, twisting and maiming its national spirit. . . .

And it is almost involuntarily that the memory evokes the image of another gnarled, old oak, described elsewhere in Russian literature, in Tolstoy's *War and Peace*:

---

6. Georges Nivat, "Essai sur la symbolique de Soljénitsyne," in *Soljénitsyne*, ed. Georges Nivat and Michel Aucouturier (Paris: L'Herne, 1971), pp. 352-364.

7. All the quotations from *The First Circle* in this essay are given in my own translation from Russian Harper & Row (New York, 1968) edition of this novel, and all page references are given to that edition.

> At the edge of the road stood an oak. . . . It was an enormous tree, its girth twice as great as a man could embrace, . . . some of its branches had been broken off and its bark scarred. With its huge ungainly limbs sprawling unsymmetrically, and its gnarled hands and fingers, it stood an aged, stern, and scornful monster. . . .[8]

The symbolic meaning of this image reveals itself only when we see the same oak again, magically transformed by the resuscitating power of spring, standing there "rapt and slightly trembling in the rays of the evening sun," "spreading out a canopy of sappy dark-green foliage," which has sprouted "through the hard century-old bark, even where there were no twigs," so that "neither gnarled fingers nor old scars nor old doubts and sorrows were any of them in evidence now" (ibid., p. 9). This oak is Tolstoy's symbol of the irrepressible forces of life eternally renewing themselves. "Life is indestructible," Tolstoy seems to say with these two contrasting images, "it is present everywhere, even under the dead bark of an old oak tree; and it breaks through—when the time is ripe for it."

Perhaps these were also the thoughts that Solzhenitsyn wanted to express when he chose the image of an old gnarled oak as the symbol of his enslaved country: "Do not despair, Russia is not dead; and it will awaken—when it is ready for it." Solzhenitsyn made a reference to this Tolstoyan symbol already in his earliest work, his play "The Love-Girl and the Innocent," written in 1954: one of its characters, the prisoner Gontoir, reads to his fellow inmates the episode from *War and Peace* "about the dead oak tree which turned green"[9]—to lift their spirits by this example of a miraculous rebirth. The strong affinity between these two images does not detract anything from the originality and relevance of Solzhenitsyn's "Maimed Oak"; on the contrary, it enriches it with some additional symbolic meanings.

BEHEADING OF OLD TRADITIONS: "THE CHURCH OF ST. JOHN THE BAPTIST"

Solzhenitsyn's interpretation of the impact of the Revolution upon the cultural traditions of pre-Revolutionary Russia is given in the symbolic vision contained in chapter 23, entitled "The Church of St. John the

---

8. Leo Tolstoy, *War and Peace*, 3 vols. in 1, tr. Louise and Aylmer Maude (London: Oxford University Press, 1965), 2: 4–5.

9. Aleksandr Solženicyn, "Olen' i šalašovka," in *Sobranie sočinenij v šesti tomakh* (Frankfurt/Main: Posev Verlag, 1969–1970), p. 102.

Baptist,"[10] which surpasses all the others in the richness and complexity of its ideas and in the sustained symbolism of its imagery.

As Solzhenitsyn sees it, the Revolution of 1917 was a violent, traumatic upheaval which senselessly destroyed Russia's old social institutions and ancient folk customs, and in doing this it also barbarously maimed the tree of Russian national culture. He conveys these views through a variety of artistic means, which involve religious and historical symbolism, literary allusions, symbolism of natural phenomena, of details, of setting, etc.

The event upon which the author builds this magnificent symbolic vision is very simple: one of the novel's heroes, Yakonov, survivor of the old intelligentsia but now a Colonel of Engineers in the State Security Service, wandering alone through Moscow at night, stumbles upon a deserted ruined church, and remembers suddenly how he had visited this same place with his fiancée some twenty-two years before, when the church was still intact and open to worshipers. This memory flashback into Yakonov's past is like a journey into some golden dream-land, full of peace and sunshine, with the church standing there, bathed in the rays of the warm setting sun, aglow with the glitter of golden icons and the peaceful flames of altar candles and colorful votive lamps, filled with the sounds of beautiful choral singing. The dramatic contrast between the grim Soviet reality of 1949 and the relative freedom of the few brief years of the NEP is expressed not only through direct authorial discourse, but also through the structural arrangement of the episode (a dark December night framing the golden, sunlit memory flashback), and particularly through a repeated juxtaposition of contrasting symbols, underscoring the difference of the seasonal background, of setting, color palette, etc.

This is how Solzhenitsyn narrates Yakonov's memory flashback.

On a warm sunny late afternoon in September, some twenty-two years before, Yakonov's fiancée, Agniya, had offered to show him "one of the most beautiful places in Moscow"—

---

10. There exists a divergency in the titling of this chapter in the existing Russian editions of *The First Circle*. Thus both the Harper & Row edition (New York, 1968), used in the present article, and that of the Possev-Verlag (Frankfurt/Main, 1969) display the above title ("The Church of St. John the Baptist"), while in the YMCA edition (Paris, 1969) of this novel, chapter 23 is called "The Church of Martyr Nikita." No explanation of this discrepancy has been offered so far (at least, to the knowledge of the present writer), either by the author himself or by his publishers. The solution to this problem might be provided by the eventual publication of the complete original version of *The First Circle*, referred to by Solzhenitsyn as "Krug-96."

. . . and led him . . . to a small brick church, painted in white and red
colors, whose altar was turned to a crooked, nameless alley.[113]

The church yard was empty, and only an old beggar woman was
standing on the church steps, crossing herself at the sounds of vesper
hymns coming from its wide-open doors. There were not many worshipers
inside, either, but the church was filled with a warm golden glow:

Through the small windows in the cupola, the sinking sun filled the
church with light, scattering in golden glitter over the top of the
iconostasis and the mosaic image of the Lord Sabbaoth.[117]

Below, under the massive arches of the nave, one could see "the
peaceful flames of altar candles and the gentle flickering of colorful
votive lamps." Soft choral singing filled the little church, alternating with
the utterances of the priest reciting the litany, and everything appeared
like a small island of peace and harmony amidst the noise and hustle
of an overcrowded city. And outside, right next to the church, towering
high over its cupola and its carved wooden belfry, a big old oak spread
its wide branches:

Right next to it, at one corner inside the fence, grew a large old oak; it
was taller than the church and its branches, already yellow, over-
shadowed both the cupola and the alley, making the church seem very
tiny. [113]

Later, when Agniya took Yakonov to the main entrance of the church,
from which opened a magnificent panorama of a Moscow sunset, he
gasped:

A long white stairway, interrupted by several terraced landings, descended in flights down the side of the hill, all the way to the Moscow
River. The river itself *burned* in the sun. On the left lay the Zamosk-
vorech'ye,[11] *blinding* one with the yellow *glitter* of its windows; . . . and
below, almost at one's feet, the *gleaming* Yauza[12] flowed into the
Moscow River; . . . and still farther off *flamed* in the sun the five
gilded cupolas of the Cathedral of Christ the Savior.
    And in all this *golden radiance*, Agniya, wrapped in her yellow shawl
which also seemed *golden*, sat there, squinting into the sun. [114, italics
added]

Yakonov was overwhelmed by the splendor and beauty of this
panorama, composed of flaming gold, yellow, and orange colors, and

11. Zamoskvorechy'e—one of the oldest parts of Moscow; the traditional seat of the
Moscow merchant community, noted for its stolid conservatism and stubborn clinging to
old national customs.

12. Yauza—a tributary of the Moskva River.

by his sudden realization that this ancient city is the very heart of Russia, the source and seat of everything truly Russian. It is here, sitting on the warm stone parapet in front of the church entrance, high above the old capital of Russia, that Yakonov and Agniya conduct one of the most significant philosophical dialogues of the novel, which reveals Solzhenitsyn's views on the role of the Orthodox church in the cultural history of Russia. This argument between Yakonov and Agniya is that between a typical Russian intellectual who rejects the church on purely rationalistic grounds and a simple devout Christian who accepts the church without questioning its dogmas or its religious practices and follows its spiritual guidance in simple-minded trustfulness (this is the symbolic meaning of the name *Agniya*, from Old Church Slavic *agnec*, Latin *agnus*—lamb).

When Agniya complains about the persecution of the church by the Communist government, Yakonov responds with some angry counter-accusations:

> And what if it is being persecuted! . . . It has been persecuted for
> ten years, but how long has it persecuted the others? Ten centuries![115]

And he proceeds to criticize the Russian church for its rigid dogmatism, its automatic support of all ruling authorities, and for its repeated failure to defend its persecuted members or to condemn the oppressors:

> . . . That's what all those beautiful churches with such majestic
> locations were built on! . . . And on the immolated schismatics!
> And on dissenters being flogged to death! [115]

Agniya's shy, poorly articulated defense of the church is no match for the eloquent criticism of Yakonov, but in this very artlessness lies the main strength of her defense, because her faith springs from that side of human nature which constitutes the primary source of all religions: namely, man's realization of his own infinite vulnerability and insignificance in relation to the universe and his instinctive search for something more perfect and permanent than himself—that unceasing spiritual search which is symbolized by the painting of Kondrashov-Ivanov, entitled "The Castle of the Holy Grail."

Within the framework of *The First Circle*, Solzhenitsyn avoids making any explicit polemical statements about the church or religion in general, but the warm, radiant colors used in his portrayal of the deeply religious Agniya and the wistful nostalgia with which he writes about the vanished little church leave us in no doubt as to what side he is on in this religious dispute.

In their more direct form, Solzhenitsyn's views of the role of the Russian Orthodox church are expressed in his short stories like "The Easter Procession," "A Journey Along the Oka," and particularly in his open letters to the heads of the Russian Orthodox hierarchy, both those in the Soviet Union and those in exile. As expressed in the above writings, his religious views seem to incorporate both the rationalistic criticism of Yakonov and the deep, instinctive religiosity of Agniya. Thus he unhesitatingly points out the various present and historical shortcomings of the official church while at the same time he acknowledges unreservedly its elevating and unifying role in the spiritual life of his country all through its history. His miniature short story "A Journey Along the Oka" is his most lyrical tribute to this beneficial influence of the Russian church:

> Traveling along country roads in Central Russia, you begin to understand why the Russian countryside has such a soothing effect. It is because of its churches.
>
> They rise over ridge and hillside, descending towards wide rivers like red and white princesses, towering above the thatch and wooden huts of everyday life with their slender, carved and fretted belfries.
>
> . . . Wherever you may wander, over the field or pasture, many miles from any homestead, you are never alone: above the wall of trees, above the hayricks, even above the very curve of the earth itself, the dome of a belfry is always beckoning to you. . . .[13]

In *The First Circle*, the little church visited by Agniya and Yakonov also stands on a hill overlooking entire Moscow, and it also towers over the people and their dwellings. And it is interesting that the fanatical Communist and convinced atheist Rubin unconsciously also feels this dominating and elevating role of the church in everyday life and in his secret "Project for Civic Temples," with which he pathetically tries to fill the spiritual and moral vacuum of Marxist ideology, also recommends the choice of elevated, majestic sites for his godless pseudo-churches.

The location of the church of St. John the Baptist is symbolic also in another respect. On the one hand, its altar is "turned to a crooked, nameless alley," and its back gate is open to the multitude of simple, "nameless" Russians from the obscure, humble walks of life, including the old beggar woman standing on its back steps. But on the other hand, its main entrance opens on a majestic elevation from which beautiful white stairs descend down to the Moscow River, as if stretching

---

13. Aleksandr Solzhenitsyn, "A Journey Along the Oka," in *Stories and Prose Poems*, trans. Michael Glenny (New York: Farrar, Straus & Giroux, Inc., 1971), p. 124.

out inviting arms to the entire city. The implication of the unifying role of the church is quite obvious: not only did the church gather under its roof ordinary Russian people from the "crooked, nameless alley," but it also opened before them the riches of the Russian past and Russian art and culture—the magnificent panorama of Moscow cathedrals and historical monuments—making them conscious of their belonging to this culture and their own national identity.

However, in spite of the vibrant, festive colors predominating in this memory flashback, its hidden symbolic message is that of doom. Every major and minor detail comprising this episode carries some symbolic implication of an imminent end: the name of the church to which Agniya takes her fiancé, the year of the episode itself, even the season and time of day at which it occurs.

Of all the symbolic details, the name of the church and the fate of its patron saint evoke the most ominous premonitions. The church is dedicated to St. John the Precursor—*Ioann Predteča*.[14] The historical fact of his beheading suggests a parallel to the annihilation ("beheading") of the cultural traditions of pre-Revolutionary Russia, while the destruction of the church itself foreshadows the subsequent devastation of churches all over Russia and a systematic uprooting of old religious traditions.

The year is 1927—the last year of that unique period of relative freedom in Soviet Russia, known as NEP, with its partial temporary return to private enterprise, the resumption of some sort of cultural exchange with the West, and the restoration—however brief and limited —of some degree of artistic freedom. Only a few months after Yakonov's and Agniya's visit to the church, this hopeful prelude was brought to an abrupt end by the introduction of the first Five-Year

---

14. A study of the historical and architectural sources seems to suggest that the church described in this chapter of *The First Circle* is actually the one named after the martyr Nikita. Thus one of the most complete historical guides to Moscow, *Moskva, ili istoričeskij putevoditel'*, in 8 volumes (Moskva: Tipografija Selivanovskogo, 1831), describes three churches dedicated to Ioann Predteča: Ioanna Predteči pod Borom (vol. 3, p. 285), Ioanna Predteči v Krečešnikakh (vol. 3, p. 335), and Ioanna Predteči v Kazennoj ulice (vol. 3, p. 373), but not one of these stands even close to the location indicated with such precision by Solzhenitsyn. On the other hand, of the two chapels and one little church dedicated to the martyr Nikita, the latter (cerkov' Nikity mučenika v Čigasakh, vol. 3, p. 377) corresponds in every detail to the description of the little church in *The First Circle*. Moreover, a study of the various maps of historical and architectural monuments of Moscow, found in the Supplement to vol. 1 of the *Istorija Moskvy* in 4 volumes (Moskva: Akademija Nauk SSSR, 1952), shows that the particular panorama of the Moscow sunset, described in the novel, could have been observed only from the hill on which stood the church of the martyr Nikita.

From the above we must conclude that Solzhenitsyn has intentionally changed the real name of the church to that of John the Baptist.

Plan with its insanely unrealistic plans of instant industrialization and collectivization, accompanied by a relentless tightening of governmental control in all spheres of economic and cultural life and wave upon wave of political purges, trials, and executions.

And it is one of the later days in September,[15] barely a week after the Orthodox feast of the Beheading of John the Baptist and just two days before another major Orthodox feast, that of the birth of the Mother of God, which are observed on September 11 and 21, respectively. It is also one of the last warm, sunny days before nature's turn towards the endless Russian winter; and the hour is that of sunset—the end of the day, with only a short time left before the onset of darkness. These last rays of the sun are the symbolic last rays of freedom that Soviet Russia has known.

Even the old oak near the church, Solzhenitsyn's symbol of Russia and its culture, also shows the signs of its near end in the grip of the approaching winter: "its branches were already yellow . . . and the flagstones of the courtyard were covered with yellow and orange leaves from the oak" (113).

From the golden memory flashback into his past Yakonov returns to reality in the gloom and cold of a wintry predawn. All the symbolic omens, woven into the narrative of his memories, have become reality by 1949: the warm, sunny September evening has turned into a freezing December night, the beautiful old church—into a deserted ruin; the towering golden oak is now an ugly dead stump; and the glittering panorama of Moscow has vanished behind an impenetrable shroud of mist.

If the centuries-old tree of Russian national traditions had not been cut down and the source of its spiritual life not sealed off and befouled, the little church would still be standing and on a Christmas night it would be filled with bright lights, festive singing, and crowds of free, unintimidated worshipers. But now only darkness and desolation surround the ruined church, the dead oak stump, and the lonely, miserable Yakonov.

In their hopes of creating a new, better future for Russia, the Communist rulers have barbarously, senselessly destroyed its religious traditions, its ancient folk customs, and all the people who were bearers of this old culture. The tragedy of this irreparable loss of an age-old national culture is aggravated by the fact that nothing new, or better, has been created to replace the spiritual values destroyed. The alien, totally materialistic Marxist ideology, which had been forced upon the

---

15. Solzhenitsyn does not give here any precise date, but from his reference to the feast of the birth of the Virgin Mary we can deduce that it was September 19 (1927).

Russian people by the new regime, was not grafted onto the tree of an old Christian culture, and in 1949, after more than three decades of Communist rule, the mutilated stump of the national culture remains barren and dead, while at the foot of the ruined church spreads a desolate waste land, cleared "for the construction of some future sky-scraper" (118)—the long-promised Communist paradise of the future.

From the analysis of this symbolic vision it is obvious that Solzhenitsyn unreservedly acknowledges the beneficial influence of the Russian Orthodox church and condemns the Soviet rulers for their wanton destruction of this church and old Russian culture, thus robbing succeeding generations of Russians of their rightful spiritual heritage and their true national identity.

RUSSIAN PRESENT: "AUTUMNAL STREAM"

A particularly poignant example of nature symbolism can be found in another landscape of Kondrashov-Ivanov through which Solzhenitsyn projects his views on the present political situation in Russia and on its prospects for the near future. It is called "Autumnal Stream" (the artist himself calls it also "Largo in D minor") and represents an ordinary autumnal landscape: a still, half-frozen stream, winding its way through a desolate meadow, covered with the first patches of snow and surrounded in the distance by the dark wall of an old dense pine forest. Everything is dead still: the trees, the air, and most of all the stream itself:

> It was almost impossible to determine the direction of its current: it did not move at all. . . . The sky was hopelessly overcast with some dirty-brown patches and the smothered sun, powerless to break through with one single direct ray, was sinking into another gloom below. [226]

The stagnation and confinement of spiritual life in present-day Russia are expressed through this half-frozen autumnal stream. It stands still because it has nowhere to go: only fierce frosts and a thick ice, and an even deadlier stillness, are ahead of it—and only an ever-tightening ideological and political control is awaiting Russia and its people.

But then this is nothing new for Russia—the gnarled, maimed tree of its history had always been lashed by the storms of national disasters, and "its skies had never known the sun." "The focus of the painting did not lie there," remarks the omniscient author, but elsewhere:

> There, in the background, was a dense forest of olive-black firs, before which flamed a single rebellious crimson birch. Behind its lonely tender fire the evergreen sentries stood even gloomier, massed together, raising their sharp spears to the sky. [226]

These two key images—the "evergreen sentries" and the "rebellious crimson birch"—express some of the most permanent characteristics of Russian history. The cultural and political life in Russia of all ages has invariably unfolded against this oppressive wall of "sentries": the autocratic government, the backward and unjust social structure, the traditional suppression of all independent political activities, etc. But if Russian history presents a picture of almost perpetual political oppression, it also can boast of a long tradition of civic rebellion and a distinguished pleiad of ideological dissenters and anti-establishment rebels. Such were the religious dissenters of the Russian Middle Ages, who preferred death at the stake to the renunciation of their own interpretation of the Orthodox dogma; such were the satirical writers and journalists of the eighteenth century who raised their voices against the cruelty and injustice of serfdom and of religious and social discrimination; and of the same rebellious kind were the aristocratic Decembrists and the socially lowlier Populists of the nineteenth century, with their high ideals of civic usefulness and self-sacrifice for the good of their country and of their less-fortunate countrymen, and finally the entire liberal Russian intelligentsia of the late nineteenth and early twentieth century—all the progressive writers, artists, social thinkers, etc., who tried to instill in Russian society the humanitarian ideals of political freedom, social justice, and respect for human dignity. The fact that present-day Russia has such rebels among its distinguished artists, scholars, and writers is an incontrovertible proof of the continuity of this tradition of civic rebellion and a reassuring sign of Russia's unshaken spiritual strength.

It would seem that the symbolism of this small painting would be exhausted at this point, but now the omniscient author steps in once more and reveals still another hidden meaning of this landscape—its "main thing":

> But not even that [the rebellious birch and the evergreen sentries] was the main thing; rather it was the stagnant water of the settling stream. It had a feeling of fullness, of depth. . . . It held in itself the balance between the autumn and winter. And still some other kind of balance. [226]

Thus it is this undefinable "other kind of balance" which Solzhenitsyn considers "the main thing" in the "Autumnal Stream." It seems to imply that life in present-day Russia has somehow adjusted itself to circumstances, has achieved some sort of "balance between the autumn and winter"—between its dark present and its even darker future. "Expect no miraculous changes," the author seems to say, "an autumn can only be followed by a winter; before Russia is ready for something better, it must live through the grim winter of its present totalitarian system."

This subtle warning of Solzhenitsyn about the fallacy of any optimistic hopes for the near future and the futility of all attempts to change the existing state of things becomes in his later writings a firm belief in the ultimate uselessness and harmfulness of all violent external interference with the organic flow of a country's history. In *August 1914*, giving for the first time a full decoding of his early symbols of the maimed oak and of the stagnating autumnal stream, he gives his most comprehensive formulation of this "organic" philosophy of history:

> History grows like a living tree. And for history reason is like an axe: you can not make it grow better by applying reason to it.
>
> Or, if you wish, history is a river; it has its own laws for its currents, twists, and turns.[16]

And obviously addressing himself to all those advocating violent overthrow of the existing order, Solzhenitsyn gives this somber warning:

> But you cannot break off the river, the river's current; if you interrupt it just one inch—the current is no more. . . . The bonds between generations, institutions, customs—this is what constitutes the continuity of the current [of history]. [Ibid.]

And elsewhere in *August 1914*:

> A reasonable man cannot be in favor of revolution, because revolution is a long and insane process of destruction. Above all, no revolution ever renews a country: it ruins it, and for a long time.[17]

Solzhenitsyn's evaluation of the nature of historical process is summarized in this momentous statement:

> History is IRRATIONAL. . . . It has its own, to us perhaps incomprehensible organic structure.[18]

His alternative to revolutionary methods is:

> . . . one must become involved in the patient process of history: work, persuade, and move ahead—little by little.[19]

---

16. *August 1914* (Paris: YMCA Press, 1971), p. 377.

This and all following quotations from *August 1914* are given in my own translation of the above edition of this novel.

17. Ibid., p. 536.

18. Ibid., p. 376.

19. Ibid., p. 537.

This organic philosophy of history is only a natural—organic!—outgrowth of all the ideas contained in their germinal form already in the symbolic vision projected by the "Autumnal Stream."

MOTHER RUSSIA OF THE TWENTIETH CENTURY: "MOSCOW, 1941"

Only one bright spot enlivens the desolate landscape in "Autumnal Stream": "the rebellious crimson birch"—Solzhenitsyn's symbol of protest and resistance.

Who are the courageous men and women in today's Russia who dare to raise their voices against the colossus of the totalitarian state and who are selfless enough to sacrifice the comfort and security of their own lives for the sake of civic freedom and justice? Have not decades of a ruthless domination crushed all remnants of rebelliousness in the Russian national character? What is the Russian national character in the middle of the twentieth century?

Ever since the appearance in Russian literature of the so-called "superfluous man,"[20] about 1850, that disenchanted heir of the romantic hero of the 1820s–1830s, the works of numerous Russian authors have abounded in various types of weak, despondent men, unable to make themselves useful to society or just to manage their own lives successfully. This character type proliferated in Russian literature particularly towards the end of the last century and came to be considered a true portrait of the typical Russian intellectual and of the Russian character in general. For a variety of reasons, stemming mainly from political and intellectual developments before and after the Revolution of 1917, this unappealing—and not entirely correct—cliché of a typical Russian intellectual remained uncontested, and was even promoted, in Soviet literature.

Solzhenitsyn unconditionally rejects this image of Russians as a nation of moral weaklings. Kondrashov-Ivanov, the authorial voice in all disputes about art, asks indignantly:

> . . . if our nature were just that, tell me, from where would our self-immolators come? Our *strel'cy*-rebels? Peter the First? The Decembrists? The People's Will revolutionaries? [227]

Solzhenitsyn's own achievements as man and artist deliver the greatest blow to the myth of the inherent weakness of the Russian character. His conception of modern Russian character is expressed through another painting of Kondrashov-Ivanov, this time the portrait of a young

---

20. The definition of a "superfluous man" has been derived from a novella of I. S. Turgenev, entitled *The Diary of a Superfluous Man* (1850), in which he portrayed an ineffective, idle dreamer incapable of finding for himself a place in society.

Russian woman, the member of a firefighting squad of Moscow citizens during an air raid of the German bombers in World War II:

> It showed a young girl dressed in a fire fighter's suit. . . . Her head was raised up; her crazed eyes were looking at something terrible, unforgettable in front of them and were filled with the tears of anger.
>
> But her figure was not girlishly weak! Her hands, ready for the struggle, were holding the straps of a gas mask, and the sharply angular folds of her black-grey fire fighter's suit shone with silver highlights along its folds—and it looked like a medieval knight's armor.
>
> The cruel and the noble mingled in the face of this resolute Komsomol girl from Kaluga, not at all beautiful, but in whom Kondrashov-Ivanov recognized and showed the Maid of Orleans! [225]

It seems that in this portrait the author wants the reader to see not only a Russian Joan of Arc but something far more relevant for us—a symbol of her entire country. Present-day Russia seems to be embodied in this fearless young woman, defending her people from foreign invaders. Ending his description of this portrait, Solzhenitsyn calls her "Madonna of wrath and vengeance" (225), associating her through the word "Madonna" with the Virgin Mary, traditionally considered the divine protector of the Russian people, and, in a bold gesture, spanning Russia's atheistic present and her mystical past with the concept of the Holy Mother Russia.

But Mother Russia of the twentieth century is not the ascetic, mystical Holy Russia of the Middle Ages: she is young, vigorous, totally materialistic, and has to endure a different kind of oppressor and to follow a different historical path. She is not lovely, this Mother Russia of our days: she is ravaged, abused, and full of pain and anger, and "the cruel and the noble mingle" in her image. But she is strong, steeled by her ordeals, and, repeating the historical events of centuries ago, she probably will some day outgrow and destroy also her native oppressors.

The interpretation of this portrait as a symbol of modern Russia is also suggested by the various details related to its creation. The painting had been ordered by the government during World War II, and was supposed to depict the horrors endured by the Russian people in the war and their heroic struggle with the invaders. The finished painting masterfully showed everything experienced by the Russian people: suffering, hatred of the enemy, and determination to fight it. But the officials unexpectedly rejected the painting—"because they were frightened by it," writes the author.

The cause of their fright is easy to guess: in this portrait the Soviet bureaucrats intuitively recognized the image of modern Russia and with their guilty consciences correctly sensed that all this hatred and readiness to fight were directed also against them.

It is one of the greatest and most tragic ironies of modern Russian history that all that wrath and vengeance which had accumulated in the Russian people against their native oppressors was fiendishly exploited by these latter and directed—and released—against the foreign enemy, so that the enslaved and abused Russians voluntarily defended their country and with it their own oppressors. All the abuses and misery of the pre-war years remained unavenged, and Kondrashov-Ivanov's "Madonna" stood all through the war in his garret, "turned against the wall," until the day of his arrest, when they both were brought to prison.

And there it stands, on the back stairs of the prison building, waiting for its day of wrath and vengeance.

RUSSIAN FUTURE: "THE ARK"

Streams and rivers have often been used in literature as symbols of life's current, of the progress of history, and of the passage of time in general. The mythological Lethe of the ancient Greeks, Derzhavin's "River of Time,"[21] the haunting evocation of centuries, floating down the river of time like a caravan of rafts, which closes the last poem in Pasternak's *Doctor Zhivago*[22]—all are manifestations of the same spontaneous association of the flow of water with the passage of time.

One of the most memorable uses of this symbol (and one closest to Solzhenitsyn in mood and conception) can be found in a poem by his distant namesake and predecessor on the battlefield of civic protest, Alexander Radishchev.[23] In his poem "The Eighteenth Century" ("Osmnadcatoe stoletie," 1801), Radishchev depicts Russian history of that century as a turbulent "bloody current," rushing its waves towards the boundless "ocean of eternity."

But if eighteenth century Russian history could be expressed adequately through the symbol of a turbulent current, the events comprising the history of Russia in the twentieth century were too overpowering in their scope and their universal impact to be expressed with one single symbolic image. The disasters of World War I, the political and social upheaval of the Revolution of 1917, the even more devastating World War II, etc.— all these involved not only Russia, but practically all the nations of the

---

21. The opening lines of the last, unfinished, poem by Derzhavin, entitled "Na tlennost' " ("On Mortality"), written in 1816: "Reka vremen v svoem stremlen'i . . .". The poem was inspired by a popular chart of world history, shown as a "River of Time."

22. Boris Pasternak, *Doctor Zhivago* (Ann Arbor, The University of Michigan Press, 1958), p. 566.

23. Aleksandr Radishchev (1749-1802), author of *Journey from Petersburg to Moscow*, directed against the institution of serfdom; founder of Russian Radicalism, pioneer of civic protest and its first martyr.

world, mixing their national destinies into one immense ocean of modern
world history.

To express the complexity of this history one needed new artistic symbols
of greater monumentality and universal relevance. Solzhenitsyn has
discovered them in the archaic, and seemingly irrelevant, biblical legend
of the Great Flood and Noah's Ark.

Reaffirming his conception of history as a spontaneous organic force,
paralleling the forces of nature, he compares the natural disaster of the
Great Flood with the political disaster of Stalinist rule which has flooded
Russia with waves of unprecedented mass terror. (The association of the
great inundation of St. Petersburgh in 1824 with the stormy reign of Peter
I in Pushkin's "Bronze Horseman" would be the closest literary parallel
to it.) Describing the building of the prison research institute in Mavrino,
which holds hundreds of imprisoned scholars and scientists, Solzhenitsyn
compares it to Noah's ark:

> Flooded with the constantly burning electric lights of the MGB, the
> two-story ark of the former estate church . . . floated unconcernedly and
> aimlessly through the black ocean of human destinies and delusions,
> leaving behind thin, faintly glowing streams of light from its port-
> holes. . . . [262][24]

Inside this prison-ark, the captive scholars, isolated from the rest of
society, deprived of their families, their possessions, and their personal
freedom, are spending their rare free hours in passionate arguments about
the meaning of life, the essence of Good and Evil, their country's present
political predicament, and its future destiny:

> From here, from the ark, confidently making its way through the dark-
> ness, one could easily survey the meandering, lost stream of accursed
> History—the entire stream at once, as if from a great height, and mi-
> nutely, down to the last pebble on the river bed, as if one dived to the
> bottom. [262]

It would be pointless to speculate whether by associating the Stalinist
mass terror with the Great Flood and a political prison with the biblical
ark Solzhenitsyn wants to suggest that this mass annihilation of innocent

---

24. This house-ark metaphor is not entirely original. Evgeny Zamyatin has used it in
one of his short stories ("Mamaj," 1920) which contains this description of Petersburg
during the first chaotic post-revolutionary years: "In the evening and at night there are no
more houses left in Petersburg: only six-storied stone ships. These ships, solitary six-storied
worlds, scud along the stone waves in the midst of other solitary six-storied worlds;
these ships gleam with the lights of countless cabins into the agitated ocean of the streets"
(*Povesti i rasskazy* [Letchford, Hertfordshire: Bradda Books, 1969], p. 148).

That Solzhenitsyn was familiar with the works of Zamyatin is obvious from his own
statements in the *Gulag Archipelago* (New York: Harper & Row, 1974), pp. 214–216.

people is some sort of divine punishment, or that political prisoners are the only righteous ones who will be saved. But it is true that political prisons in Russia harbor within their walls some of its most enlightened and independent men, whose minds preserve and perpetuate the traditions and moral values of vanished pre-Revolutionary Russian culture—and also something even more precious: the seeds of some unknown Russian culture of the future. Because once the floods of the present tyranny have receded, the seeds of these treasured spiritual values will unavoidably fall on native soil and, ravaged and exhausted as this soil will be, it still will bear a new abundant spiritual harvest.

Interpreted in this prophetic light, the symbol of Noah's ark is neither archaic nor irrelevant.

CONCLUSION

The image of modern Russia, as depicted in the preceding symbolic visions, is gloomy indeed. The age-old tree of national traditions is no more: it had been beheaded by the Revolution, and all that remains from this once powerful living organism is a huge stump. The stagnating stream of national spiritual life is at a standstill and only a long grueling winter and an even greater stillness are ahead of it. The skies over Russia are "stormy now as ever" and the "smothered sun"—the source of all life-sustaining forces—is "sinking into another gloom below."

But, paradoxically, it is this sinking sun and this dying autumnal nature, with its calm, resigned preparation for the long winter sleep, which inspires some distinctly optimistic feelings. We feel reassured because the old "maimed oak" of the Russian nation "refuses to give up" and stubbornly continues to struggle for its existence on its desolate, storm-swept cliff; and because we know instinctively that just as the gloomy sunset will be followed by the night, and the chilly autumn by the icy winter, so the darkness will be succeeded by the morning light, and the winter frosts by the warmth of the spring. And just as unfailingly, the stream of Russian national life will be freed one day from the grip of its present political system and, enriched by the waters from its melting ice chains, it will resume its natural flow towards some unknown destiny.

In summing up the discussion of the symbolic visions in *The First Circle*, we are startled by some unexpected insights. One of these is that in spite of the tragic subject matter of this novel, with its background of jails, forced deportations, and brutal abuse of human beings, in spite of the tragic fate of several of its main heroes and the gloomy grandeur of the visions themselves, the general impression left by this work is not painful or disheartening. This wholesome optimism undoubtedly stems from Solzhenitsyn's firm belief in the strong moral resilience of the Russian people, a belief born of his own experiences and observations gathered in the Soviet Army and in Soviet prisons and labor camps. The tragic last scene of the novel, which shows Nerzhin and his friends being transported to Siberia, does not create an impression of hopelessness or despair. On the contrary, this scene makes it clear that these men are not crushed morally but are more than ever determined to continue their resistance to their oppressors—even if it means a slow death in a Siberian mine or in some Arctic labor camp.

However, most startling is the realization that although in *The First Circle* Solzhenitsyn has given a devastating exposure of the secret workings of the Soviet state, based on a ruthless oppression of its citizens, it is also a work that Soviet rulers should be least afraid of because of the purely spiritual, non-violent means suggested by the author for its reformation.

Beginning with *The First Circle* and ending with the last prophetic chapters in *August 1914*, Solzhenitsyn, with an ever increasing conviction and an ever louder insistence, warns *against* any violent interference into the natural organic development of national history, *against* any sudden revolutionary changes of the existing political and social order. Solzhenitsyn's solution to his country's dilemma is not political but moral. He advocates two entirely non-violent means: first, moral emancipation of the individual conscience from its enslavement to brutal power; second, conscious *resistance to evil by non-participation in it* (Volodin's ethical imperative "Not me!"). In Solzhenitsyn's view, moral rejection of evil and non-participation in it are those positive moral actions whose cumulative force will eventually neutralize the evil and destroy it—and these moral weapons are available to even the most deprived prisoner. The liberation of Russia cannot be accomplished from outside, by some drastic changes of the existing political and social structure, but from within, through a slow, gradual, *organic* moral regeneration. Until this moral emancipation of individual conscience from evil is achieved, any forced attempts to change radically the present state of things will only lead to greater enslavement and greater misery.

Perhaps it would be suitable to conclude this interpretation of *The First Circle* with an improvised symbolic vision summing up the ideological message contained in this novel.

. . . All rivers on earth flow toward one single ocean washing the shores of all the continents, and all national histories of the different countries fall into one boundless ocean of human history. And as all seas, lakes, and rivers are only parts of one immense but interconnected body of water, so the destinies of individual nations are only different chapters in the unfinished book of modern history. If the water of only one of these rivers gets poisoned, no matter how small the amount of poison which it carries in its current, it will eventually poison the entire ocean; and if one single society in the big family of nations becomes sick, the evil emanating from it will sooner or later infect the rest of humanity.

In *The First Circle* Solzhenitsyn has shown one such sick society, his own native Soviet Russia, and his entire novel is one emphatic warning that unless some moral force will counterpoise totalitarianism, Russia could become only the first—and the best!—of the circles of some future totalitarian inferno awaiting us at the end of modern history. . . .

This seems to be the most important message which Solzhenitsyn wants to convey with this novel to his countrymen. And to the rest of the world.

A CAMP THROUGH THE EYES OF
A PEASANT:
Solzhenitsyn's *One Day In The Life of Ivan Denisovich*

BY

DAVID PIKE

ALEKSANDR SOLZHENITSYN's recent book of memoirs, *Bodalsja telenok s dubom* (*The Calf Butted Against the Oak*),[1] contains new material that recounts in detail the story of the author's decision in 1960 to emerge after twelve years of undisturbed writing in secret ("There was no longer sufficient air for me in the literary underground" [16]). Solzhenitsyn's reminiscences discuss the editorial intrigue and behind-the-scenes maneuvering that led to the appearance of *One Day in the Life of Ivan Denisovich* in the Soviet Union and established the author's name in that country and abroad. Solzhenitsyn's initial distress, following his voluntary decision to submit the work to Aleksandr Tvardovsky and *Novyj Mir*, is typical of his trepidation during the uncertain editorial process: "How, with nothing compelling me, could I have denounced myself?" (23) In *Bodalsja telenok s dubom* Solzhenitsyn draws a decidedly sympathetic portrait of Tvardovsky without disregarding the editor's shortcomings, his alcoholism, and his "thirst to believe" (49). The latter characteristic had led to Tvardovsky's honest tribute to Stalin in spite of the latter's destruction of the peasants and the ordeal of the editor's own family; and Tvardovsky's honest lament upon Stalin's death preceded equally honest dissociation from him following his exposure during the period of de-Stalinization. Solzhenitsyn also speaks of two incompatible "truths" continually in opposition to each other within Tvardovsky the editor, stemming from his sentiments toward both literature and the party: "In taking an initial liking to each manuscript out of the first feeling, Tvardovsky without fail had to submit it to the second and only then print it—as a SOVIET work" (36).

---

1. Aleksandr Solženicyn, *Bodalsja telenok s dubom, Očerki literaturnoj žizni* (Paris: YMCA Press, 1975). All references are to this edition, and page numbers are cited following each quotation. Translations are my own.

193

It is Solzhenitsyn's belief that Anna Berzer's tactics of attracting the editor Tvardovsky's attention to the manuscript of *One Day* by describing it to him as the portrayal of a "camp through the eyes of a peasant, a work very close to the people" (26) saved Ivan Denisovich from being "eaten alive" (27) by the other editors, A. Dementyev, B. Zaks, and A. Kondratovich. Solzhenitsyn strongly emphasizes the importance of this attribute in attaining the publication of *One Day*: "I won't say I planned it exactly this way, but I did have a true sense of conjecture and presentiment within me: The upper [*verkhnij*] peasant Aleksandr Tvardovsky and the supreme [*verkhovoj*] peasant Nikita Khrushchev could not remain indifferent to the peasant Ivan Denisovich" (27). It is Berzer's apt characterization of *One Day* as a "camp through the eyes of a peasant" that we shall use as our point of departure in this study.

I

The subject of literature examining the aesthetic merits of *One Day* has most frequently been the work's narrative system and its linguistic innovation; however, no critic has yet carried the analysis of Solzhenitsyn's careful and consistent manipulation of perspective and narrative mode to a logical conclusion with regard to its inevitable effect on structure, descriptive technique, and character portrayal.[2] As the various narrational voices and the techniques with which Solzhenitsyn presents them are crucial to the artistic conception of *One Day*, a brief discussion of the author's narrative construct precedes our analysis of its structural and descriptive repercussions.

Most critics[3] determine the existence of two perspectives in the book, that of a narrator and of the peasant inmate Ivan Denisovich Shukhov; they attribute to them various narrational functions. This approach proves ambiguous when logically scrutinized and tested throughout the book. In restricting the possibilities of perspective to these two voices alone, one must accordingly clarify all questions concerning point of view through the presence of either Ivan or the narrator. In previous studies this approach has often led to the combination, within each of the two perspectives, of disparate and, presumptively, incompatible narrational qualities. This is not to say that the various viewpoints in *One Day* do not

2. Vinokur hints at these connections in her article on *One Day*, but fails to develop them. See T. G. Vinokur, "O jazyke i stile povesti A. I. Solženicyna *Odin den' Ivana Denisoviča*," in *Voprosy kultury reči*, no. 6 (1965), pp.16–32.

3. Primarily: Vladimir Rus, "*One Day in the Life of Ivan Denisovich*: A Point of View Analysis," *Canadian Slavonic Papers* 13 (Summer-Fall 1971): ii–iii; Richard Luplow, "Narrative Style and Structure in *One Day in the Life of Ivan Denisovich*," *Russian Literature Triquarterly*. no. 1 (Fall 1971), pp. 399–412; and Christopher Moody, *Solzhenitsyn* (Harper and Row, 1975), particularly chap. 3, "Language and Style," pp. 50–68.

mingle and that each and every passage is clearly attributable to one of the perspectives. Such is clearly not the case. Nonetheless, I suggest the presence of three viewpoints which, despite frequent blending, are occasionally identifiable each in its own right. This interpretation seems to eliminate much of the ambiguity of previous studies while providing a more satisfactory clarification of all possibilities for point of view.

I attribute the three perspectives to Ivan, a prisoner-narrator, and an omniscient, objective narrator. It is imperative, however, to define clearly the *narrative mode* in which each perspective is presented. Therein lies both the intricacy of the formal construct as well as the key to *One Day's* efficacy in recreating the ambience of a Stalinist "destructive labor camp."

II

Our discussion of the various perspectives will begin with a brief examination of the most neutral and least personally "involved" viewpoint. Solzhenitsyn commonly calls upon the omniscient narrator for the purpose of nature descriptions and certain types of biographical and situational information. He seems to guide the dialogue and unobtrusively establishes settings. The language of the omniscient narrator is closer to a standardized literary level, relatively free of the colloquialisms and slang peculiar to Shukhov and the prisoner-narrator. It is this increased linguistic sophistication, along with his omniscience, that facilitates his identification. The passage below contains two distinct voices in obvious contiguity of perspective:

> I, dolžno, pošli perednikh dva konvoira po doroge. Kolykhnulas' kolonna vperedi, zakačala plečami, i konvoj, sprava i sleva ot kolonny šagakh v dvadcati, a drug za drugom čerez desjat' šagov,—pošel derža avtomaty nagotove. [32][4]

The result is a noticeable inharmonious impression when the omniscient narrator coalesces with a subjective and limited perspective. The initial remark is an assumption made either by the prisoner-narrator or by Ivan who are in line some distance from the front. Outward

4. Aleksandr Solženicyn, *Odin den' Ivana Denisoviča. Matrenin dvor* (Paris: YMCA Press, 1973). All references are to this edition, and page numbers are cited following each quotation. The following translation, and all subsequent ones, with page numbers cited after each are from the Bantam Book 1969 paperback edition of the Hingley-Hayward version (originally published as *One Day in the Life of Ivan Denisovich*, trans. Max Hayward and Ronald Hingley [New York: Frederick A. Praeger, 1963]), although I have made a few necessary changes. "The first two escort guards must've already started along the road. In front the column swayed, men began to swing their shoulders, and the escort guards, twenty paces away at either side of the column and with ten paces between them, started off, their tommy guns at the ready." (42)

appearances lead them to assume that the front of the column "must've" already started marching. A descriptive comment by the omniscient narrator follows immediately. Unlike the subjective narrators, he *sees* the front, hidden to those in back, and knows exactly what is happening. This criticism seems justified because of Solzhenitsyn's overall meticulous manipulation of point of view. His usage of perspective consistently avoids any "illogical" convergence of viewpoint in the same paragraph of the omniscient narrator with Ivan or the prisoner-narrator. It would only be possible in any case for "illogical" situations to arise with the omniscient narrator, for his narrational function is radically different from that of Ivan and the prisoner-narrator (as we shall demonstrate below).

The scene in the hospital involving Ivan and Vdovushkin also contains passages that clearly stem from the omniscient narrator and are identifiable as such by the lexical level of the Russian text. One may also establish their origin by the fact that Ivan and Vdovushkin are alone in the room, and the observations of a descriptive nature about the latter's situation and activity could not have been made by either of the only two people physically present:

> . . . A Vdovuškin pisal svoe. On, vpravdu, zanimalsja rabotoj "levoj," no dlja Šukhova nepostižimoj. On perepisyval novoe dlinnoe stikhotvorenie, kotoroe včera otdelal, a segodnja obeščal pokazat' Stepanu Grigor' eviču, tomu samomu vraču, poborniku trudoterapii.
>
> Kak èto delaetsja tol'ko v lagerjakh, Stepan Grigor'evič i posovetoval Vdovuškinu ob"javit'sja fel'dšerom, postavil ego na rabotu fel'dšerom, i stal Vdovuškin učit'sja delat' vnutrivennye ukoly na temnykh rabotjagakh, v č'ju dobroporjadočnuju golovu nikak by ne moglo vstupit', čto fel'dšer možet byt' vovse i ne fel'dšerom. Byl že Kolja student literaturnogo fakul'teta, arestovannyj so vtorogo kursa. Stepan Grigor'evič khotel, čtob on napisal v tjur'me to, čego emu ne dali na vole. [22][5]

In this instance, the presence of the omniscient narrator makes possible the dissemination of information beyond the range of that passed on by the freely associative sequence in the narrative of Ivan or the

---

5. "Vdovushkin was still writing away. He really was doing something on the side, something that didn't mean much to Shukhov. He was copying out a long poem that he'd given the finishing touches to the day before and had promised to show Stepan Grigoryevich today—the man who believed in work as a cure-all.

This sort of thing could only happen in a camp. It was Stepan Grigoryevich who told Vdovushkin to say he was a medic and then gave him the job. So Vdovushkin started learning how to give injections to poor, ignorant prisoners who would never let it enter their simple, trusting minds that a medic might not be a medic at all. Nikolay had studied literature at the university and had been arrested in his second year. Stepan Grigoryevich wanted him to write the sort of thing here he couldn't write 'outside'." (24)

prisoner-narrator. The omniscient narrator illuminates facts that are beyond the capacity and function of the other two narrational voices either to know or to relate; however, the scene is obviously "legitimized" by Ivan's presence in the hospital (questions of this type will be dealt with in our discussion of the structural repercussions of viewpoint). The description of Captain Buynovsky in the mess hall (Russian edition, pp. 58-9; English edition, p. 90) is another passage related by the omniscient narrator and distinguishable by the higher linguistic quality of the language.

III

Ivan and the prisoner-narrator embody, respectively, the following two narrative modes: represented discourse[6] and *skaz*. In his usage of represented discourse, an author composes his narrative through a character's own thought processes, framed by his intellectual qualities, and through the resultant linguistic peculiarities inherent in his speech; but the third person approach must be maintained. The story is related less *by* a specific character (as in *skaz*) than it is rendered *through* him by a "representor." The difference is a narrative presented basically from the inside out, rather then from outside alone. In *skaz* the author more or less subordinates overt aspects of his authorial self—opinions, observations, intellectual capabilities, speech characteristics—to those of his character who then relates in seeming independence from the author; however, both techniques rely heavily on the reproduction of the character's idiolect and intellectual capabilities. In *One Day*, where the two techniques of represented discourse and *skaz* exist contiguously, there arise formidable impediments to a clear distinction between Ivan and the *skaz* prisoner-narrator. In particular, the repercussions on their vocabulary of an overlapping camp experience and the similarity of their daily activity present one of the greatest two impediments to a clear distinction.[7] Their language is saturated with the same argot, characterized by similar semi-obscene phrases and expressions endemic to their particular closed environment; moreover, there can be little doubt that Ivan and the prisoner-narrator are akin to each other in their general outlook and in their mode of thinking.

Generally speaking, the camp account is given *glazami mužika* (through the eyes of a peasant), and not *slovami* (in his words), a formulation that requires precise definition. Ivan is the hero of the story,

---

6. This seems a suitable English equivalent for the German *erlebte Rede* and Russian *nesobstvenno-prjamaja reč'*. Vladimir Rus provides a brief discussion of alternate terms in his article "A Point of View Analysis," p. 165.

7. The second impediment is discussed on pp. 201-203.

and his predicament is presented in a twofold manner. First of all, the
story of his one day in the camp is told in terms of his mental
reaction to the empiric realities of his situation, i.e., "through his eyes."
This interiorization of his experience is given effective expression through
represented discourse; but the account is not rendered, strictly speaking,
by him in his own direct words (wide use is certainly made of his
vocabulary, but on an indirect basis through represented discourse).
The task of actually telling the story belongs not to Ivan but to the
skaz prisoner-narrator; it is he who gives us the second portrayal of
Ivan on a somewhat different level. The *skaz* narrator observes and
recounts, and the object of his observations is Ivan's physical behavior
and activity throughout the day. When a subjective rendition of the inner
workings of Ivan's mind is deemed desirable, the narrative mode
switches to represented discourse. We are then taken inside Ivan's
consciousness and its free flow of associations. He is both object and
subject in *One Day*. He serves as an object for the *skaz* narrator's
descriptive account of the daily events; but he becomes the subject when
an internal figuration of his consciousness occurs. Ivan never relates.
On the one hand, his verbal thought fragments stemming from his
mental reaction to the day are rendered in represented discourse; on
the other hand, he *physically acts* and is observed and described by the
skaz narrator. These distinctions are central to our interpretation of
narrative mode in *One Day* and will become clearer as we proceed
with separate examinations of Ivan and the *skaz* prisoner-narrator.

IV

Represented discourse reproduces a character's verbalized thought
processes through third person mimicry of speech characteristics and
mental patterns typical of his linguistic idiom and indicative of his
intellectual level. Authorial intrusion upon the character's consciousness
is restricted, and the presentation of reality is rendered in a highly
subjectivized fashion.[8] In Ivan's case the reader vicariously experiences

---

8. Edward Brown has applied the term "linguistic mimicry" to Solzhenitsyn's frequent
emphatic portrayals. See "Solzhenitsyn's Cast of Characters" in *Major Soviet Writers*
(London, Oxford, New York: Oxford University Press, 1973), pp. 351–66. Especially
noteworthy examples of this technique in other works by Solzhenitsyn are Rusanov in
Cancer Ward and Spiridon and Stalin himself in *The First Circle*. Interestingly, Solzhenitsyn's episode with Stalin has occasionally drawn criticism as a type of polemical
authorial indulgence. That Solzhenitsyn's linguistic mimicry in the case of Ivan and Spiridon
illuminates innocently moral, refreshingly naive minds, while the same technique, applied to
Stalin or Rusanov, exposes the intellection of a moral nonentity, is less tendentious
editorializing than the logical result of a consistently applied technique. While the limits of
this paper do not allow a detailed discussion of this question, it might also be noted that

the ordeal of a semi-literate, resourceful peasant slogger (*rabotjaga*) who by and large maintains his innate moral credo despite the demands placed upon it by the camp. Ivan's represented discourse is composed of personal dialectal peculiarities and prison camp speech expressed in elliptic, fragmentary sentences and thought patterns.[9] His discourse frequently begins with introductory phrases like "Shukhov noticed," "he remembered," "he could see," "Shukhov figured out," "he no longer saw," or simply brief descriptive phrases about Ivan's activity. These usually preface extended passages in which the reader is no longer explicitly reminded that Ivan's immediate train of thought is still being "represented." Luplow's contention that the represented discourse is not linked to the character-referent by such "connectives" seems invalid.[10] The reader is continually reminded of Shukhov's presence either by such "connectives" or by curt explanatory introductions to a certain passage.[11] In this fashion the scene is established for the represented discourse which follows. The passage below is just such an example. It contains descriptive remarks concerning both Senka and Ivan which establish the perspective. These comments are interspersed with and then followed by represented discourse in which Ivan's thought fragments about the day's work are mentally verbalized:

---

linguistic mimicry or represented discourse, through which Solzhenitsyn constantly performs his feats of empathy, is noticeable in most of his works, up to and including *The Gulag Archipelago*, where they find, however, more encapsulized application.

9. See the amusing but thoroughly predictable reaction on the part of Kondratovich to *One Day's* grammatical and linguistic characteristics so anomalous in the Soviet Union (in *Bodalsja telenok s dubom*, pp. 27 and 29; for instance, "the language would have to be cleaned up"). In Part III of *The Gulag Archipelago* Solzhenitsyn characterizes the zeks' language in a manner that adds much to our understanding of his usage of language in *One Day*: "In conversation with you he [the zek] will be laconic, speaking without expression—either monotonously and dully or else with servility—if it is necessary to ask you for something . . . [the language] is free of all kinds of superfluous expressions, of introductory phrases such as 'pardon me,' or 'please,' or 'if you don't object,' and also from superfluous pronouns and interjections. The speech of the zek moves straight to its goal, just as he himself pushes into the Arctic wind. He speaks as if he were punching his companion in the mug beating him with words." Aleksandr Solženicyn, *Arkhipelag GULag: 1918-1956. Opyt khudožestvennogo issledovanija* (Paris: YMCA Press, 1974) [pts. 3 & 4], p. 495. English translation by Thomas Whitney (Harper & Row, 1975), p. 508. All references are to these editions, and page numbers are cited after each quotation.

10. Luplow, "Narrative Style and Structure," p. 400. True, phrases of this type do not occur at the beginning of every paragraph, and the perspective in such cases becomes correspondingly more difficult, if not impossible, to identify with certainty.

11. Luplow's remarks seem general in nature and not exclusively directed at *One Day* alone. Consequently, it would not be superfluous to mention another Russian novel in which extensive use of represented discourse is made. Fëdor Sologub's *The Petty Demon* applies represented discourse which is continually accompanied by these very "grammatical connectives."

Nosilki skhvatil—i po trapu. [The reference is to Senka]

A Šukhov, khotja tam ego sejčas konvoj psami travi, otbežal po ploščadke nazad, gljanul. Ničego. Teper' podbežal—i čerez stenku, sleva, sprava. Èx, glaz—vaterpas! Rovno! Ešče ruka ne staritsja. [78][12]

It would be difficult to mistake this verbal patter of Ivan's waking mind for some type of oral disquisition in response to his day's work; rather it is the spontaneous mental verbalization of his thoughts, and they are rendered indirectly through represented discourse.

V

Ivan's subjective views converge with those of the *skaz* prisoner-narrator who rarely seems to leave Shukhov's side. We shall now turn our attention to the other partner in this tandem narrative relationship. In so doing we must address ourselves to some specific questions concerning the nature of *skaz*, many of which have yet to receive definitive analysis. Our purpose here is not to provide such analysis in terms of a possible broad application to literature; rather we must limit ourselves to a discussion of the nature of the *skaz* technique as it is found in *One Day*. Rice[13] insists, and rightly so, on a clear distinction between form and style in his efforts to establish *skaz* as a literary genre. In terms of form, we are precluded from speaking of a pure *skaz* in *One Day* due to the presence of other narrative modes; we shall adhere instead to Rice's advice and refer to the "skazality" or *skaz* style used by the prisoner-narrator.

Rice's proposition that the *skaz* teller does not use himself as the object of his tale is also directly applicable to *One Day*.[14] Our discussion above has demonstrated that Ivan is the primary object of the teller's tale. In our analysis of *skaz* we must look at individual passages according to two criteria: observation and "skazality." The following example contains two sentences that combine both observation and narration with a style that is clearly *skaz*. This set of characteristics eliminates the possibility of attributing the remarks to either Ivan or the omniscient narrator:

---

12. "He grabbed the hod and went down the ladder. But Shukhov—the guards could set the dogs on him for all he cared now—ran back to have a last look. Not bad. He went up and looked over the wall from left to right. His eye was true as a level. The wall was straight as a die. His hands were still good for something!" (125)

13. Martin P. Rice, "On 'Skaz'," *Russian Literature Triquarterly*, no. 12 (1975), pp. 409–424.

14. Ibid., p. 418.

Tol'ko ètogo Šukhov i ždal! Teper'-to on, kak ptica vol'naja, vyporkhnul iz-pod tamburnoj kryši—i po zone, i po zone! [97][15]

Solzhenitsyn's usage of first and third person grammatical forms in *One Day* is also central to our treatment of narrative mode. Rice establishes the third person narrative as the legitimate medium for *skaz*; the occasional appearance in a third person tale of first person plural forms such as "us," "we," or "our" is not necessarily contradictory. In particular, Rice adduces Gogol's *Overcoat* as a work where one or two first person plural forms occur.[16] Rice's determination of the third person as the most appropriate medium for *skaz* may or may not have widespread application; but most of the *skaz* prisoner-narrator's tale in *One Day* is in fact rendered in the third person. We have already pointed out one of the two main impediments to a clear distinction between represented discourse and *skaz* in their application in Solzhenitsyn's work.[17] The use of the third person in both these techniques is the second; however, scattered use is made of first person plurals. For example:

A mig—naš! Poka načal'stvo razberetsja—pritknis', gde poteplej, sjad', sidi, ešče nalomaeš' spinu. Khorošo, esli okolo pečki—portjanki pereobernut' da sogret' ikh malost'. Togda vo ves' den' nogi budut teplye. A i bez pečki—vse odno khorošo. [37][18]

A descriptive passage follows, obviously by the omniscient narrator, and then:

Tridcat' vos'maja, konečno, čužikh nikogo k peči ne dopuskaet, sama obsela, portjanki sušit. Ladno, my i tut, v ugolku, ničego. [38][19]

---

15. "That was all Shukhov was waiting for. He tore out of the package room like a bat out of hell and chased across the compound." (158)

16. Rice, "On 'Skaz'," p. 417. One of the best examples in Russian literature of pure *skaz* is Leskov's "Levša" (*The Steel Flea*). This work also adapts itself to Rice's pattern, for there are two instances of first person plural forms in the narrative ("us," "our").

17. See pp. 5-6.

18. "But this is our moment. While they [the bosses] were figuring things out, you could find some warm spot and stay there for a spell before you started breaking your back. It was good if you could get near the stove to take your footclothes off, warm them a little, and then put them on again. Then your feet would be warm all day long. But even if you couldn't get to a stove it was still great . . ." (52-3) I have made minor emendations in the translation of the passage where Solzhenitsyn's first person plural forms failed to survive the translation process.

19. "Of course, the men of Gang 38 were hogging the stove, drying out their footclothes. Okay, so the rest of us have to sit in a corner. What the hell." (53)

I suggest that the use of what Luplow considers "a striking distortion of the usual quasi-direct [or represented] discourse form,"[20] i.e., first person plurals, provides one of the few sure demarcations between the narrator-prisoner's "skazality" and Ivan's represented discourse. First person plural forms are not at all a distortion of represented discourse; rather, they represent a different narrative approach altogether. Comments like "but this is our moment" or "so the rest of us have to sit in a corner" are not represented discourse but a collective application of a *skaz* style. This does not deny that the signals for both techniques may often be identical, and without the first person plural forms in this passage a distinction would be greatly impeded; however, Solzhenitsyn's usage of first person constructions, when they occur, provides one method for certain differentiation.

Moody's attempt to attribute first person plural forms to Ivan is similarly unacceptable. Moody would have us believe that Ivan "openly takes over as narrator, using the first person 'we' " at "moments of special intensity."[21] This is simply not the case. Ivan is entirely unaware that he is the subject of literary portrayal, and it is incongruous to maintain that he should suddenly begin verbalizing his experience to some imagined listener.

Solzhenitsyn occasionally mixes his use of first and third person pronouns and possessive adjectives within a passage, but this is not out of line with the presence of a *skaz* prisoner usually in close proximity to Shukhov. The race back to camp at the end of the day, where represented discourse and *skaz* oscillate, is a case in point. Here one can easily imagine the *skaz* prisoner peering over Ivan's shoulder in the line:

> Kak khvost na kholm vyvalil, tak i Šukhov uvidel: sprava ot nikh, daleko v stepi, černelas' ešče kolonna, šla ona našej kolonne naperekos i, dolžno byt' uvidav, tože pripustila. [87][22]

When this fluctuation between the two narrative modes occurs, it is tempting to see the *skaz* prisoner himself as the "representor" of Ivan's discourse. Near Shukhov's side, he can slip in and out of his responsibility of "representing" Ivan's discourse and adding his own observations in a *skaz* style occasionally characterized by collective first

20. Luplow, "Narrative Style and Structure," p. 405.

21. Moody, *Solzhenitsyn*, p. 67 (note 3, above).

22. "Shukhov could see what it was all about when the column cleared a rise they'd been passing. Way over to the right of them on the plain there was another column heading for the camp, across our path. These fellows must've spotted our column too and put on a spurt." (142)

person plurals. The stylistic subtlety of a represented discourse *within skaz* could then result, a method that seems limitedly compatible with the dictates of both forms as narrative modes and which makes good artistic sense. This possibility would be eliminated, though, when the represented discourse requires a "representor" capable of reading thoughts as well, a task seemingly outside the human capabilities of a *skaz*-style narrator.

The description of the race home, with its frequent usage of first person plural forms, also demonstrates another important characteristic of the *skaz* prisoner-narrator. He too is obviously reacting to his situation and is very much involved in it. He is more than a mere passive observer and teller, and his passionate involvement adds to the immediacy of the experience being described. Nevertheless, the precise personality of the *skaz* prisoner-narrator remains an enigma. Our knowledge of his person must be gleaned entirely from the manner in which he relates his story and from the occasional instances where he becomes overtly yet anonymously involved in it.

In our attempt to dismantle and dissect the various tightly-woven strands of differing but related narrative modes in *One Day*, we have selected as examples those rare passages which fulfill sufficient criteria to enable their positive identification; but the merit of Solzhenitsyn's narrative approach lies precisely in his integration of the various perspectives. His amalgam of point of view and narrative mode is so intimately merged that viewpoint and technique cannot be established and identified with assurance in the majority of cases.

VI

The presence of the three viewpoints still leaves unanswered the question of Solzhenitsyn's relationship to each. There is no overt authorial presence in *One Day*; nonetheless, the occasional shift in tonality, the sarcastic or ironic *double entendre* in numerous remarks stemming ostensibly from the various perspectives can be viewed according to a substratum of authorial intent or motivation. This does not imply in the least that any of the three voices are patently autobiographical; on the contrary, the effect that Solzhenitsyn's personal experience as a prisoner has on his characters will not likely be noticed by a reader unfamiliar with the author's biography. In other instances, where Solzhenitsyn is perceptible behind the narrational façade, his authorial presence is more obvious. As we have indicated, these situations are generally marked by double layers of meaning and by the presence of an ironic or sarcastic intent beneath a surface of apparent factualism.

Apart from the three principal perspectives, the presence of other individuals who comment and react to their situation in various ways supplements and broadens further the dimensions of the narrative canvas. Thoughout the day a plethora of prisoners, guards, and other assorted characters from the camp population makes comments of varying length and importance; these are also strewn throughout the account. Solzhenitsyn's use of parenthesized commentary is a device (not peculiar to *One Day* alone) that results in highly effective encapsulized shifts in perspective. These comments come in the form of quotations, observations, obscenities, fleeting impressions, or sarcastic rejoinders. They are liberally sprinkled throughout passages presented in themselves from other points of view; the multifarious combinations provide a wide variety of interaction (ironic, ridiculing, sarcastic, factual, etc.) among all participants in the narrative. The abundance of these two devices, along with the three main perspectives, produces a panoramic portrait of many individuals that adds to the rich credibility and broad range of what is not a particularly lengthy narrative.

A brief categorization of some salient features of Solzhenitsyn's stylistic tone is also appropriate at this juncture. The following passage, in the language of the omniscient narrator, illustrates Solzhenitsyn's laconic sarcasm beneath the façade of his narrator:

> Kontora byla—rublenaja izba bliz vakhty. Dym, kak utrom, i posejčas vse valil iz ee truby. Topil ee dneval'nyj, on že i posyl'nyj, povremenku emu vypisyvajut. A ščepok da paloč'ja dlja kontory ne žalejut. [60][23]

This factual description of the warders' office concludes with an observation, the sardonic touch of which seems unmistakable in intent. Here the author's presence penetrates through his narrator and expresses itself as obvious but unobtrusive sarcasm about the warmth of the office. The comment "I Šukhov takoj že špion" (83; "Shukhov was that kind of a spy" [133]) in reference to Russian POWs arrested on charges of espionage upon their return to Russia is similarly laconic and sarcastic. Purely laconic, yet powerful in its effect, is the comment made about Gopchik: ". . . Khlopec let šestnadcati, rozoven'kij" (42; "He was a kid of about sixteen with rosy cheeks" [60]). And perhaps the best example of laconism concludes the book: "Iz-za visokosnykh godov—tri dnja lišnikh nabavljalos' . . ." (121; "The three extra ones [days] were because of the leap years . . ." [203]).

---

23. "The office was a wooden shack next to the guardroom. Smoke was still belching out of the chimney, just like in the morning. The stove was kept going by an orderly who also worked as a messenger and was given a piece rate for this. The office never ran out of firewood." (92)

Solzhenitsyn's pronounced use of matter-of-fact understatement has a definite purpose. Superlative language may rapidly become burdensome and overbearing when used to describe an inherently "superlative" situation. More effective approaches must be found, and this is certainly part of the reasoning behind Solzhenitsyn's selection of a "good" day in Ivan's life. Solzhenitsyn writes in his memoirs of a certain "law of poetry—to be above your anger."[24] He elaborates on his writer's relationship to repulsive human beings in Part III of *The Gulag Archipelago* which in general provides an excellent gloss on many counts for *One Day*. This is immediately relevant to our understanding of the restrained and dispassionate tone in *One Day*:

> I now know that a writer cannot afford to give in to feelings of rage, disgust, or contempt. Did you answer someone in a temper? If so, you didn't hear him out and lost track of his system of opinions. You avoided someone out of disgust—and a completely unknown personality slipped out of your ken—precisely the type you would have needed some day. But, however tardily, I nonetheless caught myself and realized I had always devoted my time and attention to people who fascinated me and were pleasant, who engaged my sympathy, and that as a result I was seeing society like the Moon, always from one side.
>
> But just as the Moon, as it swings slightly back and forth ("libration"), shows us a portion of its dark side too—so that chamber of monstrosities disclosed people unknown to me. [English edition: p. 268; Russian edition: p. 262]

VII

The narrative point of view in *One Day* is expressed through three principal perspectives; however, it is Ivan's activities that predominately determine the book's structure, character delineation, and situational descriptions. The story (*povest'*)[25] contains approximately twenty distinguishable "episodes" during Ivan's day, many of which are shared by Shukhov's gang but virtually none of which occur independently of Ivan's

---

24. Solženicyn, *Bodalsja telenok s dubom*, p. 12 (note 1, above).

25. Ibid., p. 31. Solzhenitsyn gives an interesting discussion here both of the original title of *One Day* (*ŠČ-854*) and of the decision to call it a *povest'*. Perhaps it would be informative to cite his comments about genre in this context: "The boundaries between genres are disappearing in our literature, and a devaluation of form is taking place. Of course *Ivan Denisovich* is a short story (*rasskaz*), though a substantial and weighty one. I would consider a novella smaller than a short story—lighter in construction and clear in its subject matter and thought. A story (*povest'*) is what we frequently call a novel: where there are several plot lines and even an almost obligatory temporal expanse. And a novel (a vile word! have we no other?) differs from a story not so much in size or temporal expanse (compactness and a dynamic quality are even part of the novel) as by the range of the large number of fates involved, the broad horizon, and the vertical line of thought."

presence. These episodes provide the structure that frames the narrative. Each episode assumes an obvious position within the chronological development of the day and creates opportunities, spontaneously keyed by the particular nature of the episode, for natural and unforced commentary by the narrative voices on camp life. *One Day's* descriptions and impressions are not merely a by-product of the rough chronological framework of one camp day; while the book offers an abundance of detail, nothing occurs that is not subordinated to the episodic nature of the narrative and to the free association within the consciousness of the narrative voices.

A number of years of Ivan's imprisonment have been spent in another labor camp, Ust-Izhma. This bit of information is introduced both episodically and associatively. A warder known by the sobriquet "The Thin Tartar" drags Ivan out of bed, takes him to the warders' room, and forces him to mop the floor. It is through this episode that we are confronted with the laziness of the orderlies, the quality of life in the warders' room (with blazing stove and checker games), Ivan's work ethic, and his experience in Ust-Izhma. The strict limitations enforced by Solzhenitsyn's use of perspective would have precluded this illumination of one of the "higher circles" in the camp had Shukhov not been forced to mop the floor. This is the episodic justification. The associative basis for the information on Ust-Izhma derives from the simple descriptive statement "On ulybnulsja prostodušno, pokazyvaja nedostatok zubov" (16; "He gave an innocent smile, which showed that some of his teeth were missing" [13]). This immediately establishes an associative point of departure for a curt comment about Ust-Izhma:

> [the teeth had been] prorežennykh cingoj v Ust'-Ižme v sorok tret'em godu, kogda on dokhodil. Tak dokhodil, čto krovavym ponosom načisto ego pronosilo, istoščennyj želudok ničego prinimat' ne khotel. A teper' tol'ko šepeljaven'e ot togo vremeni i ostalos'. [16][26]

Solzhenitsyn keeps details about that camp deliberately vague at this point, and we learn only of its physically ruinous effect on Shukhov's health. Since it is clear that the camp almost killed him, further particulars are left to the reader's imagination. In this manner the contrast with the present portrayal of a "good" day is underscored, thereby rendering Ivan's joy at his day's success all the more veracious. A less effective alternative to fragmentary dissemination of detail would have been a cohesive account of the earlier camp given at this point in

---

26. "They'd [the teeth] been thinned out by scurvy at Ust-Izhma in 1943, a time when he thought he was on his last legs. He was really far gone. He had the runs, with bleeding, and his insides were so worn out he couldn't keep anything down. But now all that was left from those days was his funny way of talking." (13)

its entirety; however, the lack of correspondence to Ivan's train of thought, conditioned and restricted by the external reality of the episode, negates this possibility. The camp was only mentioned because Ivan smiled, revealing the loss of teeth due to the implicit inhuman conditions of Ust-Izhma; and thoughts about the camp break off when this delicate associative basis is exhausted. These episodic and associative patterns of narration occur independently of any one particular perspective; they encompass and govern instead the presence of every person who appears in the narrative.

To recapitulate briefly, we have shown that two discernible approaches structure descriptions and commentary. On the one hand, they are woven tightly into the narrative fabric through episodical situations; on the other hand, they result from and are given through the remarks of the characters. The latter approach frequently derives from a free association that leads into various illuminations of the camp. As we have shown in our discussion of the Ust-Izhma comments in the warders' room, these two approaches often intermingle. Apart from the information about Ust-Izhma, other aspects of the camp likewise derive from an associative basis in this scene. Ivan prepares to mop the floor in the room, and the following remark is dropped: "Nikak ne godilos' s utra močit' valenki" (15; "It wasn't a good idea to get your felt boots wet in the morning" [11]). This both prefaces and results in an important treatment of the vicissitudes in the boot situation over the course of Shukhov's eight years in camp. The prisoners had at times gone without boots all winter and had worn only footwear made of birch bark or from the "Chelyabinsk Tractor Factory" (which left the marks of the tread behind them); however, the boot situation improved when Shukhov managed to wangle a pair of good sturdy boots in October to go along with the felt ones issued in December. For a while, "žitukha, umirat' ne nado" (15; "Life was great. You didn't have to die" [12]). But camp life oscillates regularly, and the pendulum soon swings back: Shukhov must surrender the good pair. In spite of the obvious importance of the boots, such seemingly inconsequential successes, which fill Ivan's one day, affect the prisoner far out of proportion to their "normal" significance. When Ivan loses the one pair, he feels that "ničego tak žalko ne bylo za vosem' let, kak ètikh botinkov" (15; "nothing had hit him during the whole eight years more than having to turn in those boots" [12]). It seems actually more likely that this deprivation is freshest in Shukhov's mind, while equally or even more disconcerting events have simply been forgotten or repressed. One must bear in mind that the comment is not presented factually, but more as a fleeting thought verbalized within Ivan's mind. The primary point that a prisoner should not get his boots wet early in the morning (a point emphasized

directly by Ivan's immediate situation) digresses to a type of interioralized discussion that casts much light on an important facet of life in
the camp.

The importance of these minor successes over the course of a zek's
camp term cannot be overestimated. Not allowing one's boots to become
wet could well be a crucial factor in maintaining the precarious balance
between a state of relative health and fatal illness. In Part III of
The Gulag Archipelago Solzhenitsyn cites G. Shelest, the author of
Kolyma Notes, and injects his own parenthetical remarks concerning
the long-term significance of extra bowls of mush such as Ivan twice
manages to obtain during the day:

> "Some survived thanks to *their strength of spirit* (these were some
> orthodox Communists swiping bread and cereal—A.S.), while others
> survived thanks to an extra bowl of oatmeal (that was Ivan Denisovich)."
> [English edition: p. 346; Russian edition: p. 340]

The morning march to the work compound illustrates a number of
similar techniques that Solzhenitsyn effectively applies. The prisoners
begin the march at approximately 7 A.M. They must first clear the camp
compound, and factual comments (but with parenthesized sarcasm)
correspond here to the prisoners' surroundings as they leave the camp: the
carpentry workshop "built by the prisoners," a block of living quarters
"(also built by the prisoners . . . but for the 'free' workers)," a new
club "(also the work of prisoners . . . but it was only the 'free' ones
who saw the movies there)," and so forth. The brigade then moves out
into the steppe. From this moment until the arrival at the work site a
half an hour later, the reader is made privy to Ivan's extended daydream.
The prisoners are never allowed to sleep before 10 P.M. and must
arise daily at 5 A.M.; they exist in a state of near exhaustion. In Part
III of *The Gulag Archipelago* Solzhenitsyn writes of the zeks' uncanny
ability to "fall asleep even when marching under guard to work"
(English edition: p. 346; Russian edition: p. 503). Mechanically marching
in standard groups of five, not allowed to look or step aside, and freezing
from the seventeen minus degree weather, Ivan thinks of his next letter
home and of the futility of writing:

> Pisat' teper'—čto v omut dremučij kameški kidat'. Čto upalo, čto
> kanulo—tomu otzyva net. Ne napišeš', v kakoj brigade rabotaeš', kakoj
> brigadir u tebja Andrej Prokof'evič Tjurin. Sejčas s Kil'gasom, latyšom,
> bol'še ob čem govorit', čem s domašnimi. [33][27]

---

27. "Writing now was like throwing stones into a bottomless pit. They fell down and
disappeared, and no sound came back. What was the point of telling them what gang you
worked in and what your boss was like? Now you had more in common with that Latvian
Kilgas than with your own family." (44)

He then recalls in his mind the various scraps of information contained in his family's letters, among other things, about a new boss in the kolkhoz. Shukhov's mind is numbed by lack of sleep, malnutrition, and cold; it begins wandering freely. He recollects the confused situation in the kolkhoz which was constantly being "amalgamated" or split up; this member of the kolkhoz had now lost part of his private plot, another all of it. Shukhov remembers his wife's comment that not a single new member had come to the kolkhoz since the war (an implicit authorial presence is obvious in that bit of information). Additional desultory thoughts follow, each more vaguely connected with the beginning of his daydream always associatively keyed by the previous thought. Within the framework of the march and through Ivan's meandering semi-delirious daydream, Solzhenitsyn duplicates the rambling, disorganized intellection of a tired and cold zek unable to understand the reasoning behind a kolkhoz.

Shukhov's mind skips next to another detail of his wife's last letter: a number of people are taking up "carpet painting." From here Ivan's mind digresses still further. Details of the new carpet painting business mingle with his wife's hopes that he too might one day return and get rich painting carpets, and he continues his interioralized conversation with his wife through her letter. How could Shukhov be a carpet painter if he couldn't even draw? Besides, what was so great about these carpets? Well, as his wife relates, any fool could do it. More absurd details follow: there are three designs, Troika, Stag, and imitation Persian; and they were selling at fifty rubles apiece because the real ones cost thousands. But this type of get-rich-quick business didn't appeal to Shukhov. On the other hand, he reasons, if you had been convicted with loss of rights, you could get no work anyway and weren't even allowed home. And so it continues. The march demands of a prisoner only his unthinking physical compliance and permits his mind to do as it pleases. The snowy steppe provides nothing to occupy his mind anyway, and Shukhov's tired intellect daydreams unhindered about a life far removed from his present existence. The column then arrives, and Ivan's thoughts abruptly break off. Throughout the duration of the march Solzhenitsyn has exposed us to the verbal patter of Shukhov's consciousness, loosely guided by his wife's last letter, but replete with rambling digressions; and the reader too discovers that his perception of time has been likewise dulled until a break in the narrative induced by the arrival at the work compound interrupts the lethargic state of Shukhov's mind.

Solzhenitsyn's treatment of time constitutes one of the more subtly successful aspects of *One Day*. Chronologically brief as well as extended passages can both require the same amount of pages, which demonstrates the lack of correspondence between length in the book and the amount of time an event actually occupies in the fictitious course of the day; nonetheless, one never senses temporal imbalance for Solzhenitsyn masterfully subordinates his delineation of time to Ivan's perception of it and reproduces that perception in the reader. Time and position do coincide at one point in the book: at 1:00 P.M. the prisoners return to work after lunch and a brief rest; both the day and the book are half completed.

Another example of Solzhenitsyn's subtle treatment of time issues not from Shukhov's wandering mind but from his intense concentration at work. The bricklaying episode abounds in minute details of every conceivable technical aspect of a task in which Shukhov reveals himself a past master. The episode is quite devoid of aspects outside the range of the job at hand; any additional information about the gang members (for instance, Fetyukov tilting the hod and spilling some mortar to ease his load) is strictly controlled by the thematic requirements of the minute-to-minute work of hauling mortar and laying brick.

This episode, which revolves around Ivan as the central figure, recounts the prisoners day-long work on a wall. Ivan's sudden discovery that the sun is setting is equally surprising to the reader and leads to the realization that approximately five hours have passed within only ten pages of the narrative. Just as in the march, Ivan's failure to notice the passage of time, a consequence of his intense concentration on the wall, has been successfully recreated within the reader. It is typical of Solzhenitsyn's treatment of time that the completion of the episode, fifteen minutes in length, requires several more pages. Inured to his work, Shukhov even jokingly refuses to stop working until using up the last of the mortar. He remarks to the boss: "Čto, gadstvo, den' rabočij takoj korotkij" (78; "Why do the sonsofbitches give us such a short working day?" [124]). It is true that Solzhenitsyn speaks in Part III of *The Gulag Archipelago* as well of the zeks' custom of making light of their work: "At the end of the working day (when the zeks are already exhausted and waiting for knocking-off time) they invariably joke about the detested work: 'Well, the work just got going but the day is too short' " (English edition: p. 528; Russian edition: p. 516). But Ivan Denisovich is special in his attitude to his work, and the jocular reference to the brief working day serves to cloak his more innate affinity with meaningful physical labor. The following passage, also from Part III of *The Gulag Archipelago*, casts a good deal of light on Solzhenitsyn's personal perception of camp work as well as his embodiment of that principle in the figure of Ivan:

  . . . such is man's nature that even bitter, detested work is sometimes performed with an incomprehensible wild excitement. Having worked for two years with my hands, I encountered this strange phenomenon myself: suddenly you become absorbed in the work itself, irrespective of whether it is slave labor and offers you nothing. I experienced those strange moments at bricklaying (otherwise I wouldn't have written about it), at foundry work, carpentry, even in the fervor of breaking up old pig iron with a sledge. And so surely we can allow Ivan Denisovich not to feel his inescapable labor as a terrible burden forever, not to hate it perpetually? [English edition: p. 259; Russian edition: p. 253]

The language itself reflects the frantic finish during the last few minutes of the bricklaying episode: "Rastvor! Šlakoblok! Rastvor! Šlakoblok!" (78; "Mortar, brick, mortar, brick!" [124]).

Ivan's comment to the boss about the short working day also demonstrates one aspect of Solzhenitsyn's relationship to his narrator Ivan. Shukhov and Solzhenitsyn are unmistakably synonymous within the restricted bounds of the technical particularities of bricklaying. The above citation from *The Gulag Archipelago* supports the assumption that Solzhenitsyn's experience as a bricklayer is interpolated into the copious, precise explanations of the work. It could not really be otherwise. This is certainly not to say that Ivan is autobiographical, for Shukhov's perspective remains very much his own outside of the confines of this factual description.

The short discussion in the office at the work site where Caesar spends his days provides one last example of an episode which establishes the basis for a particular description. Through Ivan's presence Solzhenitsyn creates a situation where, with Caesar and K-123 as his mouthpiece, he can polemicize with Soviet art. Caesar calls Einsenstein a genius whereupon K-123[28] criticizes the film. K-123 explodes in answer to Caesar's remark that any other treatment of the subject would not have been let through:

Akh, propustili by?! Tak ne govorite, čto genij! Skažite, čto podkhalim, zakaz sobačij vypolnjal. Genii ne podgonjajut traktovku pod vkus tiranov! [61][29]

---

28. The use of Caesar's name is justified by the fact that he belongs to Ivan's gang; Ivan knows him personally by name. He is not, however, familiar with Caesar's interlocutor and can only refer to him as K-123, the number he reads from his jacket and cap. The use of a prisoner's number as a form of address occurs at other points in the narrative when the individual involved is a stranger to Ivan.

29. "Ha! Let *through*, you say? Then don't call him a genius! Call him a toady, say he carried out orders like a dog. A genius doesn't adapt his treatment to the taste of tyrants." (94)

This episode occurs solely because of Shukhov's visit and is, in a sense, de-politicized because of Ivan's incomprehension of the "learned conversation." Ivan's struggle for survival continually transcends any overt political message in the book; in fact, the only mention of Stalin —"Bat'ka usatyj" ("the moustached old bastard")—occurs as a result of one of Solzhenitsyn's "concessions" to the editors of *Novyj Mir*. He was asked to mention Stalin's name once as the perpetrator of the horrors pictured in *One Day*![30]

What we are stressing here in our discussion of the episodic structure and fragmentary descriptions in *One Day* is perhaps less obvious than it seems. Solzhenitsyn's point of view techniques disallow a series of chronologically ordered observations and characterizations; rather, the relative "theme" of a particular segment (episodic justification) and the characters' train of thought (associative basis) establish the opportunity for the fragmentary dispersal of details. These opportunities are present in equal portions throughout the narrative; the reader obtains as many details at the end of the day as at the beginning.

Solzhenitsyn's facility in recreating the spontaneity of past impressions and the complexity of a seemingly inarticulate experience, broken down first into one concentrated day, and then dismantled moment by moment into individual utterances, words, and fleeting thoughts, is an unquestionable show of virtuosity in *One Day*. What further heightens his feat is the aesthetic figuration of these events through the consciousness of non-autobiographical characters. Solzhenitsyn firmly believes his experience in the Archipelago provided him with necessary empathetic insight into the human condition of the lower strata of humanity. A brief digression seems justified at this point, for Solzhenitsyn's conviction bears directly on our understanding of his artistic task in *One Day*.

In Part III of *The Gulag Archipelago* Solzhenitsyn elaborates upon the writer and his position in what he, Solzhenitsyn, perceives as the "four spheres of world literature (and of art in general, and ideas in general)."[31] These four spheres assume the following configuration: 1) the upper stratum portraying the upper stratum (itself); 2) the upper stratum depicting or pondering the lower; 3) the lower stratum portraying the upper; and 4) the lower stratum depicting the lower (itself). In Solzhenitsyn's mind, those of the first sphere or stratum were in the most advantageous position to master artistic techniques and disciplines

30. Solženicyn, *Bodalsja telenok s dubom*, p. 48.

31. Solzhenitsyn discusses his theory of literature on pp. 489–91 (English edition) and pp. 477–79 (Russian edition) (see note 9, above).

of thought; but "contentment always kills spiritual striving in a human being," and this frequently vitiated the products of this group. The third sphere suffered both from inexperience and, even worse, from the poison of envy and hatred, feelings nonconducive to artistic creation. Solzhenitsyn's fourth sphere contains, on an oral level, the wealth of the world's folklore and, on a written level, an embryonic, inexperienced (proletarian, peasant) literature, unsuccessful for want of know-how.

Solzhenitsyn contrasts the inherent flaws of much of the literature of these three spheres with that of the second which, "looking down from above," is the most promising in a moral sense. It would combine mature and accomplished artistry with human beings "whose goodness, striving for the truth, and sense of justice had proved stronger than their soporific prosperity." These writers' sympathy, tears, pity, and indignation notwithstanding, the major difficulty encountered here is "the incapacity generally to understand." Writers such as these view others from above, from the sidelines, and are unable to "climb into the *pelts* of the members of the lower stratum." But a transformation can occur through the aid of "external violence." Solzhenitsyn makes particular mention in this context of Cervantes and Dostoevsky, whose experience in the crucible of human suffering infused their art with important human insights. By the same token the Archipelago "opened to writers a fertile though fatal path":

> Millions of Russian intellectuals were thrown there—not for a joy ride: to be mutilated, to die, without any hope of return. For the first time in history, such a multitude of sophisticated, mature, and cultivated people found themselves, not in imagination and once and for all, inside the pelt of a slave, serf, logger, miner. And so for the first time in the world history (on such a scale) the experience of the upper and the lower strata of society *merged*. That extremely important, seemingly transparent, yet previously impenetrable partition preventing the upper strata from understanding the lower—pity—now melted.

The intellectual zeks in the Archipelago were not afflicted with the blinding pangs of conscience which had prevented previous "noble sympathizers" from the second sphere from accurately depicting the lower stratum, for these zeks now shared the same evil fate as the common people.

The relevance of Solzhenitsyn's view of literature as developed in *The Gulag Archipelago* (Part III) to his artistic intention and its realization in *One Day* becomes immediately evident toward the end of his treatise: "Only now could an educated Russian write about an enserfed peasant *from the inside*—because he himself had become a serf" (491). Yet even as the Archipelago was granting the intellectual zeks the necessary insight into the lower stratum of humanity, it was likewise eliminating forever the possibility of their ever setting pen to paper by bringing about their physical destruction:

> The experience of the upper and the lower stratum had merged—but the bearers of the merged experience perished . . .
> And thus it was that an unprecedented philosophy and literature were buried under the iron crust of the Archipelago. [491]

We have spoken of the tandem approach practiced by Solzhenitsyn in his structuring of descriptions and commentary, and we have given two lengthy examples of one of them—the episodic framework. We have also pointed out that various digressions stem directly from a spontaneous reaction to incidental remarks. For reasons of space we shall cite only one last example of an observation that results associatively from a character's comment. While laying brick the gang is being harassed by Der, the building foreman, who was "trying to rise in the world and get himself made an engineer, the damn swine" (113). He was completely ignorant about construction, and to his, Shukhov's and everybody else's way of thinking, you should build a house with your own hands before trying to become an engineer. The one word "house" releases Ivan's thoughts to a verbalized remembrance only vaguely related to the particular episode of bricklaying: "V Temgenëve kamennykh domov ne znali, izby iz dereva. I škola tože rublenaja, iz zakaznika les privozili v šest' saženej" (72; "In Shukhov's home village there were no stone houses, only wooden shacks. And the school was built of logs too— they got as much wood as they liked from the forest" [114]). But the job at hand, which commands Ivan's full attention, immediately redirects his thoughts back to bricklaying: "A v lagere ponadobilos' na kamen- ščika—i Šukhov, požalujsta, kamenščik. Kto dva dela rukami znaet, tot ešče i desjat' podkhvatit" (72; "But now in the camp he had to do a bricklayer's job. So okay, he did. Anybody who knew two trades could pick up a dozen more just like that" [114]). This particular digression is dissimilar to the march where the actual physical activity had no control over Shukhov's freely wandering thoughts. In the above passage, Ivan also mentally verbalizes his thoughts; but his consciousness is conditioned by and dependent on the events of his daily regimen.

VIII

Solzhenitsyn's character delineation is likewise a product of perspective and of the episodic structure and associative commentary. Solzhenitsyn accordingly avoids unified portrayals of characters in single passages (Tyurin is one exception). Just as all the points of Solzhenitsyn's dis- connected account are distributed equally throughout yet fully integrated into the entire narrative, so the depiction of prisoners is divided and dispersed mosaically; it is the reader's task to assemble the puzzle of fragmentary details to reconstruct the ambience of the camp.

Shukhov's gang is composed of many different strata of Soviet society: Shukhov, the simple peasant and soldier arrested as a POW, typifies the largest single group of prisoners;[32] Alyosha symbolizes the persecuted religious believer; Fetyukov, the upper echelon of arrested bureaucrats; Gopchik, young prisoners; Caesar, the intellectual and racial mix; Pavlo, the Ukrainians; and Boss Tyurin, the "lifer."

The broad dispersal of essential details of personality and biography is especially subtle in the case of the unsympathetic scavenger Fetyukov. He was "iz poslednikh brigadnikov, poploše Šukhova" (17; "He didn't count for much in the gang, even less than Shukhov" [16]) and is shown (as a counter-figure to and through the thoughts of Shukhov) totally without human dignity. He would look straight at another prisoner's mouth when he wanted a cigarette butt, often going as far as to pick them out of the spittoons. He is lazy and persists in trying to scrounge anything possible, which often leads to a beating. Yet despite the negative aspects of his personality, Solzhenitsyn requires but one factual observation to evoke sympathy even for this repellent zek: "U Fetjukova na vole detej troe, no kak sel—ot nego vse otkazalis', a žena zamuž vyšla: tak pomošči emu niotkuda" (39; "Fetyukov had three children 'outside,' but they'd all disowned him when he was arrested, and his wife had married again. So there was no one to send him things" [56]).[33] Fetyukov's case is emblematic: as a prisoner his family has disowned him (either voluntarily or through coercion of various types). The reader is likewise informed cursorily about the most important biographical detail concerning Fetyukov's former life "outside": "Fetjukov, kes' v kakoj-to kontore načal'nikom byl. Na mašine ezdil" (46; "Fetyukov was once some kind of a big shot in an office. He used to ride around in a car" [68]). This essential fact occurs as a brief mental digression as Ivan observes the Captain and Fetyukov carrying sand in hods; from it

---

32. The cook allotes Ivan's gang twenty-three bowls of mush (including Caesar's, who is not present) at lunchtime, but for some reason twenty-four in the evening. Despite this apparent minor discrepancy in the size of the gang, the statement that each gang had five such spies gives an indication of the approximate percentage of zeks imprisoned on fake charges of espionage.

33. Despite Solzhenitsyn's implacability in questions of morality, a similar somewhat understanding attitude toward others pervades *The Gulag Archipelago*, primarily in the chapter "The Bluecaps" in his discussion of good and evil. This even leads Solzhenitsyn to write: "It is after all only because of the way things worked out that they were the executioners and we weren't." Aleksandr Solženicyn, *Arkhipelag GULag: 1918–1956. Opyt khudozestvennogo issledovanija* (Paris: YMCA Press, 1973) [Pts. 1 & 2], p. 176. English translation by Whitney, p. 168 (see note 9, above).

the reader must deduce that Fetyukov belongs to the upper stratum of arrested Soviet bureaucrats. Only one additional detail is supplied in this regard, and it appears at a considerably later point in time: "U, gadskaja krov'! A direktorom byl—nebos' s rabočikh treboval?" (71; "You lazy slob. I bet you really took it out on the fellows in that factory you managed" [112]).

This pattern of always providing information about a prisoner's former life, his sentence, a few physical characteristics, and his personality is repeated in the case of most members of Shukhov's gang that appear in the story; however, the information is never allowed to occur in any predetermined order. We learn the following details about Buynovsky throughout the chronological course of the narrative: he had been a captain in the navy (5;11),[34] he had only been in prison for three months (38; 29), and he is a Communist (38; 29). He is obviously intelligent, but is deteriorating physically (41; 31). He treats camp work conscientiously, like the navy, always working hard (112; 71), and he is about forty years old (119, 75). Finally, within the framework of the prisoner count in the late afternoon, we find out the reason for his arrest (140; 86). This manner of character portrayal allows Solzhenitsyn to depict unobtrusively each prisoner in surprising detail while integrating his information according to the formal dictates of his style.

IX

Facts about Shukhov's personality and biography also abound in the book and manage to reveal most important aspects of his life. When referring to physical characteristics, however, the details become exceedingly scanty (as is also the case with the other prisoners). Senka is deaf, Caesar of uncertain racial derivation, and the boss's face is all pockmarked. Other than personal biographical details, Solzhenitsyn de-particularizes his characters by depriving them of thorough physical description. Ivan's "funny way of talking" and his near-baldness are among the relatively few peculiarities we learn about him. It has been suggested (in reference to *The First Circle* but also applicable here) that Solzhenitsyn's cursory reference to physical characteristics recreates the description contained in a prisoner's police records. Different zeks are then imagined purely in terms of the salient features mentioned in their file.[35] Another possibility suggests itself. By giving very sparse details of physical appearance Solzhenitsyn permits the millions of former camp

34. Where only the English text is cited, the page numbers refer to the English and Russian editions in that order (see note 4, above).

35. Brown, "Solzhenitsyn's Cast of Characters," p. 358 (note 8, above).

inmates to identify personally with his "fictitious" creations. The remarks
of Soviet readers of *One Day* attest to his success:

> MARKELOV: "Ivan Denisovich? That's me, sz-209. And I can give all
> the characters real names, not invented ones. Which camp? Ukhta,
> 29th encampment. Or Steplag, Balkhash, 8th section."
> N.A. IVANOV: "It's the No. 8 mine in Vorkuta."
> VOYCHENKO: "Solzhenitsyn has not even changed Tyurin's name . . . I
> shall never forget the disciplinary officer, Sorodov, introduced in the
> story as Volkovoy . . . I also knew Shukhov under another name.
> There was one like him in every brigade."[36]

As a conclusion to our examination of a camp "through the eyes of
a peasant," we shall now look at a character who is seen exactly as
Shukhov views him. This discussion involves a number of aspects
somewhat outside the realm of narrative technique; but it will nonetheless
show how Solzhenitsyn is able to work within the bounds of perspective
and its influence on the work's structure to make important statements
on questions of morality and religion.

Alyosha is perhaps the most important single figure in *One Day* apart
from Ivan, and it is obviously no coincidence that he is a Baptist.
According to the magazine *Time*, Soviet civil rights leaders have reported
that more than one-third of the known political prisoners in the Soviet
Union during the past two decades were made up of Baptists.[37]
When understood in conjunction with Solzhenitsyn's remarks made on
numerous occasions about the failures of the Russian Orthodox Church,[38]
it becomes immediately evident that the portrayal of Alyosha the Baptist
as a persecuted religious figure is an implied attack on the Orthodox
Church. This polemic culminates at the conclusion of the book, which
contains a discussion quite unlike any previous talk in the book in terms
of the subject matter (although its occurrence is understandable and
well integrated, as it takes place during what little time the prisoners
have to themselves). During the conversation Shukhov reveals the
complete hypocrisy of the priest in his, Ivan's, village parish. This does
not surprise the Baptist Alyosha, and Solzhenitsyn directs a powerful
accusation through him at the official church: "Začem ty mne o pope?

---

36. Leopold Labedz, ed., *Solzhenitsyn: A Documentary Record* (Bloomington: Indiana
University Press, 1973), pp. 44–5.

37. *Time Magazine*, 27 January 1975, pp. 86–7. I have no way of verifying these figures,
but the March, 1975, issue of *Posev*, no. 3, contains similar information about persecution of
Baptists in the Soviet Union.

38. See in particular Solzhenitsyn's letter "To Patriarch Pimen of Russia," in John B.
Dunlop, Richard Haugh, and Alexis Klimoff, eds., *Aleksandr Solzhenitsyn: Critical Essays
and Documentary Materials* (New York: Collier Books, 1975), pp. 550–56.

Pravoslavnaja cerkov' ot evangelija otošla. Ikh ne sažajut ili pjat' let dajut, potomu čto vera u nikh ne tverdaja" (118; "Why are you telling me about this priest? The Orthodox Church has gotten away from the Gospel. And the reason they don't put them in prison, or give them only five years, is because they have no true faith" [197-8]).[39]

It would obviously be a serious misreading of Solzhenitsyn to interpret his criticism as pertaining to all religious believers, and he certainly does not discount the faith of all Orthodox believers. He has consistently high praise for Christians of all denominations who fell into the Archipelago because of adherence to their faith. There are frequent references in *The Gulag Archipelago* to the steadfastness of faith the Christians evinced in the camps, and Solzhenitsyn's portrait of Alyosha may be better understood in light of the following comments (from Part IV), especially the last sentence:

> And how is it that genuine religious believers survived in camp (as we mentioned more than once)? In the course of this book we have already mentioned their self-confident procession through the Archipelago—a sort of silent religious procession with invisible candles. How some among them were mowed down by machine guns and those next in line continued their march. A steadfastness unheard of in the twentieth century! And it was not in the least for show, and there weren't any declamations. [English edition: pp. 623-4; Russian edition: p. 610]

Solzhenitsyn's character study of Alyosha is given "through the eyes of a peasant" and is emphasized by the high opinion Ivan has of the Baptist. Alyosha's everyday life evidences the morality he professes. His quiet, unobtrusive dedication to prayer and Bible study (26; 23), his refusal to relax his principles even slightly (49; 35), and his meek devotion to work (112; 71) are all sympathetically seen through Ivan's eyes. But Shukhov does not merely serve in this instance as a mouthpiece for the author's view of Alyosha alone; it is, rather, Ivan's relationship itself to Alyosha and the nature of their respective personalities that is important. The Baptist evinces one method of maintaining principles; and Shukhov has high respect for his way of life. The admiration is quite unmistakable: "S nikh [Alyosha and the Baptists] lagerja, kak s

---

39. The phrase "or give them five years" is new in the YMCA edition (in comparison with the Posev edition of Solzhenitsyn's works). One may wonder if Solzhenitsyn felt it quite inconceivable to imagine any social group escaping the Archipelago completely. And five years was astonishingly little anyway, especially when one considers that *"the sentence for nothing at all is ten years."* The Gulag Archipelago, I-II (English edition: p. 293; Russian edition: p. 299).

gusja voda. Po dvadcat' pjat' let vkatili im za baptistskuju veru—
neuž dumajut tem ot very otvadit'?"[40] The first part of that remark
also indicates the extent of Ivan's understanding of the implications of
Alyosha's belief. Shukhov's admiration for Alyosha is also given expression on other occasions as well: "Smirnyj— v brigade klad" (71; "A
meek fellow is a treasure in any gang" [112; The translation is misleading,
and I have altered it accordingly]). It is Shukhov's peasant pragmatism
that perhaps plays a large part in preventing him from accepting
Alyosha's faith:

> Bezotkaznyj ètot Aleška, o čem ego ni poprosi. Kab vse na svete
> takie byli, i Šukhov by byl takoj. Esli čelovek prosit—otčego ne posobit'?
> Èto verno u nikh. [75][41]

Interestingly enough, there are occasions where Ivan does precisely
that. The main significant difference between Ivan and Alyosha is
perhaps Shukhov's inability to associate his principles with a particular
faith. His dedication to honest hard work makes his wife's carpet idea
inherently abhorrent. Even in the camp he insisted on making his own
way, and he refused to ever lower his standards: "No on ne byl
šakal daže posle vos'mi let obščikh rabot—i čem dal'še, tem krepče
utverždalsja" (107; "After eight years of hard labor he was still no
scavenger and the more time went on, the more he stuck to his guns"
[178]). Shukhov's attitude toward other prisoners also evinces his innate
beneficence. He approves when Pavlo offers the Captain an extra bowl
of mush: "A po Šukhovu pravil'no, čto kapitanu otdali. Pridet pora,
i kapitan žit' naučitsja, a poka ne umeet" (59; "But to Shukhov's way
of thinking, it was only right to give it to the Captain. The time
would come when he'd learn the ropes, but as it was he didn't know
his way around yet" [91]). And when Caesar is caught at the night
check with his package unhidden, Ivan adroitly helps him avoid having
it stolen; not because he hoped to scrounge something more to eat, but
because he felt sorry for Caesar. Ivan's type of "ignorant perfection"

---

40. "The camp didn't worry them—it was like water off a duck's back. They hit 'em
with twenty-five years for their Baptist faith—do they really think they can get them to give
up their belief with that?" (49) The concluding sentence is new in the YMCA edition of
One Day. Again, it may be worth speculating on the reasons for the addition. It seems
likely that Solzhenitsyn wished to emphasize even further the plight of the genuine religious
believers in the Archipelago and to contrast their twenty-five year sentence with the
maximum five years given those with "no true faith."

41. "Alyosha always did whatever you asked. If only everybody in the world was like that,
Shukhov would be that way too. If someone asked you, why not help him out?
They were right on that, these people." (120)

might well be termed Christian and, in this sense, he may serve as a
paradigm for Solzhenitsyn's contention that justice and conscience are
inherent in man and not traceable to any other source.[42]

Ivan is not, however, completely without his character flaws. His
behavior is somewhat less admirable during the lunchtime break:
"Vklinilsja on za stolòm, dvukh dokhodjag sognal, odnogo rabotjagu
po-khorošemu poprosil . . ." (55; "He squeezed through to one of the
tables, chased away a couple of goners, asked another prisoner to have
a heart and go away . . ." [84-5]). Moreover, the following incident
takes place at the evening meal:

> Dones tot [S-208] do mesta, razgruzil, Šukhov skhvatilsja za podnos,
> a i tot [the other zek to whom S-208 had promised the tray]
> nabežal, komu obeščano, za drugoj konec podnosa tjanet. A sam
> ščuplej Šukhova. Šukhov ego tuda že podnosom dvinul, kuda tjanet, on
> otletel k stolbu, s podnosa ruki sorvalis'. [101][43]

These two events contribute to a more total understanding of Ivan's
character and the effect on it of his years in camp. Solzhenitsyn
draws an important distinction in Part IV of *The Gulag Archipelago*
between life in a prison cell and in a camp. The amount of bread
available was so insufficient in the latter "that one or two people have
to die for each one who survives" (English edition: p. 619; Russian
edition: p. 606). Life frequently degenerated to a simple struggle in the
camps: "You got beaten if you were weaker than all the rest, or else you
yourself beat up those weaker than you" (English edition: pp. 620-21;
Russian edition: p. 607). The point is definitely not accidental that
Shukhov notes the size of the other zek before shoving him. Solzhenitsyn
acknowledges in *The Gulag Archipelago* (Part IV) that "that's the
general trend, that's the way things are" (English edition: p. 623;
Russian edition: p. 609).[44] Solzhenitsyn's depiction of Ivan reveals an
individual with a high standard of personal morality; however, he too is
unable to avoid completely infection by the "soul mange" (*duševnyj
lišaj*) of which Solzhenitsyn speaks in *The Gulag Archipelago*. The
sympathetic overall portrait notwithstanding, Ivan too has moments of

42. In particular, see Solzhenitsyn's letter to three students in Labedz, *Solzhenitsyn*, p. 151, where this notion is unequivocally expressed.

43. "S-208 put his bowls on the table and Shukhov snatched the tray. But the other guy ran over and grabbed it by the end. He was smaller than Shukhov. So Shukhov shoved it at him and sent him flying against one of the posts holding up the roof." (166)

44. Whitney's translation (note 9, above) is somewhat misleading, and I have altered it slightly. The Russian text is: "Èto—obščee napravlenie, èto—zakonomernost'."

weakness. He will most likely survive his camp term (it is in fact almost over); but in return, one or two others (the goners? the "other guy"?) will not leave the camp alive. Ivan's shortcomings, slight as they are on a comparative scale, are probably traceable to Solzhenitsyn's hypersensitivity toward the smallest of "concessions." In *The Gulag Archipelago* he cites numerous instances where he felt he might have offered more resistance to the camp authorities.[45]

Ivan is contrasted in this way with Alyosha, whose behavior during the day is emblematic of Solzhenitsyn's view of religious prisoners. Alyosha's moral integrity is impeccable, but his chances of surviving the Archipelago are accordingly slimmer, as Solzhenitsyn points out in *The Gulag Archipelago* (Part IV): "And yet who was there among the religious prisoners whose soul was corrupted? They died—most certainly, but . . . they weren't corrupted" (English edition: p. 624; Russian edition: p. 611).

It might be worth noting an additional element to the relationship between Ivan and Alyosha that may serve to bring into sharper focus our comparison of the two. It seems inconceivable that a Russian novelist of Solzhenitsyn's stature could randomly select the names Ivan and Alyosha for his two main protagonists without some awareness of their predecessors in Dostoevsky's *The Brothers Karamazov*. This parallel might easily be developed to the point of absurdity; nonetheless, there do exist echoes of the Dostoevskian dialectic in *One Day* that surpass mere name similarity.

The plot in *One Day*, and all events and conversations occurring within it, are directly determined by the minute-to-minute reality of the camp day and the demands the daily regimen places on the individual zeks. Following the last night check, however, Ivan and Alyosha engage in a conversation about God and prayer (English edition: pp. 195–99; Russian edition: pp. 117–19) which, as we have already indicated, is quite dissimilar in nature to any preceding discussions in the book. Alyosha makes any number of attempts to convert Ivan to his, Alyosha's, religious convictions; but to the Baptist's exhortation to prayer, Ivan replies that "molitvy te, kak zajavlenija, ili ne dokhodjat, ili 'v žalobe otkazat' ' " (117; "all these prayers are like the complaints we send to the higher-ups—either they don't get there or they come back marked 'rejected' " [196]). Ivan counters all of Alyosha's lofty religious sentiments with opinions that have been formed by the experiential realities of his eight years in camp. Modes of thought outside the realm of his daily

---

45. See in particular the chapter entitled "Knock, Knock, Knock . . . " in part III of *The Gulag Archipelago*, (English edition: pp. 353–374; Russian editon: pp. 347–367).

ordeal are inaccessible to the pragmatic Ivan, for his consciousness and rational capabilities of comprehension have been indelibly stamped by his years in Soviet prison camps. Moreover, as Solzhenitsyn points out in *The Gulag Archipelago*:

> Can you think about your own grief, about the past and future, about humanity and God? Your mind is absorbed in vain calculations which for the present moment cut you off from the heavens—and tomorrow you are worth nothing. [English edition: pp. 619–20; Russian edition: pp. 606–7]

As for Dostoevsky's Ivan, the question of God's existence is not the central issue at all for Shukhov: "V Boga ja okhotno verju" (118; "I believe in God, all right" [198]). It is the notion of Heaven and Hell that is insulting to one who has been subjected to eight years of Stalin's own version of the latter: "Tol'ko vot ne verju ja v raj i v ad" (118; "But what I don't believe in is Heaven and Hell" [128]). The present simply "cuts off" Ivan from the possibility of engaging in such contemplation. One's religious beliefs and the amount of time spent in prayer change little, as Ivan points out to Alyosha: ". . . skol'ko ni molis', a sroku ne skinut. Tak ot zvonka do zvonka i dosidiš' " (118; ". . . you can pray as much as you like but they won't take anything off your sentence and you'll just have to sit it out, every day of it, from reveille to lights out" [198]). Under normal circumstances Ivan might well have been receptive to Alyosha's formal religious concepts, for the two share numerous similarities in their standards of morality; but the total senselessness of Ivan's situation renders impossible any understanding of abstract religious principles beyond the only world Ivan knows:

> Viš, Aleška,—Šukhov raz"jasnil,—u tebja kak-to ladno polučaetsja: Khristos tebe sidet' velel, za Khrista ty i sel. A ja za čto sel? Za to, čto v sorok pervom k vojne ne prigotovilis', za èto? A ja pri čem? [119][46]

Much as Ivan's opinions in *The Brothers Karamazov* have been molded by his view of the empiric reality of the world, which makes immaterial questions concerning any divine order and meaning, so Shukhov's camp experience has radically curtailed his receptivity to metaphysical arguments seeking to establish a higher purpose behind the suffering in the camps.

---

46. " 'Look, Alyoshka,' Shukhov said, 'it's all right for you. It was Christ told you to come here, and you are here because of Him. But why am *I* here? Because they didn't get ready for war like they should've in forty-one? Was that my fault?' " (199)

In spite of the formal restrictions Solzhenitsyn has imposed upon himself by his choice of perspective ("a camp through the eyes of a peasant"), he has nonetheless succeeded in grafting into his account a relationship which has implicit and far-reaching significance in its treatment of important facets of life and thought in the camp.[47] The range of implications contained, in particular, in this brief concluding conversation is quite extensive; but in much the same style that typifies Solzhenitsyn's artistry throughout the entire narrative, the integration of the discussion is effected in such a manner as to avoid completely any impression of unnatural authorial coercion or force. It is characteristic of the relationship Ivan and Alyosha share, as it is of the entire camp account, that one never has the impression Solzhenitsyn felt constrained to "say it all," to omit no detail, however small. While the amount of information in *One Day* is truly astonishing, the total unity of the narrative is a mark of the author's formal virtuosity.

---

47. As a footnote to Ivan's talk with Alyosha it might be worth noting that it was these very passages that Dementyev wanted eliminated from the story because they were "artistically pale, ideologically false, too long anyway, and only spoiled a good story." See *Bodalsja telenok s dubom*, p. 45 (note 1, above).

THE NEW YORK CROATO-GLAGOLITIC MISSAL AND ITS BACKGROUND
(PRELIMINARY COMMUNICATION)

BY

HENRIK BIRNBAUM

As I HAVE recently tried to show elsewhere (Birnbaum, 1976), considerable evidence supports the assumption—despite the doubts expressed lately by J. Hamm—that the extant copy of what is still generally regarded as the earliest known specimen of continuous Slavic text, the so-called *Kiev Folia*, originated somewhere in Dalmatian Croatia. It is my contention that it was only the immediate textual source of the *Kiev Folia*, whether itself the original or only an intermediate copy of a still earlier prototype, that was written by a Czech scribe either in the Bohemian-Moravian-Pannonian area or, after Methodius's death in 885 and the subsequent expulsion of the Slavic clergy from Greater Moravia, somewhere in the Slavic South, perhaps Macedonia. Possibly, this archaic Old Church Slavonic text could also have been written in Rome during the Thessalonian brothers' stay there prior to Constantine's demise in 869, as was suggested by G. Y. Shevelov (1957, 391), among others. Therefore, in a sense there can be said to exist a direct link between the linguistic form in which the *Kiev Folia* have come down to us, pointing to Dalmatian Croatia, and the numerous missals in Croatian Church Slavonic. The earliest Old Church Slavonic text, too, contains a mass-book according to the Roman rite, though in an abridged version—*libellus missae*—and with no exact Latin counterpart so far ascertained. By contrast to the *Kiev Folia*, the Croatian missals are written in the more recent, angular variety of the Glagolitic script characteristic of Dalmatia, including, in particular, the Croatian Littoral (Hrvatsko Primorje) and the Kvarner Archipelago. Yet it should be

Research on this paper was in part supported by a grant from the American Philosophical Society.

225

remembered that Glagolitic writing and the Slavic liturgy had been interfered with and, subsequently, explicitly banned by the Roman See in the later part of the eleventh century by the Synods of 1066/7, probably held in Omiš, and of 1075/6, convened in Split, under the Popes Alexander II and Gregory VII. It was not until nearly two hundred years later, after Pope Innocent IV had officially granted the island of Krk and the diocese of Senj as well as, shortly thereafter, the Benedictine monastery at Omišalj the right to retain or, rather, resume their tradition of conducting service in Slavic and using the ancient Slavic alphabet—decrees of 1248 and 1252—that the activity of the *glagoljaši* once again could flourish and spread. On the vicissitudes of the Slavic liturgy and Glagolitic writing in Dalmatian Croatia, cf. further, e. g., Dvornik, 1970, 236-44. In time, this renewed papal permission coincided with the acceptance of the Franciscan redaction of the *Missale plenum (Ordo Missalis secundum consuetudinem Romanae curiae)*. In this context it should also be noted, however, that the remaining fourteen folia of the eleventh century Old Church Slavonic codex *Clozianus*, a homily collection also known as *Glagolita Clozianus* and now available in an exemplary critical edition by A. Dostál, have some unmistakably Croatian features and that the manuscript whose major portion is now lost was probably first found on Krk and may well have originated in this area; cf. Dostál, 1959, 6 and 9; see also Grivec, 1960, 194, and Vlasto, 1970, 380, n. 172. And the so-called *Vienna Folia*, the oldest unambiguously Croato-Glagolitic liturgical text—dating from the twelfth century—already show the characteristically Croat ductus of the Glagolitic script with its angular shape, thus testifying to the early evolvement of this form of writing. See also Vajs, 1932, 128-30, especially n. 8, on the shape of the script found in *Clozianus*; 138-9 on that of the *Vienna Folia*; 144-6, on the general background of the flowering of Croatian writing in Glagolitic as of the mid-thirteenth century.

The oldest extant Croato-Glagolitic full missal text is the famed Vatican codex (sign. *Illir. 4*) described in detail in Vajs, 1948. It dates from the beginning of the fourteenth century, not later than sometime between 1314 and 1323. Its place of origin is in all likelihood Omišalj on the island of Krk; cf. also Vajs, 1932, 147; Vlasto, 1970, 205. From earlier times, only missal and breviary fragments are known; so, for example, besides the previously mentioned, very earliest *Vienna Folia*, there is the fragmentary *Baška Missal*, again from Krk: two narrow strips containing an excerpt from a passion reading (Mt XXVI:37-48); cf. Vajs, 1932, 140-1; 1948, 5-6; Vlasto, 1970, 205. But the bulk of Croato-Glagolitic missal texts, including all full versions, date only from the fourteenth and, especially, fifteenth centuries. The latter missals, mostly from the fifteenth century, represent a more recent, largely stereotype textual tradition. (We are disregarding in this context still later printed variants—the oldest edition of a Glagolitic missal text appeared in 1483, most probably in Venice; see Vajs, 1932, 158; 1948, 44-7.) Thus, the Vatican manuscript (*Illir. 4*) and the richly illuminated and handsomely executed *Hrvoje Missal* (also *Hrvoje's Glagolitic Missal*), dating from ca. 1404 and housed in the Library of the Topkapı Sarayı Museum in Istanbul (now available in a luxurious, scholarly edition in two volumes which cites in its critical apparatus major variant readings), can serve as fitting examples of these two varieties of what nonetheless essentially must be considered one—Franciscan—redaction of the Croato-Glagolitic version of the Roman Catholic *Missale plenum* (or *plenarium*). A survey of extant manuscripts of the missal text in Glagolitic script can be found in Vajs, 1948, 3-43, in addition to the brief, now somewhat dated account given in Vajs, 1932, previously referred to. Cf. now also Grabar-Nazor-Pantelić II, 1973, 520, and Nazor, 1975, 211-12; see further Štefanić, 1969, 57-90 (listing and briefly describing all Glagolitic missal texts, both complete and fragmentary, now housed in the Yugoslav Academy of Zagreb); Radovich, 1974 (discussing the application of a statistical method of graphic and linguistic data contained in four Glagolitic missal manuscripts primarily for dating and classifying purposes); Birk-fellner, 1974 (on a hitherto overlooked Croato-Glagolitic missal fragment in the Austrian National Library, with some general comments on relevant manuscripts in Austrian public collections); Böhm, 1959 (describing and analyzing a Croato-Glagolitic missal fragment found in Wertheim, West Germany).

Even though the bibliographic references just listed merely represent a selection of relevant titles, it is noteworthy that only in one—Grabar-Nazor-Pantelić II, 1973, 520—is there any mention made of a Croato-Glagolitic manuscript of a full missal text, purchased in 1966 by The Pierpont Morgan Library in New York City. For the manuscript, listed simply as "*New York*, Morgan Library M 931," not even a tentative date or place of origin is indicated. My own attention was drawn to this manuscript in early 1970 by the leading expert in the field, Professor Josef Hamm of Vienna University. In a letter from the Director of The Pierpont Morgan Library, Charles A. Ryskamp, dated October 20, 1970, I was granted the rights to publish a scholarly edition of this manuscript (sign. *M 931*). Preparations are now underway to arrange for such a critical edition to be published in two volumes (part I: facsimile reproduction; part II: transliteration, philological apparatus, scholarly essays, glossary) by Otto Sagner Verlag, Munich, in that publisher's series

Sagners Slavistische Sammlung, edited by Dr. P. Rehder. The collaboration of specialists from the Universities of Munich and Vienna as well as the Old Slavonic Institute (Staroslavenski institut) in Zagreb has been assured. What follows is some preliminary information on the *New York Missal*—this name henceforth to be used as its informal designation—its appearance and format, significance, and external history.

In the catalog issued by the well-known auctioneers Sotheby of London announcing the auction on Tuesday, November 29, 1966, of the "Bibliotheca Phillippica," i. e., the book and manuscript collection of Sir Thomas Phillipps, the *New York Missal* was described in some detail on pages 68–69 as follows:

[Lot] 62 MESSALE GLAGOLITHICUM [*sic* H.B.]

[WESTERN CROATIA, C. 1400-1410]

On vellum. 293 ll., apparently lacking nine leaves in the body of the work and one (or more) gatherings at the end. Gatherings mostly of ten leaves with catchwords. Double column. 30 lines. 280 x 195 mm.; 11 x 7 3/4 in. Handsomely written in black ink (the first gathering in brown) in Glagolithic script. Rubrics in red. The initial letter of most sentences has red infilling. Tear in f. 134 neatly patched and text supplied by an early hand. A little waterstaining of the first twenty-three leaves, mostly in the upper margin, and a few other stains and signs of use, but the writing throughout very clear and the whole manuscript in very sound condition. Wide outer and lower margins, many leaves having the pin-holes. English early nineteenth-century russia over thick wooden boards, which have been hollowed out to leave areas in high relief; decorated in blind; blind-tooled doublures; small projections from the edges of the boards in the manner of a 'box-binding' (perhaps by T. Witaker).

PROVENANCE

(1) Fredrick North, fifth Earl of Guilford (1766-1827), with his bookplate; his sale, Evans, 8 December 1830, lot 460, bought by Thorpe for Sir Thomas Phillipps. The underbidder was probably Sir Fredric Madden, for the British Museum.

(2) Phillipps MS. 6446. Phillipps paid the colossal price of £168 for this manuscript at the Guilford sale, and considered it one of his chief treasures. It was often produced at his 'desserts of manuscripts' for the admiration of visitors.

TEXT

This is a translation of the Roman Missal into Croat written in the Glagolithic alphabet—the ancient Slavonic alphabet peculiar to Croatia. There are both palaeographic and philological indications that it comes from the North-Western Čakavci-dialect area (i. e. the Western part) of Croatia. In its composition it resembles missals from the Lika-Krbava area (namely the Missal of Prince Novak of 1368 in Vienna, Cod. slav. 8, Bodleian Library MS. Canon. Lit. 172 also of the fourteenth century, and the later Vatican Cod. illir. 8), rather than the Glagolithic Missal of 1402 in Berlin. The absence of a calendar supports the belief that this originally formed no part of Missals from this region.

The scribe was clearly ignorant both of the Latin language and of the Roman rite, and the manuscript cannot have been intended for one of the churches on the coast. A rubric on f. 107*b* directs the choir to sing the text that follows in both Greek and Slav during Passion-week; the Greek words are given in Glagolithic transcription. From the marriage service it is clear that the Missal was for the use of nobles, and not of merchants or peasants.

Glagolithic manuscripts are of the utmost rarity. None is recorded in the U.S.A. and it is doubtful whether any has been sold at auction in England since the present one was last offered in 1830. It is entirely unpublished, and will certainly prove of both philological and liturgical importance.

Included in the lot is an autograph description of the manuscript, in Latin with Glagolithic transcripts of some passages, by Bartholomaeus Kopitar, the Croat scholar and Keeper in the Imperial Library, Vienna, signed and dated 15 December 1837, and a copy of Kopitar's *Glagolita Clozianus*, Vienna, 1836, large 4to, partly printed in Glagolithic letter, with two plates, bound in calf.

DECORATION

The great interest of the decoration is that it combines painted initials in an Italianate style (with both Venetian and Bolognese influence) with characteristically Slav penwork initials. There are seven painted initials, of which four are historiated and have foliate prolongations usually extending to both upper and lower margins.

Folio 82. The angel of St. Matthew.
Folio 88. The lion of St. Mark.
Folio 93. The bull of St. Luke.
Folio 102. The eagle of St. John.

Smaller painted initials are on f. 144*b* (tree-trunk, vase and feathers), f. 148*b* and f. 196 (deer's head holding branch).

The penwork initials are extremely numerous and vary greatly in size. They embody a wide range of foliate and interlaced ornament. They are in red with occasional use of black, but from ff. 1–9 and 41–52 most have yellow infilling, from ff. 30–41 the infilling is green, eight initials are in red and blue (ff. 1, 145*b* and 192–199*b*) and one (f. 178*b*) in red, blue and green. Six of the catchwords are accompanied by penwork ornament.

[SEE COLOUR PLATE B AND PLATE 17]

This is as far as the description in Sotheby's catalog goes. For more information on the avid British manuscript collector and bibliophile

Sir Thomas Phillipps, see the five-volume set of *Phillipps Studies* by
A. N. L. Munby, especially Munby, 1954, on the assembling of the
Phillipps Library in the years of the acquisition of the Croato-Glagolitic
missal manuscript (cf. pp. 56, 159), and Munby, 1960, on the scattering
of this unique collection; the lack of a particular reference to our manuscript in the index (see no. 6446, Munby, 1960, 124), seems to suggest,
however, that in spite of what was said in the Sotheby featuring of this
codex as being considered by Sir Thomas to be one of his chief treasures,
it is nowhere specifically mentioned in Munby's comprehensive *Phillipps
Studies*. At the Sotheby sale the manuscript was purchased by the London bookdealer Martin Breslauer for £4,000, the equivalent of $11,200
at the then rate of exchange; Sotheby's own pre-sale estimate had been
£6,000. Breslauer was planning to feature the manuscript in his catalog,
listing it at a price of £6,800. This particular section of the catalog,
available in page proof, was never published as The Pierpont Morgan
Library purchased the manuscript before the catalog went to press. The
money came from the Library's special Belle Da Costa Greene Fund,
so named after its first director, 1905-48. In The Pierpont Morgan
Library it was given its present signum, *M 931*. I am indebted to Mr.
William Voelkle, Associate Curator of Mediaeval and Renaissance Manuscripts at The Pierpont Morgan Library, for this information concerning the more recent fate of the Croato-Glagolitic missal text.

Considering the fact that the *New York Missal* to date has not been
the subject of any closer scholarly examination (none available in
published form at least), the description in the Sotheby catalog, quoted
above in extenso, undoubtedly provides some valuable data in need of
further corroboration and, in part, correction by future research. In
particular, the brief statement on the decoration of the codex, suggesting
Venetian and Bolognese influences, is of considerable art-historical and
codicological interest, as is the reference to the direction to the choir on
folio 107^V to use both Slavic and Greek, but not Latin, when singing
the liturgical chant of the passion-week. This may point either to the
retention of an ancient tradition from the period of Byzantine rule over
Dalmatia or to the existence of continued links, beyond those times, with
the Greek Orthodox liturgy of the Byzantine sphere, in addition to, and
combined with, a general adherence to the Roman rite, of course. As
for the tentative dating (ca. 1400-1410) and localization (Lika-Krbava
area, north of Zadar and southeast of Senj) of our manuscript, pending
any positive identification of possible direct indications or substantive
clues, this is in general agreement with my own initial impression, as
confirmed also by Dr. Marija Pantelić of the Zagreb Old Slavonic
Institute, whose expert advice is hereby gratefully acknowledged. (In Sir

Thomas Phillipps's own *Catalogus librorum manuscriptorum in biblio-theca D. Thomae Phillipps, Bart.,* Middle Hill, 1837, our codex is listed on p. 95 under "Additional Guilford MSS." incorrectly—as regards contents and date of origin—as follows: "6446. Novum Testamentum. Charactere Glagolitico. fol. v. s. xii. No. 460 1 vol.") A date somewhat later than 1400–1410, around 1420 perhaps, is equally conceivable if not even more likely, and Dr. Pantelić tentatively suggests the environs of Zadar, slightly south of the proposed region, as a likely place of origin. This, therefore, would not entirely rule out some parish on the Dalmatian coast, at least if we understand the Zadar area in a more narrow sense. Such a possibility was discarded by the author of the Sotheby description, presumably because of the scribe's claimed ignorance of Latin—in itself of course not necessarily a compelling argument against a localization on the Adriatic littoral—and his presumed lack of familiarity with, but hardly (as was suggested) complete ignorance of, the liturgy according to the Roman rite. Note, incidentally, that the early Slavic so-called St. Peter liturgy contained Byzantine elements (so-called *Missa Graeca*), as has been persuasively demonstrated (cf., e.g., Zagiba, 1971, 176–207, especially 184–90 and 197–8). Further, the author of the cited description of the *New York Missal* is mistaken when he calls Bartholomaeus (in his native language: Jernej) Kopitar, the great pioneer of Slavic studies, a Croat; he was, of course, a Slovene, that is to say, a member of another, if neighboring and closely related, nationality among those manifold languages and peoples that made up the colorful mosaic of the Dual Monarchy.

Not quite accurate or perhaps just awkwardly phrased is the reference to Kopitar's Latin description of the manuscript "with Glagolithic transcripts of some passages." What we have instead are five Glagolitic excerpts from the codex which were sent to Kopitar by Sir Thomas Phillipps. Most probably, these short passages were handcopied by Phillipps himself (see below, the statement to that effect in the *Review* of The Pierpont Morgan Library). On the first page is a note reading: "New Testament in the Glagolitic character. in the Libr: of Sir Thomas Phillipps: MS: 460." Of the five pieces, the first one is taken from folio 1, col. I, lines 1–3 (and is marked "pag. I."), the three following are copied from within the codex (marked "in medio"), and the fifth one, on the last page, is from folio 293^V (the last page of the manuscript), col. II, adducing the concluding five and a half lines. That passage is marked "finis:", and next to the second line from the end there is a note "rubro charact." Three capital Glagolitic letters appear immediately below the last passage.

It was obviously this text sample that Kopitar helped Sir Thomas to decipher and interpret by sending him the following information on a few handwritten sheets, now in The Pierpont Morgan Library together with the excerpts sent to Kopitar. Kopitar's note on the title page reads: "Missale Glagoliticum seculi XIV–XV. MS. 460. alias 6446. Bibliothecae Middlehillensis." On the next page follow under the heading "Facsimilium Transcriptio Cyrilliana & Interpretatio latina" the transliterated excerpts (the Cyrillic letters here being rendered in Latin transliteration, in a couple of instances Kopitar himself—apparently by oversight—using Latin script rather than Cyrillic in citing the Slavic text):

vime b̄žie i s̄te m̄rie
amenь. početie misala p
o z̄knu rimskogo dvora. prv-

in nomine Dei & S. Mariae
amen. Initium Missalis secundum
legem Romanae Curiae. I^{ma}
(Adventus).

Excita quaesumus Domine
potentiam tuam & veni. & magna

Vzbudi prosimъ ḡi silu
tvoju i pridi. i v̄likoju n̄mъ

nobis misericordia succurre, ut ab
immin-

m^{l}stiju pomozi da o naležᵗ-

———

M. věčni be. iže s̄ps̄n
ie čs̄kgo roda na drě-
vě križa postavi

Oremus. Aeterne Deus, qui salutem
humani generis in li-
gno Crucis posuisti -

Unde & memores
nos servi tui, sed & plebs tu-
a sancta Christi filii tui D̄ni n̄ri.

Otnjuduže i pametoyjušte
mi rabi tvoi na i ljudi tvo-
i s̄ti x̄a s̄na tvoego Ḡa n̄š̄-

———

　　Per eundem Dm̄ı̄m
nrum̄ Jesum Christum filium tuum
qui venturus est judi-
care vivos & mortuos
& seculum per ignem. *Sequentia
S. Evangelii secundum
Mattheum ——

T̄mde ḡmъˣ̌
n̄šmъ is̄xmъ s̄nomъ tvoimъ.
iže grędetъ sudi-
ti živomъ i mrtvomъ
i věku ognemъ. amenъ. *Naslje-
dovanie. s̄to evangelija ot
Mattěja ——

*vides dessee *verum* finem.
　(V N O) fortasse est custos paginae sequturae. ——

On the two following pages Kopitar has added:

Annotationes

1) habes ergo non quidem N. Test. integrum; sed *Missalis* Romani versionem lingua Slavorum veteri. *Missali* quantum insit non modo N. sed & V. Testamenti, facile dispicias, modo latinum textum summas ad manum. In *Breviario* habes totum psalterium, & plurimas lectiones e V. Test. ———
2) Mitto Tibi Glagolitam meum pro ulteriori hujus litteraturae notitia.
3) Cuperem vicissim uberiorem notitiam de codd. qui pro illyricis indicantur in Catalogo Hänelii Lipsiensis. Sunt autem universim *octo* sequentes:

		Celotti	
	No 936 =	157	S. Gregorii dialogi
	937 =	159	Sermoni sacri
	950 =	191	Principi d'ogni virtù
cf. retro	⎧2314 ———		Dialogi S. Gregorii glagolit.
	⎩2315		Missale slav.
	2739		Passione di S. Matteo
	2740		Meditatio passionis Christi
	2741		Tr. da psalmi

Aut potius (ut Tibi minus sim molestus) sufficiet, si neglectis latino forte charactere scriptis, glagoliticos tantum & cyrillianos quos habes placuerit indicare.

Quaero praesertim glagolitica vetustiora, e. g. reliqua *Glagolitae Cloz.* quae in *Mariano* dicebantur adesse (c. 1800). ———

Custos Kopitar
XV. Dec. 1837
Vindobonae

And on the reverse side:

Codex 2314 glagolit. est breviarii pars *diurna*, cujus partem constituunt homiliae patrum.
———2315   erit *Octoechus* cyrilliana.
Ignoratur hucusque *quid* contineant & cujus sint aetatis codices duo *russici* Bibliothecae Bodlejanae *duo*.

One can see that these notes contain information and references which go beyond the *New York Missal* and are of more general interest for Slavic philologists. The work mentioned in note 2 ("Glagolitam meum") refers, of course, to Kopitar's own early edition of the codex *Clozianus*. Incidentally, the copy referred to was part of the lot auctioned at the Sotheby sale and is therefore now also in The Pierpont Morgan

Library. The catalog indicated in note 3 is none other than the great work *Catalogi Librorum manuscriptorum qui in bibliothecis Galliae, Helvetiae, Belgii, Britanniae M., Hispaniae, Lusitaniae asservantur* by the eminent Leipzig professor Gustav Friedrich Haenel which listed, among other items, 3,133 of Phillipps's manuscripts; for more information on this legal scholar and manuscript expert, especially as concerns his relationship and dealings with Sir Thomas, see Munby's *Phillipps Studies*, in particular, 1954, 40, 60-3 125-7. The name written above the second column of numbers refers to Abbé Luigi Celotti, engaged in manuscript and book "traffic" across the Channel, from whom through Sotheby Phillipps purchased a considerable number of valuable and rare items; cf. Munby, 1954, 50-1.

In its own publications, The Pierpont Morgan Library has made mention of the *New York Missal* at least twice: once briefly in its *Review of Acquisitions 1949-1968*, the other time at greater length in its *Fifteenth Report to the Fellows*, both published in 1969. In the *Review* the Croato-Glagolit codex is listed on page 11 as follows:

> M. 931 MISSAL, use of Rome, with a Psalter and other biblical passages, in Croatian. Western Croatia; ca. 1400-1410. 293 leaves (10 7/8 x 7 3/4 inches). 2 cols., 30 lines. 4 historiated initials, numerous decorated initials. FR 1967-68: 17.

The description on pages 17-18 of the *Report* gives some additional details regarding the history of the codex:

GLAGOLITIC MISSAL

> Had the Ionian Univeristy at Corfu complied with certain conditions of the bequest of Frederick North, fifth earl of Guilford (1766-1827), its founder and first chancellor, this Glagolitic Missal would not have become the first manuscript in this rare script to come to America. The philhellenic North, in his will of 1827, bequeathed some 3,000 manuscripts, as well as other important collections, to the University, which had been inaugurated three years earlier under the auspices of Sir Frederick Adam, the lord high commissioner of the Ionian Isles. Why the Ionian Republic did not accede to the rather modest conditions of the will or if, in fact, they were even aware of them, is not known. In any case, Lord Sheffield, North's nephew and heir, ordered that all the collections be brought to England, where they were sold by Evans in 1830. The Missal, which was featured in Evans's advertisement of the sale, and was purchased by Thorpe for Sir Thomas Phillipps, brought 168 pounds, a considerable sum in those days. Indeed, it appears that Phillipps regarded the manuscript as a special treasure, for it is said that he often produced it at his "desserts of manuscripts" for visitors.

Phillipps's interest in this manuscript, moreover, was more than incidental, for he sent facsimiles of some passages, presumably in his own
hand, to Bartholomeus Kopitar, the great Slovene scholar and keeper
of the Imperial Library at Vienna. Kopitar returned the facsimiles,
along with Cyrillic transcriptions and Latin interpretations. By good
fortune both of these autograph documents were also acquired with the
manuscript.

The manuscript itself consists of a translation of the Roman Missal
and other texts, including a Psalter, into the Čakavci dialect of the
Croatian language. The book, written in the rare Glagolitic script
originally used by the Roman Catholic Croats, was executed in Western
Croatia about 1400–1410. The careful execution and sheer beauty of the
text, as well as its fine state of preservation, make it a monument of
considerable importance in spite of its rather meager illumination,
which consists of four historiated initials representing the symbols of
the four Evangelists.

The Glagolitic Missal, now M. 931, was purchased with income from
the Belle da Costa Greene Fund. It perfectly complements two other
manuscripts in the Library, M. 694 (Four Gospels, xv century) and M.
695 (Book of Psalms, xvi century), both of which were written in
Cyrillic, the script which was employed by the Orthodox Serbs.

As is apparent from references and quotations earlier in this paper,
much of the information contained in this last description stems from
those previously adduced sources, notably the 1966 Sotheby catalog
announcement (whatever its sources of information had been), and
particulars given by A. N. L. Munby in his monumental *Phillipps
Studies*, except where we find an account of certain details directly
relevant to the situation in The Pierpont Morgan Library itself. The
statement that, in addition to the translation of the Roman Missal,
the manuscript also consists of some other texts, including a Psalter,
is of course in need of further corroboration and specific identification,
possible only after a thorough textual analysis. The description of the
New York Missal, found in the publications of The Pierpont Morgan
Library, was provided by Mr. William Voelkle, its Associate Curator
of Manuscripts.

A less than accurate library-internal worksheet, dated "18. vii. 67,"
attempting a preliminary collation of our manuscript, need not be
considered here, especially as Mr. Voelkle has now been kind enough to
provide me with a collation which reliably reflects the present physical
makeup and composition (in terms of gatherings and leaves) of the *New
York Missal*. Mr. Voelkle's collation is reproduced below with his
permission; it should be noted that where gatherings are regular they
are not diagrammed; the wavy line represents the string; *cw* indicates

that the catchword matches up with the following gathering; leaves that have lines connecting them are conjoint. The collation reads as follows (here slightly modified for publication):

M. 931

I. (1-9)^9 *cw*
II. (10-19)^{10} *cw*
III. (20-29)^{10} *cw*
IV. (30-39)^{10} *cw*
V. (40-49)^{10} *cw*
VI. (50-59)^{10} *cw*
VII. (60-69)^{10} no *cw*
VIII. (70-79)^{10} *cw*
IX. (80-89)^{10} *cw*
X. (90-99)^{10} *cw*
XI. (100-109)^{10} *cw*
XII. (110-119)^{10} *cw*
XIII. (120-129)^{10} *cw*
XIV. (130-139)^{10} *cw*
XV. (140-149)^{10} *cw*
XVI. (150-159)^{10} *cw*

XVII. (160-169)^{10} *cw*
XVIII. (170-174)^5 no *cw*
XIX. (175-182)^8 *cw*
XX. (183-192)^{10} no *cw*
XXI. (193-203)^{11} *cw* (on f. 202^v)
XXII. (204-213)^{10} *cw*
XXIII. (214-223)^{10} *cw*
XXIV. (224-233)^{10} *cw*
XXV. (234-243)^{10} *cw*
XXVI. (244-253)^{10} *cw*
XXVII. (254-263)^{10} *cw*
XXVIII. (264-273)^{10} no *cw*
XXIX. (274-283)^{10} *cw*
XXX. (284-293)^{10} *cw* (thus incomplete?)

Special problems with certain gatherings:

I

1　2　3　4　5　6　7　8　9

F. 7, which has a stub, is neither sewn nor glued into the MS. A reading of the text should determine if this is the correct position. If not, it may actually have been sewn in the center of the gathering or between one of the other leaves, if it belongs in the gathering at all. The MS. is not in its original binding and the order may therefore have been disturbed in the rebinding—but any final conclusions can only be reached on the basis of textual and codicological considerations.

XVIII

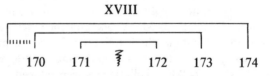

170　　171　　172　　173　　174

F. 174 has a stub which is glued to f. 170^r.

XIX

175   176   177   178   179   180   181   182

F. 179^V glued to f. 180^r even though it has a stub. F. 178^r glued to f. 177^V.

XXI

193   194   195   196   197   198   199   200   201   202   203

Here the *cw* is on f. 202^V and the stub of f. 203 goes around the gathering. The text of f. 203 must be examined to determine whether it belongs between ff. 202 and 204. The *cw* would suggest that f. 203 might have been bound elsewhere—but then a text reading may show it to be all right, especially since the *cw* links.

There can be no doubt, of course, that these preliminary findings of the collator will prove very useful for the future codicological and linguistic analysis of the *New York Missal*.

It would certainly be premature to comment here at any length on the contents and language of the *New York Missal*, or to go into the details of its paleography. Such information will be available only upon the completion of volume two of the envisaged critical edition, containing, in addition to the annotated Latin transliteration of the text itself, a number of essays on particular aspects of the codex and a select glossary. However, even a superficial scanning of the manuscript reveals it to be one of particular historical and linguistic significance, while from an artistic point of view, although splendidly written, it does not come up to some of the other Croato-Glagolitic missal texts, especially not to the high aesthetic level of rich decoration and illumination of the recently edited *Hrvoje Missal* of ca. 1404. As for our manuscript's paleographic characteristics, it is, generally speaking, quite resemblant of the *Hrvoje Missal* in its angular Glagolitic script. The *New York Missal* seems to have been written by five or six different hands. In some instances, certain of its readings appear to have exact counterparts only in the *Hrvoje Missal*, that is, in none of the other known Croato-Glagolitic versions of the *Missale plenum*. Among several linguistic features which suggest that this manuscript is of particular interest for the history of Serbo-Croatian and especially its Čakavian dialect, forms of the type *suln'ce, puln*, testifying to a special intermediate stage in the sound shift $l > u$, are worthy of note; for details, cf. e. g., Popović, 1960, 383–6, and specialized literature cited there (especially the articles by R. Strohal and I. Milčetić). I am indebted to Dr. Marija Pantelić of the Old Slavonic Institute, Zagreb, for having drawn my attention to some of the peculiarities of the *New York Missal* briefly mentioned here.

Croatian Glagolitism was to serve, literally, as the fountainhead for the revival of the Slavic liturgy of the Roman rite and the Church Slavonic tradition in fourteenth century Bohemia. Charles IV's monastic foundation of 1346, the Abbey of Emmaus in Prague (also known as *Na Slovanech*), consisted, at first, entirely of Benedictine monks from Dalmatia and the Croatian Littoral who, however, soon were joined by monks of Czech origin. And it was from here, the Prague Emmaus Monastery, that Croato-Glagolitic writing briefly spread even further—to Southern Poland, the Holy Cross Monastery at Kleparz outside Cracow (in 1390) and another monastery in Oleśnica (Oels) near Wrocław. It is therefore not particularly surprising that among students of Glagolitic Church Slavonic writing we find, in addition to numerous Croatian specialists, many of them now working in the Old Slavonic Institute (Staroslavenski institut "Svetozar Ritig") in Zagreb, also quite a few prominent Czech philologists. J. Vajs was the foremost among these Czech scholars and his example was followed by a host of other experts who combined an interest and thorough erudition in classical Old Church Slavonic and in its particular subsequent Croatian variety.

REFERENCES

BIRKFELLNER, 1974   G. Birkfellner, "Ein älteres glagolitisches Pergamentfragment (Missale romanum) in der Österreichischen Nationalbibliothek," *WSlJb* 20, 7–21.

BIRNBAUM, 1976   H. Birnbaum, "Noch einmal zur Lautgestalt der Kiever Blätter und der Frage nach ihrer Herkunft," *ZfslPh* 38, (1975), 335–48.

BÖHM, 1959   H. Böhm, *Das Wertheimer glagolitische Fragment*, Meisenheim am Glan: Anton Hain (= *Slavisch-Baltisches Seminar der Westfälischen Wilhelms-Universität Münster [Westf.], Veröff.* Nr. 2).

DOSTÁL, 1959   A. Dostál (ed.), *Clozianus. Staroslověnský hlaholský sborník tridentský a innsbrucký*, Prague: ČSAV.

DVORNIK, 1970   F. Dvornik, *Byzantine Missions among the Slavs. SS. Constantine-Cyril and Methodius*, New Brunswick, N.J.: Rutgers University Press.

GRABAR-NAZOR-PANTELIĆ I/II, 1973

B. Grabar, A. Nazor, M. Pantelić (eds.), *Missale Hervoiae Ducis Spalatensis Croatico-Glagoliticum*, I: *Facsimile*; II: *Transcriptio et Commentarium* (title also in Serbo-Croatian and English), V. Štefanić, ed. in chief, Ljubljana: Mladinska knjiga & Graz: Akademische Druck- u. Verlagsanstalt.

GRIVEC, 1960   F. Grivec, *Konstantin und Method. Lehrer der Slaven*, Wiesbaden: Harrassowitz.

MUNBY, 1954   A. N. L. Munby, *The Formation of the Phillipps Library up to the Year 1840*, Cambridge: University Press (= *Phillipps Studies* No. 3).

MUNBY, 1960   A. N. L. Munby, *The Dispersal of the Phillipps Library*, Cambridge: University Press (= *Phillipps Studies* No. 5).

NAZOR, 1975   A. Nazor, "Staroslavenski institut 'Svetozar Ritig' u Zagrebu," *Zbornik za slavistiku* 9 (Novi Sad: Matica srpska), 207–19.

PIERPONT MORGAN LIBRARY 15TH REPORT, 1969

Fifteenth Report to the Fellows of The Pierpont Morgan Library, 1967 & 1968, ed. Fr. B. Adams, Jr., New York: The Pierpont Morgan Library.

PIERPONT MORGAN LIBRARY REVIEW, 1969

The Pierpont Morgan Library: A Review of Acquisitions 1949–1968, Foreword by H. S. Morgan and Preface by A. A. Houghton, Jr., New York: The Pierpont Morgan Library.

POPOVIĆ, 1960   I. Popović, *Geschichte der serbokroatischen Sprache*, Wiesbaden: Harrassowitz.

RADOVICH, 1974   N. Radovich, *La codificazione del* Canon Missae *in quattro manoscritti glagolitici*, Naples: Istituto Universitario Orientale di Napoli (= *Euroasiatica—Folia Philologica AION-Sl Suppleta* II: 5).

SHEVELOV, 1957   G. Y. Shevelov, " 'Trъt'-type Groups and the Problem of Moravian Components in Old Church Slavonic," *SEER* 35: 85, 379–98.

SOTHEBY CATALOG, 1966

Sotheby & Co, *Bibliotheca Phillippica*, New Series: *Medieval Manuscripts*, Part II, *Catalogue of Forty-Four Manuscripts of the*

9th to the 17th century, Day of Sale: Tuesday, 29 November 1966, London: Sotheby & Co.

ŠTEFANIĆ, 1969   V. Štefanić, *Glagoljski rukopisi Jugoslavenske akademije*, I dio: *Uvod, Biblija, Apokrifi i legende, liturgijski tekstovi, egzorcizmi i zapisi, molitvenici, teologija, crkveni govori (homiletika), pjesme*, Zagreb: JAZU.

VAJS, 1932   J. Vajs, *Rukovět' hlaholské paleografie. Uvedení do knižního písma hlaholského*, Prague: "Orbis".

VAJS, 1948   J. Vajs, *Najstariji hruatskoglagoļski misal. S bibliografskim opisima svih hruatskoglagoļskih misala*, Zagreb: JAZU.

VLASTO, 1970   A. P. Vlasto, *The Entry of the Slavs into Christendom. An Introduction to the Medieval History of the Slavs*, Cambridge: Cambridge University Press.

ZAGIBA, 1971   F. Zagiba, *Das Geistesleben der Slaven im frühen Mittelalter*, Vienna-Cologne-Graz: Böhlau (= *Annales Instituti Slavici*, Bd. 7).